ARABIAN POETRY

FOR

ENGLISH READERS.

EDITED, WITH INTRODUCTION AND NOTES,

MU'ALLAQaT

Translation by
W. A. CLOUSTON.

ZuuBooks specialize in offering rare printed and ebooks for affordable prices. For more information on our products and services for authors please contact us at ilifeebooks@gmail.com

This has been a ZuuBooks.com Publication. For New and Classic titles in Audiobooks, ebooks, and Paperback please visit us at www.zuuBooks.com

Authors who are interested in publishing and distributing their works can contact us at ilifeebooks@gmail.com

BY

The Arabian Poets were the historians and moralists of the age; and if they sympathized with the prejudices, they inspired and crowned the virtues of their countrymen: the indissoluble union of generosity and valour was the darling theme of their song.—GIBBON [1881]

PREFACE.

THE history of the present volume is soon told. I was engaged in collecting material for illustration of the migrations and transformations of Popular European Tales and Fictions, and, in the course of my researches, had occasion to consult the works of Sir William Jones, where meeting with his translation of the MU'ALLAQaT, or Seven Ancient Arabic Prize Poems, the idea occurred to me that a reprint of it would be acceptable to a few personal friends, interested in Asiatic literature. The project was readily approved; and it was suggested that these Poems might be interesting to a larger section of English readers. A tentative Prospectus was then issued, proposing to privately reprint Sir W. Jones' translation of the Mu'allaqat and Carlyle's Specimens of Arabian Poetry. This proposal met with support, not only from English scholars and public libraries, but from many distinguished Orientalists; and it was resolved to add to the volume a selection from the Poetry contained in Hamilton's translation of part of the famous Arabian Romance of 'Antar. The connecting of these selections with an outline of the leading incidents of the Romance was an afterthought. Even if Hamilton's volumes were readily accessible, which they are not, few mere English readers would care to go through his diffuse translation, which is rendered more unreadable by the magnificent poetry being printed without a break, often for two or more pages together. But the Epitome included in this volume will perhaps satisfy the curiosity of readers generally regarding a work of which assuredly a complete English translation will never be attempted.

The SHORTER ARABIAN POEMS, translated by Dr. Carlyle, and entitled, "Specimens of Arabian Poetry"--first published in 1796, and again in 1810--are confessedly paraphrases in English verse rather than translations. The selections, together with the translator's anecdotal notices of some of the authors, furnish, nevertheless, a concise history of Arabian literature during the most flourishing period of the Muslim empire.

But this volume must possess an interest and value far beyond what might otherwise possibly attach to it, in containing the famous BURDA POEMS of K'AB and EL-BuSiRi, which are here presented for the first time in English, by Mr. J. W. Redhouse, whose high reputation for scholarship will be a sufficient guarantee to the English reader that the translations are as accurate as it is possible to render such enigmatical compositions into our language.

It may perhaps be thought somewhat strange that a mere English scholar--for my knowledge of Arabic is as "nothing, and less than nothing, and vanity"--should have undertaken the task of editing a thesaurus of Arabian Poetry. But the original plan was very simple; and, to be perfectly candid, I thought myself not altogether incompetent to judge of what would likely be of interest to intelligent English readers. How the task has been performed, readers will, of course, decide for themselves.

The want of uniformity in the spelling of Arabic proper names in the several sections of the book is thus explained: Sir W. Jones' translation of the MU'ALLAQaT is reprinted literatim as well as verbatim; and the same has been done in the case of Carlyle and others whose translations have been reproduced. Nearly every English Arabist of eminence has his own pet system of transliteration; and where doctors differ, who shall decide? In the Introduction, however, I have generally adopted Mr. Redhouse's system, confident that in so doing I followed a safe guide.

The subjects of the Introduction are necessarily treated with brevity: the volume exceeds in bulk by two-thirds the limit originally proposed; but the Appendix Notes will be found to supply much of what may appear wanting in the introductory matter.

I take this opportunity to gratefully acknowledge the valuable help which Mr. Redhouse has rendered me in the course of my work: I had but to make known to him my difficulties in order to have them promptly removed; but all the shortcomings and blunders must be ascribed to myself alone.

I have also to express my best thanks to all who have supported this humble attempt to popularize Arabian Poetry among English readers. By members of the Royal Asiatic Society generally the project has been warmly encouraged; and--although it can add nothing to their reputation--it affords me great pleasure to record that Mr. William Platt, Colonel W. Nassau Lees, Sir William Muir, Professor E. B. Cowell, of Cambridge, Rev. Professor R. Gandell, of Oxford, Professor W. Wright, of Cambridge, Rev. Professor W. P. Dickson, and Rev. Professor James Robertson, both of Glasgow University, were among the foremost to kindly express an interest in this little enterprise. I can but regret that the result, as here presented, should fall so far short of what it might have been in abler hands.

It only remains to add, that, in the course of this work, much out-of-the-way information had to be sought for, and I must have sorely tried the courtesy of my obliging friends: Mr. J. T. Clark, of the Advocates' Library, Edinburgh; Mr. James Lymburn, of the Glasgow University Library; and Mr. F. T. Barrett, of the Mitchell Public Library, Glasgow; who afforded me all the assistance in their power--directing my attention to little-known works, and furnishing me with useful bibliographical notes.

W. A. CLOUSTON.
GLASGOW, December, 1880.

THE FRONTISPIECE.

THIS is a lithographed reproduction, in facsimile (but only in black and white), of a page of a beautifully written and splendidly illuminated Arabic manuscript volume, in the possession of Mr. E. J. W. Gibb, whose translation of Mesihi's Ode on Spring enriches the Appendix to the present work. The page contains the eleven first couplets of El-Busiri's celebrated Qasida (Poem, or rather, Hymn) in praise of Muhammad, of which an English translation, by Mr. J. W. Redhouse, will be found in pages <page 319>-<page 341>. It is hardly necessary to state, what almost every English reader must already know, that Arabic, like most Oriental languages, is written from right to left; but it may be explained that the space in the centre of the page separates the first and second hemistichs of each verse. For example: the first couplet is contained in the first line, at the top of each column; the second couplet, in the second line of each column; and so on, reading across the central division. Mr. Redhouse has favored me with a transliteration of this page (not every Arabist can correctly read any Arabic manuscript), and a translation of the titles and the customary invocation. The titles of the poem and of the first section, at the top of the page, are: qasidatun burdatun faslun fi ta'dili 'n-nafsi

A Poem; a Mantle. A Section on the Justification of the Carnal Man.

Then follows the invocation which is invariably placed at the beginning of every Muslim composition, whether secular or religious:

bi 'smi 'llahi 'r-rahmani 'r-rahimi

In the name of GOD, the Most Merciful, the All-Compassionate.

Our old European authors in like manner always headed their writings with the sign of the cross, +. Thus, in the King's Quair, by James I., of Scotland:

And forthwithal my pen in hand I took,
 And made a +, and thus began my book.

Modern Christians do not so literally follow the scriptural injunction: "In all thy ways acknowledge Him, and He shall direct thy paths." But with Muslims it is no empty form.

The English reader will be interested in observing, in the following four first couplets of El-Busiri's Poem, in italic characters, the movement of the qasida rhyme:

1 e min tezekkuri jiramin bi dhi-selemi
  mezejta dem'an jera min muqletin bi demi

2 em hebeti 'r-rihu min tilqa'i katzimetin

wa ewmadza 'l-barqu fi 'tz-tzalma'i min idzami

3 fa ma li 'ayney-ke in qulta 'kfufa hemeta
wa ma li qalbi-ke in qulta 'stefiq yehimi

4 e yahsibu 's-sabbu enna 'l-hubba munketimun
ma beyna munsejimin min-hu wa mudztarimi

The two halves of the first distich, as above, rhyme; and the final syllable (mi) of the second half of every succeeding distich, to the end of the poem, is the same as those of the hemistichs of the opening verse.

W. A. C.

CONTENTS.

[7]

[9]

INTRODUCTION.

An indescribable charm surrounds the early poetry of the Arabs. Dwelling in the wonderful creations of their genius with these ancient poets, you live, as it were, a new life. Cities, gardens, villages, the trace of even fields, left far out of sight, you get away into the free atmosphere of the desert; and--the trammels and conventionalities of settled society cast aside--you roam with the poet over the varied domain of Nature in all its freshness, artlessness, and freedom.--SIR WILLIAM MUIR, K. C. S. I., LL.D.

INTRODUCTION.

I.--THE ANCIENT ARABS.

IN the modern history of the world, no race or nation has figured so largely, or so widely and permanently influenced the destinies of mankind, as the race of shepherds, dwelling in tents, who have occupied the peninsula of Arabia almost since the Deluge. Roused, from the fatal lethargy of the gross idolatry into which they had long been sunk, by the enthusiasm of one man, who substituted for their vain superstitions the simple but sublime formula of belief, "There is but ONE sole GOD," in the space of less than a hundred years these people had overrun and conquered a great part of the then known world, which they held subject for several centuries, until, in their turn, they had to yield to more vigorous races. But wherever the Muslim gained footing, there his footprints are still to be seen; and the influence of the enlightened descendants of the first Arabian conquerors, who gave the nations the choice of the Qur'an or the scimitar, remains in European arts, sciences, and literature to this day.

The early history of the Arabs, like that of other very ancient nations, is involved in great obscurity. Their country, or most part of it, seems from remote antiquity to have been called 'Ariba, a name which it still retains. Regarding the origin of this name learned men differ in opinion. According to some, the name of 'Ariba was derived from 'Arba, a district of Tamana, where Ishmael dwelt; others say there was a town of this name in the neighbourhood of Makka. Tradition asserts that the name was derived from Ya'ruh son of Qahtan, or Joktan, the grandson of Eber; while certain learned Hebraists would have it to be of Hebrew original, since the term araba in that language signifies west, and in the Scriptures the western part of the peninsula is called eretz arab, or ereb--the western country.

Ptolemy's division of Arabia into the "Stony," the "Desert," and the "Happy" was altogether unknown to the Arabs themselves. The best Oriental writers divide the peninsula into five provinces or kingdoms, namely: Yaman; Hijaz; Tahama; Najd; and Yamama. Of these the two first call for special notice.

The province of Yaman has always been famed for the fertility of its soil, and the mildness of its climate, which seems to realise the dreams of the poets in being a perpetual Spring. "The beauties of Yemen," says Sir W. Jones, are proved by the concurrent testimony of all travellers, by the descriptions of it in all the writings of Asia, and by the nature and situation of the country itself, which lies between the eleventh and fifteenth degrees of northern latitude, under a serene sky, and exposed to the most favourable influence of the sun: it is enclosed on one side by vast rocks and deserts, and defended on the other by a tempestuous sea; so that it seems to have been designed by Providence for the most secure as well as the most beautiful region of the East. Its principal cities are: Sanaa, usually considered as its metropolis; Zebid, a commercial town, that lies in a large plain near the Sea of Oman; and Aden, surrounded with pleasant gardens and woods. It is observable that Aden, in the Eastern dialects, is precisely the same word with Eden, which we apply to the garden of Paradise. It has two senses, according to a slight difference in its pronunciation: its first meaning is, a settled abode; its second, delight, softness, or tranquillity. The word Eden had probably one of these senses in the sacred text, though we use it as a proper name. We may also observe that Yemen itself takes its name from a word which signifies verdure and felicity; for in those sultry climates, the freshness of the shade and the coolness of water are ideas almost inseparable from that of happiness; and this may be a reason why most of the Oriental nations agree in a tradition concerning a delightful spot where the first inhabitants of the earth were placed before their fall. The ancients, who gave the name of Eudaimon, or Happy, to this country, either meant to translate the word Yemen, or, more probably only alluded to the valuable spice trees and balsamic plants that grow in it, and, without speaking poetically, give a real perfume to the air." Such a charming land and climate may well be supposed to have been the seat of pastoral poetry; and, indeed, the best poets which ancient Arabia produced were those of Yaman.

The province of Hijaz is so named, either because it divides Najd from Tahama, or because it is surrounded by mountains. Its principal cities, Makka and Madina, are most sacred in the estimation of every Muslim. Makka is the Qibla, or place in the direction of which Muslims everywhere turn their faces in prayer: it contains the Sacred Ka'ba, or Cubical House,--the Baytu-'llah, or House of GOD--whither flock unnumbered pilgrims from all parts of the world of Islam once every year; [**] and the sacred well, Zem Zem-- the self-same well, saith tradition, near which Hagar sat with her son Ishmael when she was comforted by the angel. Moreover, Makka is the birthplace of Muhammad. El-Madina--"the city," emphatically--was called Yathrub before the Prophet retreated thither: it contains his tomb, which is, of course, also visited by the devout.

Oriental writers divide the inhabitants of Arabia into two classes: the old lost Arabs, descended from 'Ad and Thamud (who were destroyed by GOD because of their unbelief), and others famous in tradition; and the present Arabs, who are sprung from two different stocks: Qahtan, the same with Joktan the son of Eber, the fourth in descent from Noah; and 'Adnan, who was descended in a direct line from Ishmael, the son of Abraham and Hagar. [**] Those descended from Qahtan are called 'al-'Arabu-'l-'ariba, genuine or pure Arabs (some authors, however, consider the old lost tribes as the only pure Arabs);

[12]

those from 'Adnan, 'al-'Arabu-'l-musta'riba, naturalised or insititious Arabs.--For several centuries many of the Arabian tribes were under the government of the descendants of Qahtan: Ya'rub, one of his sons, having founded the kingdom of Yaman, and Jurhum, another son, that of Hijaz.

"The perpetual independence of the Arabs," says Gibbon, "has been the theme of praise among strangers and natives; and the arts of controversy transform this singular event into a prophecy and a miracle, in favour of the posterity of Ishmael. Some exceptions, that can neither be dissembled nor eluded, render this mode of reasoning as indiscreet as it is superfluous: the kingdom of Yemen has been successively subdued by the Abyssinians, the Persians, the Sultans of Egypt, and the Turks; the holy cities of Mecca and Medina have repeatedly bowed under a Scythian tyrant; and the Roman province of Arabia embraced the peculiar wilderness in which Ishmael and his sons must have pitched their tents in the face of their brethren. Yet these exceptions are temporary or local; the body of the nation has escaped the yoke of the most powerful monarchies: the arms of Sesostris and Cyrus, of Pompey and Trajan, could never achieve the conquest of Arabia; the present sovereign of the Turks may exercise a shadow of jurisdiction, but his pride is reduced to solicit the friendship of a people whom it is dangerous to provoke and fruitless to attack. The obvious causes of their freedom are inscribed on the character and country of the Arabs. Many ages before Mahomet, their intrepid valour had been severely felt by their neighbours in offensive and defensive war. The patient and active virtues of a soldier are insensibly nursed in the habits and discipline of a pastoral life. The care of the sheep and camels is abandoned to the women of the tribe; but the martial youth, under the banner of the emir, is ever on horseback and in the field, to practise the exercise of the bow, the javelin, and the scimitar. The long memory of their independence is the firmest pledge of its perpetuity; and succeeding generations are animated to prove their descent and to maintain their inheritance."

The religion of most of the Arabs before the time of Muhammad was rank idolatry. The Sabian religion--worship of the sun, the fixed stars, and the planets, and of angels and lower intelligences--overran the whole nation, although there also existed among them a considerable number of Christians, Jews, and Magians. It was perhaps natural for the Arabs to be led into the worship of the celestial luminaries: a pastoral life requiring continual observation of their motions, in order to forecast changes of the weather, they would be very easily induced to ascribe the blessing of rain to a divine power that resided in them. The constellations, which divide the zodiac into twenty-eight parts, through one of which the moon passes every night, were called anwa', or the Houses of the Moon. In the Temple of Makka were 360 idols, one for each day of their year; of these the chief were Lat and 'Uzza, by which they were wont to swear, though such an oath was not considered so binding as the following, from which it will be seen that, besides their imaginary deities, they also believed in a supreme GOD: "I swear, by Him who rendered the lofty mountains immovable, the Giver of life and death, that I will never betray you, either in word or in deed." If a man broke this oath, the same day he would bark like a dog, and the flesh would fall off his bones.

[13]

Some tribes believed in a future state, and when a warrior died his camel was tied to his grave and there left to perish, in order that its master should ride it on the Day of Reckoning, as befitted his rank; others had no faith either in a past creation or a resurrection, ascribing the origin of all things to nature and their dissolution to age. But, for the most part, the pagan Arabs concerned themselves but little as to their future destiny--content if their daily wants were supplied, they hardly looked beyond the present.

Of their virtues and their vices much may be learned from the reliques of their ancient poetry. Hospitality was greatly esteemed among them, while avarice, in men, was held in supreme contempt. The bitterest taunt by one tribe to another was to say that their men had not the heart to give, nor their women to deny: men being esteemed for liberality and courage; women, for parsimony and beauty. The fires which they kindled on the tops of hills, and kept burning during the night, to guide travellers to their tents, and hence called "hospitality fires," are often referred to in their early poetry. But their system of morals, observes Sir W. Jones, "generous and enlarged as it seems to have been in the minds of a few illustrious chiefs, [**] was on the whole miserably depraved for a century at least before Muhammad: the distinguishing virtues which they boasted of inculcating and practising were, a contempt of riches and even of death," but in the age immediately before the time of the Prophet, "their liberality had deviated into mad profusion, their courage into ferocity, and their patience into an obstinate spirit of encountering fruitless dangers."

The general mode of life of the tent-dwelling pagan Arabs was much the same as that of their descendants the Bedawis of the present day. The wants of a pastoral life are few. To the Arab of the desert, the camel--like the reindeer to the Laplander--is an invaluable gift of Providence. Strong and patient, the camel is capable of carrying a load weighing a thousand pounds, and of making a journey of several days' duration without water; while the dromedary, of a lighter and more active build, is celebrated by their poets as outstripping the ostrich in speed. The long and fine hair of the camel, which is cast periodically, was woven into cloth for their tents and their garments; its milk, cooled in the wind, furnished a refreshing and nourishing drink; its flesh was their chief food, together with the flesh of horses on festal occasions. Camel's milk, however, was not their only beverage: the old Arabs--those of the deserts as well as those of the cities-- seem to have been greatly addicted to wine-drinking, and intoxication was the rule rather than the exception at their frequent feasts. Even the women appear to have freely indulged in wine--in the absence of their lords, if not with their sanction and in their presence. The pre-Islamite bards all celebrate the exhilarating effects of wine, and some even boast of their ability to drink the whole store of the vintner, "at one sitting." It was therefore not without reason perhaps that Muhammad, the great Lawgiver, sternly interdicted the use among Muslims of that salutary yet perilous beverage, and of all other intoxicating drinks.--The Arabs are praised by all ancient writers for their respect for women; their scrupulously keeping their word; and for their quickness of apprehension and their penetration, and--the desert tribes especially--the vivacity of their wit. On the other hand, they were characterised by an eager desire for the property of

[14]

their neighbours, an unconquerable fondness for strife and bloodshed, and by their vengeful disposition.

One of the barbarous customs which prevailed among the independent tribes of Arabia was the system of private war, or tribal and family feuds, similar in their origin, duration, and ferocity to those feuds which existed among the Highland clans of Scotland until within comparatively recent times. The murder of an Arab chief by the people of another tribe was sufficient to kindle a sanguinary war between the two tribes and their collateral branches, which often lasted for a generation, and even longer. For every relative that had been slain, the Arabian, when his tribe were victorious over that of the slayer, singled out a captive, and, as a point of honour, coolly put them to death. But avarice sometimes mitigated this brutal custom: the nearest relative of the deceased was permitted to waive the blood-vengeance in consideration of a fine, the amount of which, about the time of Muhammad's birth, seems to have been ten camels. The Prophet endeavoured to soften or regulate the vengeful disposition of his countrymen by several passages in the Qur'an; and in later times, in the Sunnat, or Traditions, almost equal in authority with the Qur'an itself, the amount of the bloodwit was increased to one hundred camels. "In the East," says Richardson, "the relations of the principals in a quarrel seem to have been bound by honour and custom to espouse their party and to revenge their death: one of the highest reproaches with which one Arabian could upbraid another being an accusation of having left the blood of his friend unrevenged."

The custom of setting apart certain months of the year, during which all warfare was unlawful, must have acted as a wholesome check upon the sanguinary disposition of the pagan Arabs. The eleventh, twelfth, first, and seventh months were thus held sacred; the twelfth, Dhu'l-hajj, being, as the name implies, the month of pilgrimage to Makka. "During these months whoever was in fear of his enemy lived in security; so that if a man met the murderer of his father or his brother, he durst not offer him violence." Similar in object, though not in observance, to the sacred months of the old Arabs, were the Treuga Dei and the Pax Regis of Europe during the Middle Ages. [**] Muhammad retained the sacred months, but gave permission to attack the enemies of Islam at all times.

The unnatural practice, which prevailed among some tribes, of burying their female children alive as soon as they were born, had its origin perhaps in a desire to save them from the ill-usage to which female captives were often subjected. [*+] They also sacrificed them to their idols, in common with some of the neighbouring nations. It is said that even the Greeks themselves in the earlier ages destroyed their female offspring. Muhammad, of course, abolished this horrible custom.

Divination and augury were much in vogue among the old Arabs. Arrows, without heads or feathers, were employed in divination, and were usually kept in the temples dedicated to local or favourite idols.

The idol Habal in the Temple of Makka, which was destroyed by Muhammad himself when he purified the Ka'ba, had seven such arrows in its hand; but three was the number

[15]

commonly used. On one of these was written: "Command me, Lord!" on another: "Forbid me, Lord!" and the third was blank. If the blank arrow happened to be drawn, they were again mixed (in a sack), and drawn until a decisive answer was obtained. No enterprise of moment was undertaken without consulting either these divining arrows or the flight of a bird: if it flew to the right, it was ominous of good fortune: but if to the left, the intended journey or enterprise was abandoned.

The principal dialects spoken by the Arab tribes were those of Himyar (or Yaman) and of the Quraysh. The language of Himyar seems to have been but little cultivated; that of the Quraysh, called the pure, and styled in the Qur'an, "the perspicuous and clear Arabic," ultimately became the language of all Arabia. The Quraysh were the most learned and refined of all the Western Arabs: carrying on an extensive trade with every neighbouring state, and being, for many generations before the time of Muhammad, the custodians of the Ka'ba, to which a vast number of pilgrims flocked once a year from all parts of Arabia, and from every country where the Sabian religion prevailed, refinement and learning were a natural consequence of their intercourse with strangers of the best classes.

Poetry and eloquence, but especially poetry, were assiduously cultivated by the Arabs. "With them," says Professor E. H. Palmer, "it was not merely a passion, it was a necessity; for, as their own proverb has it, 'the records of the Arabs are the verses of their bards.' What the Ballad was in preserving the memory of the Scottish Border wars, such was the Eclogue in perpetuating the history and traditions of the various tribes of the Arabian peninsula. The peculiar construction of their language and the richness of its vocabulary afforded remarkable facilities for the metrical expression of ideas; and accordingly the art of Munazarah, or poetical disputation, in which two rival chieftains advanced their respective claims to pre-eminence in extemporary verse, was brought to the highest perfection among them."

To their poetry, indeed, the Arabians have been chiefly indebted even for the preservation of their language. The old Arabs set great store by the genealogy of their families, and as this was the subject of frequent and bitter disputes, their poems preserved the distinction of descents, the rights of tribes, and the memory of great actions. The principal occasions of rejoicing among the desert tribes were: the birth of a boy; the fall of a foal of generous breed; and the rise of a great poet capable of vindicating their rights, and of immortalising their renown.

Such, in brief, were some of the characteristics of those ancient people, who, under the banner of Islam, spread like an inundation over Asia: "delighting in eloquence, acts of liberality, and martial achievements, they made the whole earth red as wine with the blood of their foes, and the air like a forest of canes with their tall spears": and in a very few years created an empire larger than that of the Romans themselves.

Footnotes

^xx:* According to Arab tradition, Abraham built the first Ka'ba on the same spot where the present building stands. Muslim writers go farther, and say that Adam himself erected a temple there, and that it was built and rebuilt ten times. (For a full description and history of the Ka'ba, see Burton's Pilgrimage to el-Medinah and Meccah, vol. iii., chapter xxvi.) Putting idle legends aside, the antiquity of the Ka'ba reaches far beyond the Christian era: we learn from Greek writers that the Temple at Makka had been visited by pilgrims time out of mind.

^xxi:* From the uncertainty of the descents between Ishmael and 'Adnan, the Arabs of this stock usually reckon their genealogies no higher than 'Adnan.

^xxiv:* Hatim, chief of the tribe of Ta'i, and Hasn, of the tribe of Fazara, are greatly celebrated for their profuse hospitality. The name of Hatim is still synonymous in the East with the utmost liberality.

^xxviii:* The Treuga Dei, or Truce of God, was adopted about the year 1032, in consequence of a pretended revelation of a bishop of Aquitaine. It was published in the time of a general calamity; and it made so deep an impression on the minds of men, that a general cessation of private hostilities was observed, we are told, for seven years; and a resolution formed, that no man should in time to come molest his adversary from Thursday evening till Monday morning. The Pax Regis, or Royal Truce, was an ordinance of Louis VIII., King of France, A.D. 1245; by which the friends or vassals of a murdered or injured person were prohibited from commencing hostilities till forty days after the commission of the offence.--Richardson.

^xxviii:+ See Epitome of the Romance of Antar, in the present volume--pp. <page 244> and <page 249>.

II.--THE MU'ALLAQAT;

OR, SEVEN ANCIENT ARABIC PRIZE POEMS.

ABOUT the end of the sixth century--the most brilliant period in the ancient history of the Arabs--the Arabic language attained its greatest perfection, in consequence, it is said, of the poetical contests which took place at the annual fair that was held at 'Ukatz during the month of pilgrimage (Dhu'l-hajj). "For, as every tribe had many words peculiar to itself," says Sir W. Jones, "the poets, for the convenience of the measure, or sometimes for their singular beauty, made use of them all; and as the poems became popular these words were by degrees incorporated with the whole language: like a number of little streams which meet together in one channel, and, forming a most bountiful river, flow rapidly into the sea." The several tribes of the peninsula vied with each other in sending their best poets to represent them at the 'Ukatz assembly. The bards having recited their eclogues--in which there was little variety of subject: most of them commencing with a lament for the departure of a fair one, and a description of her personal charms; passing abruptly to an account of the noble qualities of the poet's horse or camel, or a eulogium

on his tribe, and his own prowess in battle--judgment was impartially passed on their respective merits; and those poems which were considered as most excellent were afterwards written upon silk, in characters of gold, and hung up in the Temple--hence, it has been supposed, they were called Mu'allaqat, or "Suspended," and also Mudhahhabat, or "Gilded" (not "Golden," as the term is usually rendered). [**] Of these "Prize Poems" seven, entitled THE MU'ALLAQaT, par excellence, are preserved in many of the European libraries: they are the composition of IMRA'U-'L-QAYS; TARAFA; ZUHAYR; LEBiD; 'ANTARA; 'AMR; and EL-HaRITH;
and in the Pocock MSS., No. 174, preserved in the Bodleian Library at Oxford, are some forty others which were also hung up in the Ka'ba.

To Sir William Jones, who first directed the attention of the learned in Europe to the rich treasures contained in the ancient literature of Hindustan, belongs also the honour of having been the first to translate the Seven Arabic Prize Poems into a European language. In 1782 was published his English translation of the MU'ALLAQaT, with Arguments, and the original texts in Roman characters. [**] And this was
not only the first, but it remains the only complete English translation of these remarkable compositions; for, strange as it may appear, no attempt has been made by our modern English Arabists to give their unlearned countrymen a more accurate translation than was perhaps possible in the time of Sir W. Jones.

The original metre employed in Arab poetry was the Rajaz, a short iambic verse, always ending with the same rhyme: this was the measure of the rude songs of the camel-drivers; and it was well adapted for extemporary verse, to express defiance, contempt, or panegyric. The Mu'allaqa Poems are composed in verses, or couplets (called bayts), of double the length of the Rajaz, and consisting of two halves or hemistichs; the two hemistichs of the first bayt invariably rhyming with each other, and with the second hemistich of each succeeding couplet. This form of verse is called the Qasida (Kasidah, or Casida); and, being that adopted in the composition of the Prize Poems, it has been thought that the term was derived from the word Qasd, which signifies an object or aim: these poems (or Qasidas) having been composed with the special object of obtaining preeminence at the poetical contests. [**] But this generally received interpretation of the term Qasida is rejected by Professor Ahlwardt, who ascribes it to another signification of the word Qasd--"the breaking of things into halves": each bayt, or verse, being divided into hemistichs (as is shown in the Frontispiece to the present volume), the whole poem may be said to consist of two halves. Sixteen different measures are known in Arabian prosody, four of which are adopted in the Mu'allaqa Poems; but the movement of the rhyme (qasida) is the same in them all.

The authors of the MU'ALLAQaT were all men of high poetical genius, although they were in no sense possessed of literary culture--indeed, it is almost certain that scarcely one of them could read and write. They were natural poets, whose ignorance of letters was fully compensated by a nice sense of rhythm and the faculty of clearly and vigorously expressing in their rich and copious language what they thought and felt;-- impulsive children of the desert, whose passions had free scope for good and evil; who

[18]

were capable of the most intense affection, and of the most bitter hatred: whose strong feelings found vent in flowing verse.

A century had elapsed after the rise of Islam when the fragments of the early poetry, and anecdotes of the most famous bards of the Arabian peninsula--especially the poets of Yaman--which had been handed down orally from generation to generation, were finally reduced to writing. How much of the traditions regarding the pagan Arab poets is fabulous cannot now be ascertained; but to the task of investigating the authenticity of the so-called reliques of ancient Arabic poetry the most learned scholars of Germany have for some time been devoted, with results which are more or less conclusive, and which will be touched upon in the next section of this Introduction. The following particulars regarding the several authors of the MU'ALLAQaT are gleaned from the best Oriental writers.

IMRA'U-'L-QAYS

[paragraph continues] the son of Hujr, the son of Harith, was a prince of the tribe of Kinda. His real name was Hunduj, and he acquired the epithet of Imra'u-'l-Qays ("the man of adversity") from his misfortunes. [**] Muhammad called him el-Maliku 'dz-Dziltil, "the most erring prince," as being the best of the pagan Arab poets, whom, he also said, Imr' would head on their way to the place of woe. His love adventure with a damsel of another tribe, alluded to in vv. 8-43 of his Mu'allaqa, and detailed in the translator's Argument, so exasperated his father that he expelled him from the tribe; and for many years the poet led a wandering, reckless life among the Arabs of the desert, a life of peril and often of privation; occasionally varied by a halt at some well-watered spot, where he and his comrades feasted on camel's flesh and caroused, while singing-girls amused them with their lively songs. The poet was thus engaged, drinking and gaming, when a messenger from his tribe arrived, and announced that his father had been slain by his rebellious subjects. Imra'u-'l-Qays made no answer; and on his companion stopping his game, he simply said: "Play on." But when the game was finished, he remarked to his comrade: "I would not have thy game interrupted;" and then, turning to the messenger, he inquired minutely into all the circumstances of his father's assassination. Having learned the particulars, he said: "As a youth, my father banished me from his house; as a man, it is my duty to avenge his death. But to-day we shall drink; to-morrow, sobriety: wine, to-day; business, to-morrow."

With an army of the tribes of Taglib and Bakr (who were not then at variance), Imra'u-'l-Qays marched against his rebellious people, who, however, escaped his vengeance, by placing themselves under the protection of the King of Hira. Upon this his followers forsook him, and he then sought help of the Himyarite prince Marthad el-Khayr, who promised him 500 men, but died soon afterwards; and his successor showed little disposition to assist the unfortunate prince.

At this juncture, Imra'u-'l-Qays had recourse to divination, as was customary among the pagan Arabs before any enterprise of moment was undertaken. The prince drew the lot with the three arrows of "order," "defence," and "expectation"; and having drawn the second one three times in succession, he broke the arrows and threw them in the face of the idol, exclaiming: "If they had killed thy father, thou wouldst not limit thyself to defence alone!"

Finding he could obtain no assistance from the prince of Yaman, he next proceeded to the court of the Emperor Justinian; but unfortunately an Arab was there whose father had been killed by the poet's father, and he prejudiced the Emperor's mind against Imra'u-'l-Qays, who quitted the court with all speed. But the Emperor, incited by his Arab courtier, sent a messenger after him with a poisoned garment. The poet was overtaken at Ancyra, and no sooner had he put on the fatal garment than he was seized with dreadful pains, his body was covered with ulcers, and soon afterwards he expired in great agony. His last words were: "He, from whose lips flowed eloquence, at whose sword-strokes flowed the blood of his enemies, at whose feasts flowed rich wine--he came to Ancyra, and no farther."

TARAFA

The son of El-'Abd, the son of Sufyan, was of the tribe of Muzayna, a branch of the Banu Bakr (sons of Bakr, or Becr), and hence he was surnamed El-Muzani. He may be said truly to have "lisped in numbers," for at the tender age of seven he gave proof of his poetical genius. He was travelling with his uncle, and, the party resting for the night on the banks of a clear stream, Tarafa--boy-like--set snares to catch larks; but not having succeeded when they resumed their journey in the morning, the little poet expressed himself on the occasion in verses to the following effect:

Rejoice, O lark! in the expanse of the plain: thou enjoyest free air--sing, then, and increase in security. Fly round about, and pick up all that thou canst desire: the bird-catcher is gone--rejoice then at his departure! The snare is removed, and thou hast nothing more to fear;--but yet fear thou always; for at length thou shalt be taken!

The occasion which gave rise to his Mu'allaqa--the loss of the camels belonging jointly to himself and his elder brother--is related in the translator's Argument. C. de Perceval states that 'Amr the son of Marthad, one of the noble chiefs whom the poet compliments in v. 81, sent for Tarafa, and said to him: "Children GOD alone can give thee; but as to goods I will set thee on the same footing with my own sons." He then called his seven sons and three grandsons, and ordered each of them to give the poet ten camels; thus making good the loss upon which his brother had so bitterly reproached him.

The most remarkable event in Tarafa's brief life is his tragical end. 'Amr the son of Hind, king of Hira, had sent Tarafa and Mutalammis, also a famous poet, to be companions to his younger brother Qabus, whom he intended for his successor. Qabus, it appears, was greatly addicted to drinking, and was often discovered intoxicated; and both poets composed some very satirical verses on him and the King. Enraged at these lampoons (which probably came to his knowledge through some "good-natured friend"), 'Amr gave each of the poets a "Bellerophon letter" to the governor of Bahrayn, in which he was ordered to put the bearer to death. Mutalammis, suspecting the designs of the King, broke open his letter, and showed it to a friend, who read it to him; and on learning the contents, he destroyed it, and advised Tarafa to turn back with him. But Tarafa, perhaps thinking that his friend had been imposed upon by the reader of the letter, [**] declined his advice, and continued his fatal journey. On delivering his letter, the governor of Bahrayn, carrying out the orders of 'Amr, cut off the poet's hands and feet, and then caused him to be buried alive. Tarafa was only twenty-six years old when he thus miserably perished.

ZUHAYR

The son of Abu Sulma, Rabi'a, was distinguished from early youth for his poetical genius. He was a special favourite of his grand-uncle Bashama, who was himself a famous poet; yet, when the old man felt his end approaching, he divided his goods among his relations and left nothing to Zuhayr. "Wilt thou leave me nothing?" asked Zuhayr.--"I leave thee," said the patriarch, "the finest part of my inheritance--my talent for poetry."--"But that is already mine," replied Zuhayr.--"Nay," said the old man, "all Arabia knows that poesy is an inheritance of my family, and that it went from me to thee." Zuhayr got a legacy, nevertheless.

His Mu'allaqa was composed, on the conclusion of the War of Dahis, in honour of el-Harith son of 'Auf and Harim son. of Sinan, the peace-makers. Zuhayr also composed a great number of eclogues in praise of Harim, the son of Salma, who had sworn not only to grant all the poet's requests, but to give him, for every poem he composed in his praise, either a female slave or a horse. This liberality rendered Zuhayr so bashful in the presence of his patron, that whenever the poet chanced to enter a company in which Harim was, he would say: "I salute you all, excepting Harim, although he is the best among you."

A son of Harim having recited to the Khalif 'Omar one of Zuhayr's eclogues in praise of his family, 'Omar remarked: "Zuhayr has said many beautiful things about you."--"True," answered the son of Harim; "but we have made him as many fine presents."--"What you gave him," said 'Omar, "will perish through course of time; but his praises will endure for ever."--'Omar, though no great friend of poets or admirer of poetry, always spoke favourably of Zuhayr, because in his poems he had praised only such as really deserved praise, as Harim the son of Salma.

Umm Aufa, whom he mentions in the first verse of his Mu'allaqa, was Zuhayr's first wife, whom he divorced on account of her jealousy, but of this he afterwards repented. The children she bore him died young. A second wife gave him two sons: Ka'b, author of the celebrated qasida entitled el-Burda, or the Mantle (generally known throughout the East as the Banat Su'adu, from the opening words of the poem: "Su'ad hath departed"), which he recited before Muhammad (A.D. 630), when he made his peace with the Prophet, and professed himself a Muslim; and Bujayr, who was an early convert to Islam.

[21]

According to the Kitabu-'l-Agani (Book of Songs), compiled by Abu-'l-Faraj el-Isfahani, Muhammad saw Zuhayr when he was a hundred years old, and exclaimed: "GOD grant me a refuge from his Devil"--meaning, his cunning in song; and it is added that before the Prophet had quitted the house, Zuhayr was dead. Another account is that Zuhayr foretold to his sons Ka'b and Bujayr the advent of Muhammad, and earnestly recommended them to give ear to the Apostle's teaching when he did come; but that Zuhayr was dead before Muhammad began his mission.

LEBID

(Or Labid) was the son of Rabi'a, of the Band Kilab, who, because of his great liberality, was called Rabi'atu-'l-muqtirin, that is, "The Spring of the indigent ones." Lebid's kunya, or bye-name, was Abu 'Aqil. His uncle was 'Abu Biza'ir, 'Amir, son of Malik, surnamed Mula'ibu-'l-'Asinna,--"the player with lances." While yet a mere youth, Lebid accompanied a deputation of his tribe, headed by his famous uncle, to the court of Nu'man of Hira, where, by a satirical poem, which he composed almost extempore and recited before the king, he effected the disgrace of a courtier who was obnoxious to his tribe.

Lebid is one of the poets who belonged to "the time of the Ignorance" and also to Islam. Various accounts are given of the circumstance which led to his conversion. According to the Agani, Lebid was one of a deputation that waited upon the Prophet after the death of the poet's brother 'Arbad (who was killed by a stroke of lightning a day or two after he had made an impious speech against the fundamental doctrine of Islam), and the aged poet then and there professed himself a convert. Others say that it was the custom for poets in those days to affix their verses to the gate of the Ka'ba, as a general challenge against the next assembly at 'Ukatz, and that Lebid had put up the following poem (translated by Mr. C. J. Lyall):

Yea, everything is vain, except only GOD alone,
  and every pleasant thing must one day vanish away!

And all the race of men--there shall surely come among them
  a Fearful Woe, whereby their fingers shall grow pale:

And every mother's son, though his life be lengthened out
  to the utmost bound, comes home at last to the Grave:

And every man shall know one day his labour's worth,
  when his loss or gain is cast up on the Judgment Day.

These verses were universally admired, and for some time no one ventured to rival them, until Muhammad placed the opening passages of the second chapter of the Qur'an by the side of them. Lebid was struck with their sublimity, and, declaring that they must have been written by divine inspiration, tore down his own verses, and immediately professed

[22]

himself a Muslim. From that time he renounced all poetry; having, it is said, only composed one couplet after his conversion:

Praise be to GOD, that my end came not
  till He had clad me with the robe of Islam!

Muhammad acknowledged that no pagan poet had ever produced nobler verses than those of Lebid above quoted.

After his conversion, Lebid settled in the city of Kufa, where he died, about the end of the reign of Mu'awiya (A.D. 660), at the age of 157, says Ibn Qutayba, or 145, according to the notice of him in the Agani, "of which he lived ninety in the Ignorance, and the rest under Islam." The following is a translation of the verses Lebid is said to have composed when he was considerably over a hundred and twenty years old:

Time in his lengthened chain of years has bound
 Our mortal race, nor e'er his conqueror found:
 I've seen him pass by day, I've seen by night,
 And still, unchanged, return with morning's light.
 Time, like Lebid, grows older every day,
 But waxes stronger, while I waste away.

The governor of Kufa once sent for Lebid and desired him to recite one of his poems. Lebid recited the second chapter of the Qur'an (entitled "The Cow"), saying, when he had finished, "GOD has given me this in exchange for poesy since I became a Muslim." The Khalif 'Omar, on being informed of this, added 500 dirhems to the 2000 Lebid was already allowed. When Mu'awiya became Khalif, he purposed retrenching the poet's stipend, but Lebid reminded him that he was not likely to live much longer: Mu'awiya's heart was touched, and he despatched the poet's allowance in full, but Lebid died before it reached Kufa.

Lebid's last words, remarks Dr. Carlyle, breathe more of the spirit of a wit than that of a devotee: "I am going to enjoy the novelty of death; but it is a novelty by no means agreeable."

'ANTARA,

The son of Shaddad, [**] the renowned warrior and poet, of the tribe of 'Abs, was born in the beginning of the sixth century. His mother was an Abyssinian slave, captured in a predatory incursion; and for many years his father refused to recognise him as his son, until, by his heroic achievements, he had rendered himself worthy of that honour. 'Antara is invariably described as being of a very dark complexion, and having his lower-lip cloven.

[23]

The tents of 'Abs having been suddenly attacked and plundered, the father of 'Antara promised him his freedom if he rescued the women who had been taken captive, a feat which the hero accomplished, after slaying many of the enemy single-handed. From this time 'Antara was recognised as the champion of his tribe; yet envious spirits did not scruple frequently to taunt him with his base birth. One of these having insultingly called his mother a negress, the hero retorted: "If it were a question of mutual help, neither thou, nor thy father, nor thy grandfather, would ever be invited to a feast; for thou wouldst never be placed at the head of those that make gains [i.e., spoils]." And when Qays son of Zuhayr said that the victory they had gained over an enemy was owing to the son of a negress, 'Antara replied, in verse: "One half of me is of the purest blood, the other half is my sword: therefore it is, that, when you are in trouble you call upon me to relieve you, rather than those who can reckon up a host of noble ancestors."

'Antara's heroic exploits and his excellent poetry. preserved by oral tradition, furnished material for the celebrated Romance of chivalry which purports to recount his life and adventures. Allowing for its hyperbolical style (which never, in the opinion of Orientals, invalidates the truth of history), "the whole work," says Von Hammer, "may be esteemed as a faithful account of the principal tribes of the Arabs, particularly of the tribe of 'Abs, from which sprung 'Antara, in the time of Nushirvan, King of Persia."

The circumstance of 'Antara's death, as related by some authors--echoing the voice of tradition--though hardly so striking, is perhaps not less in accordance with the rules of poetical justice than that which concludes the Romance. It is said that, returning home with a herd of camels, of which he had robbed a clan of the tribe of Ta'i, 'Antara was struck with a spear, thrown at him by one of the plundered tribe, who had followed the party unseen, until a favourable opportunity offered for revenge. Mortally wounded, and now an old man, 'Antara had still sufficient strength left to ride home to his tribe, where he died soon after his arrival.

Muhammad was fascinated by the stories related of 'Antara's prowess and poetry: "I have never heard an Arab described," said the Prophet, "whom I should like to have seen so much as 'Antara." 'AMR the son of Kulthum, was a prince of the tribe of 'Araqim (i.e., "the speckled snake"), a branch of the Banu Taglib. His mother, Layla, was the daughter of Muhalhil and Hind; and at her birth, according to the barbarous custom of the pagan Arabs, Muhalhil gave order that she should be immediately buried alive. But hearing in his sleep a voice that told him his daughter should be the mother of heroes, he asked for the infant, and, finding that she was still alive, allowed her to be brought up. In course of time Layla was married to Kulthum, and shortly before 'Amr was born, she dreamed that a supernatural being assured her that her son should prove the bravest of warriors.

The tribes of Taglib and Bakr having been long at war, in consequence of the murder of Kulayb the son of Rabi'a, it was mutually agreed to terminate the feud by referring the dispute to the decision of 'Amr the son of Hind, king of Hira--the same who had so foully caused the murder of the poet Tarafa. 'Amr the son of Kulthum appeared as the advocate of the Banu Taglib, and el-Harith the son of Hilliza, on behalf of the Banu Bakr. The arguments employed by 'Amr on this occasion are contained in his Mu'allaqa; and his boastful--even minatory--declamation was little calculated to please the royal arbiter. The King of Hira gave judgment in favour of the Banu Bakr, and not long afterwards he was slain by 'Amr the son of Kulthum--in revenge, as some think, for the murder of Tarafa; but others allege, perhaps with more reason, in retaliation for the judgment he had pronounced against the tribe of Taglib.

The circumstances of the King's death are thus related. The King having asked some one, "Do you know an Arab whose mother would refuse to serve my mother?" the reply was: "Only Layla, the mother of 'Amr son of Kulthum; for her father and uncle were the most honoured among the Arabs." Piqued at this reply, the king sent a messenger to the poet, desiring him and his mother to visit at his court. 'Amr set out, with his mother in a litter, and accompanied by a troop of horsemen. The king had erected a pavilion between Hira and the Euphrates, and there, with his mother Hind, he awaited the arrival of the poet and his mother Layla. When the latter entered the royal pavilion, Hind desired Layla to reach her the keys, who boldly replied: "Let them rise and do thy bidding whom such service befits." At this refusal, Hind began to insult Layla, and even to use violence against her, which 'Amr the son of Kilthum seeing, his wrath knew no bounds; and, seizing the only sword (the King's) that hung upon the wall, he smote King 'Amr on the head and killed him.

Besides his Mu'allaqa, 'Amr the son of Kulthum composed a number of bitter satires upon King Nu'man of Hira and his mother, who was the daughter of a goldsmith.

'Amr is reported to have attained the great age of a hundred; and to his descendants, gathered round his death-bed, he thus spoke: "I have lived longer than my forefathers, and I am now going to join them. Hear, then, the counsel of my experiences. Each time I blamed another, I was the object of well-founded or ill-founded blame. He who attacks will be attacked: guard, therefore, against offending any one. Be benevolent and hospitable towards your friends: thus you will gain their esteem. It is better to refuse a request, than to promise and break your word. When a man speaks to you, listen to him attentively: when you speak, be brief; for long speeches are not free of folly. The bravest warrior is he that returns to the attack; and the best death is that on the battle-field."

EL-HARITH the son of Hilliza, [**] when over a hundred years old, but still comparatively vigorous, was sent to the court of 'Amr son of Hind, King of Hira, to represent the tribe of Bakr when the dispute between them and the Banu Taglib was submitted to that prince as arbiter. His Mu'allaqa contains the arguments he made use of on that occasion in behalf of his tribe; and such was the effect of his reasoning, his eloquence, and skilful praise of the prince of Hira, that the royal arbiter decided in favour of the Banu Bakr; and, as a mark of special honour to the poet, the prince cast off the seven veils in which he was enveloped during the recitations of the rival-chiefs, and caused Harith to sit beside him. For this decision there is reason to believe the King soon afterwards lost his life at the hand of 'Amr son of Kulthum, as has been already mentioned. [**]

[25]

IT has been said of translation in general that "the wrong side of tapestry will represent more truly the figures on the right, notwithstanding the floss that blurs them, than the best version the beauties of the original." This remark would seem to apply with special force to English translations of early Arabic poetry, of which indistinctness is said to be the very essence. "The language," says Burton, "'like a faithful wife, following the mind, and giving birth to its offspring,' and free from that 'luggage of particles' which clogs our modern tongues, leaves a mysterious vagueness between the relation of word to word, which materially assists the sentiment, not sense, of the poem. When verbs and nouns have--each one--many different significations, only the radical or general idea suggests itself. Rich and varied synonyms, illustrating the finest shades of meaning, are artfully used: now scattered to strike us by distinctness; now to form, as it were, a star, about which dimly seen satellites revolve." Yet even in an English translation the more striking beauties of the MU'ALLAQaT are not altogether lost.

The Poem of IMRA'U-'L-QAYS is the most picturesque--even dramatic--of the whole seven: it presents a series of scenes of desert life, graphic, yet without the least attempt at detail: rapidly sketched, like the cartoons of a great artist, yet full of colour and vraisemblance, like finished pictures. We see the poet at supper in the sandhills, with the maidens whom he had surprised at their primitive bath; and while they all ply the leathern bottle of generous wine, we fancy we can hear their merry laughter at the jests of the wild young prince. We follow the bold youth at midnight, as he threads his way--not without a beating heart--among the tents of a hostile tribe, to the dwelling of the maiden for whose sake he thus carries his life in his hand: we see the expectant damsel (for evidently the visit was pre-arranged) peeping timidly from the opening of her tent: we see them stealing softly away together, while she "draws over their footsteps the train of her pictured robe."--A weird journey through the desert on a gloomy night, when the darkness seems to enfold the solitary wayfarer as with a garment, and he starts ever and anon at the gaunt bones of camels and their riders that have been bleached on the sands by the noontide sun.--An exciting chase of the wild cow--a primitive feast on the game--a thunderstorm.

TARAFA is the only one of the Seven Poets who compares camels to ships. In his opening verses, the camels that bore away his beloved are likened to "ships sailing from Aduli"; and in verse 28, he says that the neck of his own camel "resembles the stern of a ship floating high on the billowy Tigris." Nearly one third of the poem is taken up with what Sir W. Jones terms "a long and no very pleasing description" of the poet's camel; yet we must suppose this minute detail of the points of an animal so indispensable to desert life in Arabia to have been very highly appreciated by the poet's countrymen; and the reader is recompensed for his patience by the fine simile with which it concludes: "She floats proudly along with her flowing tail, as the dancing-girl floats at the banquet of her lord, and spreads the long white skirts of her trailing robe"--a simile which suggests a pleasing image to the reader's mind. After the long panegyric on his camel, the poet proceeds to speak of his own prowess in battle; then to hint at his pleasant way of life, in company of gay youths like himself, and beautiful singing-girls; followed by a series of Horatian maxims: life is brief--therefore let me enjoy the fleeting moments--let me drink my full draught of wine to-day, come what may to-morrow. Once more he refers to his warlike performances, armed with a scimitar which is no mere pruning-hook, but the genuine brother of confidence--one stroke of which renders a second needless. He concludes with a sagacious observation, which Muhammad said was prophetic of his own great mission: "Time will produce events of which thou canst have no idea; and he to whom thou gayest no commission will bring thee unexpected news." [**]

Bold metaphor is a marked characteristic of the Poem of ZUHAYR--that of War as a foul monster, the mother of twin-born Famine and Desolation, being particularly striking and apposite: not less so perhaps is the poet's description of the contending parties in the fierce and protracted War of Dahis, under the figure of camels driven out to pasture on noxious weeds and to drink from foul and loathsome pools. The maxims tagged to the Poem, for the most part, express sentiments such as must occur to all thoughtful minds, matured by time and observation of life. [**]

The elegiac verses with which LEBiD'S Poem opens, by their natural and unembellished touches of pathos, must, even in an English translation, come home to every feeling heart. Six of the Mu'allaqa Poems commence with the conventional lament for the departure of a mistress, but this elegy of Lebid excels them all, for beauty of imagery and tenderness of expression--contrasting agreeably with the artificial eclogues of some modern European poets, whose aim has been rather to dazzle by contrast of words and brilliancy of diction than to reach the heart by natural thoughts conveyed in natural language. His camel the poet compares to a wild he-ass, hastening with his mate from the hills after the winter is past; and to a wild cow chased by the hunters. Like the Scottish poet Burns, whose large heart welled-up in sympathy for all natural objects--a crushed daisy--a ruined field mouse--little birds on a winter's night--like all true poets, the old Arabian bard could feel pity for the wild cow who had lost her young one, and who passed the night in agony, roaming restlessly to and fro, while the rain fell continuously upon her back. There is no such humane feeling as this expressed in any of the other Poems, unless indeed it be in that of 'Antara, who seems to have pitied his wounded steed, who, he says, upbraided him with his eyes, and would have spoken if he could. Bright sketches of Arab life are furnished in this masterpiece of early poetry: outlines, but boldly and clearly defined, of which the reader is left to fill in the details from his own imagination. We see the poet, chief among his gay companions at the tavern, drinking rich wine long hoarded in leathern bottles, while the nimble fingers of the fair lutanist skilfully touch the strings of her instrument. We find him superintending the gaming, with headless and featherless arrows, for camels, which the poet himself generously provides as the prizes. We see him rise early in the morning and mount his horse, to defend his tribe against invaders. And at the opening of his tent we behold crowds of the poor and the needy--the widow and the fatherless--all partaking largely of his bounty.

The Poem of 'ANTARA is a curious medley of gentle pastoral utterances and fierce breathings of slaughter and revenge. The passage (vv. 14 to 19) in which the poet compares the mouth of his beloved to a fragrant bower, which the gentle rains have kept in perennial verdure, is perhaps finer than anything in the other six Poems. Interesting glimpses of Arab life are afforded us in this mosaic of poetical fragments: the breaking up of a family-camp in the desert at night--the camels, laden and bridled, grazing on khimkhim grains; young ostriches flocking round the parent male bird, like a herd of black camels of Yemen assembling at the call of their keeper: the poet-hero quaffing old wine, bought with shining coin--frequently replenishing his crystal goblet from a well-stoppered jug: a stolen interview with a beautiful damsel of a hostile tribe: protracted and fierce single combats with the most renowned warriors.

The Poem of 'AMR the son of Kulthum is the only Mu'allaqa which does not begin with an address to a real or imaginary mistress. 'Amr calls loudly for his morning draught of wine in a capacious goblet, and goes on to praise the magical influence of the generous beverage in causing the miser to forget for a time his golden hoard, and in diverting even the lover from his passion. Nevertheless the inevitable departure of his mistress is referred to, and her charms very minutely described, in the tenth to the twenty-second verses. The rest of his Poem consists of an arrogant panegyric on the Banu Taglib--their greatness and power, rich possessions and glorious achievements; and the beauty of their women, and the high estimation in which they were held by all their brave warriors.

Of a sober and staid cast, as befitted his venerable years, is the Poem of EL-HARITH, in reply to the intemperate harangue of his boastful opponent; yet he does not scruple to claim for his tribe all the virtues which should characterise a noble race.

"The range of thought in the early Arab poetry," remarks Sir William Muir, [**] "is of limited extent. Past experiences and the sentiment of the moment are described with illustrations drawn from pastoral life. The future is not thought of, nor is the attempt made to draw lessons from the past. Childlike, it is in the present that the Arab poet lives. . . The pastoral life is pictured in the simple imagery of undisturbed rural scenery. The cavalcade, bearing the whole worldly goods of the tribe--the matrons and maidens borne in litters on the camels' backs--passes along the desert with its scant and scattered foliage of hardy shrubs, and, after a weary march, encamps, it may be, in a vale where the springs break forth from the slope of an adjacent hill. The clustering tents darken the background, while the grateful fountain, with its green environs and its grove of date-trees, stands in delightful contrast to the wild bleak scenery around. [*+] The maidens go forth with their pitchers to the spring; and the herds of goats return with full udders from the pasture, or still sweeter but scanty foliage of the stunted acacia-trees.

"Arab life lives, truly, a life of its own. There is no advancing civilization wherewith to rehabilitate the surrounding imagery. The nearest approach in our own language to Arabian Poetry is the Book of Job, with its illustrations of the conies, the goats, and the wild ass; and even such is still the life of the desert at the present day. Cut off from the world by wilderness and by nomad habits, the Arab maintains unchanged his simplicity, affected as little by the luxury and civilization of surrounding nations as by their politics. The eclogues of the classics are ever bordering upon urban life; but here the freshness and freedom of the wild desert is untainted by the most distant approach of the busy

[28]

world. The din of the city, even the murmur of the rural hamlet, is unheard. The poet is unconscious of their existence."

Footnotes

^xxxii:* The actual meaning of these terms, as applied to the "Seven Ancient Arabic Prize Poems," is, however, a vexed question among modern European Arabists. The current interpretations, that these Poems were entitled Mu'allaqat (in the singular, Mu'allaqa), either because they were suspended on the Ka'ba, or because each of the so-called Poems consists of fragments or short pieces "hung" or strung together, are utterly rejected by Professor W. Ahlwardt, the eminent German Orientalist; as also the surmise of Herr Von Kremer, that the terns is derived from another meaning of the word--"written down from the dictation of the Rawis" (Reciters of Poetry): he rather regards the name as being analogous with the other term, Mudhahhabat, or gilded, and to signify "set with ornaments "pre-eminent, or "golden" verses. The same learned Professor moreover considers the accounts of poetical contests, at 'Ukatz and other places, as mere fictions of Oriental writers.

^xxxiii:* In quarto, entitled: The Moallakat; or Seven Arabian Poems which were Suspended on the Temple at Mecca, with a Translation and Arguments. By William Jones, Esq. London, 1782. From the "Advertisement" prefixed to this work we learn that Sir W. Jones purposed furnishing a Preliminary Discourse which was to comprise "observations on the antiquity of the Arabian language and letters; on the dialects and characters of Himyar and Koraish, with accounts of some Himyarick poets; on the manners of the Arabs in the age immediately preceding that of Mahomed; on the temple at Mecca, and the Moallakat, or pieces of poetry suspended on its walls or gate; lastly, on the lives of the Seven Poets, with a critical history of their works, and the various copies or editions of them preserved in Europe, Asia and Africa." There were also to be Notes, giving "authorities and reasons for the translation of controverted passages; elucidating all the obscure couplets, and exhibiting or proposing amendments of the text; directing the reader's attention to particular beauties, or pointing out remarkable defects; and throwing light on the images, figures, and allusions of the Arabian poets, by citations, either from writers of their own country, or from such of our European travellers as best illustrate the ideas and customs of Eastern [p. xxxiv] nations." This elaborate scheme, however, was never carried out.--From a letter addressed to his learned Dutch friend, H. A. Schultens, in June, 1781, we learn that Sir W. Jones was guided in his translation of the Mu'allaqat by the Commentary of Tabrizi, the paraphrase of Zauzani, and other native grammarians.

It may be added, that, in issuing his translation of the Mu'allaqat, with the original texts transliterated into European characters, Sir W. Jones solicited the co-operation--the strictures and annotations--of continental scholars. "But," he remarks, "the Discourse and Notes are ornamental only, and not essential to the work"--surely a curious statement, from an English reader's point of view, at least; since without some previous knowledge of the habits and manners of the old Arabs, and some notes explanatory of obscure allusions, these compositions must be in a great measure unintelligible to general readers. But Sir W. Jones doubtless meant that the proposed Discourse and Notes were unnecessary to scholars, who might consult the native commentaries. However this may be, it is probable that to the absence of explanatory notes is due the circumstance that his translation of the Mu'allaqat had not been reprinted since it was included in the editions of his collected works: 6 vols., quarto, 1799, and 13 vols., octavo, 1807.

^xxxv:* Some commentators say that praise-poems, or eclogues in praise of great men, which were always composed in this form of verse, first obtained the name of Qasidas: panegyric being their special object or aim. Even the nature of the Qasida is variously reported: some have said that it must be over three distichs (the lowest Arabic plural); others, over seven; and others, over sixteen.--A specimen of the Qasida rhyme, in English verse, is given in page <page 367> of this volume.

^xxxvii:* In Sir W. Jones' "Genealogy of the Seven Poets," prefixed to his translation of the Mu'allaqat, the father of Imra'u-'l-Qays ('Amrio'l-Kais) is called Maiah; his grandfather, Rabeiah (who was the father of Kulayb, the proud chief, whose murder caused a long and bloody war between the tribes of Taglib and Bakr); and his great grandfather, Hareth. Possibly "Maiah" was another name of Hujr, the father of Imra'u-'l-Qays; however, the asterisk after the name in Sir W. Jones' list evidently indicates that it was doubtful.--According to Professor Ahlwardt, the poet was also styled Abu Zayd (father of a son called Zayd), son of Hujr, son of Harith.

^xli:* From this it would appear that the poet Mutalammis, and probably Tarafa also, could not read.

^xlvi:* So this poet is generally styled by Oriental writers; and according to Sir W. Jones' "Genealogy of the Seven Arabian Poets" (prefixed to his translation of the Mu'allaqat in this volume), 'Antara was the son of Shaddad, the son of Mu'awiya; but Professor Palmer and other modern authorities reverse this order of descent, and make Mu'awiya the father of 'Antara, and Shaddad his grandfather.

^li:* According to Sir W. Jones' "Genealogy of the Seven Arabian Poets." D'Herbelot (Bibliotheque Orientale) says that he was "either el-Harith son of 'Amr, or 'Amr son of el-Harith."

^lii:* The order in which the several poems of the Mu'allaqat are placed seems purely arbitrary; since they are not arranged either according to merit, date, length, or the rank of the authors. In the order of poetical merit, doubtless the Qasida of Imra'u-'l-Qays would still retain the first place; that of Lebid would come next, followed by 'Antara, Tarafa, and Zuhayr; and 'Amr, and el-Harith, whose compositions are political declamations rather than eclogues, would occupy, as they do at present, the last places in the poetical Pleiades. If they were arranged in chronological order, they would probably stand thus: Tarafa; el-Harith; 'Amr; 'Antara; Imra'u-'l-Qays; Zuhayr; Lebid. In the order of length: 'Amr, whose poem contains 108 verses; Tarafa, 103; Lebid, 89; el-Harith, 85; 'Antara, 81;

[30]

Imra'u-'l-Qays, 75; and Zuhayr, 64 verses. According to social rank, Imra'u-'l-Qays again would take precedence of the others, while 'Antara would- occupy the last place, as being the son of a slave-woman. Between these two extremes--Imra'u-'l-Qays, the prince, and Antara, the son of a slave--would stand the five others, of whom at least four were connected with the court of Hira, where the great poets of Arabia assembled in the century before the time of Muhammad.--In some editions of the "Seven Poets" the poems of en-Nabiga of Dubyan and el-'Asha take the places of those of 'Amr and el-Harith.

^liv:* A "dark" saying, which seems a parallel to that of Agatho, who remarks that "it is extremely probable that the most improbable things will occur"; as well as to the favourite saying of Lord Beaconsfield, that "it is always the unexpected that happens."

^lvi:* Verse 62, for instance, offers a parallel to the well-known Greek epigram of Palladius, which has been thus rendered into English verse:

A blockhead as long as he is silent is wise;
 For his talk is a sore he should hide from all eyes.

^lix:* In an excellent paper on "Ancient Arabic Poetry," published in the Journal of the Royal Asiatic Society, 1879.

^lix:+ And they came to Elim, where were twelve wells of water, and three score and ten palm trees; and they encamped there by the waters.--Genesis xv. 27.

III.--GENUINENESS OF THE EARLY ARABIC POETRY.

LIKE the ILIAD of Homer, which was formed from the songs of the Rhapsodists, the Qasidas of the MU'ALLAQaT are not regular compositions, but consist of short effusions and fragments strung together. But there is this difference, remarks Von Hammer-Purgstall, that "the authorship of the old Arab Prize Poems has been undisputed; and no Arabian wolf has torn the MU'ALLAQaT, like the ILIAD, and thrown the fragments to various authors." This "difference," however, no longer exists; for, while the authenticity of the MU'ALLAQaT as a whole is still allowed, the genuineness of certain passages is questioned by distinguished German scholars. And if we consider that the songs of the pre-Islamite Arabs, like the Scottish Border Ballads, were preserved for many generations by oral tradition alone (for the art of writing, although known among the tribes of Arabia, was but little used), it will appear more than probable that interpolations exist in the early Arabic poetry. When the collectors, about the end of the seventh century, began to commit the songs of the old Arabs to writing, they found only fragments--but very numerous fragments--remaining among the desert tribes; and they were exposed to very much the same kind of errors and even frauds as were our own literary antiquaries when they went about the pastoral districts gathering fragments of traditionary ballads from the lips of "oldest inhabitants": verses of one particular song found their way into another; and artful rhymesters, who had a fatal knack of imitating the external form and language of the old Border Ballads, occasionally imposed upon

[31]

enthusiastic and all too credulous collectors of legendary ballad lore. In like manner, it would seem that the collectors of early Arab poetry were sometimes the dupes of knavish Rawis, or Reciters, many of whom were themselves no mean poets, but could extemporaneously compose verses so like in style and sentiment to the genuine old poetry as to render detection almost impossible. Nor are the collectors even above suspicion of helping out the sense of an obscure fragment by interweaving, here and there, a verse or two of their own composition.

Professor Ahlwardt, Herr Von Kremer, and other eminent German Orientalists have of late years subjected the reliques of ancient Arabic poetry to a thorough critical examination, with the object of separating the spurious from the genuine verses. The sudden transition from one subject to another, so common in the longer qasidas, furnished most favourable opportunities for interpolation. To distinguish such interpolated passages must necessarily be a work of no small difficulty; and very frequently the student can only detect errors and inaccuracies by finding the rules of Qasida composition violated. For instance, only the hemistichs of the opening bayt, or couplet, should rhyme with each other; and if two or more such couplets are found in the same poem, they must be interpolations, or opening verses of other poems. Again, it is the rule, with very few exceptions (for which there are always obvious reasons), that a Qasida begin with an address to a mistress--lamenting her departure, generally; and where this is wanting the poem is incomplete, if not altogether spurious. But errors of this kind must be obvious to every student, and require no great critical acumen for their discovery.

A much more difficult task is, the recognition and separation of verses which have been ingeniously composed and inserted by the Reciters, or even by the collectors, in order to connect fragments together. It is not easy to bring to the investigation of such a subject as this a mind perfectly unprejudiced. If the student brings to his task a pre-conceived notion of what the old Arabs would (or should) say about certain things, and finds in the poetry sentiments which go against his theory, he is prone to consider them as interpolations; and thus, consciously or unconsciously, the critic, in the process of investigation, will be more disposed to establish his theory than to elicit the truth. But the learned Orientalists who are engaged in sifting the early Arab poetry are certainly actuated by no such narrow motives; and the importance of the work they have undertaken can hardly be over-rated; since, without being assured of the genuineness of the pre-Islamite poetical remains, accurate knowledge of the old Arabs themselves is impossible. Nevertheless, some of the conclusions at which they have arrived have been questioned by other scholars.

We are told that the collectors and critics were led by a strong religious sentiment to eliminate from the early poetry all allusions to pagan customs and false deities; yet in two of the Seven Prize Poems references to pagan superstitions still remain. Lebid, in verse 76 of his Poem, alludes to the "camel doomed to die at her master's tomb"; and 'Antara, verse 70, refers to the pagan superstition of "birds of the brain," a belief strictly forbidden by the Qur'an. [**] In the Romance of 'Antar, said to have been composed in the 8th century, allusions to pagan deities and idolatrous customs of the old Arabs are very

[32]

frequent; but perhaps the "strong religious sentiment" had evaporated on the introduction of profane science into Islam. However, if the collectors were imbued with so fervent a religious spirit as to eliminate references to idolatry from the early poetry, it seems strange that they should have allowed the numerous allusions to wine-drinking to remain: for the frequent mention of wine in modern Oriental poetry is to be explained by its mystical meaning.

But the same pious critics, who so carefully eliminated from the poetry all reference to pagan superstitions, substituted, it is said, sentiments in consonance with the doctrines of the Qur'an. This, it is well known, was done by the authors of the Thousand and One Nights, in the case of Tales derived from Hindu sources; but it does not follow that the native poetry of the old Arabs was treated after the same manner. Herr Von Kremer takes exception to verses 27 and 28 of Zuhayr's Mu'allaqa, in which mention is distinctly made of the omniscience of GOD and of the Book of Reckoning, as being alien from the spirit of the old poetry. The same objection, if just, would also apply to verses 85 and 86 of Lebid, where the dispensations of Providence are recognised, and to verse 25 of Imra'u-'l-Qays, and verse 81 of Tarafa, where the Creator is plainly mentioned. But, besides their numerous false deities--for which the Arabs seem to have entertained but small reverence about the period when Muhammad began his great mission--there existed, more or less, among the several tribes of the Peninsula a belief in ALLAH--the GOD. Indeed, as Mr. C. J. Lyall has very justly observed, [**] "without assuming such a faith as already well known to the people, a great portion of the Qur'an would be impossible: that revelation is addressed to men who join other gods with GOD, not to those who deny Him;" and to bring them back to the worship of the one sole GOD--to concentrate their faith in Him alone--was the great object of the Prophet's mission.

That the remains of Ancient Arabic Poetry have been tampered with--altered and interpolated--by the grammarians, collectors, critics, and others, is
now, however, proved most clearly: such is also the case with our own early traditionary poetry; and human nature is essentially the same in Bussora and Kufa, and in London and Edinburgh. But it is gratifying to know, on the authority of so learned, acute, and painstaking a scholar as Professor Ahlwardt, that, while much of the so-called Ancient Arabic Poetry is decidedly spurious, and not a little doubtful, there still remains much that is the genuine offspring of the untutored but brilliant and vigorous genius of the pre-Islamite bards.

Footnotes

^lxiv:* In verse 57 of his Mu'allaqa, Imra'u-'l-Qays, according to Sir W. Jones' translation, alludes to idolatrous rites: "virgins, in black trailing robes, who dance round [the idol] Dewaar"; but this rendering seems to be erroneous. The original

fa 'anna la na sirbun, ka-anna ni'aja hu
'adhara dawarin fi mela'in mudhayyali
is thus translated by Mr. J. W. Redhouse:

[33]

"Then there appeared unto us a herd [of wild oxen], the heifers whereof [from their tails] were, as it were, maidens of Dawar in long-trained mantles."

^lxv:* In the interesting and valuable Notes to his translation of Zuhayr's Mu'allaqa: Journal of the Bengal Asiatic Society, 1877.

IV.--ARABIAN LITERATURE UNDER THE KHALIFATE.

DURING most part of the first century after the rise of Islam, the successors of Muhammad were too much engrossed in extending their dominions to bestow any patronage on science and literature. The standard of pure Arabic had been early fixed by the grammarians of Bussora and Kufa, who, for this purpose only, collected fragments of the pre-Islamite poetry that still lived in the hearts of the people of Yaman and Hijaz; but under the dynasty of 'Umayya, Arabian literature was confined to commentaries on the Qur'an and poetry in the native language. "But," says Abu-'l-Faraj, "when GOD called the family of Hashim [i.e., the house of 'Abbas] to the government, and surrendered to them the command, the hearts returned from their indolence, the minds awoke from their torpor." Under the patronage of El-Mansur, the second Khalif of the house of 'Abbas, the study of profane science was begun, and his zeal for the advancement of learning was imitated by his successors. Indeed it is usually said that Arabian literature arose, as well as flourished and decayed, with this dynasty, which continued from A.D. 749 till 1258. The literary treasures of Ancient Persia that had escaped destruction at the hands of the early Muslim conquerors were now even more esteemed than they were formerly despised. It was during the reign of El-Mansur (A.D. 754-775) that the Pahlavi version of the celebrated Hindu Fables of Vishnusarman was translated into Arabic, under the title of Kalila wa Dimna--a work which has since been rendered into more languages than any book extant, with the sole exception of the Bible. In the same century, El-Asma'i, the famous philologer and poet, wrote the great chivalric romance of 'Antar. Early in the ninth century, El-Ma'mun, the seventh Khalif of the family of 'Abbas, founded academies at Bagdad, Bussora, Kufa, and Bukhara, and caused the writings of Aristotle, Hippocrates, Galen, Dioscorides, Theophrastus, Euclid, Archimedes, and Ptolemy to be translated into Arabic. "He was not ignorant," remarks Abu-'l-Faraj, "that they are the elect of GOD--His best and most useful servants--whose lives are devoted to the improvement of their rational faculties. . . The teachers of wisdom are the true luminaries and legislators of a world which without their aid would again sink into ignorance and barbarism." About this period also were erected at Bagdad and Damascus observatories for the study of astronomy. And a generous vazir built, at the cost of 200,000 pieces of gold, a magnificent college at Bagdad, and endowed it with a yearly income of 15,000 dinars. At this establishment, it is said, several thousands of students, from the sons of noblemen to the sons of mechanics, were at the same time instructed in all the learning of the age; the professors were in the receipt of adequate stipends, and ample provision was made for indigent students.

From Samarkand and Bukhara to Fez and Cordova, the entire Muslim empire was full of song: intellectual life was healthy and vigorous. Poetry, although it had lost the freshness of the desert, now took a wider range, and, no longer dwelling solely in the present, became reflective, and ultimately philosophical. [**] The courts of the Khalifs at Bagdad were adorned with a brilliant constellation of men of learning and genius, drawn thither from all parts of the world. Nor were these princes merely the liberal and enlightened patrons of science and literature: many were themselves poets of very considerable genius, and proficients in the theory and practice of music. The descendants of the fanatics who ruthlessly destroyed the famous library at Alexandria, and all but annihilated the ancient literature of Persia, became, during the Dark Ages of European history, the zealous and intelligent conservators of the remains of the learning of antiquity. And at a period when a single copy of the Bible was valued at a sum equivalent to the cost of building an ordinary church, and when many of the Christian priests of Europe mumbled over masses which they could not understand, the library of the Muslim Kings of Spain contained 600,000 volumes, and there were 70 public libraries in the cities of Andalusia; while the library of the Egyptian Sultans comprised 100,000 manuscripts, beautifully transcribed and elegantly bound, which were freely lent to the scholars of Cairo. [**]

The false sciences of astrology and alchemy, to which the Arabians (and, in imitation of them, European dreamers) were so long ardently devoted--fondly hoping, by means of the first, to read the secrets of futurity in the movements of the planets, and, by the latter, to discover the arts of transmuting the baser metals into pure gold and of indefinitely prolonging life--these, it is well known, led to most important discoveries, and finally to the exact sciences of astronomy and chemistry.

To the descendants of the enlightened Muslims who settled in Spain early in the eighth century are Europeans indebted for not a few useful arts and appliances of daily life; among others, for the art of making paper from cotton, which rendered practicable the noble art of printing--the cheap multiplication of books. And the Arabic decimal system of numerical notation (for which the Arabians themselves were indebted to the Hindus) was introduced into Europe by Gilbert of Aurillac, afterwards Pope Sylvester II., who studied at the Muslim university of Cordova in the tenth century. It was moreover through Arabic versions in Spain that the attention of the schoolmen was first drawn to the writings of Aristotle.

But especially in European literature is the influence of the Arabians to be clearly traced. The Trouveres of northern France and their tuneful brethren the gay Troubadours of sunny Provence, whose genius kindled the torch of Italian literature, were largely indebted to the wondrous fictions and the brilliant poetry of the East for the groundwork of their Fabliaux and the fanciful allusions in their Lays. In short, the fascinating fictions of the Arabians had permeated the literature of Europe from a very early period; and the worthy ecclesiastic, who read to his congregation the "moral tales" of the Gesta Romanorum, little dreamt that he was repeating the ingenious inventions of the hated

Muslims and of the despised race of Abraham;--for many of the stories in that famous mediaeval collection are derived from Arabian and Talmudic sources.

It is usual for a sketch of Arabian literature to conclude somewhat in this manner: "On the fall of the Khalifate, A.H. 656 (A.D. 1258), literature rapidly declined in the East: it was still cultivated, however, under the rule of the Sultans of Egypt, but with indifferent success; and on the eruption of the Turks, the sun of Oriental learning was virtually extinguished." But it is utterly false to say that Arabian literature was extinguished (or "irrecoverably blighted," as Dr. Carlyle expresses it) by the Turks. "Timur and his successors in the East," writes Mr. Redhouse, the greatest living authority on this vast subject, "as the Osmanlis in the West, were patriotic enough to love their own beautiful language and to use it for all daily and literary purposes; but they patronised crowds of Persian poets and of Arabian grammarians, legists, &c. Arabic, being no longer dominant, had now only a share of attention, but this was a very large share--the scientific; as Persian had the ornamental, and Turkish the useful. Colleges innumerable were founded, for Arabic, in Turkey, in India, in Persia, in Russia--all by Turks. The Softas of Constantinople are all collegians, studying Arabic alone."

A popular English history of Arabian literature is a great desideratum. Germans have long had the rich stores of Arabic Poetry laid before them by the zeal and industry of Von Hammer-Purgstall and later scholars, among whom Ahlwardt, Von Kremer, and Rukert are pre-eminent. Yet England can at the present day boast of a trio not less distinguished for ripe scholarship, in Chenery, Palmer, and Wright: may we hope that these great Arabists will, at no distant date, open up for their unlearned countrymen the treasures of Arabian literature?

Footnotes

^lxviii:* The sentiments expressed in the Arabian didactic poetry are always just; being based on an intimate acquaintance with human nature, and an accurate observation of the course of life. The subjects are necessarily those which have formed the chief themes of moralists from Solomon downwards: they "lament the deceitfulness of hope, the fugacity of pleasure, and the frequency of calamity; and for palliatives of these incurable miseries, they recommend kindness, temperance, and [p. lxix] fortitude." But these familiar lessons of life have an additional force when they are accompanied, as in many of the Arabian poems, by illustrations which attract by their novelty, and interest and impress the heart by their beauty and appositeness.--Not less striking are the similitudes employed in the lighter effusions; as, for example, the comparison of the blue eyes of a beautiful woman weeping to violets dropping dew; or of wine, before it is mixed, to the cheek of a mistress, and, after the water is added, to the paleness of a lover.

^lxx:* Yet such was the extreme scarcity of books in England at a later period, that a manuscript, dated 1250, which is still preserved, containing the Proverbs of Solomon, Ecclesiastes, Canticles, and Wisdom (one of the books of the Apocrypha), bears the following inscription: "This book belongs to the monastery of Rochester; given by the prior John. If any remove it, or conceal it when taken away, or fraudulently efface this inscription, let him be anathema, Amen."

THE GENEALOGY OF THE SEVEN ARABIAN POETS.

THIS Table is reprinted from the Genealogy prefixed to Sir W. Jones' translation of the MU'ALLAQaT, as given in the tenth volume of the octavo edition of his works. The mode of transliterating Arabic proper names adopted by Sir W. Jones is different from most of the systems in use among modern English Arabists: the letter Qaf he represents by K, and Kaf by C; 'Ayn, for which there is no corresponding letter in our alphabet, and which is now generally represented by ['] or, when Hamza is not represented, by ['], he seems often to transliterate by aa, or a; and the strongly aspirated Ha, by hh.

It has been remarked, in the first section of the Introduction, that those Arabs who claim to be descended from Ishmael usually trace their genealogies no higher than 'Adnan, because of the uncertainty of the descents between 'Adnan and Ishmael. According to Sale, "the most approved series enumerates eight generations between these two persons, in the following order: ISMAEL, Kidar, Hamal, Nabet, Salaman, al-Homeisa, al-Yasa, Odad, Odd, ADNAN."

THE GENEALOGY OF THE SEVEN ARABIAN POETS

In-order, depth-first transcription of the above:

THE GENEALOGY OF THE SEVEN ARABIAN POETS

'ADNaN > MAAD > NIZaR.
NIZaR > RABEIAH and MODHaR.
RABEIAH > 'Asad > Jodeilah > Daamai > 'Aksai > Heneb > Kasith > Wayel.
Wayel > TAGLEB and BECR.
TAGLEB > Ganem > 'Amru > Hhabeib > BECR > JOSHAM > Zohair.
Zohair > Morrah and Saad.
Morrah > Hhareth > Rabeiah
Rabeiah > COLEIB and Maiah* and MOHALHIL
Maiah* > 'AMRIO'LKAIS.
Saad > 'Attab > Malec > Celthum > 'AMRU.
BECR > YASHCOR and 'Alei.
YASHCOR > Cenanah > Dhobyan > Josham > Maad > 'Adb > Malec > 'Abdallah > Bodheil > Macruh > Hhilizah > HHARETH.
'Alei > 'Saab > Accabah > Thalebah > Kais > Dhobeiah > Malec > Saad > Sofyan > 'Alabd > THARAFAH.
MODHaR > Alyas and Gailan.

Alyas > Thabekhah > 'Odd* > Mozeinah > 'Othman > Lathim > Hormah > Thur >
Thalebah > Hhilawan > MaZEN > Hareth > Kerth > 'Awamer > Reiahh > Abu Solmai >
ZOHAIR.
Gailan > Kais
Kais > Khasafah and Saad.
Khasafah > Acremah > Mansur > Hawazen > Becr > Moawiah > Sasa'ah > AAMER >
Rebeiah > Celab > Jafer > Malec > Rabeiah > LEBEID.
Saad > Gathfan > Raith > Bageidh.
Bageidh > DHOBYaN and 'ABS.
DHOBYaN > Saad > 'Auf > MORRAH > GAIDH.
'ABS > Katheiah > 'Aud > Makhzum > Nezar > Korad > Moawiah > 'ANTARAH.

THE
MOALLAKAT,
OR
SEVEN ARABIAN POEMS,
WHICH WERE SUSPENDED ON
THE TEMPLE AT MECCA.

TRANSLATED, WITH ARGUMENTS,

BY

SIR WILLIAM JONES.

The Poems entitled Almoallakat exhibit an   exact picture of their virtues and their
vices, their wisdom and their folly;   and show what may be constantly expected from
men of open hearts and boiling passions, with no law to control, and little religion to
restrain ahem.--Six   W. JONES: Discourse on The Arabs.

THE
POEM
OF
AMRIOLKAIS.
THE ARGUMENT.

THE Poet, after the manner of his countrymen, supposes himself attended on a journey
by a company of friends; and as they pass near a place where his mistress had lately
dwelled, but from which her tribe was then removed, he desires them to stop awhile, that
he might indulge the painful pleasure of weeping over the deserted remains of her tent.
They comply with his request, but exhort him to show more strength of mind, and urge
two topics of consolation, namely, that he had before been equally unhappy, and that he

[38]

had enjoyed his full share of pleasures. Thus, by recollection of his past delight, his imagination is kindled, and his grief suspended.

He then gives his friends a lively account of his juvenile frolics, to one of which they had alluded. It seems he had been in love with a girl named Onaiza, and had in vain sought an occasion to declare his passion. One day, when her tribe had struck their tents, and were changing their station, the women, as usual, came behind the rest, with the servants and baggage, in carriages fixed on the backs of camels. Amriolkais advanced slowly at a distance, and, when the men were out of sight, had the pleasure of seeing Onaiza retire with a party of damsels to a rivulet or pool, called Daratjuljul, where they undressed themselves, and were bathing, when the lover appeared, dismounted from his camel, and sat upon their clothes, proclaiming aloud that whoever would redeem her dress must present herself naked before him.

They adjured, entreated, expostulated; but, when it grew late, they found themselves obliged to submit, and all of them recovered their clothes except Onaiza, who renewed her adjurations, and continued a long time in the water: at length she also performed the condition, and dressed herself. Some hours had passed, when the girls complained of cold and hunger. Amriolkais therefore instantly killed the young camel on which he had ridden, and having called the female attendants together, made a fire and roasted him. The afternoon was spent in gay conversation, not without a cheerful cup, for he was provided with wine in a leathern bottle. But, when it was time to follow the tribe, the prince (for such was his rank) had neither camel nor horse; and Onaiza, after much importunity, consented to take him on her camel, before the carriage, while the other damsels divided among themselves the less agreeable burden of his arms and the furniture of his beast.

He next relates his courtship of Fatima, and his more dangerous amour with a girl of a tribe at war with his own, whose beauties he very minutely and luxuriantly delineates. From these love-tales he proceeds to the commendation of his own fortitude, when he was passing a desert in the darkest night; and the mention of the morning which succeeded leads him to a long description of his hunter, and of a chase in the forest, followed by a feast on the game which had been pierced by his javelins.

Here his narrative seems to be interrupted by a storm of lightning and violent rain;--he nobly describes the shower, and the torrent which it produced down all the adjacent mountains; and, his companions retiring to avoid the storm, the drama (for the poem has the form of a dramatic pastoral) ends abruptly.

The metre is of the first species, called long verse, and consists of the bacchius or amphibrachys, followed by the first epitrite; or, in the fourth and eighth places of the distich, by the double iambus, the last syllable being considered as a long one: the regular form, taken from the second chapter of "Commentaries on Asiatic Poetry," is this:

"Amator | puellarum | miser sae | pe fallitur

[39]

Ocellis | nigris, labris | odoris, | nigris comis."

THE POEM OF AMRIOLKAIS

STAY!--Let us weep at the remembrance of our beloved, at the sight of the station where her tent was raised, by the edge of yon bending sands between Dahul and Haumel,

2. "Tudam and Mikra; a station, the marks of which are not wholly effaced, though the south wind and the north have woven the twisted sand."

3. Thus I spoke, when my companions stopped their coursers by my side, and said: "Perish not through despair: only be patient."

4. "A profusion of tears," answered I, "is my sole relief; but what avails it to shed them over the remains of a deserted mansion?"

5. "Thy condition," they replied, "is not more painful than when thou leftest Howaira, before thy present passion, and her neighbour Rebaba, on the hills of Masel."

6. "Yes," I rejoined, "when those two damsels departed, musk was diffused from their robes, as the eastern gale sheds the scent of clove-gillyflowers:

7. "Then gushed the tears from my eyes, through excess of regret, and flowed down my neck, till my sword-belt was drenched in the stream."

8. "Yet hast thou passed many days in sweet converse with the fair: but none so sweet as the day which thou spentest by the pool of Daratjuljul."

9. On that day I killed my camel, to give the virgins a feast; and, oh! how strange was it that they should carry his trappings and furniture!

10. The damsels continued till evening helping one another to the roasted flesh, and to the delicate fat, like the fringe of white silk finely woven.

11. On that happy day I entered the carriage, the carriage of Onaiza, who said: "Wo to thee! thou wilt compel me to travel on foot."

12. She added (while the vehicle was bent aside with our weight), "O Amriolkais, descend, or my beast also will be killed!"

13. I answered: "Proceed, and loosen his rein; nor withhold from me the fruits of thy love, which again and again may be tasted with rapture.

14. "Many a fair one like thee--though not, like thee, a virgin--have I visited by night; and many a lovely mother have I diverted from the care of her yearling infant, adorned with amulets:

15. "When the suckling behind her cried, she turned round to him with half her body; but half of it, pressed beneath my embrace, was not turned from me."

16. Delightful, too, was the day when Fatima first rejected me on the summit of yon sand-hill, and took an oath, which she declared inviolable.

17. "O Fatima!" said I, "away with so much coyness; and if thou hadst resolved to abandon me, yet at last relent!

18. "If indeed my disposition and manners are unpleasing to thee, rend at once the mantle of my heart, that it may be detached from thy love.

19. "Art thou so haughty, because my passion for thee destroys me; and because whatever thou commandest my heart performs?

20. "Thou weepest; yet thy tears flow merely to wound my heart with the shafts of thine eyes--my heart, already broken to pieces and agonizing."

21. Besides these, with many a spotless virgin, whose tent had not yet been frequented, have I held soft dalliance at perfect leisure.

22. To visit one of them, I passed the guards of her bower, and a hostile tribe, who would have been eager to proclaim my death.

23. It was the hour when the Pleiads appeared in the firmament, like the folds of a silken sash variously decked with gems.

24. I approached: she stood expecting me by the curtain; and, as if she was preparing for sleep, had put off all her vesture but her night-dress.

25. She said: "By Him who created me," and gave me her lovely hand, "I am unable to refuse thee; for I perceive that the blindness of thy passion is not to be removed."

26. Then I rose with her; and as we walked she drew over our footsteps the train of her pictured robe.

27. Soon as we had passed the habitations of her tribe, and come to the bosom of a vale, surrounded with hillocks of spiry sand,

28. I gently drew her towards me by her curled locks, and she softly inclined to my embrace;--her waist was gracefully slender, but sweetly swelled the part encircled with ornaments of gold.

29. Delicate was her shape; fair her skin; and her body well proportioned: her bosom was as smooth as a mirror,

30. Or, like the pure egg of an ostrich, of a yellowish tint blended with white, and nourished by a stream of wholesome water not yet disturbed.

31. She turned aside, and displayed her soft cheek: she gave a timid glance with languishing eyes, like those of a roe in the groves of Wegera looking tenderly at her young.

32. Her neck was like that of a milk-white hind, but, when she raised it, exceeded not the justest symmetry; nor was the neck of my beloved so unadorned.

33. Her long coal-black hair decorated her back, thick and diffused, like bunches of dates clustering on the palm-tree.

34. Her locks were elegantly turned above her head; and the riband which bound them was lost in her tresses, part braided, part dishevelled.

35. She discovered a waist taper as a well-twisted cord; and a leg both as white and as smooth as the stem of a young palm, or a fresh reed, bending over the rivulet.

36. When she sleeps at noon, her bed is besprinkled with musk: she puts on her robe of undress, but leaves the apron to her handmaids.

37. She dispenses gifts with small, delicate fingers, sweetly glowing at their tips, like the white and crimson worm of Dabia, or dentrifices made of esel-wood.

38. The brightness of her face illumines the veil of night, like the evening taper of a recluse hermit.

39. On a girl like her, a girl of a moderate height, between those who wear a frock and those who wear a gown, the most bashful man must look with an enamoured eye.

40. The blind passions of men for common objects of affection are soon dispersed; but from the love of thee my heart cannot be released.

41. O how oft have I rejected the admonitions of a morose adviser, vehement in censuring my passion for thee; nor have I been moved by his reproaches!

42. Often has the night drawn her skirts around me, like the billows of the ocean, to make trial of my fortitude in a variety of cares;

43. And I said to her, when she seemed to extend her sides, to drag on her unwieldy length, and to advance slowly with her breast:

44. "Dispel thy gloom, O tedious night! that the morn may rise; although my sorrows are such, that the morning-light will not give more comfort than thy shades.

45. "O hideous night!--a night in which the stars are prevented from rising, as if they were bound to a solid cliff with strong cables!"

46. Often, too, have I risen at early dawn, while the birds were yet in their nests, and mounted a hunter with smooth short hair, of a full height, and so fleet as to make captive the beasts of the forest;

47. Ready in turning, quick in pursuing, bold in advancing, firm in backing; and performing the whole with the strength and swiftness of a vast rock which a torrent has pushed from its lofty base;

48. A bright bay steed, from whose polished back the trappings slide, as drops of rain glide hastily down the slippery marble.

49. Even in his weakest state he seems to boil while he runs; and the sound which he makes in his rage is like that of a bubbling cauldron.

50. When other horses that swim through the air are languid and kick the dust, he rushes on like a flood, and strikes the hard earth with a firm hoof.

51. He makes the light youth slide from his seat, and violently shakes the skirts of a heavier and more stubborn rider;

52. Rapid as the pierced wood in the hands of a playful child, which he whirls quickly round with a well-fastened cord.

53. He has the loins of an antelope, and the thighs of an ostrich; he trots like a wolf, and gallops like a young fox.

54. Firm are his haunches; and when his hinder parts are turned towards you, he fills the space between his legs with a long thick tail, which touches not the ground, and inclines not to either side.

55. His back, when he stands in his stall, resembles the smooth stone on which perfumes are mixed for a bride, or the seeds of coloquinteda are bruised.

56. The blood of the swift game, which remains on his neck, is like the crimson juice of hinna on gray flowing locks.

57. He bears us speedily to a herd of wild cattle, in which the heifers are fair as the virgins in black trailing robes, who dance round the idol Dewaar:

58. They turn their backs, and appear like the variegated shells of Yemen on the neck of a youth distinguished in his tribe for a multitude of noble kinsmen.

59. He soon brings us up to the foremost of the beasts, and leaves the rest far behind; nor has the herd time to disperse itself.

60. He runs from wild bulls to wild heifers, and overpowers them in a single heat, without being bathed, or even moistened, with sweat.

61. Then the busy cook dresses the game, roasting part, baking part on hot stones, and quickly boiling the rest in a vessel of iron.

62. In the evening we depart; and when the beholder's eye ascends to the head of my hunter, and then descends to his feet, it is unable at once to take in all his beauties.

63. His trappings and girths are still upon him: he stands erect before me, not yet loosed for pasture.

64. O friend, seest thou the lightning, whose flashes resemble the quick glance of two hands, amid clouds. raised above clouds?

65. The fire of it gleams like the lamps of a hermit, when the oil poured on them shakes the cord by which they are suspended.

66. I sit gazing at it, while my companions stand between Daaridge and Odhaib; but far distant is the cloud on which my eyes are fixed.

67. Its right side seems to pour its rain on the hills of Katan, and its left on the mountains of Sitaar and Yadbul.

68. It continues to discharge its waters over Cotaifa till the rushing torrent lays prostrate the groves of canahbel-trees.

69. It passes over mount Kenaan, which it deluges in its course, and forces the wild goats to descend from every cliff.

70. On mount Taima it leaves not one trunk of a palm tree, nor a single edifice, which is not built with well-cemented stone.

[44]

71. Mount Tebeir stands in the heights of the flood, like a venerable chief wrapped in a striped mantle.

72. The summit of Mogaimir, covered with the rubbish which the torrent has rolled down, looks in the morning like the top of a spindle encircled with wool.

73. The cloud unloads its freight on the desert of Ghabeit, like a merchant of Yemen alighting with his bales of rich apparel.

74. The small birds of the valley warble at daybreak, as if they had taken their early draught of generous wine mixed with spice.

75. The beasts of the wood, drowned in the floods of night, float, like the roots of wild onions, at the distant edge of the lake.

THE
POEM
OF
TARAFA.

THE ARGUMENT.

THIS Poem was occasioned by a little incident highly characteristic of pastoral manners. Tarafa and his brother Mabed jointly possessed a herd of camels, and had agreed to watch them alternately, each on his particular clay, lest, as they were grazing, they should be driven off by a tribe with whom their own clan was at war. But our poet was so immersed in meditation, and so wedded to his muse, that he often neglected his charge, and was sharply reproved by his brother, who asked him, sarcastically, whether, if he lost the camels, they could be restored by his poetry. "You shall be convinced of it," answered Tarafa; and persisted so long in his negligence that the whole herd was actually seized by the Modarites.

This was more than he really expected; and he applied to all his friends for assistance in recovering the camels; among others, he solicited the help of his cousin Malec, who, instead of granting it, took the opportunity of rebuking him with acrimony for his remissness in that instance, and for his general prodigality, libertinism, and spirit of contention; telling him that he was a disgrace to his family, and had raised innumerable enemies.

The defence of a poet was likely to be best made in poetical language; and Tarafa produced the following composition in vindication of his character and conduct, which he boldly justifies in every respect, and even claims praise for the very course of life which had exposed him to censure.

He glories in his passion for women, and begins, as usual, with lamenting the departure of his beloved Khaula (or, the "tender fawn"), whose beauty he describes in a very lively strain. It were to be wished that he had said more of his mistress, and less of his camel, of which he interweaves a very long, and no very pleasing, description.

The rest of the poem contains an eloge on his own fortitude, sprightliness, liberality, and valour, mixed with keen expostulations on the unkindness and ingratitude of Malec, and with all the common topics in favour of voluptuousness: he even triumphs on having slain and dressed one of his father's camels, and blames the old man for his churlishness and avarice.

It is a tradition preserved by Abu Obeida, that one of the chiefs, whom the poet compliments in the eighty-first couplet, made him a present of a hundred camels, and enabled him, as he had promised, to convince his brother that poetry could repair his loss.

The metre is the same with that used by Amriolkais.

THE POEM OF TARAFA.

THE mansion of Khaula is desolate, and the traces of it on the stony hills of Tahmed faintly shine, like the remains of blue figures painted on the back of a hand."

2. While I spoke thus to myself, my companions stopped their coursers by my side, and said, "Perish not through despair, but act with fortitude."

3. Ah, said I, the vehicles which bore away my fair one on the morning when the tribe of Malec departed, and their camels were traversing the banks of Deda, resembled large ships

4. Sailing from Aduli; or vessels of the merchant Ibn Yamin, which the mariner now turns obliquely, and now steers in a direct course;

5. Ships, which cleave the foaming waves with their prows, as a boy at his play divides with his hand the collected earth.

6. In that tribe was a lovely antelope, with black eyes, dark ruddy lips, and a beautiful neck, gracefully raised to crop the fresh berries of erac--a neck adorned with two strings of pearls and topazes.

7. She strays from her young, and feeds with the herd of roes in the tangled thicket, where she browses the edges of the wild fruit, and covers herself with a mantle of leaves.

8. She smiles, and displays her bright teeth, rising from their dark-coloured bases, like a privet-plant in full bloom, which pierces a bank of pure sand moistened with dew:

[46]

9. To her teeth the sun has imparted his brilliant water; but not to the part where they grow, which is sprinkled with lead-ore, while the ivory remains unspotted.

10. Her face appears to be wrapped in a veil of sunbeams; unblemished is her complexion, and her skin is without a wrinkle.

11. Such cares as this, whenever they oppress my soul, I dispel by taking adventurous journeys on a lean yet brisk camel, who runs with a quick pace both morning and evening;

12. Sure-footed, firm, and thin as the planks of a bier; whose course I hasten over long-trodden paths, variegated like a striped vest.

13. She rivals the swiftest camels, even of the noblest breed, and her hind-feet rapidly follow her fore-feet on the beaten way.

14. In the vernal season, she grazes on yon two hills among others of her race, whose teats are not yet filled with milk, and depastures the lawns, whose finest grass the gentle showers have made luxuriantly green.

15. She turns back at the sound of her rider's voice; and repels the caresses of a thick-haired russet stallion with the lash of her bushy tail,

16. Which appears as if the two wings of a large white eagle were transfixed by an awl to the bone, and hung waving round both her sides:

17. One while it lashes the place of him who rides hindmost on her; another while it plays round her teats, which are become wrinkled and flaccid like a leathern bag, their milk no longer distending them.

18. Her two haunches are plump, and compact as the two smooth valves of a lofty castle-gate.

19. Supple is her backbone: her ribs are like the strongest bows; and her neck is firmly raised on the well-connected vertebres.

20. The two cavities under her shoulders are spacious as two dens of beasts among the wild lotus plants; and stiff bows appear to be bent under her sinewy loins.

21. Her two thighs are exceedingly strong, and, when she moves, they diverge like two buckets carried from a well in the hands of a robust drawer of water.

22. Her joints are well knit, and her bones are solid, like a bridge of Grecian architecture, whose builder had vowed that he would enclose it with well-cemented bricks.

23. The hair under her chin is of a reddish hue: her back is muscular: she takes long yet quick steps with her hind-feet, and moves her fore-feet with agility;

24. She tosses them from her chest with the strength and swiftness of cables firmly pulled by a nervous arm; and her shoulders are bent like the rafters of a lofty dome:

25. She turns rapidly from the path: exceedingly swift is her pace; long is her head; and her shoulder-bones are strongly united to her sides.

26. The white and hollow marks of the cords, with which her burdens have been tied to her back, resemble pools of water on the smooth brow of a solid rock;

27. Marks which sometimes unite, and sometimes are distinct, like the gores of fine linen, which are sewed under the arms of a well-cut robe.

28. Long is her neck; and when she raises it with celerity, it resembles the stern of a ship floating aloft on the billowy Tigris.

29. Her skull is firm as an anvil; and the bones, which the sutures unite, are indented, and sharp as a file.

30. Her cheek is smooth and white as paper of Syria; and her lips, as soft as dyed leather of Yemen, exactly and smoothly cut.

3r. Her two eyes, like two polished mirrors, have found a hiding-place in the caverns of their orbits, the bones of which are like rocks, in whose cavities the water is collected:

32. Thou beholdest them free from blemish or spot, and resembling in beauty those of a wild-cow, the mother of playful young, when the voice of the hunter has filled her with fear.

33. Her ears truly distinguish every sound, to which she listens attentively in her nightly journeys, whether it be a gentle whisper or a loud noise;

34. Sharp ears, by which the excellence of her breed is known!--ears like those of a solitary wild-bull in the groves of Haumel.

35. Her heart, easily susceptible of terror, palpitates with a quick motion, yet remains firm in her chest as a round solid stone striking a broad floor of marble.

36. If I please, she raises her head to the middle of her trappings, and swims with her fore-legs as swift as a young ostrich.

37. If I please, she moves more slowly; if not, she gallops, through fear of the strong lash formed of twisted thongs.

[48]

38. Her upper-lip is divided, and the softer part of her nose is bored: when she bends them towards the ground her pace is greatly accelerated.

39. On a camel like this I continue my course, when the companion of my adventure exclaims: "Oh, that I could redeem thee, and redeem myself from the impending danger!"

40. While his soul flutters through fear, and, imagining that he has lost the way, he supposes himself on the brink of perdition.

41. When the people say aloud: "Who is the man to deliver us from calamity?" I believe they call upon me, and I disgrace not their commission by supineness or folly.

42. I shake the lash over my camel, and she quickens her pace, while the sultry vapour rolls in waves over the burning cliffs.

43. She floats proudly along with her flowing tail, as the dancing-girl floats in the banquet of her lord, and spreads the long white skirts of her trailing vest.

44. I inhabit not the lofty hills through fear of enemies or of guests; but when the tribe or the traveller demand my assistance, I give it eagerly.

45. If you seek me in the circle of the assembled nation, there you find me; and if you hunt me in the bowers of the vintner, there too you discover your game.

46. When you visit me in the morning, I offer you a flowing goblet; and, if you make excuses, I bid you drink it with pleasure, and repeat your draught.

47. When all the clan are met to state their pretensions to nobility, you will perceive me raised to the summit of an illustrious house, the refuge of the distressed.

48. My companions in the feast are youths, bright as stars, and singing-girls, who advance towards us, clad in striped robes and saffron-coloured mantles:

49. Large is the opening of their vests above their delicate bosoms, through which the inflamed youth touches their uncovered breasts of exquisite softness.

50. When we say to one of them, "Let us hear a song," she steps before us with easy grace, and begins with gentle notes, in a voice not forced:

51.* When she warbles in a higher strain, you would believe her notes to be those of camels lamenting their lost young.

52. Thus I drink old wine, without ceasing, and enjoy the delights of life; selling and dissipating my property, both newly acquired and inherited;

[49]

53. Until the whole clan reject me, and leave me solitary, like a diseased camel smeared with pitch:

54. Yet even now I perceive that the sons of earth (the most indigent men) acknowledge my bounty, and the rich inhabitants of yon extended camp confess my glory.

55. Oh, thou, who censurest me for engaging in combats and pursuing pleasures, wilt thou, if I avoid them, insure my immortality?

56, If thou art unable to repel the stroke of death, allow me, before it comes, to enjoy the good which I possess.

57. Were it not for three enjoyments which youth affords, I swear by thy prosperity, that I should not be solicitous how soon my friends visited me on my death-bed:

58. First, to rise before the censurers awake, and to drink tawny wine, which sparkles and froths when the clear stream is poured into it.

59. Next, when a warrior, encircled by foes, implores my aid, to bend towards him my prancing charger, fierce as a wolf among the gadha-trees, whom the sound of human steps has awakened, and who runs to quench his thirst at the brook.

60. Thirdly, to shorten a cloudy day, a day astonishingly dark, by toying with a lovely delicate girl under a tent supported by pillars,--

61. A girl, whose bracelets and garters seem hung on the stems of oshar-trees, or of ricinus, not stripped of their soft leaves.

62. Suffer me, whilst I live, to drench my head with wine, lest, having drunk too little in my life-time, I should be thirsty in another state.

63. A man of my generous spirit drinks his full draught to-day, and to-morrow, when we are dead, it will be known which of us has not quenched his thirst.

64. I see no difference between the tomb of an anxious miser, gasping over his hoard, and the tomb of the libertine, lost in the maze of voluptuousness.

65. You behold the sepulchres of them both raised in two heaps of earth, on which are elevated two broad piles of solid marble among the tombs closely connected.

66. Death, I observe, selects the noblest heroes for her victims, and reserves as her property the choicest possessions of the sordid hoarder.

67. I consider time as a treasure decreasing every night; and that which every day diminishes soon perishes for ever.

68. By thy life, my friend, when Death inflicts not her wound, she resembles a camel-driver who relaxes the cord which remains twisted in his hand.

69. What causes the variance, which I perceive, between me and my cousin Malec, who, whenever I approach him, retires and flees to a distance?

70. He censures me, whilst I know not the ground of his censure; just as Karth, the son of Aabed, reproved me in the assembly of the tribe.

71. He bids me wholly despair of all the good which I seek, as if we had buried it in a gloomy grave;

7 2. And this for no defamatory words which I have uttered, but only because I sought, without remissness, for the camels of my brother Mabed.

73. I have drawn closer the ties of our relation, and I swear by thy prosperity, that in all times of extreme distress, my succour is at hand.

74. Whenever I am summoned on momentous enterprises, I am prepared to encounter peril; and whenever the foe assails thee impetuously, I defend thee with equal vehemence.

75. If any base defamers injure thy good name by their calumnies, I force them, without previous menace, to drain a cup from the pool of death;

76. Yet, without having committed any offence, I am treated like the worst offender--am censured, insulted, upbraided, rejected.

77. When any other man but Malec my cousin, he would have dispelled my cares, or have left me at liberty for a season.

78. But my kinsman strangles me with cruelty, even at the very time when I am giving thanks for past, and requesting new favours; even when I am seeking from him the redemption of my soul!

79. The unkindness of relations gives keener anguish to every noble breast than the stroke of an Indian scimitar.

80. Permit me then to follow the bent of my nature, and I will be grateful for thy indulgence, although my abode should be fixed at such a distance as the mountains of Darghed.

[51]

81. Had it pleased the Author of my being, I might have been as illustrious as Kais, the son of Khaled; had it pleased my Creator, I might have been as eminent as Amru, the son of Morthed:

82. Then should I have abounded in wealth; and the noblest chiefs would have visited me, as a chieftain equally noble.

83. I am light, as you know me all, and am nimble; following my own inclinations, and briskly moving as the head of a serpent with flaming eyes.

84. I have sworn that my side should never cease to line a bright Indian blade with two well-polished and well-sharpened edges:

85. A penetrating scimitar! When I advance with it in my defence against a fierce attack, the first stroke makes a second unnecessary: it is not a mere pruning-sickle,

86. But the genuine brother of confidence, not bent by the most impetuous blow; and when they say to me, "Gently," I restrain its rage, and exclaim, "It is enough!"

87. When the whole clan are bracing on their armour with eager haste, thou mayst find me victorious in the conflict, as soon as my hand can touch the hilt of this scimitar.

88. Many a herd of slumbering camels have I approached with my drawn sabre, when the foremost of them, awakening, have fled through fear of me:

89. But one of them has passed before me, strong-limbed, full-breasted, and well-fed, the highly-valued property of a morose old churl, dry and thin as a fuller's club.

90. He said to me, when the camel's hoof and thigh were dismembered, "Seest thou not how great an injury thou hast done me?"

91. Then he turned to his attendants, saying, "What opinion do you form of that young wine-drinker, who assails us impetuously, whose violence is preconcerted?

92. "Leave him," he added, "and let this camel be his perquisite; but, unless you drive off the hindmost of the herd, he will reiterate his mischief."

93. Then our damsels were busy in dressing the camel's foal, and eagerly served up the luscious bunch.

94. O daughter of Mabed, sing my praises, if I am slain, according to my desert, and rend thy vest with sincere affliction!

95. Compare me not with any man, whose courage equals not my courage; whose exploits are not like mine; who has not been engaged in combats, in which I have been distinguished:

96. With a man slow in noble enterprises, but quick in base pursuits; dishonoured in the assembly of the tribe, and a vile outcast.

97. Had I been ignoble among my countrymen, the enmity of the befriended and the friendless might have been injurious to me;

98. But their malevolence is repelled by my firm defiance of them, by my boldness in attack, by my solid integrity, and my exalted birth.

99. By thy life, the hardest enterprises neither fill my day with solicitude, nor lengthen the duration of my night:

100. But many a day have I fixed my station immoveably in the close conflict, and defended a pass, regardless of hostile menaces,

101. On my native field of combat, where even the boldest hero might be apprehensive of destruction; where the muscles of our chargers quake, as soon as they mingle in battle;

102. And many an arrow for drawing lots have I seen well hardened and made yellow by fire, and then have delivered it into the hand of the gamester noted for ill fortune.

103. Too much wisdom is folly; for time will produce events, of which thou canst have no idea; and he, to whom thou gayest no commission, will bring thee unexpected news.

THE
POEM
OF
ZOHAIR.

THE ARGUMENT.

THE war of Dahis, of which Amriolkais is by some supposed to have been the cause, had raged near forty years, if the Arabian account be true, between the tribes of Abs and Dhobyan, who both began at length to be tired of so bloody and ruinous a contest. A treaty was therefore proposed and concluded; but Hosein, the son of Demdem, whose brother Harem had been slain by Ward, the son of Habes, had taken a solemn oath, not unusual among the Arabs, that he would not bathe his head in water, until he had avenged the death of his brother, by killing either Ward himself, or one of his nearest relations. His head was not long unbathed; and he is even supposed to have violated the law of

[53]

hospitality by slaying a guest, whom he found to be an Absite descended lineally from the common ancestor Galeb.

This malignant and vindictive spirit gave great displeasure to Hareth and Harem, two virtuous chiefs of the same tribe with Hosein; and when the Absites were approaching in warlike array to resent the infraction of the treaty, Hareth sent his own son to the tent of their chief with a present of a hundred fine camels, as an atonement for the murder of their countryman, and a message importing his firm reliance on their honour, and his hope that "they would prefer the milk of the camels to the blood of his son." Upon this Rabeiah, the prince of Abs, having harangued his troops, and received their approbation, sent back the youth with this answer, that he "accepted the camels as an expiatory gift, and would supply the imperfection of the former treaty by a sincere and durable peace."

In commemoration of this noble act, Zohair, then a very old man, composed the following panegyric on Hareth and Harem; but the opening of it, like all the others, is amatory and elegiac: it has also something of the dramatic form.

The poet, supposed to be travelling with a friend, recognises the place where the tent of his mistress had been pitched twenty years before; he finds it wild and desolate; but his imagination is so warmed by associated ideas of former happiness, that he seems to discern a company of damsels, with his favourite in the midst of them, of whose appearance and journey he gives a very lively picture; and thence passes, rather abruptly, to the praises of the two peace-makers and their tribe; inveighs against the malignity of Hosein; personifies War, the miseries of which he describes in a strain highly figurative; and concludes with a number of fine maxims, not unlike the proverbs of Solomon, which he repeats to his friend as a specimen of his wisdom acquired by long experience.

The measure is the same with that of the first and second Poems.

THE POEM OF ZOHAIR.

ARE these the only traces of the lovely Ommaufia? Are these the silent ruins of her mansion in the rough plains of Derraage and Mothatallem?

2. Are the remains of her abode, in the two stations of Rakma, become like blue stains renewed with fresh woad on the veins of the wrist?

3. There the wild cows with large eyes, and the milk-white deer, walk in slow succession, while their young rise hastily to follow them from every lair.

4. On this plain I stopped, after an absence of twenty summers, and with difficulty could recollect the mansion of my fair one after long meditation;

5. After surveying the black stones on which her cauldrons used to be raised, and the canal round her tent, like the margin of a fish-pond, which time had not destroyed.

[54]

6. Soon as I recollected the dwelling-place of my beloved, I said to the remains of her bower,--"Hail, sweet bower! may thy morning be fair and auspicious!"

7. But, I added, look, my friend! dost thou not discern a company of maidens seated on camels, and advancing over the high ground above the streams of Jortham?

8. They leave on their right the mountains and rocky plains of Kenaan. Oh, how many of my bitter foes, and how many of my firm allies, does Kenaan contain!

9. They are mounted in carriages covered with costly awnings, and with rose-coloured veils, the linings of which have the hue of crimson andem-wood.

10. They now appear by the valley of Subaan, and now they pass through it: the trappings of all their camels are new and large.

11. When they ascend from the bosom of the vale, they sit forward on the saddle-cloths, with every mark of a voluptuous gaiety.

12. The locks of stained wool, that fall from their carriages whenever they alight, resemble the scarlet berries of night-shade not yet crushed.

13. They rose at day-break; they proceeded at early dawn; they are advancing towards the valley of Ras, directly and surely, as the hand to the mouth.

14. Now, when they have reached the brink of yon blue gushing rivulet, they fix the poles of their tents, like the Arab with a settled mansion.

15. Among them the nice gazer on beauty may find delight, and the curious observant eye may be gratified with charming objects.

16. In this place, how nobly did the two descendants of Gaidh, the son of Morra, labour to unite the tribes, which a fatal effusion of blood had long divided!

17. I have sworn by the sacred edifice, round which the sons of Koraish and Jorham, who built it, make devout processions;

18. Yes, I have solemnly sworn, that I would give due praise to that illustrious pair, who have shown their excellence in all affairs, both simple and complicated.

19. Noble chiefs! You reconciled Abs and Dhobyan after their bloody conflicts: after the deadly perfumes of Minsham had long scattered poison among them.

20. You said: "We will secure the public good on a firm basis: whatever profusion of wealth or exertions of virtue it may demand, we will secure it."

[55]

21. Thence you raised a strong fabric of peace; from which all partial obstinacy and all criminal supineness were alike removed.

22. Chiefs, exalted in the high ranks of Maad, father of Arabs! may you be led into the paths of felicity! The man who opens for his country a treasure of glory should himself be glorified.

23. They drove to the tents of their appeased foes a herd of young camels, marked for the goodness of their breed, and either inherited from their fathers or the scattered prizes of war.

24. With a hundred camels they closed all wounds: in due season were they given, yet the givers were themselves free from guilt.

25. The atonement was auspiciously offered by one tribe to the other; yet those who offered it had not shed a cupful of blood.

26. Oh, convey this message from me to the sons of Dhobyan, and say to the confederates: Have you not bound yourselves in this treaty by an indissoluble tie?

27. Attempt not to conceal from God the designs which your bosoms contain; for that which you strive to hide God perfectly knows.

28. He sometimes defers the punishment, but registers the crime in a volume, and reserves it for the day of account; sometimes He accelerates the chastisement, and heavily it falls!

29. War is a dire fiend, as you have known by experience; nor is this a new or a doubtful assertion concerning her.

30. When you expelled her from your plains, you expelled her covered with infamy; but when you kindled her flame, she blazed and raged.

31. She ground you, as the mill grinds the corn with its lower stone; like a female camel, she became pregnant: she bore twice in one year; and at her last labour, she was the mother of twins:

32. She brought forth Distress and Ruin, monsters full-grown, each of them deformed as the dun camel of Aad; she then gave them her breast, and they were instantly weaned.

33. Oh, what plenty she produced in your land! The provisions which she supplied were more abundant, no doubt, than those which the cities of Irak dispense to their inhabitants, weighed with large weights, and measured with ample measures!

34. Hail, illustrious tribe! They fix their tents where faithful allies defend their interests, whenever some cloudy night assails them with sudden adversity.

35. Hail, noble race! among whom neither can the revengeful man wreak his vengeance, nor is the penitent offender left to the mercy of his foes.

36. Like camels were they turned loose to pasture between the times of watering; and then were they led to copious pools, horrid with arms and blood:

39. They dragged one another to their several deaths; and then were they brought back, like a herd, to graze on pernicious and noxious weeds.

38. I swore by my life, that I would exalt with praises that excellent tribe, whom Hosein, the son of Demdem, injured, when he refused to concur in the treaty.

39. He bent his whole mind to the accomplishment of his hidden purpose: he revealed it not; he took no precipitate step.

40. He said, "I will accomplish my design; and will secure myself from my foe with a thousand horses well caparisoned."

41. He made a fierce attack, nor feared the number of tents, where Death, the mother of vultures, had fixed her mansion;

42. There the warrior stood armed at all points, fierce as a lion with strong muscles, with a flowing mane, with claws never blunted:

43* A bold lion, who, when he is assailed, speedily chastises the assailant; and, when no one attacks him openly, often becomes the aggressor.

44. Yet I swear by thy life, my friend, that their lances poured not forth the blood of Ibn Neheic, nor of Mothallem, cruelly slain;

45. Their javelins had no share in drinking the blood of Naufel, nor that of Waheb, nor that of Ibn Mojaddem.

46. The deaths of all those chiefs I myself have seen expiated with camels free from blemish, ascending the summits of rocks.

47. He, indeed, who rejects the blunt end of the lance, which is presented as a token of peace, must yield to the sharpness of the point, with which every tall javelin is armed.

48. He who keeps his promise escapes blame; and he who directs his heart to the calm resting-place of integrity will never stammer nor quake in the assemblies of his nation.

49. He who trembles at all possible causes of death falls in their way: even though he desire to mount the skies on a scaling-ladder.

50. He who possesses wealth or talents, and withholds them from his countrymen, alienates their love, and exposes himself to their obloquy.

51. He who continually debases his mind by suffering others to ride over it, and never raises it from so abject a state, will at last repent of his meanness.

52. He who sojourns in foreign countries mistakes his enemy for his friend; and him, who exalts not his own soul, the nation will not exalt.

53. He who drives not invaders from his cistern with strong arms will see it demolished; and he who abstains ever so much from injuring others will often himself be injured.

54. He who conciliates not the hearts of men in a variety of transactions will be bitten by their sharp teeth, and trampled on by their pasterns.

55. He who shields his reputation by generous deeds will augment it; and he who guards not himself from censure will be censured.

56. I am weary of the hard burdens which life imposes; and every man who, like me, has lived fourscore years will assuredly be no less weary.

57. I have seen Death herself stumble like a dim-sighted camel; but he whom she strikes falls; and he whom she misses grows old, even to decrepitude.

58. Whenever a man has a peculiar cast in his nature, although he supposes it concealed, it will soon be known.

59. Experience has taught me the events of this day and yesterday; but as to the events of to-morrow, I confess my blindness.

60.* Half of man is his tongue, and the other half is his heart: the rest is only an image composed of blood and flesh.

61.* He who confers benefits on persons unworthy of them changes his praise to blame, and his joy to repentance.

62.* How many men dost thou see whose abundant merit is admired, when they are silent, but whose failings are discovered, as soon as they open their lips!

63.* An old man never grows wise after his folly; but when a youth has acted foolishly he may attain wisdom.

64.* We asked, and you gave; we repeated our requests, and your gift also was repeated; but whoever frequently solicits will at length meet with a refusal.

THE
POEM
OF
LEBEID.

THE ARGUMENT.

ALTHOUGH the opening of this Poem be that of a love-elegy, and the greater part of it be purely pastoral, yet it seems to have been composed on an occasion more exalted than the departure of a mistress, or the complaints of a lover. For the poet, who was also a genuine patriot, had been entertained at the court of Nomaan, King of Hira in Mesopotamia, and had been there engaged in a warm controversy with Rabeiah, son of Zeiad, chief of the Absites, concerning the comparative excellence of their tribes. Lebeid himself relates, what might be very naturally expected from a man of his eloquence and warmth, that he maintained the glory of his countrymen and his own dignity against all opponents; but, in order to perpetuate his victory, and to render his triumph more brilliant, he produced the following poem at the annual assembly, and having obtained the suffrages of the critics, was permitted, we are told, to hang it up on the gate of the Temple.

The fifteen first couplets are extremely picturesque, and highly characteristic of Arabian manners. They are followed by an expostulatory address of the poet himself, or of some friend who attended him on his rambles, on the folly of his fruitless passion for Nawara, who had slighted him, and whose tent was removed to a considerable distance. Occasion is hence taken to interweave a long description of the camel on which he intended to travel far from the object of his love, and which he compares for swiftness to a cloud driven by the wind, or a wild-ass running to a pool, after having subsisted many months on herbage only; or rather to a wild-cow hastening in search of her calf, whom the wolves had left mangled in the forest;--the last comparison consists of seventeen couplets, and may be compared with the long-tailed similes of the Greek and Roman poets.

He then returns to Nawara, and requites her coyness with expressions of equal indifference; he describes the gaiety of his life, and the pleasures which he can enjoy even in her absence; he celebrates his own intrepidity in danger and firmness on his military station; whence he takes occasion to introduce a short but lively description of his horse; and, in the seventieth couplet, alludes to the before-mentioned contest, which gave rise to the poem: thence he passes to the praises of his own hospitality; and concludes with a panegyric on the virtues of his tribe.

[59]

The measure is of the fifth class, called perfect verse, which regularly consists of the compound foot benedicerent, six times repeated, in this form:

"Tria grata sunt | animo meo, ut | melius nihil,
  Oculi nigri, | cyathus nitens, | roseus calyx."

But when the couplet admits the third epitrite, pastoribus, and the double iambus, amantium, it may be considered as belonging to the seventh, or tremulous, class; between which and the perfect the only distinction seems to be that the tremulous never admits the anapestic foot. They are both, in the language of European prosody, iambics, in which the even places are invariably pure, and the odd places always exclude the dactyl: when the uneven feet are trochees or pyrrhics, the verses become choriambic or peonic; but of this change we have no instance in the poem before us.

THE POEM OF LEBEID.

DESOLATE are the mansions of the fair, the stations in Minia, where they rested, and those where they fixed their abodes! Wild are the hills of Goul, and deserted is the summit of Rijaam.

2. The canals of Rayaan are destroyed: the remains of them are laid bare and smoothed by the floods, like characters engraved on the solid rocks.

3. Dear ruins! Many a year has been closed, many a month, holy and unhallowed, has elapsed, since I exchanged tender vows with their fair inhabitants!

4. The rainy constellations of spring have made their hills green and luxuriant: the drops from the thunder-clouds have drenched them with profuse as well as with gentle showers:

5. Showers, from every nightly cloud, from every cloud veiling the horizon at day-break, and from every evening cloud, responsive with hoarse murmurs.

6. Here the wild eringo-plants raise their tops: here the antelopes bring forth their young, by the sides of the valley: and here the ostriches drop their eggs.

7. The large-eyed wild-cows lie suckling their young, a few days old--their young, who will soon become a herd on the plain.

8. The torrents have cleared the rubbish, and disclosed the traces of habitations, as the reeds of a writer restore effaced letters in a book;

9. Or as the black dust, sprinkled over the varied marks on a fair hand, brings to view with a brighter tint the blue stains of woad.

10. I stood asking news of the ruins concerning their lovely habitants; but what avail my questions to dreary rocks, who answer them only by their echo?

11. In the plains, which now are naked, a populous tribe once dwelled; but they decamped at early dawn, and nothing of them remains, but the canals which encircled their tents, and the thumaam-plants, with which they were repaired.

12. How were thy tender affections raised, when the damsels of the tribe departed; when they hid themselves in carriages of cotton, like antelopes in their lair; and the tents, as they were struck, gave a piercing sound!

13. They were concealed in vehicles whose sides were well covered with awnings and carpets, with fine-spun curtains, and pictured veils:

14. A company of maidens were seated in them, with black eyes and graceful motions, like the wild heifers of Tudah, or the roes of Wegera tenderly gazing on their young.

15. They hastened their camels, till the sultry vapour gradually stole them from thy sight; and they seemed to pass through a vale, wild with tamarisks and rough with large stones, like the valley of Beihsa.

16. Ah, what remains in thy remembrance of the beautiful Nawara, since now she dwells at a distance, and all the bonds of union between her and thee, both strong and weak, are torn asunder?

17. A damsel, who sometimes has her abode in Faid, and sometimes is a neighbour to the people of Hejaaz!--how can she be an object of thy desire?

18. She alights at the eastern side of the two mountains, Aja and Salma, and then stops on the hills of Mohajjer; Rokhaam also and Ferda receive her with joy.

19. When she travels towards Yemen, we may suppose that she rests at Sawayik; and baits at the stations of Wahaaf and Telkhaam.

20. Break then so vain a connection with a mistress whose regard has ceased; for hapless is a union with a maid who has broken her vow!

21. When a damsel is kind and complacent, love her with ardent affection; but when her faith staggers and her constancy is shaken, let your disunion be unalterably fixed.

22. Execute thy purpose, O Lebeid, on a camel, wearied by long journeys, which have left but little of her former strength;--a camel whose sides are emaciated, and on whose back the bunch is diminished;

23. Yet even in this condition, when her flesh is extenuated, and her hair thin, when, after many a toilsome day, the thong of her shoes is broken,--

24. Even now she has a spirit so brisk, that she flies with the rein, like a dun cloud driven by the south wind, after it has discharged its shower;

25. Or like a female wild-ass, whose teats are distended with milk, while the male, by whom she is with foal, is grown lean with driving his rivals from her, with biting and kicking them in his rage.

26. He runs with her up the crooked hills, although he has been wounded in his battles; but her present coyness, compared with her late fondness, fills him with surprise.

27. He ascends the sandy hillock of Thalbut, and explores its deserted top, fearing lest an enemy should lurk behind the guide-stones.

28. There they remain till the close of the sixth month, till the frosty season is past; they subsist on herbage without water: their time of fasting and of retirement is long.

29. The thorns of the buhma-plant wound their hind-legs, and the sultry winds of summer drive them violently in their course.

30. At length they form in their minds a fixed resolution of seeking some cool rivulet, and the object of their settled purpose is nearly attained.

31. They alternately raise high clouds of dust with an extended shade, as the smoke rises from a pile of dry wood newly kindled and flaming,

32. When fresh arfadge-plants are mingled in the heap, and the north wind plays with the blazing fire.

33. He passes on, but makes her run before him; for such is his usual course, when he fears that she will linger behind.

34. They rush over the margin of the rivulet, they divide the waters of the full stream, whose banks are covered with the plants of kolaam,--

35. Banks, which a grove of reeds, part erect and part laid prostrate, overshades or clothes, as with a mantle.

36. Is this the swiftness of my camel? No; rather she resembles a wild-cow, whose calf has been devoured by ravenous beasts, when she has suffered him to graze apart, and relied for his protection on the leader of the herd;

37. A mother with flat nostrils; who, as soon as she misses her young one, ceases not to run hastily round the vales between the sand-hills, and to fill them with her mournful cries;

38. With cries for her white-haired young, who now lies rolled in dust, after the dun wolves--hunters of the desert--have divided his mangled limbs, and their feast has not been interrupted.

39. They met him in the moment of her neglect; they seized him with eagerness; for, oh, how unerring are the arrows of death!

40. She passes the night in agony; while the rain falls in a continued shower, and drenches the tangled groves with a profuse stream.

41. She shelters herself under the root of a tree, whose boughs are thick, apart from other trees, by the edge of a hill, whose fine sands are shaken by her motion;

42. Yet the successive drops fall on her striped hack, while the clouds of night veil the light of the stars.

43. Her white hair glimmers when the darkness is just coming on, and sparkles like the pearls of a merchant, when he scatters them from their string.

44. At length, when the clouds are dispersed, and the dawn appears, she rises early, and her hoofs glide on the slippery ground.

45. She grows impatient, and wild with grief: she lies frantic in the pool of Soayid for seven whole days with their twin-sisters, seven nights;

46. And now she is in total despair; her teats, which were full of milk, are grown flaccid and dry, though they are not worn by suckling and weaning her young.

47. She now hears the cry of the hunters; she hears it, but sees them not; she trembles with fear: for she knows that the hunters bring her destruction.

48. She sits quivering, and imagines that the cause of her dread will appear on one side and the other, before and behind her.

49. When the archers despair of reaching her with their shafts, they let slip their long-eared hounds, answering to their names, with bodies dry and thin.

50. They rush on: but she brandishes against them her extended horns, both long and sharp as javelins made by the skilful hand of Samhar,

51. Striving to repel them; for she knows that, if her effort be vain, the destined moment of her death must soon approach:

52. Then she drives the dog Casaab to his fate; she is stained with his blood; and Sokhaam is left prostrate on the field.

53. On a camel like this, when the flashes of the noontide vapour dance over the plain, and the sultry mist clothes the parched hills,

54. I accomplish my bold design, from which I am not deterred by any fear of reprehension from the most censorious man.

55. Knowest thou not, O Nawara, that I preserve the knot of affection entire, or cut it in two, as the objects of it are constant or faithless?

56. That I would leave without reluctance a country not congenial to my disposition, although death were instantly to overtake my soul?

57. Ah, thou knowest not how many serene nights, with sweet sport and mirthful revelry,

58. I pass in gay conversation; and often return to the flag of the wine-merchant, when he spreads it in the air, and sells his wine at a high price:

59. I purchase the old liquor at a dear rate, in dark leathern bottles long reposited, or in casks, black with pitch, whose seals I break, and then fill the cheerful goblet.

60. How often do I quaff pure wine in the morning, and draw towards me the fair lutanist, whose delicate fingers skilfully touch the strings!

61. I rise before the cock to take my morning draught, which I sip again and again, when the sleepers of the dawn awake.

62. On many a cold morning, when the freezing winds howl, and the hand of the North holds their reins, I turn aside their blast from the travellers, whom I receive in my tent.

63. When I rise early to defend my tribe, my arms are borne by a swift horse, whose girths resemble my sash adorned with gems.

64. I ascend a dusty hill to explore the situation of the foe, and our dust, flying in clouds, reaches the hostile standard.

65. At length, when the sun begins to sink into darkness, and the veil of night conceals the ambuscade and the stratagems of our enemy,

66. I descend into the vale; and my steed raises his neck like the smooth branch of a lofty palm, which he who wishes to cut it cannot reach:

67. I incite him to run like a fleet ostrich in his impetuous course, until, when he boils in his rage and his bones are light,

68. His trappings are strongly agitated; a shower flows down his neck; and his surcingle is bathed in the scalding foam.

69. He lifts his head: he flies at liberty with the loose rein; and hastens to his goal, as a dove hastens to the brook when her feverish thirst rages.

70. There is a mansion (the palace of Nomaan) filled with guests, unknown to each other; hoping for presents and fearing reproof:

71. It is inhabited by men, like strong-necked lions, who menace one another with malignant hate, like the demons of Badiya, with feet firmly riveted in the conflict.

72. I disputed their false pretensions, yet admitted their real merit, according to my judgment; nor could the noblest among them surpass me in renown.

73. Oft have I invited a numerous company to the death of a camel bought for slaughter, to be divided by lot with arrows of equal dimensions:

74. I invite them to draw lots for a camel without a foal, and for a camel with her young one, whose flesh I distribute to all the neighbours.

75. The guest and the stranger, admitted to my board, seem to have alighted in the sweet vale of Tebaala, luxuriant with vernal blossoms.

76. To the cords of my tent approaches every needy matron, worn with fatigue, like a camel doomed to die at her master's tomb, whose vesture is both scanty and ragged.

77. There they crown with meat, while the wintry winds contend with fierce blasts, a dish flowing like a rivulet, into which the famished orphans eagerly plunge.

78. When the nations are assembled, some hero of our tribe, firm in debate, never fails by superior powers to surmount the greatest difficulty.

79. He distributes equal shares; he dispenses justice to the tribes; he is indignant when their right is diminished; and, to establish their right, often relinquishes his own.

80. He acts with greatness of mind and with nobleness of heart: he sheds the dew of his liberality on those who need his assistance;--he scatters around his own gains and precious spoils, the prizes of his valour.

81. He belongs to a tribe whose ancestors have left them a perfect model; and every tribe that descends from us will have patterns of excellence, and objects of imitation.

82. If their succour be asked, they instantly brace on their helmets, while their lances and breast-plates glitter like stars.

83. Their actions are not sullied by the rust of time, or tarnished by disgrace; for their virtues are unshaken by any base desires.

84. He hath raised for us a fabric of glory with a lofty summit, to which all the aged and all the young men of our tribe aspire.

85. Be content, therefore, with the dispensations of the Supreme Ruler; for He, who best knows our nature, has dispensed justice among us.

86. When peace has been established by our tribe, we keep it inviolate; and He, who makes it, renders our prosperity complete.

87. Noble are the exertions of our heroes, when the tribe struggle with hardships: they are our leaders in war, and in peace the deciders of our claims:

88. They are an enlivening spring to their indigent neighbours, and to the disconsolate widows, whose year passes heavily away:

89. They are an illustrious race; although their enviers may be slow in commending them, and the malevolent censurer may incline to their foe.

THE
POEM
OF
ANTARA.

THE ARGUMENT.

THIS Poem appears to have been a little older than that of Zohair; for it must have been composed during the wars of Dahis, which the magnanimity of the two chiefs, extolled by Zohair, "so nobly terminated." Antara, the gallant Absite, distinguished himself very early in the war by his valour in attacking the tribe of Dhobyan, and boasts in this composition that he had slain Demdem, the father of Hosein and of Harem, whom Ward, the son of Habes, afterwards put to death. An old enmity subsisted, it seems, between our poet and those two young men, who, as Antara believed, had calumniated him without provocation; and his chief object in this poem was to blazon his own achievements and exploits, and to denounce implacable resentment against the calumniators, whom his menaces were likely to intimidate. Yet so harsh an argument is tempered by a strain in some parts elegiac and amatory: for even this vengeful impetuous warrior found himself obliged to comply with the custom of the Arabian poets, "who had left," as he complains, "little new imagery for their successors."

He begins with a pathetic address to the bower of his beloved Abla, and to the ruins of her deserted mansion: he bewails her sudden departure, the distance of her new abode, and the unhappy variance between their respective clans: he describes his passion and the beauties of his mistress with great energy: thence he passes to his own laborious course of life, contrasted with the voluptuous indolence of the fair, and gives a forcible description of his camel, whom he compares to a male ostrich hastening to visit the eggs, which the female (whose usual neglect of them is mentioned by naturalists) had left in a remote valley. He next expatiates on his various accomplishments and virtues: his mildness to those who treat him kindly, his fierceness to those who injure him; his disregard of wealth, his gaiety, liberality, and, above all, his military prowess and spirit of enterprise, on which he triumphantly enlarges through the rest of the poem, except four couplets, in which he alludes obscurely to a certain love-adventure; and after many animated descriptions of battles and single combats, he concludes with a wish that he may live to slay the two sons of Demdem, and with a bitter exultation on the death of their father, whom he had left a prey to the wild beasts and the vultures.

The metre is iambic, like that of the poem immediately preceding.

THE POEM OF ANTARA.

HAVE the bards who preceded me left any theme unsung? What, therefore, shall be my subject? Love only must supply my lay. Dost thou then recollect, after long consideration, the mansion of thy beloved?

2. O bower of Abla, in the valley of Jiwaa, give me tidings of my love! O bower of Abla, may the morning rise on thee with prosperity and health!

3. There I stopped my camel, large as a tower, the anguish of my passion having delayed the accomplishment of my bold enterprise,

4. Whilst Abla was dwelling in Jiwaa, and our tribe were stationed in Hazn, and Samaan, and Motathallem.

5. Hail, dear ruins! with whose possessors I had old engagements; more dreary and more desolate are you become, after the departure of my beloved Omm Alheitham!

6. She dwells in the land of my foes, like roaring lions: oh, how painful has been my search after thee, fair daughter of Makhrem!

7. I felt myself attached to her at our first interview, although I had slain her countrymen in battle: I assure thee, by the life of thy father, that of my attachment there can be no doubt.

8. Thou hast possessed thyself of my heart; thou hast fixed thy abode in it (imagine not that I delude thee), and art settled there as a beloved and cherished inhabitant.

9. Yet how can I visit my fair one, whilst her family have their vernal mansion in Oneizatain, and mine are stationed in Ghailem?

10. Surely thou hast firmly resolved to depart from me, since the camels of thy tribe are bridled even in so dark a night.

11. Nothing so much alarms me with a signal of her destined removal as my seeing the camels of burden, which belong to her tribe, grazing on khimkhim-berries in the midst of their tents:

12. Among them are forty-two milch-camels, dark as the plumes of a coal-black raven.

13. Then, Antara, she pierced thee to the heart with her well-pointed teeth exquisitely white, the kiss of which is delicious, and the taste ravishingly sweet!

14. From the mouth of this lovely damsel, when you kiss her lips, proceeds the fragrance of musk, as from the vase of a perfumer;

15. Or like the scent of a blooming bower, whose plants the gentle rains have kept in continual verdure, which no filth has sullied, and to which there has been no resort:

16. Every morning-cloud, clear of hail, has drenched it with a plentiful shower, and has left all the little cavities in the earth both round and bright as coins of silver:

17. Profusely and copiously it descends; and every evening the stream, which nothing intercepts, gushes rapidly through it.

18. The flies remain in it with incessant buzzing, and their murmurs are like the song of a man exhilarated with wine:

19. Their sound, when they strike their slender legs against each other, is like the sound of a flint, from which the sparks are forced by a man with one arm, intent upon his labour.

20. While thou, fair Abla, reclinest both evening and morning on the lap of a soft couch, I pass whole nights on the back of a dark-coloured horse well caparisoned:

21. My only cushion is the saddle of a charger with firm thick feet, strong-sided, and large in the place of his girths.

22. Shall a camel of Shaden bear me to thy tent, a camel, far removed from her country, destitute of milk, and separated from the herd?

23. She waves her tail in her playful mood, and proudly moves her body from side to side, even at the end of her nightly excursion: she strikes the hills with her quickly-moving and firmly-trampling hoofs.

24. Thus the bird without ears, between whose feet there is but a small space, the swift ostrich beats the ground in his evening course.

25. The young ostriches gather themselves around him, as a multitude of black Yemenian camels assemble round their Abyssinian herdman, who is unable to express himself in the language of Arabia.

26. They follow him, guided by the loftiness of his head, which resembles the carriage of travelling damsels, raised on high, and covered like a tent.

27. His head, though lofty, is small: when he is going to visit the eggs, which his female left in Dhulasheira, he looks like an Ethiop with short ears in a trailing garment of furred hides.

28. My camel drinks the water of Dehradhain, but starts aside with disdain from the hostile rivulets of Dailem.

29. She turns her right side, as if she were in fear of some large-headed screamer of the night,--

30. Of a hideous wild-cat fixed to her body, who, as often as she bent herself towards him in her wrath, assailed her with his claws and his teeth.

31. I continue all day on the well-cemented tower of her back, strongly raised, and firm as the pillars of him who pitches a tent.

32. When she rests, she crouches on the soft bank of Ridaa, and groans through fatigue, like the soft sounding reed, which she presses with her weight.

33. Her sweat resembles thick rob or tenacious pitch, which the kindled fire causes to bubble in the sides of a caldron;

34. It gushes from behind her ears, when she boils with rage, exults in her strength, and struts in her pride, like the stallion of her herd, when his rivals assail him.

[69]

35. O Abla, although thou droppest thy veil before me, yet know, that by my agility I have made captive many a knight clad in complete armour.

36. Bestow on me the commendation which thou knowest to be due; since my nature is gentle and mild, when my rights are not invaded;

37. But, when I am injured, my resentment is firm, and bitter as coloquinteda to the taste of the aggressor.

38. I quaff; when the noontide heat is abated, old wine, purchased with bright and well-stamped coin;

39. I quaff it in a goblet of yellow glass variegated with white streaks, whose companion is a glittering flagon, well secured by its lid from the blasts of the north:

40. When I drink it, my wealth is dissipated, but my fame remains abundant and unimpaired;

41. And when I return to sobriety, the dew of my liberality continues as fresh as before: give due honour, therefore, to those qualities which thou knowest me to possess.

42. Many a consort of a fair one, whose beauty required no ornaments, have I left prostrate on the ground; and the life-blood has run sounding from his veins, opened by my javelin, like the mouth of a camel with a divided lip:

43. With a nimble and double-handed stroke, I prevented his attack; and the stream that gushed from the penetrating wound bore the colour of anemones.

44. Go, ask the warriors, O daughter of Malec, if thou art ignorant of my valour, ask them that which thou knowest not;

45. Ask how I act, when I am constantly fixed to the saddle of an elegant horse, swimming in his course, whom my bold antagonists alternately wound;

46. Yet sometimes he advances alone to the conflict, and sometimes he stands collected in a multitudinous throng of heroes with strong bows:

47. Ask, and whoever has been witness to the combat will inform thee that I am impetuous in battle, but regardless of the spoils.

48. Many a warrior, clad in a suit of mail, at whose violent assault the boldest men have trembled, who neither had saved himself by swift flight nor by abject submission,

49. Has this arm laid prone with a rapid blow from a well-straightened javelin, firm between the knots:

[70]

50. Broad were the lips of the wound; and the noise of the rushing blood called forth the wolves, prowling in the night, and pinched with hunger:

51. With my swift lance did I pierce his coat of mail; and no warrior, however brave, is secure from its point.

52. I left him, like a sacrificed victim, to the lions of the forest, who feasted on him between the crown of his head and his wrists.

53. Often have I burst the interior folds of a well-wrought habergeon, worn by a famed warrior appointed to maintain his post;

54. Whose hands were brisk in casting lots, when winter demands such recreation: a man censured for his disregard of wealth, and for causing the wine-merchant to strike his flag, by purchasing all his store.

55. When he saw me descend from my steed, and rush towards him, he grinned with horror, but with no smile of joy.

56. My engagement with him lasted the whole day, until his head and fingers, covered with clotted gore, appeared to be stained with the juice of idhlim.

57. Then I fixed him with my lance; I struck him to the heart with an Indian scimitar, the blade of which was of a bright water, and rapid was the stroke it gave:

58. A warrior, whose armour seemed to be braced on a lofty tree; a chief, who, like a king, wore sandals of leather stained with Egyptian thorn: a hero, without an equal.

59. O lovely heifer! what a sweet prey was she to a hunter permitted to chase her! To me she was wholly denied: oh, would to heaven that she had not been forbidden me!

60. I sent forth my handmaid, and said to her: "Go, ask tidings inquisitively of my beloved, and bring me intelligence."

61. She said: "I have seen the hostile guards negligent of their watch, and the wild heifer may be smitten by any archer who desires to shoot her."

62. Then she turned towards me with the neck of a young roe, well grown, of an exquisite breed among the gazals of the wood: a roe with a milk-white face.

63. I have been informed of a man ungrateful for my kindness; but ingratitude turns the mind of a benefactor from any more beneficence.

64. The instructions which my valiant uncle gave me I have diligently observed; at the time when the lips are drawn away from the bright teeth,

65. In the struggle of the fight, into whose deepest gulfs the warriors plunge themselves without complaint or murmur.

66. When my tribe has placed me as a shield between them and the hostile spears, I have not ignobly declined the danger, although the place where I fixed my foot was too narrow to admit a companion.

67. When I heard the din of Morra raised in the field, and the sons of Rabeia in the thick dust;

68.* And the shouts of Dhohol at the moment of assault, when they rush in troops to the conflict with all their sharp-biting lions;

69. When even the mildest of the tribes saw the skirmish under their standards (and Death spreads havoc under the standard of the mildest nation),

70. Then I knew with certainty, that, in so fierce a contest with them, many a heavy blow would make the perched birds of the brain fly quickly from every skull:

71. As soon as I beheld the legions of our enemies advancing, and animating one another to battle, I too rushed forward, and acted without reproach.

72. The troops called out "Antara!" while javelins, long as the cords of a well, were forcibly thrust against the chest of my dark steed.

73. I ceased not to charge the foe with the neck and breast of my horse, until he was mantled in blood.

74. My steed, bent aside with the stroke of the lances in his forehead, complained to me with gushing tears and tender sobbing:

75. Had he known the art of discourse, he would have addressed me in a plaintive strain; and had he possessed the faculty of speech, he would have spoken to me distinctly.

76. In the midst of the black dust, the horses were impetuously rushing with disfigured countenances; every robust stallion and every strong-limbed short-haired male.

77. Then my soul was healed, and all my anguish was dispersed by the cry of the warriors, saying, "Well done, Antara: charge again!"

78. My camels too are obedient to my will, as often as I desire to kindle the ardour of my heart, and press it on to some arduous enterprise.

79. Yet I fear lest death should seize me before the adverse turn of war has overtaken the two sons of Demdem:

80. Men who attacked my reputation, when I had given them no offence, and vowed, when I had never assailed them, to shed my blood;--

81. Yes, they injured me: but I have left their father, like a victim, to be mangled by the lions of the wood, and by the eagles advanced in years.

THE
POEM
OF
AMRU.

THE ARGUMENT.

THE discordant and inconsistent accounts of the commentators, who seem to have collected without examination every tradition that presented itself, have left us very much in the dark on the subject of the two following poems; but the common opinion, which appears to me the most probable, is that they are, in fact, political and adverse declamations, which were delivered by Amru and Hareth at the head of their respective clans, before Amru the son of Hinda, King of Hira in Mesopotamia, who had assumed the office of mediator between them after a most obstinate war, and had undertaken to hear a discussion of their several claims to pre-eminence, and to decide their cause with perfect impartiality. In some copies, indeed, as in those of Nahas and of Zauzeni, the two poems are separated; and in that of Obaidalla the poem of Hareth is totally omitted.

Were I to draw my opinion solely from the structure and general turn of Amru's composition, I should conceive that the King of Hira, who, like other tyrants, wished "to make all men just but himself, and to leave all nations free but his own," had attempted to enslave the powerful tribe of Tagleb, and to appoint a prefect over them, but that the warlike possessors of the deserts and forests had openly disclaimed his authority, and employed their principal leader and poet to send him defiance, and magnify their own independent spirit.

Some Arabian writers assert, what there is abundant reason to believe, that the above-mentioned king was killed by the author of the following poem, who composed it, say they, on that occasion; but the king himself is personally addressed by the poet, and warned against precipitation in deciding the contest; and where mention is made of "crowned heads left prostrate on the field," no particular monarch seems to be intended; but the conjunction copulative has the force, as it often has in Arabic, of a frequentative particle.

[73]

Let us then, where certainty cannot be obtained, be satisfied with high probability, and suppose, with Tabreizi, that the two tribes of Becr and Tagleb, having exhausted one another in a long war, to which the murder of Coleib the Taglebite had given rise, agreed to terminate their ruinous quarrel, and to make the King of Hira their umpire; that on the day appointed the tribes met before the palace or royal tent, and that Amru the son of Celthum, prince of the Taglebites, either pronounced his poem, according to the custom of the Arabs, or stated his pretensions in a solemn speech, which he afterwards versified, that it might be more easily remembered by his tribe and their posterity.

The oration, or poem, or whatever it may be called, is arrogant beyond all imagination, and contains hardly a colour of argument. The prince was most probably a vain young man, proud of his accomplishments, and elate with success in his wars; but his production could not fail of becoming extremely popular among his countrymen; and his own family, the descendants of Josham the son of Beer, were so infatuated with it that (as one of their own poets admits) "they could scarce ever desist from repeating it, and thought they had attained the summit of glory, without any farther exertions of virtue."

He begins with a strain perfectly Anacreontic; the elegiac style of the former poems not being well adapted to his eager exultation and triumph: yet there is some mixture of complaint on the departure of his mistress, whose beauties lie delineates with a boldness and energy highly characteristic of unpolished manners. The rest of his work consists of menaces, vaunts, and exaggerated applause of his own tribe for their generosity and prowess, the goodness of their horses, the beauty of their women, the extent of their possessions, and even the number of their ships;--which boasts were so well founded that, according to some authors, if Mohammed had not been horn, the Taglebites would have appropriated the dominion of all Arabia, and possibly would have erected a mighty state, both civil and maritime.

This poem is composed in copious verse, or metre of the fourth species, according to the following form:

"Amatores | puellarum | misellos
  Ocellorum | nitor multos | fefellit."

But the compound foot amore furens is used at pleasure, instead of the first epitrite; as,

"Venusta puel | la, tarda venis | ad hortum,
  Parata lyra est, | paratus odor | rosarum."

THE POEM OF AMRU.

HOLLA!--Awake, sweet damsel, and bring our morning draught in thy capacious goblet; nor suffer the rich wines of Enderein to be longer hoarded:

[74]

2. Bring the well-tempered wine, that seems to be tinctured with saffron, and, when it is diluted with water, overflows the cup.

3. This is the liquor which diverts the anxious lover from his passion; and, as soon as he tastes it, he is perfectly composed:

4. Hence thou seest the penurious churl, when the circling bowl passes him, grow regardless of his pelf:

5.* When its potent flames have seized the discreetest of our youths, thou wouldst imagine him to be in a frenzy.

6. Thou turnest the goblet from us, O mother of Amru; for the true course of the goblet is to the right hand:

7. He is not the least amiable of thy three companions, O mother of Amru, to whom thou hast not presented the morning bowl.

8.* How many a cup have I purchased in Balbec! how many more in Damascus and Kasirein!

9. Surely our allotted hour of fate will overtake us; since we are destined to death, and death to us.

10. O stay a while, before we separate, thou lovely rider on camels, that we may relate to thee our sorrows, and thou to us thy delights!

11. O stay!--that we may inquire whether thou hast altered thy purpose of departing hastily, or whether thou hast wholly deceived thy too confident lover:

12. In the hateful day of battle, whilst he struggles amid wounds and blows, may the Ruler of the world refresh thy sight with coolness, and gratify it with every desired object!

13. O Amru, when thou visitest thy fair one in secret, and when the eyes of lurking enemies are closed in rest,

14. She displays two lovely arms, fair and full as the limbs of a long-necked snow-white young camel, that frisks in the vernal season over the sand-banks and green hillocks;

15. And two sweet breasts, smooth and white as vessels of ivory, modestly defended from the hand of those who presume to touch them:

16. She discovers her slender shape, tall and well proportioned, and her sides gracefully rising with all their attendant charms;

[75]

17.* Her hips elegantly swelling, which the entrance of the tent is scarce large enough to admit, and her waist, the beauty of which drives me to madness;

18.* With two charming columns of jasper or polished marble, on which hang rings and trinkets making a stridulous sound.

19. My youthful passion is rekindled, and my ardent desire revives, when I see the travelling camels of my fair one driven along in the evening;

20. When the towns of Yemama appear in sight, exalted above the plains, and shining like bright sabres in the hands of those who have unsheathed them.

21. When she departs, the grief of a she-camel who seeks her lost foal, and returns despairing with piercing cries, equals not my anguish;

22. Nor that of a widow, with snowy locks, whose mourning never ceases for her nine children, of whom nothing remains, but what the tomb has concealed.

23. Such is our fate! This day and the morrow, and the morning after them, are pledges in the hand of destiny for events of which we have no knowledge.

24. O son of Hinda, be not precipitate in giving judgment against us: hear us with patience, and we will give thee certain information;--

25. That we lead our standards to battle, like camels to the pool, of a white hue, and bring them back stained with blood, in which they have quenched their thirst;

26. That our days of prosperity, in which we have refused to obey the commands of kings, have been long and brilliant.

27. Many a chief of his nation, on whom the regal diadem has been placed, the refuge of those who implored his protection,

28. Have we left prostrate on the field, while his horses waited by his side, with one of their hoofs bent, and with bridles richly adorned.

29.* Often have we fixed our mansions in Dhu Thaluh, towards the districts of Syria, and have kept at a distance those who menaced us.

30. We were so disguised in our armour, that the dogs of the tribe snarled at us; yet we stripped the branches from every thorny tree (every armed warrior) that opposed us.

31. When we roll the millstone of war over a little clan, they are ground to flour in the first battle;

32. From the eastern side of Najd the cloth of the mill is spread, and whatever we cast into it soon becomes impalpable powder.

33. You alight on our hills as guests are received in their station, and we hasten to give you a warm reception, lest you should complain of our backwardness:

34. We invite you to our board, and speedily prepare for your entertainment a solid rock, which, before daybreak, shall reduce you to dust.

35. Surely hatred after hatred is manifested by thee, O hostile chief! and thy secret rancour has been revealed:

36. But we have inherited glory, as the race of Maad well knows; we have fought with valour till our fame has been illustrious.

37. When the falling pillars of our tents quiver over our furniture, we defend our neighbours from the impending min.

38. We disperse our gifts to our countrymen, but disdain to share their spoils; and the burdens which we bear we support for their advantage.

39* When the troops of the foe are at a distance from us, we dart our javelins; and when we close in the combat, we strike with sharp sabres;--

40. Our dark javelins, exquisitely wrought of Khathaian reeds, slender and delicate; our sabres, bright and piercing:

41. With these we cleave in pieces the heads of our enemies; we mow--we cut down their necks as with sickles:

42. Then might you imagine the skulls of heroes on the plain to be the bales of a camel thrown on rocky ground.

43. Instead of submitting to them, we crush their heads; and their terror is such, that they know not on which side the danger is to be feared.

44. Our scimitars, whose strokes are furiously interchanged, are as little regarded by us as twisted sashes in the hands of playful children.

45. Their armour and ours, stained reciprocally with our blood, seems to be dyed or painted with the juice of the crimson syringa-flower.

46. At a time when the tribe is reluctant to charge the foe, apprehensive of some probable disaster,

47. Then we lead on our troop, like a mountain with a pointed summit; we preserve our reputation, and advance in the foremost ranks,

48. With youths, who consider death as the completion of glory, and with aged heroes experienced in war:

49. We challenge all the clans together to contend with us, and we boldly preclude their sons from approaching the mansion of our children.

50. On the day when we are anxious to protect our families, we keep vigilant guard, clad in complete steel;

51. But on the day when we have no such anxiety for them, our legions assemble in frill council.

52. Led by a chief among the descendants of Josham the son of Becr, we bruise our adversaries, both the weak and the strong.

53.* Oh, the nations remember not the time when we bowed the neck, or ever flagged in the conflict!

54. Oh, let no people be infatuated and violent against us; for we will requite their infatuation, which surpasses the folly of the most foolish!

55. On what pretence, O Amru, son of Hinda, should we be subject to the sovereign whom thou wouldst place over us?

56. By what pretence, O Amru, son of Hinda, dost thou yield to our calumniators, and treat us with indignity?

57. Thou hast menaced us: thou hast thought to intimidate us; but, gently, O King!--say, when were we ever the vassals of thy mother?

58. Our javelins, O Amru, disdain to relax their vehemence before thee in assailing our foes:

59. Whenever a man uses force to bend them, they start back, and become inflexibly rigid,-

60. So rigid, that when they return to their former state, they ring with a shrill noise, piercing the neck and forehead of him who touches them.

61. Hast thou ever been informed that Josham the son of Becr, in battles anciently fought, was at any time remiss?

62. We have inherited the renown of Alkama the son of Saif, who by dint of valour obtained admission for us into the castles of glory.

63. We are heirs to Mohalhil, and to Zoheir, the flower of his tribe: O of how noble a treasure were they the preservers!

64. From Attab also and from Celthum we have received the inheritance transmitted from their progenitors.

65. By Dhu'lborra, of whose fame thou hast heard the report, have we been protected; and through him we protect those who seek our aid.

66. Before him the adventurous Coleib sprung from us: and what species of glory is there which we have not attained?

67. When our antagonists twist against us the cords of battle, either we burst the knot or rend the necks of our opponents.

68. We shall be found the firmest of tribes in keeping our defensive alliance, and the most faithful in observing the bond of our treaties.

69. When the flames were kindled in the mountain, on the morning of an excursion, we gave succour more important than the aid of other allies.

70. To give immediate relief, we kept all our herds confined in Dhu Orathei, until our mulch-camels of a noble breed were forced to graze on withered herbs.

71. We protect with generosity the man who submits to us; but chastise with firmness him by whom we are insulted.

72. We reject the offers of those who have displeased us; but accept the presents of those with whom we are satisfied.

73. We succoured the right wing, when our troops engaged in combat, and our valiant brothers gave support to the left.

74. They made a fierce attack against the legions which opposed them, and we not less fiercely assailed the squadrons by which we were opposed.

75. They returned with booty and with rich spoils, and the sons of kings were among our captives.

76. To you, O descendants of Becr, to you we address ourselves;--have you not yet learned the truth concerning us?

[79]

77. Have you not experienced with what impetuosity our troops have attacked your troops, and with what force they have darted their javelins?

78. We are armed with bright sabres, and clad in habergeons made in Yemen; our scimitars are part straight, part bent.

79. We have coats of mail that glitter like lightning; the plaits of which are seen in wrinkles above our belts:

80. When at any time our heroes put them off, you may see their skin blackened with the pressure of the steel.

81. The plaits of our hauberks resemble the surface of a pool which the winds have ruffled in their course.

82. On the morning of attack, we are borne into the field on short-haired steeds, which have been known to us from the time when we weaned them, and which we rescued from our foes after they had been taken.

83.* They rush to the fight, armed with breastplates of steel; they leave it with their manes dishevelled and dusty, and the reins, tied in knots, lie on their necks.

84. We inherited this excellent breed from our virtuous ancestors; and on our death they will be inherited by our sons.

85. All the tribes of Maad perfectly know, when their tents are pitched in the well-watered valleys,

86. That we support the distressed in every barren year, and are bountiful to such as solicit our bounty;

87.* That we defend the oppressed, when we think it just; and fix our abode in Arabia, where we find it convenient;

88. That we give succour to those that are near us, when the bright scimitars make the eyes of our heroes wink.

89. We entertain strangers at our board whenever we are able; but we hurl destruction on those who approach us hostilely.

90. We are the tribe who drink water from the clearest brooks; whilst other clans are forced to drink it foul and muddy.

91. Go, ask the sons of Tamah and of Domia, how they have found us in the conflict!

[80]

92. Behind us come our lovely, our charming damsels, whom we guard so vigilantly that they cannot be made captive, or even treated with disrespect:

93. Fair maidens, descended from Josham the son of Becr, who comprise every species of beauty, both in the opinion of men and in truth.

94. They have exacted a promise from their husbands, that, when they engaged with the hostile legions, distinguished by marks of valour,

95. They would bring back, as spoils, coats of mail and scimitars, and captives led chained in pairs.

96.* Thou mayst behold us sallying forth into the open plain, whilst every other tribe seeks auxiliaries through fear of our prowess.

97. When our damsels are on foot, they walk with graceful motions, and wave their bodies like those of libertines heated with wine.

98. They feed with their fair hands our coursers of noble birth, and say to us: "You are no husbands of ours, unless you protect us from the foe."

99. Yes, if we defend not them, we retain no possessions of value after their loss, nor do we think even life desirable:

100. But nothing can afford our sweet maids so sure a protection as the strokes of our sabres, which make men's arms fly off like the clashing wands of playful boys.

101.* We seem, when our drawn scimitars are displayed, to protect mankind, as fathers protect their children.

102.* Our heroes roll the heads of their enemies, as the strong well-made youths roll their balls in the smooth vale.

103. This world is ours, and all that appears on the face of it; and when we do attack, we attack with irresistible force.

104. When a tyrant oppresses and insults a nation, we disdain to degrade ourselves by submitting to his will.

105. We have been called injurious, although we have injured no man; but if they persist in calumniating us, we will show the vehemence of our anger.

106. As soon as a child of our tribe is weaned from his mother, the loftiest chiefs of other clans bend the knee and pay him homage.

[81]

107.* We force our enemies to taste the unmixed draught of death; and heavy is the overthrow of our adversaries in battle.

108. We fill the earth with our tents, until it becomes too narrow to contain them; and cover the surface of the ocean with our ships.

THE
POEM
OF
HARETH.

THE ARGUMENT.

WHEN Amru had finished his extravagant panegyric on the tribe of Tagleb, and had received the loud applause of his own party, Hareth arose, and pronounced the following poem, or speech in verse; which he delivered, according to some authors, without any meditation, but which, as others assert, with greater appearance of probability, he had prepared and gotten by heart.

Although, if we believe Asmai, the poet was considerably above a hundred years old at this time, yet he is said to have poured forth his couplets with such boiling ardour, that, without perceiving it, "he cut his hand with the string of his bow, on which," after the manner of the Arabian orators, "he leaned while he was speaking."

Whatever was his age, the wisdom and art of his composition are finely contrasted with the youthful imprudence of his adversary, who must have exasperated the King, instead of conciliating his good will, and seems even to have menaced the very man from whom he was asking a favourable judgment. Hareth, on the contrary, begins with complimenting the Queen, whose name was Asoma, and who heard him behind the tapestry: he appears to have introduced another of his favourites, Hinda, merely because that was the name of the king's mother; and he celebrates the monarch himself, as a model of justice, valour, and magnanimity. The description of his camel, which he interweaves according to custom, is very short; and he opens the defence of his tribe with coolness and moderation; but as he proceeds his indignation seems to be kindled, and the rest of his harangue consists of sharp expostulations and bitter sarcasms, not without much sound reasoning, and a number of allusions to facts, which cannot but be imperfectly known to us, though they must have been fresh in the memory of his hearers.

The general scope of his argument is that no blame was justly imputable to the sons of Becr for the many calamities which the Taglebites had endured, and which had been principally occasioned by their own supineness and indiscretion.

[82]

The oration, or poem, or whatever it may be denominated, had its full effect on the mind of the royal umpire, who decided the cause in favour of the Becrites, and lost his life for a decision apparently just. He must have remarked the fiery spirit of the poet Amru, from the style of his eloquence, as Caesar first discovered the impetuous vehemence of Brutus' temper from his speech delivered at Nice, in favour of King Deiotarus: but neither the Arabian nor the Roman tyrant were sufficiently on their guard against men whom they had irritated even to fury.

This poem is composed in light verse, or metre of the eleventh class, consisting of epitrites, ionic feet, and paeons, variously intermixed, as in this form:

"Amarylli, | dulci lyra | modulare
  Molle carmen | sub arbore | fusa sacra."

Sometimes a molossus ends the distich, as:

"Dulce carmen | sub arbore | fusa sacra
  Modulare, | dum sylvulae | respondent."

The close of a couplet in this measure has often the cadence of a Latin or Greek hexameter; thus, v. 20:

Tis'-hali khailin khilala dhaca rogao--

that is, literally,

Hinnitus modulantur equi, fremitusque cameli.

THE POEM OF HARETH.

DOTH fair Asoma give us notice of her departure? Oh, why are sojourners so frequently weary of their sojourning?

2. She is resolved to depart, after our mutual vows among the sandy hillocks of Shamma, and in the nearer station of Khalsa;--

3. Vows, repeated in Mohayat, Sifah, and Aglai, in Dhu Fitak, Adhib, and Wafa;--

4. Vows, renewed in the bowers of Katha, and the dales of Shoreib, in the Two Valleys, and in the plains of Ayla.

5. I see no remains of the troth which she plighted in those stations; and I waste the day in tears, frantic with grief; but oh, what part of my happiness will tears restore?

[83]

6. Yet, O Hareth, a new passion invites thee; for Hinda is before thy eyes, and the fire which she kindles at night in the hills will direct thee to her abode:

7. She kindles it with abundance of wood between the hilly stations of Akeik and Shakhsein, and it blazes like the splendour of the sun.

8. I have been contemplating her fire from a distance on the hill whence our excursions are made; but oh, the scorching heat and the calamities of war prevent me from approaching her

9. But I seek assistance in dispelling my care, when the sojourner of the tent hastily leaves his abode through fear of some impending calamity,

10. On a camel, swift as an ostrich, the mother of many young ones; the long-necked inhabitant of the desert,

11. Who hears a soft sound, and dreads the approach of the hunter, in the afternoon, just before the dusk of evening:

12. Then mayst thou see behind her, from the quick motion of her legs, and the force with which she strikes the earth, a cloud of dust, thin as the gossamer,

13. And the traces of her hoofs, which are such as to be soon effaced by the winds blowing over the sandy plain.

14. With her I disport myself in the sultry noon, whilst every son of valour is like a blind camel devoted to death.

15. Yet misfortunes and evil tidings have brought on us affairs which give us affliction and anguish;

16. For our brethren, the family of Arakem, the dragon-eyed, have transgressed the bounds of justice against us, and have been vehement in their invectives:

17. They have confounded the blameless among us with the guilty, and the most perfect innocence has not escaped their censure.

18. They have insisted that all who pitch their tents in the desert are our associates, and that we are involved in their offences.

19. They assembled their forces at night, and as soon as the dawn appeared, there was nothing heard among them but a tumultuous noise

20. Of those who called and those who answered; the neighing of horses, and, among the rest, the lowing of camels.

21. O thou, who adornest thy flowery speeches concerning us before Amru, can this falsehood be long undetected?

22. Imagine not that thy instigation will animate him against us, or humiliate us; since long before thee our enemies have openly calumniated us;

23. Yet we continued advancing ourselves in defiance of their hate, with laudable self-sufficiency and exalted reputation.

24. Before this day, the eyes of nations have been dazzled by our glory, and have been moved by envious indignation and obstinate resentment.

25. Fortune seemed to raise for us a dark rock,. with a pointed summit, dispelling the clouds;

26. Thick and firm, secured from calamity; not to be weakened by any disaster, however grievous and violent.

27.* Intrust to our wisdom every momentous affair from which you desire to be extricated, and by which the assemblies of chiefs are made unhappy.

28.* If you inquire concerning our wars between Milaha and Dhakib, you will find on their plains many an unavenged and many an avenged corse:

29.* Or, if you examine diligently the questions in which all tribes are deeply interested, you will see the difference between your offences and our innocence.

30.* But if you decline this fair discussion, we shall turn from you with resentment, concealing hatred in our bosoms, as the mote is concealed in the closed eyelids.

31.* Reject, if you please, the terms which we offer; but of whom have you heard that surpasses us in glory?

32.* You have perfectly known us on the days when the warriors have assailed one another with rapacious violence, when every tribe has raised a tumultuous din;

33.* When we brought up our camels from the palm-groves of Bahrein, and drove them by rapid marches, till we reached the plain of Hisa.

34. Then we advanced against the sons of Tameim, and when the sacred month required a cessation of our war, we carried away the daughters of their tribe for our handmaids.

35. In opposition to us, neither could the valiant man keep his ground on the level field, nor did precipitate flight avail the faint-hearted.

[85]

36. No; the coward, who ran hastily from the plain, was not saved by the summit of rocks or the roughness of craggy paths.

37. By these exertions we maintained our preeminence over the tribes, until Mondir, son of the beautiful Maisema, obtained the dominion.

38. He was a prince who bore witness to our valour on the day of Hayarain, when the calamity of war was, in truth, a calamity:

39. A prince who subjected nations; whose equal in magnanimity could not be found among them.

40. Desist then from vaunting and from hostility: you have indeed pretended ignorance of our claims, but from that pretended ignorance will proceed your woe.

41. Remember well the oaths taken in Dhu'lmejaaz: the covenants and vows of amity, which were made there of old.

42. Beware of injustice and violence; nor let your intemperate passions impel you to violate your contracts written on tablets.

43. Know, that we and you, on the day when we made our treaty, were equally bound by our respective engagements.

44. Are we responsible for the crimes of Canda? Shall their conquering chief have the spoils, and shall reprisals be made upon us?

45. Are we responsible for the excesses of Haneifa, and for all the conflicts which the dusty plain has seen accumulated?

46. Must we answer for the offences of the sons of Ateik? No: whoever has broken his covenant, we are innocent of their war.

47. Doth the guilt of Ibaad hang on our heads, as the burden is suspended on the centre of the camel's girths?

48. Has the blame due to Kodhaa fallen upon us? or, rather, are we not secure from a single drop of their faults?

49. Are we responsible for the crimes of Iyaad, as it was said to the tribe of Thasm, "Your brethren are rebels?"

50. Those who raised the dissension belong not to us, neither Kais, nor Jondal, nor Hadda.

51. Vain pretexts! Unjust aspersions! That we should suffer for others, as the roe is sacrificed in the place of the sheep!

52. Fourscore warriors, indeed, advanced from Taureim, and their hands carried lances, whose points were Fate;

53. Yet they profaned not the hallowed places of the sons of Rizaah on the hills of Nitaa, when they called on them for mercy.

54. They left them, however, wounded on the plain, and returned with captive herds and flocks so numerous, that the drivers of them were deafened with their cries.

55. The vanquished tribe came afterwards to implore restitution, but not a single beast, either black or of a bright hue, was restored to them.

56. So they retired with heart-breaking afflictions, nor could any stream of water quench their ardent rage.

57. After this a troop of horsemen, led by the impetuous Ghallaak, assailed them without remorse or pity:

58. Full many a son of Tagleb has been smitten, whose blood has flowed unrevenged, while the black dust covered his corse.

59. Are your cares comparable to those of our tribe, when Mondir waged war against them? Are we, like you, become subject to the son of Hinda?

60. When he fixed his abode in the lofty turrets of Maisuna, and sojourned in the nearer stations of Khaltha,

61. From every tribe there flocked around him a company of robbers, impetuous as eagles:

62. He led them on, and supplied them with dates and with water; so the will of God was accomplished, and afflicted men doomed to affliction.

63. Then you invited them to attack you by your want of circumspection; and the vain security of your intemperate joy impelled them to be hostile.

64. They surprised you not, indeed, by a sudden assault; but they advanced, and the sultry vapour of noon, through which you saw them, increased their magnitude.

65. O thou inveterate and glozing calumniator, who inveighest against us before King Amru, will there be no end of thy unjust invectives?

[87]

66. Between Amru and us many acts of amity have passed, and from all of them, no doubt, has benefit arisen.

67. He is a just prince, and the most accomplished that walks the earth: all praise is below his merit:

68. A prince descended from Irem! A warrior like him ought ever to be encircled with troops of genii, for he protects his domain, and refuses to punish even his opponents:

69. A monarch who knows us by three infallible signs, by each of which our excellence is decided:--

70. The first is, the conspicuous token of our valour, when all Arabia came forth in the rocky vales, each tribe of Maad under their banner,

71. And assembled, in complete armour, round the warlike Kais, that valiant prince of Yemen, who stood firm and brilliant like a white cliff.

72. Then came a legion of high-born youths, whom nothing could restrain but our long and glittering spears;

73. But we repelled them with strokes, which made their blood gush from their sides, as the water streams from the mouth of a bottle which contains it.

74. We drove them for refuge to the craggy hills of Thahlaan; we thrust them before us, till the muscles of their thighs were breeched in gore.

75. We did with them a deed, the name of which God only knows; and no revenge could be taken for the blood of men who sought their own fate.

76. Next advanced Hojar, son of Ommi Kathaam, with an army of Persians, clad in discoloured brass:

77. A lion in the conflict, of a ruddy hue, trampling on his prey; but a vernal season of beneficence in every barren year.

78. Yet we smote them on the foreheads with the edges of our scimitars, which quivered in their flesh, like buckets drawn from a deep well encircled with stone.

79. Secondly, we broke the chains of Amriolkais, after his long imprisonment and anguish.

80. We forcibly revenged the death of Mondir, king of Gassaan, that his blood might not flow in vain.

81. We redeemed our captives with nine kings of illustrious race, whose spoils were exceedingly precious.

82. With the horses, with the dark horses of the sons of Aus, came whole squadrons, fierce as eagles with crooked beaks:

83. We scarce had passed through the cloud of dust when they turned their backs; and then how dreadfully blazed the fire of our vengeance!

84. Lastly, we gave birth to Amru, the son of Omm Ayaas; for not long ago were the bridal gifts presented to us, as kinsmen.

85. May our faithful admonition reach all our kindred tribes, extended as wide as our consanguinity, in plains beyond plains!

SHORTER PIECES
OF
ARABIAN POETRY.

TRANSLATED INTO ENGLISH VERSE,

BY J. D. CARLYLE, BD.

As the following translations were attempted at different times and with different impressions, their execution is, no doubt, very unequal: in general they will, I trust, be found as literal as the nature of two languages, so little resembling each other in their structure, will admit; in some few instances I have indulged myself in a greater latitude, and have given rather an imitation than a version;--in such a manner, however, I hope, as not in any place to have lost sight of the original idea of the writer.--From the Translator's Preface.

Most of the Translator's interesting Biographical Notices of the Authors and the subjects of these little pieces are, with some additional Notes, placed in the Appendix to this volume.--ED.

ON THE
TOMB OF MANO.
BY HASSAN ALASADY.

FRIENDS of my heart, who share my sighs!
 Go seek the turf where Mano lies,
 And woo the dewy clouds of Spring
 To sweep it with prolific wing.

Within that cell, beneath that heap,
 Friendship and Truth and Honour sleep.
 Beneficence, that used to clasp
 The world within her ample grasp,
 There rests entombed--of thought bereft;
 For were one conscious atom left,
 New bliss, new kindness to display,
 'T would burst the grave, and seek the day.

But though in dust thy relics lie,
 Thy virtues, Mano, ne'er shall die:
 Though Nile's full stream be seen no more,
 That spread his waves from shore to shore,
 Still in the verdure of the plain
 His vivifying smiles remain.

ON THE
TOMB OF SAYID.
BY ABD ALMALEC ALHARITHY.

BLEST are the tenants of the tomb!
  With envy I their lot survey;
 For Sayid shares the solemn gloom,
  And mingles with their mouldering clay.

Dear youth! I'm doomed thy loss to mourn,
  When gathering ills around combine;
 And whither now shall Malec turn?
  Where look for any help but thine?

At this dread moment, when the foe
  My life with rage insatiate seeks,
 In vain I strive to ward the blow--
  My buckler falls, my sabre breaks.

Upon thy grassy tomb I knelt,
  And sought from pain a short relief:
 Th' attempt was vain--I only felt
  Intenser pangs and livelier grief.

The bud of woe, no more represt,
  Fed by the tears that drenched it there,
 Shot forth and filled my labouring breast,
  Soon to expand and shed despair.

But though of Sayid I'm bereft,
   From whom the stream of bounty came,
Sayid a nobler meed has left--
   Th' exhaustless heritage of fame.

Though mute the lips on which I hung,
   Their silence speaks more loud to me
Than any voice from mortal tongue:
   "What Sayid was, let Malec be!"

ON THE
DEATH OF HIS MISTRESS.
BY ABU SAHER ALHEDILY.

DOST thou wonder that I flew
 Charmed to meet my Leila's view?
 Dost thou wonder that I hung
 Raptured on my Leila's tongue?--
 If her ghost's funereal screech
 Through the earth my grave should reach,
 On that voice I loved so well
 My transported ghost would dwell:
 If in death I can descry
 Where my Leila's relics lie,
 Saher's dust will flit away,
 There to join his Leila's clay.

ON AVARICE.
BY HATEM TAI.

HOW frail are riches and their joys!
 Morn builds the heap which eve destroys;
 Yet can they leave one sure delight--
 The thought that we've employed them right.

What bliss can wealth afford to me,
 When life's last solemn hour I see?--
 When Mavia's sympathising sighs
 Will but augment my agonies?

Can hoarded gold dispel the gloom
 That death must shed around his tomb?

Or cheer the ghost which hovers there,
And fills with shrieks the desert air?

What boots it, Mavia, in the grave,
 Whether I loved to waste or save?
 The hand that millions now can grasp
 In death no more than mine shall clasp.

Were I ambitious to behold
 Increasing stores of treasured gold,
 Each tribe that roves the desert knows
 I might be wealthy, if I chose.

But other joys can gold impart;
 Far other wishes warm my heart;--
 Ne'er may I strive to swell the heap
 Till want and woe have ceased to weep.

With brow unaltered I can see
 The hour of wealth or poverty:
 I've drunk from both the cups of Fate,
 Nor this could sink, nor that elate.

With fortune blest, I ne'er was found
 To look with scorn on those around;
 Nor for the loss of paltry ore,
 Shall Hatem seem to Hatem poor.

ON THE BATTLE OF SABLA.
BY JAAFER BEN ALBA.

SABLA, thou saw'st th' exulting foe
 In fancied triumphs crowned;
 Thou heard'st their frantic females throw
 These galling taunts around:

Make now your choice--the terms we give,
 Desponding victims, hear:
 These fetters on your hands receive,
 Or in your hearts the spear."

"And is the conflict o'er?" we cried;
 "And lie we at your feet?
 And dare you vauntingly decide

The fortune we must meet?

"A brighter day we soon shall see,
  Though now the prospect lowers;
And conquest, peace, and liberty
  Shall gild our future hours."

The foe advanced;--in firm array
  We rushed o'er Sabla's sands;
And the red sabre marked our way
  Amidst their yielding bands.

Then, as they writhed in Death's cold grasp,
  We cried, "Our choice is made:
These hands the sabres' hilt shall clasp,
  Your hearts shall have the blade!"

VERSES
ADDRESSED TO A KINDRED TRIBE AT VARIANCE WITH THE ONE TO WHICH
THE POET BELONGED.

BY ALFADHEL IBN ALABAS.

WHY thus to passion give the rein?
  Why seek your kindred tribe to wrong?
Why strive to drag to light again
  The fatal feud entombed so long?

Think not, if fury ye display,
  But equal fury we can deal;
Hope not, if wronged, but we repay
  Revenge for every wrong we feel.

Why thus to passion give the rein?
  Why seek the robe of peace to tear?
Rash youths, desist! your course restrain;
  Or dread the wrath ye blindly dare!

Yet friendship we nor ask from foes,
  Nor favour hope from you to prove:
We loved you not, great Allah knows!
  Nor blamed you that ye could not love.

To each are different feelings given;

This slights, and that regards his brother:
'Tis ours to live--thanks to kind Heaven--
Hating and hated by each other.

ON HIS FRIENDS.
BY MESKIN ALDARAMY.

WITH conscious pride I view the band
Of faithful friends that round me stand;
With pride exult, that I alone
Can join these scattered gems in one:
    For they're a wreath of pearls, and I
    The silken cord on which they lie.

'Tis mine their inmost souls to see;
Unlocked is every heart to me;
To me they cling, on me they rest,
And I've a place in every breast:
    For they're a wreath of pearls, and I
    The silken cord on which they lie.

ON TEMPER.
BY NABEGAT BENI JAID.

YES, Leila, I swore, by the fire of thine eyes,
  I ne'er could a sweetness unvaried endure;
The bubbles of spirit that sparkling arise
  Forbid life to stagnate, and render it pure.

But yet, my dear maid, though thy spirit's my pride,
  I'd wish for some sweetness to temper the bowl:
If life be ne'er suffered to rest or subside,
  It may not be flat, but I fear 't will be foul.

THE SONG OF MAISUNA.

[MAISUNA was a daughter of the tribe of Calab; a tribe, according to Abulfeda,
remarkable both for the purity of dialect spoken in it and for the number of poets it had
produced. She was married, whilst very young, to the Khalif Mowiah; but this exalted
situation by no means suited the disposition of Maisuna; and, amidst all the pomp and
splendour of Damascus, she languished for the simple pleasures of her native desert.

[94]

These feelings gave birth to the following simple stanzas, which she took the greatest delight in singing, whenever she could find an opportunity to indulge her melancholy in private. She was unfortunately overheard one day by Mowiah, who was of course not a little offended, both with the discovery of his wife's sentiments, and with the contemptuous manner in which she had expressed herself with regard to her husband; and, as a punishment for her fault, he ordered her to retire from court. Maisuna immediately obeyed, and, taking her infant son Yezid with her, returned to Yemen; nor did she revisit Damascus till after the death of Mowiah, when Yezid ascended the throne.]

THE russet suit of camel's hair,
    With spirits light and eye serene,
 Is dearer to my bosom far
    Than all the trappings of a queen.

The humble tent, and murmuring breeze
    That whistles through its fluttering walls,
 My unaspiring fancy please,
    Better than towers and splendid halls.

Th' attendant colts, that bounding fly
    And frolic by the litter's side,
 Are dearer in Maisuna's eye
    Than gorgeous mules in all their pride.

The watch-dog's voice, that bays whene'er
    A-stranger seeks his master's cot,
 Sounds sweeter in Maisuna's ear
    Than yonder trumpet's long-drawn note.

The rustic youth, unspoiled by art,
    Son of my kindred, poor but free,
 Will ever to Maisuna's heart
    Be dearer, pampered fool, than thee!

VERSES
OF YEZID TO HIS FATHER, MOWIAH,
WHO REPROACHED HIM FOR DRUNKENNESS.

MUST then my failings from the shaft
    Of anger ne'er escape?
 And dost thou storm because I've quaffed
    The water of the grape?

[95]

That I can thus from wine be driven,
  Thou surely ne'er canst think--
Another reason thou hast given
  Why I resolve to drink:

'Twas sweet the flowing cup to seize,
  'Tis sweet thy rage to see;
And, first, I drink myself to please,
  And, next--to anger thee!

ON FATALISM.
BY THE IMAM SHAFAY MOHAMMED BEN IDRIS.

NOT always wealth, not always force,
  A splendid destiny commands;
The lordly vulture gnaws the corse
  That rots upon yon barren sands.

Nor want nor weakness still conspires
  To bind us to a sordid state;
The fly, that with a touch expires,
  Sips honey from the royal plate.

TO THE KHALIF
HAROUN ALRASHID,
ON HIS UNDERTAKING A PILGRIMAGE TO MECCA.
By IBRAHIM BEN ADHEM.

RELIGION'S gems can ne'er adorn
  The flimsy robe by Pleasure worn:
Its feeble texture soon would tear,
  And give those jewels to the air.

Thrice happy they who seek th' abode
  Of peace and pleasure, in their God!
Who spurn the world, its joys despise,
  And grasp at bliss beyond the skies.

ON THE
INAUGURATION OF HAROUN ALRASHID,
AND THE

APPOINTMENT OF YAHIA
TO BE HIS VIZIER.
BY ISAAC ALMOUSELY.

TH' affrighted sun erewhile had fled,
  And hid his radiant face in night;
A cheerless gloom the world o'erspread--
  But Haroun came, and all was bright.

Again the sun shoots forth his rays;
  Nature is decked in beauty's robe:
  For mighty Haroun's sceptre sways,
And Yahia's arm sustains the globe.

ON THE
RUIN OF THE BARMECIDES.

NO, Barmec! time hath never shown
  So sad a change of wayward fate;
Nor sorrowing mortals ever known
  A grief so true, a loss so great.

Spouse of the world! thy soothing breast
  Did balm to every woe afford;
And now, no more by thee caressed,
  The widowed world bewails her lord.

EPIGRAM
ON
TAHER BEN HOSEIN,
WHO WAS AMBIDEXTER AND ONE-EYED.

A PAIR of right hands and a single dim eye
 Must form not a man, but a monster, they cry:
 Change a hand to an eye, good Taher, if you can,
 And a monster perhaps may be changed to man.

THE ADIEU.
BY ABU MOHAMMED.

THE boatmen shout, "'Tis time to part,
  No longer we can stay; "

'Twas then Maimuna taught my heart
  How much a glance could say.

With trembling steps to me she came;
  "Farewell," she would have cried,
But ere her lips the word could frame,
  In half-formed sounds it died.

Then bending down, with looks of love,
  Her arms she round me flung,
And as the gale hangs on the grove,
  Upon my breast she hung.

My willing arms embraced the maid,
  My heart with raptures beat;
While she but wept the more and said,
  "Would we had never met!"

VERSES
ADDRESSED TO HIS MISTRESS, WHO HAD FOUND FAULT WITH HIM FOR
PROFUSION.

BY ABU TEMAN HABIB.

UNGENEROUS and mistaken maid,
  To scorn me thus because I'm poor
Canst thou a liberal hand upbraid,
  For dealing round some worthless ore?

To spare's the wish of little souls;
  The great but gather to bestow:
Yon current don the mountain rolls,
  And stagnates in the swamp belay.

TO A FEMALE CUPBEARER.

BY ABD ALSALAM BEN RAGBAN.

COME, Leila, fill the goblet up--
  Reach round the rosy wine;
Think not that we will take the cup
  From any hand but thine.

A draught like this 'twere vain to seek,

No grape can such supply
It steals its tint from Leila's cheek,
  Its brightness from her eye.

SONGS
BY MASHDUD, RAKEEK, AND RAIS,
THE THREE MOST CELEBRATED IMPROVISATORI POETS IN BAGDAD, AT AN
ENTERTAINMENT GIVEN BY ABU ISY, SON OF THE KHALIF MOTAWAKKEL.

THE preface with which these Poems are accompanied in the Mostatraf, at the same time
that it explains the cause of their composition, gives no bad picture of Arabian manners
during the flourishing period of the Khalifate:--

I was one day going to the mosque [says Abu Akramah, an author who supported himself
at Bagdad by the profits of his pen], in order to see if I could pick up any little anecdote
which might serve for the groundwork of a tale. As I passed the gate of Abu Isy, son of
the Khalif Motawakkel, I saw Mashdud, the celebrated extempore poet, standing near it.

Mashdud saluted me, and asked whither I was going. I answered, to the mosque, and
confessed without reserve the business which drew me thither. The poet, upon hearing
this, pressed me to accompany him to the palace of Abu Isy. I declined, however,
complying with his solicitations, conscious of the impropriety of intruding myself
uninvited into the presence of a person of such rank and consequence. But Abu Isy's
porter, overhearing our conversation, declared that he would put an end to my difficulties
in a moment, by acquainting his master with my arrival. He did so; and in a short time
two servants appeared, who took me up in their arms, and carried the into a most
magnificent apartment, where their master was sitting.

Upon my introduction, I could not help feeling a little confused, but the Prince soon made
me easy, by calling out in a good-natured manner, "Why do you stand blushing there, you
simpleton? Take a seat." I obeyed: and in a few minutes a sumptuous collation was
brought in, of which I partook. Nor was the juice of the grape forgotten: a cupbearer,
brilliant as the morning star, poured out wine for us, more sparkling than the beams of the
sun reflected by a mirror.

After the entertainment I arose, and having invoked every blessing to be showered down
upon the head of my bounteous host, I was preparing to withdraw. But Abu Isy prevented
me, and immediately ordered Mashdud, together with Rakeek and Rais, two musicians,
whose fame was almost equal to Mashdud's, to be called in. They appeared accordingly
and having taken their places, Mashdud gave us the following satiric song:

MASHDUD ON THE MONKS OF KHABBET.
TENANTS of yon hallowed fane!
  Let me your devotions share:

There unceasing raptures reign--
  None are ever sober there.

Crowded gardens, festive bowers,
  Ne'er shall claim a thought of mine:
You can give in Khabbet's towers--
  Purer joys and brighter wine.

Though your pallid faces prove
  How you nightly vigils keep,
'Tis but that you ever love
  Flowing goblets more than sleep.
Though your eyeballs, dim and sunk,
  Stream in penitential guise,
'Tis but that the Hine you've drunk
  Bubbles over from your eyes.

He had no sooner finished. than Rakeek began, and in the same versification, and to the same air, sung as follows:

RAKEEK TO HIS FEMALE COMPANIONS.

THOUGH the peevish tongues upbraid,
  Though the brows of wisdom scowl,
Fair ones, here on roses laid,
  Careless will we quaff the bowl.

Let the cup, with nectar crowned,
  Through the grove its beams display;
It can shed a lustre round,
  Brighter than the torch of Day.

Let it pass from hand to hand,
  Circling still with ceaseless flight,
Till the streaks of gray expand
  O'er the fleeting robe of Night.

As Night flits, she does but cry.
  "Seize the moments that remain":
Thus our joys with yours shall vie,
  Tenants of yon hallowed fane!

It was Rais' turn next, who charmed us with this plaintive little dialogue, supposed to pass betwixt himself and a Lady:

DIALOGUE BY RAIS.
RAIS.

MAID of sorrow, tell us why
   Sad and drooping hangs thy head?
Is it grief that bids thee sigh?
   Is it sleep that flies thy bed?

LADY.

AH! I mourn no fancied wound;
   Pangs too true this heart have wrung,
Since the snakes which curl around
   Selim's brows my bosom stung.

Destined now to keener woes,
   I must see the youth depart;
He must go, and, as he goes,
   Rend at once my bursting heart.

Slumber may desert my bed;
   'Tis not slumber's charms I seek:
'Tis the robe of beauty spread
   O'er my Selim's rosy cheek.

TO A LADY WEEPING.
BY EBN ALRUMI.

WHEN I beheld thy blue eye shine
   Through the bright drop that Pity drew,
I saw beneath those tears of thine
   A blue-eyed violet bathed in dew.

The violet ever scents the gale,
   Its hues adorn the fairest wreath;
But sweetest through a dewy veil
   Its colours glow, its odours breathe.

And thus thy charms in brightness rise:
   When Wit and Pleasure round thee play;
When Mirth sits smiling in thine eyes,
   Who but admires their sprightly ray?
But when through Pity's flood they gleam,

[101]

Who but must love their softened beam?

ON A VALETUDINARIAN.
BY THE SAME.

SO careful is Isa, and anxious to last,
   So afraid of himself is he grown,
He swears through two nostrils the breath goes too fast,
   And he's trying to breathe through but one.

ON A MISER.
BY THE SAME.

HANG her--a thoughtless, wasteful fool,
   She scatters corn where'er she goes!"
Quoth Hassan, angry at his mule,
   That dropped a dinner to the crows.

TO CASSIM OBID ALLAH,
ON THE DEATH OF ONE OF HIS SONS.
BY ALI BEN AHMED BEN MANSOUR.

POOR Cassim! thou art doomed to mourn,
   By Destiny's decree;
Whatever happen, it must turn
   To misery for thee.

Two sons hadst thou, the one thy pride,
   The other was thy pest;
Ah, why did cruel Death decide
   To snatch away the best?

No wonder thou shouldst droop with woe,
   Of such a child bereft:
But now thy tears must doubly flow,
   For ah,--the other's left!

TO A FRIEND,
ON HIS BIRTHDAY.

WHEN born, in tears we saw thee drowned,

While thine assembled friends around
 With smiles their joy confessed:
So live, that at thy parting hour,
They may the flood of sorrow pour,
 And thou in smiles be dressed.

ON A CAT,
THAT WAS KILLED AS SHE WAS ATTEMPTING TO ROB A DOVE-HOUSE.
BY IBN ALALAF ALNAHARWANY.

POOR Puss is gone!--'tis Fate's decree--
 Yet I must still her loss deplore;
For dearer than a child was she,
 And ne'er shall I behold her more.

With many a sad presaging tear,
 This morn I saw her steal away,
While she went on without a fear,
 Except that she should miss her prey.

I saw her to the dove-house climb,
 With cautious feet and slow she stept,
Resolved to balance loss of time
 By eating faster than she crept.

Her subtle foes were on the watch,
 And marked her course, with fury fraught;
And while she hoped the birds to catch,
 An arrow's point the huntress caught.

In fancy she had got them all,
 And drunk their blood and sucked their breath;
Alas! she only got a fall,
 And only drank the draught of death.
Why, why was pigeon's flesh so nice,
 That thoughtless cats should love it thus?
Hadst thou but lived on rats and mice,
 Thou hadst been living still, poor Puss!

Cursed be the taste, howe'er refined,
 That prompts us for such joys to wish;
And cursed the dainty where we find
 Destruction lurking in the dish!

[103]

EPIGRAM
ON
EBN NAPHTA-WAH.
BY MOHAMMED BEN ZEID ALMOTAKALAM.

[IN order to understand Ben Zeid's Charade. we must remark that, in Arabic, Naphta signifies a combustible not very much unlike our gunpowder, and that Wah is an exclamation of sorrow.]

BY the former with ruin and death we are curst;
   In the latter we grieve for the ills of the first;
And as for the whole where together they meet,
   It's a drunkard, a liar, a thief, and a cheat.

FIRE: A RIDDLE.

THE loftiest cedars I can eat,
   Yet neither paunch nor mouth have I;
I storm whene'er you give me meat;
   Whene'er you give me drink, I die.

TO A LADY,
ON SEEING HER BLUSH.
BY THE KHALIF RADHI BILLAH.

LEILA, whene'er I gaze on thee
   My altered cheek turns pale;
While upon thine, sweet maid, I see
   A deep'ning blush prevail.

Leila, shall I the cause impart
   Why such a change takes place?--
The crimson stream deserts my heart
   To mantle on thy face.

ON THE VICISSITUDES OF LIFE.
BY THE SAME.

MORTAL joys, however pure,
   Soon their turbid source betray;
Mortal bliss, however sure,

Soon must totter and decay.

Ye who now, with footsteps keen,
  Range through Hope's delusive field,
Tell us what the smiling scene
  To your ardent grasp can yield?

Other youths have oft before
  Deemed their joys would never fade,
Till themselves were seen no more--
  Swept into oblivion's shade.

Who, with health and pleasure gay,
  E'er his fragile state could know,
Were not age and pain to say--
  Man is but the child of woe?

TO A DOVE.
BY SERAGE ALWARAK.

THE Dove, to ease an aching breast,
  In piteous murmurs vents her cares;
Like me, she sorrows, for, oppressed,
  Like me, a load of grief she bears.

Her plaints are heard in every wood,
  While I would fain conceal my woes:
But vain's my wish--the briny flood,
  The more I strive, the faster flows.

Sure, gentle bird, my drooping heart
  Divides the pangs of love with thine;
And plaintive murm'rings are thy part,
  And silent grief and tears are mine.

ON A THUNDER-STORM.
BY IBRAHIM BEN KHIRET ABU ISAAC.

BRIGHT smiled the morn, till o'er its head
 The clouds in thickened foldings spread
  A robe of sable hue;
 Then, gathering round Day's golden King,
 They stretched their wide o'ershadowing wing,

And hid him from our view.

The rain his absent beams deplored,
 And, softened into weeping, poured
   Its tears in many a flood;
 The lightning laughed, with horrid glare;
 The thunder growled, in rage; the air
   In silent sorrow stood.

TO HIS FAVOURITE MISTRESS.
BY SAIF ADDAULET, SULTAN OF ALEPPO.

I SAW their jealous eyeballs roll,
  I saw them mark each glance of mine;
 I saw thy terrors, and my soul
   Shared every pang that tortured thine.

In vain, to wean my constant heart,
  Or quench my glowing flame, they strove:
 Each deep-laid scheme, each envious art,
   But waked my fears for her I love.

'Twas this compelled the stern decree
  That forced thee to those distant towers,
 And left me nought but love for thee,
   To cheer my solitary hours.

Yet let not Abla sink depressed,
  Nor separation's pangs deplore:
 We meet not--'tis to meet more blest;
   We parted--'tis to part no more.

ON THE
CRUCIFIXION OF EBN BAKIAH.
BY ABU HASSAN ALANBARY.

WHATE'ER thy fate, in life and death,
  Thou'rt doomed above us still to rise,
 Whilst at a distance far beneath
   We view thee with admiring eyes.

The gazing crowds still round thee throng,
  Still to thy well-known voice repair,

As when erewhile thy hallowed tongue
  Poured in the mosque the solemn prayer.

Still, generous Vizier, we survey
  Thine arms extended o'er our head,
As lately, in the festive day,
  When they were stretched thy gifts to shed.

Earth's narrow bound'ries strove in vain
  To limit thy aspiring mind;
And now we see thy dust disdain
  Within her breast to be confined.

The earth's too small for one so great;
  Another mansion thou shalt have--
The clouds shall be thy winding-sheet,
  The spacious vault of heaven thy grave.

ON THE
CAPRICES OF FORTUNE.
BY SHEMS ALMAALI CABUS,
THE DETHRONED SULTAN OF GEORGIA.

WHY should I blush that Fortune's frown
  Dooms me life's humble paths to tread?
To live unheeded and unknown!
  To sink forgotten to the dead!

'Tis not the good, the wise, the brave,
  That surest shine, or highest rise:
The feather sports upon the wave,
  The pearl in ocean's cavern lies.

Each lesser star that studs the sphere
  Sparkles with undiminished light:
Dark and eclipsed alone appear
  The Lord of Day, the Queen of Night.

LIFE.

LIKE sheep, we're doomed to travel o'er
  The fated track to all assigned;
These follow those that went before,

And leave the world to those behind.

As the flock seeks the pasturing shade,
  Man presses to the future day;
 While Death, amidst the tufted glade,
  Like the dun robber, [**] waits his prey.

Footnotes

^134:* i.e.--The Wolf.

TO LEILA.

LEILA, with too successful art,
  Has spread for me Love's cruel snare;
 And now, when she has caught my heart,
  She laughs, and leaves it to despair.

Thus the poor sparrow pants for breath,
  Held captive by a playful boy;
 And while it drinks the draught of death,
  The thoughtless child looks on with joy.

Ah! were its fluttering pinions free,
  Soon would it bid its chains adieu;
 Or did the child its sufferings see,
  He'd pity and relieve them too.

EXTEMPORE VERSES
ON THE SULTAN CARAWASH, HIS PRINCIPAL MUSICIAN BARKAIDY, HIS
VIZIER EBN FADHI, AND HIS CHAMBERLAIN ABU JABER.

BY EBN ALRAMACRAM.

TOWERING as Barkaidy's face,
  The wintry night came in,
 Cold as the music of his bass,
  And lengthened as his chin.

Sleep from my aching eyes had fled,
  And kept as far apart
 As sense from Ebn Fadhi's head,
  Or virtue from his heart.

The dubious paths my footsteps balked,
  I slipped along the sod,
As if on Jaber's faith I'd walked,
  Or on his truth had trod.

At length the rising King of Day
  Burst on the gloomy wood,
Like Carawash's eye, whose ray
  Dispenses every good.

ON THE
DEATH OF A SON.
BY ALI BEN MOHAMMED ALTAHMANY.

TYRANT of Man! Imperious Fate!
  I bow before thy dread decree;
Nor hope in this uncertain state
  To find a seat secure from thee.

Life is a dark, tumultuous stream,
  With many a care and sorrow foul;
Yet thoughtless mortals vainly deem
  That it can yield a limpid bowl.

Think not that stream will backward flow,
  Or cease its destined course to keep;
As soon the blazing spark shall glow
  Beneath the surface of the deep.

Believe not Fate, at thy command,
  Will grant a meed she never gave;
As soon the airy tower shall stand
  That's built upon a passing wave.

Life is a sleep of threescore years;
  Death bids us wake and hail the light;
And man, with all his hopes and fears,
  Is but a phantom of the night.

ON MODERATION IN OUR PLEASURES.
BY ABU ALCASSIM EBN TABATABA.

HOW oft does passion's grasp destroy

[109]

The pleasure that it strives to gain!
How soon the thoughtless course of joy
   Is doomed to terminate in pain!

When Prudence would thy steps delay,
   She but restrains to make thee blest;
Whate'er from joy she lops away
   But heightens and secures the rest.

Wouldst thou a trembling flame expand
   That hastens in the lamp to die?
With careful touch, with sparing hand,
   The feeding stream of life supply.

But if thy flask profusely sheds
   A rushing torrent o'er the blaze,
Swift round the sinking flame it spreads,
   And kills the fire it fain would raise.

ON THE
VALE OF BOZAA.
BY AHMED BEN YOUSEF ALMENAZY.

THE intertwining boughs for thee
   Have wove, sweet dell, a verdant vest,
And thou in turn shall give to me
   A verdant couch upon thy breast.

To shield me from Day's fervid glare,
   Thine oaks their fostering arms extend,
As, anxious o'er her infant care,
   I've seen a watchful mother bend.

A brighter cup, a sweeter draught,
   I gather from that rill of thine,
Than maddening drunkards ever quaffed,
   Than all the treasures of the vine.

So smooth the pebbles on its shore,
   That not a maid can thither stray,
But counts her strings of jewels o'er,
   And thinks the pearls have slipped away.

TO ADVERSITY.

BY ABU MENBAA CARAWASH, SULTAN OF MOUSEL.

HAIL, chastening friend, Adversity! 'tis thine
 The mental ore to temper and refine;
 To cast in Virtue's mould the yielding heart,
 And Honour's polish to the mind impart.

Without thy wakening touch, thy plastic aid,
 I'd lain the shapeless mass that Nature made;
 But formed, great artist, by thy magic hand,
 I gleam a sword, to conquer and command.

ON
THE INCOMPATIBILITY OF PRIDE
AND TRUE GLORY
BY ABU ALOLA.

THINK not, Abdallah, Pride and Fame
  Can ever travel hand in hand;
 With breast opposed, and adverse aim,
  On the same narrow path they stand.

Thus Youth and Age together meet,
  And Life's divided moments share:
 This can't advance till that retreat;
  What's here increased, is lessened there.

And thus the falling shades of Night
  Still struggle with the lucid ray,
 And ere they stretch their gloomy flight,
  Must win the lengthened space from Day.

ON THE
DEATH OF NEDHAM ALMOLK,
VIZIER TO THE THREE FIRST SELJUK
SULTANS OF PERSIA.
BY SHEBAL ADDAULET.

THY virtues, famed through every land,
  Thy spotless life in age and youth,
 Prove thee a pearl, [**] by Nature's hand
  Formed out of purity and truth.

[111]

Too long its beams of orient light
  Upon a thankless world were shed:
 ALLAH has now revenged the slight,
  And called it to its native bed.

Footnotes

^142:* Nedham, in Arabic, signifies a string of pearls.

VERSES
ADDRESSED BY WALADATA, DAUGHTER OF MOHAMMED
ALMOSTAKFI BILLAH, KHALIF OF SPAIN, TO SOME
YOUNG MEN, WHO HAD PRETENDED A PASSION
FOR HERSELF AND HER COMPANIONS.

WHEN you told us our glances, soft, timid, and mild,
  Could occasion such wounds in the heart,
 Can ye wonder that yours, so ungoverned and wild,
  Some wounds to our cheeks should impart?

The wounds on our cheeks are but transient, I own,
  With a blush they appear and decay;
 But those on the heart, fickle youths, ye have shown
  To be even more transient than they.

VERSES
ADDRESSED TO HIS DAUGHTERS, DURING HIS IMPRISONMENT,
BY MOTAMMED BEN ABAD, SULTAN OF SEVILLE.

["UPON a certain festival," says Ebn Khocan, a contemporary writer, "during the confinement of Motammed, he was waited upon by his children, who came to receive his blessing, and to offer up their prayers for his welfare. Amongst these some were females, and their appearance was truly deplorable. They were naturally beauteous as the moon, but, from the rags which covered them, they seemed like the moon under an eclipse: their feet were bare and bleeding, and every trace of their former splendour was completely effaced. At this melancholy spectacle their unfortunate father gave way to his sorrow in the following verses."]

WITH jocund heart and cheerful brow,
  I used to hail the festal morn:
 How must Motammed greet it now?--
  A prisoner, helpless and forlorn;

[112]

While these dear maids, in beauty's bloom,
  With want oppressed, with rags o'erspread,
By sordid labours at the loom
  Must earn a poor, precarious bread.

Those feet, that never touched the ground
  Till musk or camphor strewed the way,
Now, bare and swoll'n with many a wound,
  Must struggle through the miry clay.

Those radiant cheeks are veiled in woe,
  A shower descends from every eye;
And not a starting tear can flow
  That wakes not an attending sigh.

Fortune, that whilom owned my sway,
  And bowed obsequious to my nod,
Now sees me destined to obey,
  And bend beneath oppression's rod.

Ye mortals, with success elate,
  Who bask in Hope's delusive beam,
Attentive view Motammed's fate,
  And own that bliss is but a dream.

A SERENADE
TO HIS SLEEPING MISTRESS.
BY ALI BEN ABD ALGANY, OF CORDOVA.

SURE Harut's [**] potent spells were breathed
  Upon that magic sword, thine eye;
For if it wounds us thus while sheathed,
  When drawn 'tis vain its edge to fly.

How canst thou doom me, cruel fair,
  Plunged in the hell [*+] of scorn, to groan?
No idol e'er this heart could share
  This heart has worshipped thee alone.

Footnotes

^146:* A wicked angel, who is permitted to tempt mankind by teaching them magic: see
the legend respecting him in Sale's Koran.

[113]

^146:+ The poet here alludes to the punishments denounced in the Koran against those who worship a plurality of gods: "their couch shall be in hell, and over them shall be coverings of fire." Sur. 2.

THE INCONSISTENT.
TO A LADY, UPON HER REFUSAL OF A PRESENT OF
MELONS, AND HER REJECTION OF THE
ADDRESSES OF AN ADMIRER.

WHEN I sent you my melons, you cried out with scorn,
  "They ought to be heavy, and wrinkled, and yellow:"
When I offered myself, whom those graces adorn,
  You flouted, and called me an ugly old fellow!

ON THE
CAPTURE OF JERUSALEM,
IN THE FIRST CRUSADE.
BY ALMODHAFER ALABIWERDY.

FROM our distended eyeballs flow
 A mingled stream of tears and blood;
 Nor care we feel, nor wish we know,
 But who shall pour the largest flood.

But what defence can tears afford?
 What aid supply in this dread hour?
 When, kindled by the sparkling sword,
 War's raging flames the land devour!

No more let sleep's seductive charms
 Upon your torpid souls be shed:
 A crash like this, such dire alarms,
 Might burst the slumbers of the dead.

Think where your dear companions lie--
 Survey their fate, and hear their woes:
 How some through trackless deserts fly,
 Some in the vulture's maw repose;

While some, more wretched still, must bear
 The tauntings of a Christian's tongue;--
 Hear this--and blush ye not to wear
 The silken robe of peace so long?

[114]

Remember what ensanguined showers
 The Syrian plains with crimson dyed;
 And think how many blooming flowers
 In Syrian forts their beauties hide.

Arabian youths! in such a cause
 Can ye the voice of glory slight?
 Warriors of Persia! Can ye pause,
 Or fear to mingle in the fight?

If neither piety nor shame
 Your breasts can warm, your souls can move,
 Let emulation's bursting flame
 Wake you to Vengeance and to Love!

TO A LADY,
WHO ACCUSED HER LOVER OF FLATTERY.

O, Abla, no--when Selim tells
 Of many an unknown grace that dwells
     In Abla's face and mien;
 When he describes the sense refined
 That lights thine eye, and fills thy mind,
     By thee alone unseen,--

'Tis not that, drunk with Love, he sees
 Ideal charms which only please
     Through Passion's partial veil;
 'Tis not that Flattery's glozing tongue
 Hath basely framed an idle song,
     But Truth that breathed the tale.

Thine eyes unaided ne'er could trace
 Each opening charm, each varied grace,
     That round thy person plays:
 Some must remain concealed from thee,
 For Selim's watchful eye to see,
     For Selim's tongue to praise.

One polished mirror can declare
 That eye so bright, that face so fair,
     That cheek which shames the rose;.
 But how thy mantle waves behind,
 How float thy tresses on the wind,

[115]

Another only shows.

EPIGRAM
ON
ABU ALCHAIR SELAMU,
AN EGYPTIAN PHYSICIAN.
BY GEORGE, A PHYSICIAN OF ANTIOCH.

WHOEVER has recourse to thee
　　Can hope for health no more:
He's launched into perdition's sea,
　　A sea without a shore.

Where'er admission thou canst gain,
　　Where'er thy phiz can pierce,
At once the Doctor they retain,
　　The mourners and the hearse.

TO A LITTLE MAN WITH A VERY LARGE BEARD.
BY ISAAC BEN KHALIF.

HOW can thy chin that burden bear?
　　Is it all gravity to shock?
Is it to make the people stare,
　　And be thyself a laughing-stock?

When I behold thy little feet
　　After thy beard obsequious run,
I always fancy that I meet
　　Some father followed by his son.

A man like thee scarce e'er appeared;
　　A beard like thine, where shall we find it?
Surely thou cherishest thy beard,
　　In hopes to hide thyself behind it!

LAMIAT ALAJEM.
BY MAUID EDDIN ALHASSAN ABU ISMAEL ALTOGRAI.

[THE sccnc lics in the desert, where the poet is supposed to he travelling along with a caravan. The time is midnight, and while he is kept awake by his sorrows, his fellow-travellers are slumbering around him.

[116]

The author opens the poem with a panegyric upon his own integrity, and the magnanimity he has shown under various misfortunes; these he is proceeding to recount, when he seems suddenly struck with the sight of a friend lying asleep at some distance from him. The poet adjures this friend to arise, and accompany him in an enterprise, the object of which was to visit a lady, whose habitation was in the neighbourhood. Fired with the idea of his mistress, he breaks forth into a description of the happiness of those who are admitted to her society, and resolves that nothing shall divert him from his purpose. His friend, however, appearing unmoved by his solicitations, he at length gives up his intention in despair, and after many bitter invectives against cowardice and sloth, returns to the subject of his misfortunes, and concludes the poem with an ardent exhortation to mistrust mankind, and in every contingence to rely solely upon our own prudence and fortitude.]

NO kind supporting hand I meet,
 But Fortitude shall stay my feet;
 No borrowed splendours round me shine,
 But Virtue's lustre all is mine:
 A fame unsullied still I boast,
 Obscured, concealed, but never lost--
 The same bright orb that led the day
 Pours from the west his mellowed ray.

 Zaura, farewell! No more I see
 Within thy walls a home for me;
 Deserted, spurned, aside I'm tossed,
 As an old sword whose scabbard's lost:
 Around thy walls I seek in vain,
 Some bosom that will soothe my pain--
 No friend is near to breathe relief,
 Or brother to partake my grief.

 For many a melancholy day
 Through desert vales I've wound my way;
 The faithful beast whose back I press
 In groans laments her lord's distress;
 In every quivering of my spear
 A sympathetic sigh I hear;
 The camel, bending with his load,
 And struggling through the thorny road,
 Midst the fatigues that bear him down,
 In Hassan's woes forgets his own;--
 Yet cruel friends my wanderings chide,
 My sufferings slight, my toils deride.

 Once wealth, I own, engrossed each thought;

[117]

There was a moment when I sought
The glittering stores Ambition claims
To feed the wants his fancy frames;
But now 'tis past: the changing day
Has snatched my high-built hopes away,
And bade this wish my labours close,--
Give me not riches, but repose.

'Tis he! that mien my friend declares,
That stature, like the lance he bears;
I see that breast which ne'er contained
A thought by fear or folly stained,
Whose powers can every change obey,
In business grave, in trifles gay,
And formed each varying taste to please,
Can mingle dignity with ease.

What though, with magic influence, sleep
O'er every closing eyelid creep!
Though, drunk with its oblivious wine,
Our comrades on their bales recline,
My Selim's trance I sure can break--
Selim, 'tis I, 'tis I who speak!
Dangers on every side impend,
And sleep'st thou, careless of thy friend?
Thou sleep'st, while every star from high
Beholds me with a wakeful eye;
Thou changest, ere the changeful Night
Hath streaked her fleeting robe with white.

'Tis Love that hurries me along,
I'm deaf to Fear's repressive song;
The rocks of Idham I'll ascend,
Though adverse darts each path defend,
And hostile sabres glitter there,
To guard the tresses of the fair.

Come, Selim, let us pierce the grove,
While night befriends, to seek my love. [p. 156]
The clouds of fragrance, as they rise,
Shall mark the place where Abla lies.
Around her tent my jealous foes,
Like lions, spread their watchful rows;
Amidst their bands her bower appears,
Embosomed in a wood of spears--

[118]

A wood still nourished by the dews
Which smiles and softest looks diffuse.

 Thrice happy youths! who midst yon shades
Sweet converse hold with Idham's maids!
What bliss to view them gild the hours,
And brighten Wit and Fancy's powers,
While every foible they disclose
New transport gives, new graces shows!
'Tis theirs to raise with conscious art
The flames of love in every heart;
'Tis yours to raisc with festive glee
The flames of hospitality:
Smit by their glances lovers lie,
And helpless sink, and hopeless die;
While, slain by you, the stately steed
To crown the feast is doomed to bleed--
To crown the feast, where copious flows
The sparkling juice that soothes your woes,
That lulls each care and heals each wound,
As the enlivening bowl goes round.

 Amidst those vales my eager feet
Shall trace my Abla's dear retreat; [p. 157]
A gale of health may hover there,
To breathe some solace to my care.
I fear not Love--I bless the dart
Sent in a glance to pierce the heart:
With willing breast the sword I hail
That wounds me through a half-closed veil;
Though lions, howling round the shade,
My footsteps haunt, my walks invade,
No fears shall drive me from the grove,
If Abla listen to my love.

 Ah, Selim! shall the spells of ease
Thy friendship chain, thine ardour freeze?
Wilt thou, enchanted thus, decline
Each generous thought, each bold design?
Then far from men some cell prepare,
Or build a mansion in the air;
But yield to us ambition's tide
Who fearless on its waves can ride;--
Enough for thee, if thou receive
The scattered spray the billows leave.

[119]

Contempt and want the wretch await
Who slumbers in an abject state--
Midst rushing crowds, by toil and pain,
The meed of Honour we must gain;
At Honour's call, the camel hastes
Through trackless wilds and dreary wastes,
Till in the glorious race she find
The fleetest coursers left behind: [p. 158]
By toils like these alone, he cries,
Th' adventurous youths to greatness rise:
If bloated indolence were fame,
And pompous ease our noblest aim,
The orb that regulates the day
Would ne'er from Aries' mansion stray.

I've bent at Fortune's shrine too long;
Too oft she heard my suppliant tongue;
Too oft has mocked my idle prayers,
While fools and knaves engrossed her cares;
Awake for them, asleep to me,
Heedless of worth she scorned each plea.
Ah! had her eyes, more just, surveyed
The different claims which each displayed,
Those eyes, from partial fondness free,
Had slept to them, and waked for me.

But midst my sorrows and my toils,
Hope ever soothed my breast with smiles;
Her hand removed each gathering ill,
And oped life's closing prospects still.
Yet spite of all her friendly art,
The specious scene ne'er gained my heart:
I loved it not, although the day,
Met my approach, and cheered my way;
I loath it, now the hours retreat,
And fly me with reverted feet.

My soul, from every tarnish free,
May boldly vaunt her purity; [p. 159]
But ah, how keen, however bright
The sabre glitter to the sight,
Its splendour's lost, its polish vain,
Till some bold hand the steel sustain.

[120]

Why have my days been stretched by Fate
To see the vile and vicious great,
While I, who led the race so long,
Am last and meanest of the throng?
Ah, why has Death so long delayed
To wrap me in his friendly shade?--
Left me to wander thus alone,
When all my heart held dear is gone!

But let me check these fretful sighs--
Well may the base above me rise,
When yonder planets, as they run,
Mount in the sky above the sun.
Resigned I bow to Fate's decree,
Nor hope his laws will change for me:
Each shifting scene, each varying hour,
But proves the ruthless tyrant's power.

But though with ills unnumbered cursed,
We owe to faithless man the worst;
For man can smile with specious art,
And plant a dagger in the heart.
He only's fitted for the strife
Which fills the boist'rous paths of life,
Who, as he treads the crowded scenes,
Upon no kindred bosom leans. [p. 160]
Too long my foolish heart had deemed
Mankind as virtuous as they seemed;
The spell is broke, their faults are bare,
And now I see them as they are:
Truth from each tainted breast has flown,
And Falsehood marks them all her own.
Incredulous I listen now
To every tongue and every vow,
For still there yawns a gulf between
Those honeyed words and what they mean.
With honest pride elate I see
The sons of Falsehood shrink from me,
As from the right line's even way
The biassed curves deflecting stray.--
But what avails it to complain?
With souls like theirs reproof is vain;
If honour e'er such bosoms share,
The sabre's point must fix it there.

But why exhaust life's vapid bowl,
And suck the dregs with sorrow foul,
When long ere this my youth has drained
Whatever zest the cup contained?
Why should we mount upon the wave
And ocean's yawning horrors brave,
When we may swallow from the flask
Whate'er the wants of mortals ask?

Contentment's realms no fears invade,
No cares annoy, no sorrows shade; [p. 161]
There, placed secure, in peace we rest,
Nor aught demand to make us blest.
While Pleasure's gay fantastic bower,
The splendid pageant of an hour,
Like yonder meteor in the skies,
Flits with a breath, no more to rise.

As through life's various walks we're led,
May Prudence hover o'er our head!
May she our words, our actions guide,
Our faults correct, our secrets hide!
May she, where'er our footsteps stray,
Direct our paths and clear the way!
Till, every scene of tumult past,
She bring us to repose at last--
Teach us to love that peaceful shore,
And roam through Folly's wilds no more!

TO YOUTH.
BY EBN ALRABIA, IN HIS OLD AGE.

YES, Youth, thou'rt fled, and I am left,
  Like yonder desolated bower,
By Winter's ruthless hand bereft
  Of every leaf and every flower.

With heaving heart and streaming eyes,
  I wooed thee to prolong thy stay,
But vain were all my tears and sighs--
  Thou only fled'st more fast away.

Yet though thou fled'st away so fast,
  I can recall thee if I will;

[122]

For I can talk of what is past,
    And while I talk, enjoy thee still.

ON LOVE.
BY ABU ALI, THE MATHEMATICIAN.

[ABU ALI flourished in Egypt about A.H. 530, and was equally celebrated as a mathematician and as a poet. In the following odd composition he seems to have united these two discordant characters.]

I NEVER knew a sprightly fair
    That was not dear to me;
And freely I my heart could share
    With every one I see.

It is not this or that alone
    On whom my choice would fall:
I do not more incline to one
    Than I incline to all.

The circle's bounding line are they;
    Its centre is my heart;
My ready love, the equal ray
    That flows to every part.

A REMONSTRANCE WITH A DRUNKARD.
BY YAHIA BEN SALAMET.

[THIS author was a native of Syria, and died at Miafarakir, in the year of the Hejra 553.]

AS drenched in wine, the other night,
    Zeid from the banquet sallied,
Thus I reproved his drunken plight,
    Thus he my prudence rallied:

"In beverage so impure and vile
    How canst thou thus delight?"
"My cups," he answered, with a smile,
    "Are generous and bright."

"Beware those dangerous draughts," I cried;
    "With love the goblet flows."
"And cursed is he," the youth replied,

[123]

"Who hatred only knows!"

"Those cups too soon, with sickness fraught,
   Thy stomach shall deplore."
 "Then soon," he cried, "the noxious draught
   And all its ills are o'er."

"Rash youth! thy guilty joys resign"--
   "I will," at length he said:
 "I vow I'll bid adieu to wine--
   As soon as I am dead!"

VERSES
ADDRESSED BY THE KHALIF ALMOKTAFI LIAMRILLAH
TO A LADY, WHO PRETENDED A PASSION FOR
HIM IN HIS OLD AGE.

THOUGH such unbounded love you swear,
   'Tis only art I see:
 Can I believe that one so fair
   Should ever doat on me?

Say that you hate, and freely show
   That Age displeases Youth;
 And I may love you, when I know
   That you can tell the truth.

ON PROCRASTINATION.
BY HEBAT ALLAH IBN ALTALMITH.

YOUTH is a drunken, noisy hour,
   With every folly fraught;
 But man, by Age's chastening power,
   Is sobered into thought.

Then we resolve our faults to shun,
   And shape our course anew;
 But ere the wise reform's begun,
   Life closes on our view.

The travellers thus, who wildly roam,
   Or heedlessly delay,
 Are left, when they should reach their home,

Benighted on the way.

ON THE
EARLY DEATH OF ABU ALHASSAN ALI,
SON OF THE KHALIF ALNASSAR LEDIN ALLAH.
BY CAMAL EDDIN BEN ALNABIT.

SOON hast thou run the race of life,
    Nor could our tears thy speed control:
Still in the coursers' gen'rous strife
    The best will soonest reach the goal.

As Death upon his hand turns o'er
    The different gems the world displays,
He seizes first, to swell his store,
    The brightest jewel he surveys.

Thy name, by every breath conveyed,
    Stretched o'er the globe its boundless flight;
Alas! in eve the length'ning shade
    But lengthens to be lost in night!

If gracious ALLAH bade thee close
    Thy youthful eyes so soon on day,
'Tis that he readiest welcomes those
    Who love him best, and best obey.

THE INTERVIEW.
A SONG IN THE RHYTHM OF THE ORIGINAL, WITH THE MUSIC ANNEXED.

[THE music to this little piece was written down, by a friend, from, the singing of David
Zamir, a native of Bagdad, who resided with the translator for some time at Cambridge.]

DARKNESS closed around, loud the tempest drove,
 When through yonder glen I saw my lover rove,
    Dearest youth!
 Soon he reached our cot, weary, wet, and cold,
 But warmth, wine, and I to cheer his spirits strove,
    Dearest youth!

"How, my love," cried I, "durst thou hither stray
 Through the gloom, nor fear the ghosts that haunt the grove,
    Dearest youth?"
 "In this heart," said he, "fear no seat can find,

When each thought is filled alone with thee and love,
   Dearest maid!"

THE
ROMANCE OF ANTAR:
AN EPITOME
OF
THE FIRST PART, TRANSLATED BY
TERRICK HAMILTON, ESQ.,
WITH SELECTIONS FROM THE POETRY.
BY THE EDITOR.

I have only seen the fourteenth volume of this work, which comprises all that is elegant and noble in composition. So lofty, so various, and so bold is its style, that I do not hesitate to rank it amongst the most finished poems.--Sir W. Jones.

This is the work, and not, as is generally supposed, the "Thousand and One Nights," which is the source of the stories that fill the tents and cottages of Arabia and Egypt.--Von Hammer.

THE
ROMANCE OF ANTAR.
EDITOR'S PREFACE.

IT is generally believed that this celebrated Arabian Romance was composed, in the eighth century, from traditionary tales which had been long current in the East, by El-Asma'ee, a famous philologist and poet at the court of Haroon Er-Rasheed. Other authors and sources (for instance, Johainah and Abu Obeidah) are mentioned in the work, but these, according to Von Hammer, have been inserted by story-tellers in the coffeehouses. Lane, in his admirable work on the Modern Egyptians, remarks that the 'Ulama (learned men) "in general despise the romance, and ridicule the assertion that El-Asma'ee was its author": their opinion, however, on a question of this kind, is of little value.

The complete work is usually bound up in forty-five volumes of various sizes--presenting a mass sufficient to appal the most indefatigable of translators; not to speak of the impossibility of finding European readers who would wade through the translation, if published. An abridged copy of this voluminous work, done by some learned Syrians (and hence called the Shamiyeh, or Syrian Antar, to distinguish it from the original, which was known as the Hijaziyeh, or Arabian Antar), having been obtained by Mr Terrick Hamilton, during his residence at Constantinople, in his capacity of Oriental Secretary to the British Embassy there, he was induced by its comparative brevity to undertake the task of translating it into English.

[126]

In the year 1819 the first fruits of his labours in this direction appeared at London in the form of a small octavo volume of about 300 pages, entitled, "Antar, a Bedoueen Romance, translated from the Arabic," &c., with a short introduction by a friend who had seen the volume through the press. Next year (1820) three more volumes were issued, completing the first of the three parts into which Mr Hamilton intended dividing his translation, and bringing down Antar's adventures to his marriage with Abla.

The work was very favourably noticed by the leading reviewers of the day, some of whom ventured to predict for it a popularity in this country as great as that accorded to the fascinating "Thousand and One Nights." The anticipations of the translator, and of his friendly critics, were, however, not realised: the marvellous exploits of the Absian hero, and the wild and fiery, the tender and beautiful, effusions of natural poetry with which the narrative is interspersed, had little interest or charm for the bulk of English readers,-- familiar only with absurd imitations of Eastern fiction, adapted from the French, and bearing as little resemblance to Oriental story as the stage sailor of transpontine melodrama bears to the seaman of real life,--and, as a consequence, the translation of Antar was not completed; but Mr Hamilton gives an outline of the contents of the remainder, as follows:--

"The Second Part includes the period when the hero suspends his Poem at Mecca. This grand point he at length attains, not only by the friendly dispositions of his former associates, and the continuance of his own heroic deeds, but also by the means of his two sons and a brother, whom he discovers amongst the heroes of the desert. Encouraged by their counsels, and urged by his own ambition, after various conflicts and conquests, he resolves to crush the envious malice of his domestic foes, and in despite of all the machinations contrived against him, and the hostilities of all the most potent kings of Arabia, he succeeds in accomplishing this second object of his ambition.

"The Third Part comprises the death of Antar, and most of his comrades and relations; in the course of which he wages endless wars against the more distant tribes,--visits Constantinople and Europe, and invades that part of Arabia inhabited by the Ethiopians, amongst whom he discovers his mother's relations, and finds out that she was the daughter of a mighty monarch, and himself thus descended in both lines from a majestic race. His last conquest is over his domestic enemies. His death is consonant with the rules of poetical justice. He falls under the hand of one whom he might have justly punished with death, but who was the object of cruelty he had never practised on any one before, not even his most inveterate foes."

This singular work is the only record of the every-day life of the Arabs ere yet they had come under the influence of El-Islam. "Even in a translation," says a judicious critic, "Antar must be perused with pleasure by those to whom the simple modes of life afford matter of interesting speculation, and by those who are gratified with flowing and luxuriant descriptions, united to lively and picturesque sketches of events and characters." Here the virtues and the vices of these Children of the Desert are faithfully portrayed:

hospitable, brave, vindictive; at once liberal and avaricious; withal possessing a punctilious sense of honour: such were the pre-Islamite Arabs, whom the pen of El-Asma'ee has so vividly delineated. The Poetry with which the work is richly jewelled is the poetry of nature, abounding in touches of pathos, far beyond the reach of art.

I regret that I have been unable to obtain any German or French translation of the account of Antar's suspending his Kasidah on the Kaaba; but my friend Mr. E. J. W. Gibb, of Lochwood, Lanarkshire, a young Orientalist of much promise, has favoured me with a translation of the Death of Antar--one of the noblest of heroic poems--from the French version of M. Caussin de Perceval, which is appended to the following rough sketch of the leading incidents in the First Part, according to Mr Hamilton's translation.

THE adventures of Antar naturally suggest the question of the origin of romantic fiction, or chivalric romance, in Europe, which has long been, and perhaps is still, the subject of dispute among men of learning. By some, romantic fiction is held to be of purely Gothic origin, brought from the North by the Scalds who accompanied the army of Rollo into France; others, again, allege that its introduction into Europe is traceable to the Saracens who settled in Spain early in the 8th century. The truth seems to be that European mediaeval romances were composed, in unequal parts, of classical tales of antiquity, Northern legends, and Oriental fictions.

It is far from improbable that the famous Arabian Romance of Antar furnished the model for the earliest of the regular romances of chivalry which were current in Europe during the middle ages; indeed a comparison of incidents in the work of El-Asma'ee with others found in the so-called Gothic romances will show some very striking parallels, sufficient of themselves to lead to this conclusion.

Many of the tales and fictions which were popular in Europe in mediaeval times, and which, collected from oral tradition, have been preserved in such works as the "Clericali Disciplina" of Petrus Alphonsus, and the "Gesta Romanorum," have been traced to Eastern sources--to Arabia and Syria, and thence to India, through Persia. These fictions probably came into Europe, partly through the Saracens of Spain, partly through intercourse with the East during the Crusades.

But in the 8th, 9th, and 10th centuries there was free intercourse between the Eastern and Western countries of the Roman world. Haroon Er-Rasheed and Charlemagne interchanged presents and messages of good-will; and the wondrous adventures of Antar may well have become known to early European writers of Chivalric Romance, when communication was thus open between Asia and Europe.

If, however, we must seek in the Far East for the cradle of popular European tales and fictions, the task of tracing back even Eastern stories to their originals (for regarding popular fictions especially does Solomon's sweeping assertion hold good--"there is nothing new under the sun") becomes more complicated as we pursue our researches into remote antiquity.

[128]

We have it on the high authority of Lane that the "Thousand and One Nights" furnish exact pictures of Arabian manners and customs at the period when they were composed; but the groundwork of many of these charming tales is unquestionably of Persian or Indian origin. For example: the story, familiar to every schoolboy, of El-'Ashshar (the "Alnaschar" of our common English translation of Galland's garbled French version) and his basket of glass-ware finds a parallel in the "Pankatantra," a collection of Sanskrit Fables, where the same story is told of a Brahman and his pot of rice. But even in this ancient work we do not find the true original of the Arabian Tale. Professor Benfey has proved these Fables to have been borrowed from Buddhistic sources; and Professor Max Muller thinks "we may go a step farther, and maintain that not only the general outline of these Fables, but in some cases the very words, were taken over from Pali into Sanskrit."--The general plan of the "Thousand and One Nights" is said to have been borrowed from that of a similar Pehlevi collection of Tales. It is moreover identical in plan with that of the Parables of Sendabad, of Hindu origin, and known in various old English versions under the title of the "Seven Wise Masters."

But it is thought that the Romance of Antar must be essentially original, since there existed no work of the same kind to serve

for a model. This may be true; and yet it appears to me not impossible that some of the heroic adventures ascribed to Antar in this work may have been derived indirectly from the old Pehlevi Romances so bitterly denounced by the Kur'an. One of these was brought into Arabia by a merchant on his return from Persia, at the time when the Prophet was promulgating his new religion. The Arabs, it is said, were charmed with the stories of giants and dragons, and preferred them to the moral instructions of Muhammad: hence the passage in the Kur'an (chapter xxxi.) against romances and idle tales. The Muslim conquerors of Persia, it is well known, ruthlessly destroyed nearly all the literary treasures of that ancient kingdom, and we may be sure that works of fiction were the objects of their special abhorrence. But oral tradition may have preserved scenes and incidents from the old Persian Romances; and since it is said that to the obscurity of time do the ancients owe their reputation for originality, so to sources, which are now for ever lost, may El-Asma'ee, whose memory was richly stored with traditionary as well as with written lore, have been indebted for some of the adventures described in the Romance of Antar.

FROM THE TRANSLATOR'S PREFACE.

ANTAR is no imaginary person: he is well known as a celebrated warrior, and as the author of one of the Seven Poems suspended on the Kaaba at Mecca. His intrepidity is often mentioned by Abulfeda, as being the subject of poetry; though it does not appear that any precise composition relating to his feats in arms is extant, some detached pieces may have survived; still it must be supposed that oral tradition alone has commemorated in verse, current among succeeding generations, those various proofs of heroism which

Asma'ee afterwards embodied in his work. That he was the son of Shedad, an Absian chief, is also well attested; though it does not so clearly appear that he was born of a slave-woman.

It is not to be understood that Asma'ee merely intended to compose a faithful history of those times: his view seems rather to comprise in a pleasing tale numerous isolated facts, and the most striking traits of the manners and usages prevalent at that period; and therefore we may presume that he has embellished his narrative with every additional circumstance that could possibly throw an interest over his hero, or attract the attention of his readers.

And that he has succeeded among those for whom the work was composed, there cannot be the smallest doubt. It is also true that many who at this day have read it in the original have expressed the delight and unwearied admiration they have felt in the perusal of its endless volumes.

It may be assumed that it is one of the most ancient books of Arabian literature; composed during the second century of the
Hijrah, at a time when the arts were most successfully cultivated amongst the Asiatic conquerors, and encouraged more particularly under the influence of the Arab princes of Bagdad. Its language is therefore uncommonly pure, equally remote from the harshness of the earlier, or the conceits of the later, authors; and when we consider that it was originally written in the Cufic character, and has for a thousand years been transcribed chiefly for the use of the Bedouins, and often by persons who probably did not comprehend one word they were writing, it is a matter of surprise how it has retained so much purity and correctness. Some few Persian and Turkish words, subject to Arabic inflexions, are now and then to be observed; some other modern terms may also have been inserted. These are corruptions; and M. Hammer thinks that many interpolations have been made by the copyist. Words often occur which are not to be found in any dictionary; and some expressions there are, which, though current to this day among the Arabs of the Desert, are not susceptible of the same acceptation in any lexicon.

The style of the work as a composition is very plain and easy in construction; but abounding in an endless variety of diction, couched in the most choice and appropriate terms. The sentences are short, much in the style of the Bible; the prose is even in rhythm throughout, continuing uninterrupted but by a change of termination, according to the powers of the author, or the redundancy of expressions with the same sound;--this is reckoned the greatest beauty in Oriental compositions. Thus, with short rhythmical periods of various lengths, the author proceeds, for five or six lines, to the end of his subject, and then recommences other matter with a different rhyme. This is particularly striking in all his descriptions of battles, where the pauses are very frequent, all with the same terminations; the periods being often formed of only two words, sometimes of three, and thus hurrying on, with apparent rapidity and great variety and spirit, throughout a whole page.

This species of composition produces the necessity of continued repetitions; and though Asma'ee has proved that his memory was supplied with an infinity of expression, unrivalled by any Oriental author, yet the frequent recurrence of similar scenes and thoughts must of course occasion such repetitions as almost to weary his warmest admirers; but when translated into another tongue that admits of, comparatively speaking, no diversity of terms to express the same meaning, they become most tedious and disgusting.

The poetry has the charm of a more elevated style; and a wider range for the imagination has been eagerly seized by the poet. Infinitely more difficult in its construction, it is still natural, and devoid of those conceits and absurdities that abound in almost all Asiatic compositions. It comprises every variety to which poetry is applied. The heroic, the complimentary, the laudatory, the amatory, the ludicrous, the merry, the elegiac, are all combined in the utmost profusion; even the pastoral is not omitted. . . .

The heroic is, of course, a mixture of all that is bold in imagery and inflated in expression; exaggeration and personal vanity run throughout the whole: perhaps these are the legitimate characteristics of such poetry; certainly we have the highest authority for its currency in a poet whose writings are considered as the standard for whatever is grand and majestical in that species of poetical composition.

The elegiac has drawn tears from persons whose sympathies and tenderness were fashioned to be roused by such scenes as are described in this work, and are therefore as true to nature as those feelings which are recognised in a more refined state of society.

The ludicrous and satirical are in some instances too gross, often indelicate, but not obscene. There is something pretty and original in the amatory style; and the merry can move to mirth in its innocence and playfulness. As to the complimentary, it is, as is the case in all languages, the least entitled to commendation, abounding in ridiculous conceits and unintelligible panegyric.

With respect to the magic and enchantments that occur in the work, it may be proper to add, for the benefit of those who indulge in the still controverted point of the birth-place of sorcery, that instances are to be found of supernatural agency; though in the portion now published no mention is made of any such influence over the minds and actions of the heroes who figure in the story. The belief that ghosts, or hobgoblins, or genii, inhabited some peculiar spot generally prevailed; and we perceive that Shiboob, Antar's brother, is often taken for one of those august personages, owing to the rapidity with which he transfers himself from place to place.

The effects of an amulet ring (first worn by a Christian warrior, who at his death bequeaths it to Antar), in relieving a person from fits, are noticed more than once. Sorceresses were also sufficiently celebrated, even at that distant period, to be here recorded: more for the iniquities than for the good they were called upon to perform. One endeavours to inveigle Abla to her destruction, by means of two daemon emissaries she

[131]

employs, and a magic fire she kindles. Another fortifies her castle with the illusion of supernatural flames and smoke; whilst the sister of this wicked enchantress dispels these seeming horrors by her more potent spells. . . .

Allusions to genii frequently occur: one of Antar's sons is slain by them. They are described as most hideous monsters, having their eyes slit upwards, and uttering most terrific sounds. Antar restores to the human form one of the genii who had been metamorphosed into a horse; and, in return, he aids his deliverer in avenging his son's murder. . . . Antar's sword is certainly of original manufacture; and, though not enchanted, may be cited by the side of Durindana. Indian blades, Davidean armour, and Aadite casques are invested with all the properties of magic weapons, whether of offence or defence. . . . The frequent allusion to dragons and sea monsters in the poetry, and in the description of assailing heroes, proves that in those days the introduction of fabulous animals, distinct from those mentioned in Persian books, was considered a legitimate embellishment in romantic fiction. . . .

And thus, with all the paraphernalia of chivalrous equipment, heroes come forth, not only in fields of battle, or in single combat, but also at marriages and entertainments, merely for trials of skill in arms in the midst of a course, to tilt and joust with barbless spears in the presence of kings and chiefs, who proclaim the merits of the victor and the vanquished; sometimes distributing prizes, or awarding a contested point, or even deciding the fate of some damsel, the object of amorous contention between two devoted champions; and not unfrequently do these combats, which commence innocently, end in bloodshed.

It is also worthy of remark, that these chiefs, when bound on a marauding enterprise, often meet with extraordinary adventures: sometimes forlorn maidens, whose distresses they relieve; or matrons, whose husbands and sons have been slain; and even heroes of inferior stamp, whose cause they will adopt, and thus either soften his sorrows or die in his defence. It must be acknowledged that they sometimes take advantage of the unprotected state to which females are reduced, when their attendants have resisted the assaults of a stranger; but instances of the purest generosity, and the most chivalrous sentiments of honour and decency, will often mark their acts, and induce us to marvel how nations so barbarous in blood could ever be melted into pity and tenderness.

. . . A nation of shepherds, dwelling in tents, surrounded by deserts, appears, at first sight, as the very antipodes of those nations whose usages and habits have supplied matter for romance and historic fiction. In minds thus savagely constituted, where could love dwell? Where could courtesy, discretion, and those nameless decencies and distinctions, persons of cultivated manners can only feel and express, find a place? And without minds thus happily organised, and without sensibilities as easily roused as lasting, pliant or obdurate, according to the object that excites them into action, or bidding defiance to repulse, inconstancy, and danger--how could chivalry feed its enthusiasm, or imagination awaken into life?

But in this work we find all these anomalies reconciled. We see heroes capable of the wildest enterprises, and subject to the most vehement emotions, to secure the approbation of their mistresses. We see damsels braving every peril, smiling in captivity, to meet the objects of their love. We moreover meet with heroines cased in armour covering hearts at once steeled against the lance's point or falchion's edge, and a prey to the utmost ecstasies of enthusiastic fondness and refined irritability.

Such are the personages who are found to have inhabited the wilderness of sands, under no cultivation of mind, and bound by no moral restraints, but what love and friendship excited and established. Few could read or write. None were philosophers--wisdom had its only support in the influence attached to advanced years. Their sages were superior in age, and enjoyed a confidence among the tribes that no one could uproot, and which Antar only, by his martial prowess and universally admitted superiority, could thwart.

THE
ROMANCE OF ANTAR.
THE HERO'S BIRTH AND EARLY YEARS.

TEN famous horsemen of the tribe of Abs went forth from the land of Shurebah on a plundering expedition. They travelled by night, and lay concealed during the day; and when they reached the country of Cahtan, in a valley between two hills they discovered the flourishing tribe of Jezreela. Fearing openly to attack a people so numerous and powerful, they proceeded to their pasture ground, where they saw a large herd of camels grazing, and a black woman of great beauty and fine proportions, with her two children, in charge of them. They seized the woman and her children, and drove away the camels; but had not gone far when they were pursued by the warriors of the tribe, upon whom they turned, and after a fierce contest, compelled them to fly. Returning home, the Absians, having arrived in their own country, sat down by the bank of a stream to divide their plunder. One of the party, Shedad, the son of Carad, known as the Knight of Jirwet, from the celebrated mare of that name which he rode, was become so enamoured of the black woman, whose name was Zebeebah, that he chose her and her two boys--Jereer and Shiboob--for his share, leaving to his companions all the camels and other property.

In course of time Zebeebah gave birth to a boy, "black and swarthy as an elephant,--his shape, limbs, form, and make resembled Shedad," who was delighted to look upon him for days together, and called him ANTAR. As the boy grew up he became noted for his great strength and courage. He accompanied his mother to the pasture, and helped her in watching the cattle. One day, when he was but ten years old, he slew a wolf that had dispersed the flocks, and carried home the head and legs of the beast in a basket, and presented the trophies of his prowess to his mother. On hearing of this adventure Shedad cautioned his son not to stray far into the desert, lest he should meet with some mischief. But Antar was not to be restrained: riding about the country, and hurling, his reed-spear at the trunks of trees, he soon became an excellent horseman, and could throw the javelin with unerring precision. And thus passed the early years of Antar the son of Shedad, until

[133]

an incident, strikingly characteristic of Bedouin life, occurred, which proved the turning point of the future hero's career:

"Now King Zoheir had two hundred slaves that tended his herds of he and she-camels, and all his sons had the same. Shas was the eldest of his sons, and heir to his possessions; and Shas had a slave whose name was Daji, and he was a great bully. Shas was very fond of him on account of his vast bodily strength; and there was not a slave but feared him and trembled before him: Antar, however, made no account of him, and did not care for him.

"One day the poor men, and widows, and orphans met together, and were driving their camels and their flocks to drink, and were all standing by the water-side. Daji came up and stopped them, and took possession of the water for his master's cattle. Just then an old woman belonging to the tribe of Abs came up to him, and accosted him in a suppliant manner, saying: 'Be so good, master Daji, as to let my cattle drink; they are all the property I possess, and I live by their milk. Pity my flock: have compassion on me and grant my request, and let them drink.' But he paid no attention to her demand, and abused her. She was greatly distressed, and shrunk back.

"Then came another old woman and addressed him: 'O master Daji, I am a poor weak old woman, as you see: time has dealt hardly with me--it has aimed its arrows at me; and its daily and nightly calamities have destroyed all my men. I have lost my children and my husband, and since then I have been in great distress. These sheep are all I possess: let them drink, for I live on the milk they produce. Pity my forlorn state; I have no one to tend them; therefore grant my request, and be so kind as to let them drink.'

"As soon as Daji heard these words, and perceived the crowd of women and men, his pride increased, and his obstinacy was not to he moved, but he struck the woman on the stomach, and threw her down on her back, and uncovered her nakedness, whilst all the slaves laughed at her. When Antar perceived what had occurred, his pagan pride played throughout all his limbs, and he could not endure the sight. He ran up to the slave, and calling out, 'You bastard!' said he, 'what mean you by this disgusting action? Do you dare to violate an Arab woman? May God destroy your limbs, and all that consented to this act!'

"When the slave heard what Antar said, he almost fainted from indignation: he met him, and struck him a blow over the face that nearly knocked out his eyes. Antar waited till he had recovered from the blow, and his senses returned; he then ran at the slave, and seizing him by one of the legs, threw him on his back. He thrust one hand under his thighs, and with the other he grasped his neck, and raising him by the force of his arm, he dashed him against the ground. And his length and breadth were all one mass. When the deed was done his fury was unbounded, and he roared aloud even as a lion. And when the slaves perceived the fate of Daji, they shrieked out to Antar, saying, 'You have slain the slave of Prince Shas! What man on earth can now protect you? They attacked him with staves and stones, but he resisted them all: he rushed with a loud yell

[134]

upon them, and proved himself a hardy warrior, and dealt among them with his stick as a hero with his sword."

With all his courage and strength, however, Antar was likely to have fallen a victim to the rage of his assailants, when fortunately Prince Malik, one of the King's sons, beloved by all for his mild and gentle disposition, came upon the scene, and put an end to the unequal contest; and on learning its occasion, promised Antar his protection. When King Zoheir was informed of what the hero had done, he warmly applauded his conduct, saying: "This valiant fellow has defended the honour of women; he will shine a noble warrior, and destroy his opponents." And on Antar's return home that day, the women all crowded round him, praising him for his gallant behaviour; and among them was Antar's fair cousin Abla, the daughter of Malik, his father Shedad's brother.

THE DAWN OF LOVE.

Antar had frequent opportunities of seeing Abla, one of his duties being to serve the women of his father's and uncles' families with the camel's milk which, previously cooled in the wind, it was the custom of Arab women to drink every morning and evening. Coming into his uncle Malik's tent one day while Abla's long flowing hair was being dressed by her mother, Antar's soul was filled with the image of her beauty, and when he retired he thus expressed his feelings:

THAT fair maid lets down her ringlets, and she is completely hid in her hair, which appears like the dark shades of night.

It is as if she were the brilliant day, and as if the night had enveloped her in obscurity.

It is as if the full moon was shining in its splendour, and all the stars were concealed by its lustre.

Her charms bewitch all around her, and all are anxious to offer their services:

They live in her beauties and loveliness; and they are imbued with sweetness from her perfections, and receive new spirit from her graces.

Revile me not for my love of her, for I am distracted for her, and live but as the victim of my love.

I will conceal my affection in my soul, till I can see that I am sufficiently fortunate one day to serve her.

And on another occasion, seeing Abla playing and singing among other maidens at a feast, Antar addressed her in eloquent verses:

[135]

THE lovely virgin has struck my heart with the arrow of a glance, for which there is no cure.

Sometimes she wishes for a feast in the sand-hills, like a fawn whose eyes are full of magic.

My disease preys on me; it is in my entrails: I conceal it; but its very concealment discloses it.

She moves: I should say it was the branch of the tamarisk, that waves its branches to the southern breeze.

She approaches: I should say it was the frightened fawn, when a calamity alarms it in the waste.

She walks away: I should say her face was truly the sun when its lustre dazzles the beholders.

She gazes: I should say it was the full moon of the night when Orion girds it with its stars.

She smiles: and the pearls of her teeth sparkle, in which there is the cure for the sickness of lovers.

She prostrates herself in reverence towards her God; and the greatest of men bow down to her beauties.

O Abla! when I most despair, love for thee and all its weaknesses are my only hope!

Should fortune or my father assist me, I will requite myself for its vicissitudes by my fearless spirit.

Love had now become the master-passion of the hero's soul; for all his subsequent exploits as a warrior were undertaken and performed mainly with the view of raising himself above the circumstance of his birth, and of becoming worthy of his cousin. But already Antar had many bitter enemies among his own people, who sought every means of depriving him of the favour and protection of King Zoheir, and of his son Prince Malik. Wandering one day far from the tents of his tribe, and brooding over his forlorn condition and his love for Abla, he composed the following verses:

ABLA'S spirit appeared to me in my sleep, and thrice I kissed her within her veil.

It bade me adieu, but it deposited in me a flame that I feel burning through my bones.

[136]

Were I not left in solitude, and could I not quench the fire of my passion with tears, my heart would melt.

But I do not complain; though all my fears are on thy account, O thou perfect full moon!

O daughter of Malik! how can I be consoled, since my love for thee originated from the time I was weaned?

But how can I ever hope to approach thee, whilst the lions of the forest guard thy tent?

By the truth of my love for thee, my heart can never be cured but by patience.

O thou noble maid! till I exalt myself to the heights of glory with the thrusts of my spear, and the blows of my sword, I will expose myself to every peril wherever the spears clash in the battle-dust--then shall I be either tossed upon the spear-heads, or be numbered among the noble.

EARLY WARLIKE EXPLOITS.

King Zoheir having summoned Shedad, the father of Antar, with his other warriors, to accompany him on an expedition against a neighbouring tribe, Antar was left behind in charge of the women; and here follows a graphic description of the amusements of Arab women in those days:

"The horsemen being now absent, the children, and women, and slaves, male and female, were left behind. Semeeah, the wife of Shedad, gave a magnificent entertainment at the lake of Zatool Irsad. Sheep were slaughtered, and wine flowed, and the girls carried their instruments. Antar stood amongst the attendants, and was in transports on seeing Abla appear with the other women. She was indeed like an amorous fawn; she was decorated with variegated necklaces; and when Antar was attending her, he was overwhelmed in the ocean of his love, and became the slave of her sable tresses. They sat down to eat, and the wine-cups went merrily round. It was the spring of the year, when the whole land shone in all its glory: the vines hung luxuriantly in the arbours; the flowers shed around ambrosial fragrance; every hillock sparkled in the beauty of its colours; the birds in responsive melody sang sweetly from each bush, and harmony issued from their throats; every ear was enchanted; the ground was covered with flowers and herbs; whilst the nightingales filled the air with their softest notes. Then the damsels beat the cymbals, and recited the following verses:

THE shades have spread their canopy, and the flowers spread their pillows.

The streams roll along their shores of flowers, some white, some red, some yellow, some sweet-scented.

[137]

See the waters gliding through the gardens; and the trees and their fruits resemble bracelets and chaplets;

The birds sing melodiously upon them in every variety of note.
The nightingale and the dove pour their plaintive strain, and make every lover weep.
The gentle zephyrs whisper along, and the branches move in softest measure.
The boughs dance in the groves, among the trees, in the graceful movement.
The dew-drops fall, and the flowers and the trees are studded with its pearls.
The season is delightful; let it pass in enjoyment, and misfortunes, begone!
The opportunity is delicious; let us grasp in haste its sweets:
Be merry, and wild with joy, and let not a day pass without amusement.
"Then another set took the musical instruments, and beating the cymbals with their hands, thus sang:--
THE gardens sparkle with all they boast of lovely damsels;
Every sportive virgin is possessed of languishing glances, and enchanting movements:
Their beauty is perfection--they are loveliness itself;
Their elegant shapes glance like the well-proportioned spears;
Their tresses float down their backs, like branches of the grape-vine;
They are slayers and piercers with their arrows and their darts
Archers and strikers--the enchantresses of men.

"They now formed a dance and took off their robes: the damsels danced while the servants sang, and carried round the goblets of wine. Roses were spread over their cheeks, and their bosoms heaved. And Abla joined her associates in the dance, and exhibited her charms, and laughed. Fire shot from their eyes, and the cups of wine were united to the honey of their mouths. The imagination of Antar was inflamed and overpowered in the sea of anxiety; he hesitated whether he should violate the modesty of love by the fingers of passion, when to! on a sudden there appeared a cloud of dust; and a vast clamour arose, and in a moment there came forth a troop of horses and their riders, about seventy in number, armed with cuirasses, and coats of mail, and Aadite helmets, crying out, 'O by Cahtan!' and rushed towards the women. At the instant joy was converted into grief, and smiles into tears: in a moment they seized the women and the virgins, made them prisoners, and placed them on their horses behind them."

Antar, however, was not the man to stand by and allow the enemy thus to ravish his fair charges before his eyes. To rush after and overtake the horseman who had captured Abla, and to hurl him a lifeless and shapeless mass on the ground, and to take possession of his horse and armour, was to Antar mere child's play. Then he overtook the rest of the enemy, and with his single arm performed such wonders, that those who escaped the stroke of his death-dealing sword fled in dismay, leaving the women and the plunder they had taken.

This was Antar's first warlike exploit; and when King Zoheir returned, and heard of his prowess, he publicly praised him, and presented him with a robe of honour.

Shortly afterwards Antar put to flight a large party of a hostile tribe that had surrounded the King's sons and their attendants; and this was his song of triumph as the hero returned to his tent:

I WILL not cease to exalt myself by my deeds, till I reach Orion in my ambitious projects.

Here I care not for those who abuse me, fearful of death and separation from life.

But I will reduce my foes and my railers by force, and I will be patient under sufferings and in praise.

I will strive to attain what I desire, till Death snatch me away.

I will arm my mind against worldly lusts, that I may be considered noble-minded and faithful.

Whoever would check me, let him look to himself, where'er he may be concealed.

My complexion is no injury to me, nor the name of Zebeebah, when I exercise my courage amongst the foe.

I will work wonders and marvels; and I will protect myself from the tongues of the wicked.

The King was naturally grateful for the good service which Antar had thus rendered, and at a grand feast held in celebration of the escape of the princes, he caused the hero to sit beside him, and commanded Shedad no longer to employ his son as a keeper of camels, but to allow him to take rank among the warriors of the tribe.

ANTAR AND ABLA'S MOTHER.

Antar was now become celebrated for his verses as well as for his remarkable strength and courage; and, as may be readily supposed, he was making considerable progress in winning the affection of his beloved Abla. But in the eyes of the maiden's father, Malik, he was far from being a desirable match; and even her mother ridiculed Antar's amorous poetry, and his love for her daughter. One day she sneeringly asked him to recite some of his verses about Abla, and he thus complied:

I LOVE thee with the love of a noble-born hero; and I am content with thy imaginary phantom.

Thou art my sovereign in my very blood, and my mistress; and in thee is all my confidence.

[139]

O Abla, my description cannot portray thee, for thou comprehendest every perfection.

Were I to say thy face is like the full moon of heaven--where, in that full moon, is the eye of the antelope?

Were I to say thy shape is like the branch of the erak tree: O thou shamest it in the grace of thy form.

In thy forehead is my guide to truth; and in the night of thy tresses I wander astray.

Thy teeth resemble stringed jewels; but how can I liken them to lifeless pearls?

Thy bosom is created as an enchantment;--O may God protect it ever in that perfection!

To be connected with thee is to be connected with every joy; but separated from all my world is the bond of thy connection.

Under thy veil is the rosebud of my life, and thine eyes are guarded with a multitude of arrows: round thy tent is a lion-warrior, the sword's edge, and the spear's point.

O thy face is like the full moon of heaven, allied to light, but far from my hopes!

These eloquent verses so far mollified Abla's mother that she proposed marrying Antar to her daughter's maid, Khemisa.

"No!" said Antar, boldly; "I shall marry only a freeborn woman: and no one shall I marry but her whom my soul adores!"

"May God accomplish thy wishes," whispered Abla; "and may he grant thee the woman thou lovest, and may thou live in peace and happiness!"

ANTAR OFFENDS HIS FATHER.

To a wedding among a friendly tribe Antar had the honour of escorting a party of Absian women of rank, among whom was the fair Abla, with their attendants. On the way thither some brigands attack them, but Antar, crying, "O by Abs! I am ever the lover of Abla!" dealt his sword-blows among the enemy to such good purpose that many were slain, and the rest fled in dismay. The return of the party from the wedding feast furnished the hero with further opportunities for the display of his prowess; and after encountering several hostile parties, and killing many renowned horsemen, Antar brings home the women of Abs in safety and in triumph.

Shedad naturally exulted in the fame of his slave-son, and even declared his intention of ennobling Antar forthwith; but he was dissuaded from this by his brother Malik, who threatened to quit the tribe should Antar be raised above the condition of a slave. And one night, when Antar, emboldened with wine, presented himself before his father, and demanded the rank of an Arab chief, Shedad was enraged at his presumption and threatened to kill him. Antar seeks the counsel and protection of his friend Prince Malik, who expresses his regret that he should thus have offended his father. There is a deal of nature in Antar's reply: "Do not, my lord, reprove my ambition, which often robs me of my wits and discretion; but had I not been intoxicated, this would not have happened, and I should have concealed my wishes, and submitted patiently to my misfortunes till death had overtaken me. But in all circumstances, thou art my master. Ah, my lord!" continued he, "how often have I relieved them from their foes, and no one ever assisted me! Know, too, that I love Abla, the daughter of my uncle Malik, and she drives away sleep from my eyelids, and in my sleepless nights I am united to her; but my father Shedad has cut off all my hope, and misfortunes upon misfortunes overpower me. I only demanded to be recognised as his son, that I might be united to her; but truly all my hopes of her are completely destroyed. No joy now remains for me, and the light of the day is the darkness of night in my eyes. I have no home hut among the wild beasts and the reptiles!" And tears gushed from the eyes of the hero as he expressed his anguish and passion.

The Prince endeavoured to soothe Antar's distress, by the promise of his influence and protection, and Antar remained all that night with Prince Malik.

HOW ANTAR OBTAINED HIS HORSE ABJER.

At daybreak Antar stole out of the Prince's tent, and mounting his horse, wandered into the desert, where he chanced to meet forty Absian horsemen, led by Ghegadh the son of Nasshib, bent on a marauding enterprise. Antar joins them, and the Absians proceed to the land of Cahtan, where they saw "a great quantity of cattle, with some high raised tents and lofty pavilions; many horses running about and camels grazing; and the people unsuspicious of a reverse of fortune." Antar, while his companions were engaged in plundering the tents, drove away the cattle, and had proceeded some distance, when he discovered a knight, "mounted on a dark-coloured colt, beautiful and compact; and it was of a race much prized by the Arabs: his hoofs were as flat as the beaten coin; when he neighed he seemed as if about to speak; and his ears like quills: his sire was Wasil, and his dam Hemama." Perceiving the beauty and speed of the horse, Antar eagerly longed for it, and pursued the rider till sunset, when the strange knight stopped, and Antar, coming up to him, made overtures for the purchase of the beautiful steed. The knight, however, would only part with it in exchange for the cattle taken from his tribe, to which Antar very readily agreed; and thus he became possessed of Abjer, the famous horse on which he performed so many wonderful exploits.

A BRIDAL PARTY ATTACKED.

Next day Antar and his companions meet with a numerous bridal party; the bride's howdah--richly ornamented with velvet, and on its top a crescent of gold--was preceded by damsels and slaves wearing bright-coloured robes, and behind came a troop of seventy horsemen. The Absians attack the escort, and take the bride prisoner. But while Ghegadh and the others are disputing with Antar about his share of the plunder, the father of the damsel, Yezid the son of Handhala, surnamed the Blood-drinker, arrives, with 300 warriors. "In a moment swords clashed; every heart was roused: heads flew off like balls, and hands like leaves of trees. The Teyans rushed upon the race of Abs; the Blood-drinker assailed them in his courage, and released his daughter. The Absians quitted their plunder, for their souls could not stand fire, and they fled over the wilds." Antar, to punish his sordid companions, had thus far remained an inactive spectator of the conflict, but seeing the Absians give way, he rushed down on the Teyans, and slew with his own hand eighty of their bravest warriors; and the rest, with the renowned Blood-drinker and his daughter, spread themselves over the plain and escaped. The Absians had hardly returned from pursuing the Teyans, when Nakid, the husband of the bride, came up, with a large body of horsemen, and a fierce battle immediately ensued. The tribe of Abs were overpowered, and were about to retreat, when Antar turned the fortune of the day, by encountering and slaying Nakid.

Meanwhile King Zoheir had sent a slave in search of Antar, who returned with the news that he was engaged with the tribe of Maan in deadly conflict. The King at once despatched his son Prince Malik with a party of warriors to Antar's assistance, but when they reached him, the enemy was already vanquished. Antar and Prince Malik then returned to their own land, and as they drew near the tents of their tribe Antar exclaimed:

WHEN the breezes blow from Mount Saadi, their freshness calms the fire of my love and transports. Let my tribe remember I have preserved their faith; but they feel not my worth, and preserve not their engagements with me.

Were there not a maid settled in the tents, why should I prefer their society to absence?

Slimly made is she, and the magic influence of her eye preserves the bones of a corpse from entering the tomb.

The sun, as it sets, turns towards her, and says: Darkness obscures the land--do thou rise in my absence; and the brilliant moon calls out to her: Come forth!--for thy face is like me when I am at the full, and in all my glory!

The tamarisk trees complain of her in the morn and the eve, and say: Away, thou waning beauty, thou form of the laurel!

She turns away abashed, and throws aside her veil, and the roses are scattered from her soft fresh cheeks.

She draws her sword from the glances of her eyelashes, sharp and penetrating as the blade of her forefathers, and with it her eyes commit murder, though it be sheathed:

[142]

Is it not surprising that a sheathed sword should be so sharp against its victims?

Graceful is every limb; slender her waist; love-beaming are her glances; waving is her form.

The damsel passes the night with musk under her veil, and its fragrance is increased by the still fresher essence of her breath.

The lustre of Day sparkles from her forehead, and by the dark shades of her curling ringlets Night itself is driven away.

When she smiles, between her teeth is a moisture, composed of wine, of rain, and of honey.

Her throat complains of the darkness of her necklace;--alas! alas! the effects of that throat and that necklace!

Will fortune ever, O daughter of Malik! ever bless me with thy embrace, that would cure my heart of the sorrows of love?

If my eye could see her baggage-camels, and her family, I would rub my cheeks on the hoofs of her camels. I will kiss the earth where thou art; mayhap the fire of my love and ecstacy may be quenched.

Shall thou and I ever meet as formerly on Mount Saadi? or will the messenger come from thee to announce thy meeting? or will he relate that thou art in the land of Nejd?

Shall we meet in the land of Shurebah and Hima, and shall we live in joy and happiness?

I am the well-known Antar, the chief of his tribe, and I shall die; but when I am gone, history shall tell of me.

King Zoheir and the chiefs of the tribe came out to meet Antar, and congratulate him on his return. The hero, after the King had greeted him kindly, ran to his father Shedad, and asked his forgiveness; and the whole tribe were astonished at his prowess.

PLOTS AGAINST THE HERO.

Old Malik, Antar's uncle, and his faction were, however, more than ever resolved to thwart the hero's union with Abla; and, envious of the honours bestowed on him by the King, and enraged at his presumption in professing love for his daughter, Malik proposes to his son Amru that Antar should be put to death. Other and more formidable enemies lay plans for his destruction. Antar's mother, Zebeebah, in the simplicity of her heart, advises him to resume his old occupation of tending the flocks and the camels, and no

[143]

longer expose his life to perils. The hero smilingly replies that she should yet be proud of her son.

Prince Shas (who had never forgiven Antar for killing his insolent slave) complains to his father of his favour of Antar, and of the hero's presumption in desiring union with Abla. King Zoheir reproves his son for his evident ill-feeling towards the hero, telling him that it may be decreed of God that Antar should be the recipient of divine favours. Antar, overhearing this conversation, entered the tent, and thus recited:

THIS flame is for Abla, O my friend!--her lustre illumines the darkest night. She blazes--her form is in my heart, and the fire of love is in my soul.

Her gently-waving form has kindled it like the branches whose motion refreshes the breeze.

Her breath diffuses a lively odour, and in her perfumes I pass the night in paradise.

She is a maid whose breath is sweeter than honey, whenever she sips the juice of the grape.

When I taste a coolness from her lips, she leaves in my mouth a hot burning flame.

The moon has stolen her charms, and the antelope has borrowed the magic of her eyes.

O grant me thy embrace, O light of my eyes! and save me from thy absence, and mine own griefs.

Be just, if thou wishest, or persecute me: for in thee is my paradise, and in thee is my hell.

No happiness is there for me in my troubles, but my lord, who is called the generous Zoheir.

Wherever he goes Death anticipates him; and he destroys his foes before he meets them.

Let them not abuse him if he aid a solitary creature, who spends the live-long night without sleep, and in tears.

He is my support and stay against those who, when they see my exaltation, would trouble me the more.

He is a king to whose name princes shall bow, and Shall point at him to pay their homage.

He is the asylum of all who refer to him to dissipate their sorrows, as he relieves my griefs.

May fortune never deprive me of my King! May he ever live in the purest joy and felicity!

The King courteously thanked Antar for his verses, and confessed his inability to adequately reward him--"even were I to give you all I possess; for my property will pass away, as if it had never been; but thy praises will endure for ever." He presented Antar with two virgin slaves, beautiful as moons, two rows of rare jewels, and some perfumes; after which Antar withdrew, and going to the tents of the family of Carad, found the men absent, and the women sitting up to hear an account of his exploits, and the fair Abla most anxious of all; upon which he thus addressed them:--

DARKNESS hovers o'er, and my tears stream down in copious torrents;--I conceal my love, and complain to no one.

I pass the night, regarding the stars of night in my distraction, and the tears rush violently from my eyes like a hail-storm.

Ask the night of me, and it will tell thee that I am indeed the ally of sorrow and anguish.

I live desolate; there is no one like me: a lover without friends or a companion!

I am the friend of sorrow and desire. I am o'erwhelmed by them, and I am worn out with patience and trials in my grief.

I complain to God of my afflictions and my love; and to no one else do I complain.

Abla was deeply moved by Antar's evident distress, for she loved him both for his courage and his eloquence. "Where," said she, playfully, "is my share of thy plunder, cousin? Am I now of no consequence to thee?"--"Truly," replied he, "I gave all to thy father and thy uncles." He then gave her the two female slaves and the jewels he had received from the King; but the perfumes he divided among his aunts, telling Abla that she had no need of them, her breath being sweeter than any perfumes.

ANTAR RESCUES HIS FATHER AND UNCLES.

Antar then learns that his father Shedad and his uncles are gone in pursuit of a knight, called Kais, who had taken some cattle from their tribe, and immediately mounts his horse Abjer and sets off to their assistance. He finds his father and uncles tied ignominiously across their horses, prisoners of Kais, at which he roared, "Ye dastards!--come forth!" and Kais no sooner heard the challenge than he pricked on his horse till he came up to Antar, and thus addressed him:

[145]

I AM renowned in every nation for the thrust of the spear and the blow of the sword.

I am the destroyer of horsemen with the lance, when the spears are interwoven under the dust.

How many contests have I waged on the day of battle, whose terrors would turn gray the heads of infants!

Long ago have I drunk the blood of horsemen, with which they fed me before I was weaned. This day will I prove my words when the blood streams from my sword.

This foul wretch will I slay with the edge of my sword, that cleaves through the flesh before the bones.

His dwellings shall this eve be found waste and desolate, and I will not swerve from my word: his body shall lie on the deserts, cut down, and his face thou mayst see grovelling in the dust.

To these insolent verses Antar replied, saying, "Silence!--may thy mother bewail thee":--

VERILY, thy spirit has urged thee to abuse me, and thou hast spoken the words of a vile dastard:

Thou art ignorant of my exploits in every battle, from the land of Irak to the sacred shrine:

Thou shalt have no time to reply--no justice but the sword; for ignorance among mankind conducts them to their death.

This is the scene of conflict, and in it doubtless will be proved the skill of the coward and the base-born.

Let him repent who has only shown his vanity; and let him prefer flight to resistance.

I am Antar; and my name is far spread for the thrust of my spear and the blow of my sword.

Having thus exclaimed, Antar "drew forth his sword and struck Kais between the eyes, and split his helmet and wadding, and his sword worked down to his thighs, down even to the back of his horse: and he cried out--'Thou wretch! I will not be controlled! I am still the lover of Abla!'" He then rushed among the tribe of Dibgan, who fled in dismay, leaving all their plunder behind.

A GALLANT KNIGHT OF MAZIN.

The Absians return home in triumph, and King Zoheir comes to meet them at the lake Zatool-irsad, where he gives a grand feast to celebrate the exploits of Antar. In the midst of the entertainment a gallant knight of the tribe of Mazin, with a hundred followers, comes riding up to the royal pavilion, and implores the King's succour. He is Hassan, the foster-brother of Prince Malik. He had, he informs the King, long loved Naeema, the beautiful daughter of his uncle Nedjem. A wealthy chief named Awef had come as a suitor for his fair cousin, and her father feared to offend so powerful a knight by a refusal. Hassan, however, had settled the matter in his own favour by encountering Awef and dismounting him, and only spared his life on the intercession of his uncle Nedjem, who reminded him that Awef had eaten his bread and been under his protection; but he cuts off his hair and sends him away in ignominy. Thus far, all was well; but Hassan had nothing for his cousin's dowry; so he sets off to procure one in the usual way, by plundering some other tribe. He returns with immense wealth, and finds that Oosak, a still more powerful chief, had demanded his betrothed in marriage, and had been refused by her father; and now Oosak, with all the warriors of Cahtan, was on his way to attack the tribe--and therefore he had come to beg the help of King Zoheir in repelling the threatened invasion.

No sooner had Hassan finished his story than Antar started to his feet, and eagerly offered his services, and Zoheir gave Prince Malik leave to accompany the hero, with a thousand chosen warriors.

HOW ANTAR FOUND THE SWORD DHAMI.

"They travelled on for three days, and on the fourth (for the Lord of Heaven had decreed the glory of Antar, and that none should exceed him in prosperity), Antar, happening to stray a little out of the way, descended into a deep valley, and to! there were two horsemen engaged in desperate combat. Antar urged on his steed, and coming up to them, 'Stop, ye Arabs!' he cried, 'and tell me the cause of your quarrel.' At the instant one of them stepped aside, and came up to Antar. 'Noble horseman of the desert and the town,' said he, 'I refer myself to you, for you are able to protect me.'--'I will take your part,' said Antar, 'I will protect you--I pledge myself to you. But acquaint me with your story, and what has rendered necessary this combat between you.'

"'Know, then, noblest knight of the age,' said the youth, 'that I and this horseman are brothers, of the same father, and the same mother; he is the eldest and I am the youngest; and our father was one of the Arab chieftains, and he was called Amru, the son of Harith, the son of Teba; and Teba was our ancestor. And one day as he was sitting down, his flocks strayed away, and one of his camels was lost, and as he was very partial to it, he questioned some of the herdsmen about it. One of them said: "Know, my lord, yesterday this camel strayed away from the pasture; I followed behind it, and it still continued to run away, and I after it, till I became tired, and perceiving that it lagged behind, I stretched out my hand and took up a stone, black in appearance, like a hard rock, brilliant and sparkling. I struck the camel with it, and it hit the camel on the right side and issued

[147]

out on the left, and the camel fell to the ground dead. On coming up to it I found the stone by its side, and the camel was weltering in its blood."

"'On hearing this my ancestor mounted his horse, and, taking the herdsman with him, went to find out the pasture. They passed on till they came to the camel, which they found dead, and the stone lying near it. My ancestor took it in his hand, and considered it very attentively, and he knew it was a thunderbolt; so he carried it away and returned home. He gave it to a blacksmith, and ordered him to make a sword of it. He obeyed, and took it and went his way; and in three days he returned to my ancestor with a sword two cubits long and two spans wide. My ancestor received it, and was greatly pleased when he saw it, and turned towards the blacksmith and said: "What name have you given it?" So the blacksmith repeated this distich:

"The sword is sharp, O son of the tribe of Ghalib,
  Sharp indeed: but where is the striker for the sword?"

And my ancestor waved the sword with his hand, and said: "As to the smiter--I am the smiter!" and struck off the head of the blacksmith, and separated it from his body. He then cased it with gold, and called it Dhami, on account of its sharpness. He laid it by amongst his treasures, and when he died it came in succession to my father with the rest of the arms; and when my father perceived his death was at hand, he called me to him privately. "O my son," said he, "I know your brother is of a tyrannical, obstinate disposition, one that likes violence and hates justice, and I am aware that at my death he will usurp my property."--"What measures shall I take?" said I.--He answered: "Take this sword and conceal it, and let no one know anything about it: and when you see that he takes forcible possession of all my property, cattle and wealth, do you be content, my son, with this sword, for it will be of great benefit to you: for if you present it to Nushirvan, king of Persia, he will exalt you with his liberality and favours; and if you present it to the Emperor of Europe, he will enrich you with gold and silver."

"'When I heard these words I consented to what he demanded, and took it out in the darkness of the night, and having buried it in this place, I returned to my father and stayed with him till he died. We buried him, and returned home; but my brother took possession of all my father had, and gave me nothing--not a rope's end; and when he searched for the arms, and saw not the Dhami, he asked me for it. I denied knowing anything about it; he gave me the lie, and abused me most violently; at last I confessed, and told him I had buried it in such a spot; so he came with me hither, and searched for it but could not find it. Again he asked me where I had buried it; and when he saw me roaming about from place to place, he rushed upon me, and cried out, saying: "Vile wretch! you know where the sword is, and act thus to deceive me." He attacked me, and sought to slay me. I defended myself until you arrived, and now I demand your protection.'

"When Antar heard this his heart pitied him; he left the youth, and turning to his brother, said: 'Why do you tyrannize over your brother, and do not divide with him the property

[148]

your father left?'--'Base slave!' cried he, highly incensed, 'look to yourself, and interfere not so arrogantly'; and he turned upon Antar, thinking him a common man; but Antar gave him no time to wheel, or direct his reins, ere he pierced him through the chest with his spear, and thrust it ten spans through his back, and threw him down dead. 'And now, young man,' said he to the other, 'return to your family, and assume the rank of your father; and should any one molest you, send and inform me: I will come and tear his life out of his sides.' The youth thanked him and expressed his gratitude: 'Now my brother is no more,' said he, 'I have no other enemy'; and he departed home.

"But Antar fixed his spear in the ground, and dismounted from Abjer, and sat down to rest himself; and as he was moving the sand with his fingers, he touched a stone; on removing what was about it, behold! the sword the youth had been seeking! He still cleared away, and drew it forth, and seized hold of it, and it was a sword two cubits in length, and two spans wide, of the metal of Almalec, like a thunderbolt. And Antar was convinced of his good fortune, and that everything began and ended in the most high God."

RESCUE OF THE TRIBE OF MAZIN.

On the following day the Absians encounter five hundred horsemen, all clad in steel, and led by Gheidac, a haughty chief, whose father Antar had killed in one of his former expeditions. Gheidac and his troops were advancing to assist Oosak in his purposed attack on the tribe of Mazin, when they fell in with the warriors of Abs. "They all rushed forward, and horsemen encountered horsemen. Cowards fled, and the weak-hearted were disgraced; but the bold were firm in the assault, and the equals in courage met each other in the field. The earth trembled under the trampling of the horses; the heavens were obscured with the clouds of dust; the warriors were covered with wounds, and the swords laboured in the cause of death: exertion was alive, and all jest was at an end." Thus the battle raged till mid-day, when Antar and Gheidac met, and after a desperate combat, the Absian hero, having wearied his antagonist, at length struck him a blow with Dhami, and cleft him--and his horse as well.

On seeing their chief fall, Gheidac's warriors took to flight, and the Absians, after collecting the horses and plunder, resumed their journey and proceeded until they reached the tribe of Mazin. Here all was confusion and dismay; for Oosak and his horsemen were already busy plundering the women's quarter, and Antar, who was ever "solicitous in the cause of women," rushed with his warriors upon the dastards, scattering them to the right and left--"mighty was every act, and fate descended among them."

"Antar eagerly sought after the plume that floated above the head of Oosak, and he stopped not in attack until he was beneath the standard where Oosak was waiting for his people to bring him Naeema; neither could he be roused till Antar came before him and encountered him. Then ensued a dreadful engagement. The combat lasted an hour; when nerveless sunk the arm of Oosak. Antar, seeing the state he was in, clung to him, and grappled him; and drawing his sword from the scabbard, he aimed a blow at his head, but

[149]

Oosak received it on his shield. The sword of Antar came down upon it and shivered it in two, and split his vizor in twain, and it penetrated even to his thighs, down to the back of the horse; and the rider and the horse fell in four parts; and he cried out--'O by Abs! I am ever the lover of Abla! never will I be controlled! I will not be restrained!'

Oosak's followers then wheeled about their horses and sought security among the rocks of the desert. The horsemen of Abs and of Mazin, having pursued them out of the land, returned to the tents, where Hassan entertained Antar and his comrades at feasts during seven days, and on the eighth night he was married to his beloved Naeema. Next day the warriors of Abs returned to their own country.

ANOTHER SUITOR FOR ABLA.

While Antar was gone to assist the tribe of Mazin, something happened which marred his hopes of winning his beloved Abla, and commenced a series of troubles to himself, to his family, and even to the whole tribe of Abs. This was the betrothal of Abla to a noble Absian named Amarah: "a conceited coxcomb, very particular in his dress, fond of perfumes, and always keeping company with women and young girls." The fame of Abla's beauty having reached this Bedouin exquisite, he sent a female slave to the tents of the family of Carad, to discover whether Abla was as beautiful as was reported of her; and the girl returning with a glowing account of Abla's charms, Amarah conceived a violent passion for her--"his ears fell in love before his eyes." He visits old Malik, and demands his daughter in marriage, promising a handsome dowry. Malik the perfidious is overjoyed at the prospect of such a son-in-law, and very readily gives his consent--hoping, no doubt, that Antar is by this time become food for the ravens and the vultures.

Next day, as Amarah was hastening to Abla's father with the dowry and marriage presents, a messenger arrived to announce the return of Antar and Prince Malik, and the whole tribe went out to welcome them. Antar remained that night with his mother Zebeebah, from whom he learned that Abla was betrothed to Amarah; and "the light was darkened in his eyes." In the morning he acquaints Prince Malik of his uncle's perfidy, and the Prince offers to secure Abla for his friend, by "putting his name on her," and thus keeping off any suitor till Antar was in possession of his wife. Prince Malik then goes to Shedad, and requests him to formally recognise Antar as his son, that he may take rank among the chiefs of the tribe. But Shedad would not consent to do what no Arab chief had ever done before--ennoble his slave-son. The Prince replied that no other chief ever had such a son as Antar: "Let other Arabs follow your example," said he; "good practices are to be admired, even though they are new." But all that the Prince's arguments could effect in favour of Antar was a promise from Shedad that "he would consider the matter."

In the meantime, Antar meets his rival riding away from old Malik's tent, where he had been visiting. Amarah, in the excess of his vanity, addressed the hero in insolent language, to which Antar replied by seizing the coxcomb, and dashing him senseless to the ground. Amarah's followers rushed upon the hero, who would probably have been soon overpowered had not Prince Malik, returning from his interview with Shedad, come to his rescue, and, gallantly crying, "Verily Antar is a rare onyx among a people who know not his worth!--Come on, Antar!--now for the family of Zeead!" lustily plied his sword among them, until the King came up and separated the combatants.

Although the coxcomb Amarah richly deserved the punishment he received from Antar, yet for a slave to raise his hand against a noble Absian was an unpardonable offence in the opinion of the hero's enemies; and his father Shedad was therefore compelled to send Antar back to his former occupation of tending the flocks and camels. At the same time Antar had to endure the mortification of seeing the warriors of Abs prepare to resist a threatened attack of the tribe of Tey. But his mother Zebeebah brings him a message of love and consolation from his faithful Abla "Soothe the heart of my cousin Antar; and tell him that, if my father even makes my grave my resting-place, none but him do I desire-- none but him will I choose."

BATTLE OF THE TRIBES OF ABS AND TEY--ANTAR TO THE RESCUE!

The Absians meet the Teyans, and are defeated; their bravest warriors retreat, and the women of Abs are taken captive. In their extremity the Absian chiefs recollect the prowess of Antar, whom their envy and malice have caused to be degraded from the rank of the foremost warrior of the age to the condition of a keeper of flocks and camels. A messenger is despatched to solicit his assistance. Antar puts on his armour, girds his sword Dhami to his side, and mounting Abjer, joins the chiefs of Abs. His father Shedad solemnly promises, if he will pursue the enemy and rescue the women and plunder, to recognise him as his son; and his uncle Malik swears that, if he will but rescue Abla, he shall have her for his wife. On these conditions Antar agreed to redeem the honour of the tribe, and thus he exclaimed:

SOON shall ye behold my deeds this day with the foe in the field of spear-thrusts and the battle-fire; and my furious courage amongst the tribes; so that in my sublimity, I will mount above the Pisces.

I plunge into the flames of war with the cleaving scimitar, and I extirpate them with the goring lance. I drive back the horses on their haunches, from the lofty seat of my thin-flanked Abjer, and with the blade of my sword Dhami, at whose edge flow the waves of death over the enemy.

This day will I exhibit my ardent soul with my Indian sword, and I will meet the chests of the horse with my thrusts.

I will establish the market of war in its field on the top of my steed, in the protection of my country. My sword is my father, and the spear in my hand is my father's brother; and I am the son of my day in the heights of the deserts!

[151]

The first object of his attack was the horseman who had captured Abla. Antar pierced him through the side with his spear, and he caught Abla in his arms, like a frightened bird, but unhurt. He then rushed upon the enemy with irresistible impetuosity--his sword Dhami played among them, causing the heads of warriors to fly through the air like balls, and scattering their limbs like the leaves of trees. The Absians are again collected together and attack the Teyans, who, seeing their leader Rebeeah fall, slain by Antar, fly in terror of the hero's sword; and the tribe of Abs, after driving them out of their country, return to their own tents, with Antar at their head, chanting his song of triumph:

I HAVE abused fortune, but how can she humiliate such as I?--I, too, that have a spirit would cut down mountains!

I am the warrior of whom it is said, "He tended the he and she camels of his tribe!"

When I assaulted Kendeh and Tey, their hands brandishing the long spears, with armies, that when I thought of them, I imagined the whole earth filled with men;

And as their hardy steeds trampled our lands, whilst you might see them talking and exulting--'twas then their steeds fled away horrified at me, and the redoubled thrusts that gored them as they sought the fight.

The noble hero feels no fatigue: him no challenger need call to the combat.

It was the slave alone that drove back the horsemen whilst the flame of battle was blazing!

Then speeded away their troops, in terror of my arm;--light they fled, burthened though they had been!

Crushing were the stamps and tramplings on their necks, and the horse-shoes dashed and pounded their skulls.

How many warriors were laid low by my sword, whilst they tore, in very rage, their hands with their teeth!

I rescued the maidens and virgins, and not one did I leave but bereft of sense.

Mine is a spirit for every enterprise: high is my fame!--exalted is my glory!

ANTAR PROCLAIMED CHAMPION OF ABS.

At length the hero is duly admitted by the Absian warriors to the honour and rank of an Arab. King Zoheir causes a great feast to be prepared to celebrate the overthrow of the Teyans, at which he presents Antar with a robe worked with gold, girds on him a trusty sword, and placing in his hand a pike of Khata, and mounting him on a fine Arab horse,

[152]

proclaims him the champion of Abs and Adnan. And thus, apparently, was removed the chief obstacle to Antar's union with Abla; moreover, the maiden's father had solemnly sworn that she should be married to the hero if he rescued her from the Teyans. But the treacherous Malik never meant to keep his word; although, the King favouring Antar's cause, he had no choice but to profess his willingness to bestow his daughter on the saviour of the tribe. Old Malik, however, was a perfect master of craft and cozenage; and he devised a plan of exposing Antar to almost certain death. He requires him to procure for Abla's dowry a thousand Asafeer camels--the property of Monzar the son of Massema, king of the Arabs, and lieutenant of Nushirvan of Persia: if Antar once venture among the tribe of Shiban, Malik confidently assures his complotters, he will never return to trouble them again. For such a prize as Abla, however, Antar would willingly encounter even greater dangers, and therefore he undertakes the desperate enterprise with alacrity.

ANTAR'S EXPEDITION FOR THE ASAFEER CAMELS.

Accompanied only by his faithful brother Shiboob,--his trusty henchman, who frequently rendered the hero important service by his dexterity as an archer, and whose fleetness of foot had gained him the soubriquet of Son of the Wind,--Antar departed at night from the tents of Abs, and proceeded towards the land of Irak. Traversing the wilds and the deserts by secret paths, well known to Shiboob, one day they came upon a single tent pitched beside a spring, and near it was an aged sheikh, bent with years:

AN old man was walking along the ground,
 And his face almost touched his knees.
So I said to him, "Why art thou thus stooping?"
He said, as he waved his hands towards me:
 "My youth is lost somewhere on the ground,
And I am stooping in search of it."

The venerable solitary presented the travellers with a draught of milk, cooled in the wind, and set food before them; and when they had satisfied their hunger, he inquired of Antar whence he came, and on what business he was bound. The hero related his story: how he was betrothed to his fair cousin Abla, and how her father had engaged him to procure a thousand Asafeer camels, for her dowry. The old man earnestly advised him to abandon an enterprise beset with so many perils, but in vain; and having reposed that night in the sheikh's tent, they resumed their journey at daybreak. As they proceeded, the recollection of his beloved Abla, and of all that he had endured for her sake, occurring to Antar's mind, his feelings found expression in these verses:

IN the land of Shurebah are defiles and valleys; I have quitted them, and its inhabitants live in my heart:

Fixed are they therein, and in my eyes; and even when they are absent from me they dwell in the black of mine eye;

And when the lightning flashes from their land, I shed tears of blood, and pass the night leagued with sleeplessness.

The breeze of the fragrant plants makes me remember the luscious balmy airs of the Zatool-irsad.

O Abla! let thy visionary phantom appear to me, and infuse soft slumbers over my distracted heart!

O Abla! were it not for my love of thee, I would not be with so few friends and so many enemies!

I am departing, and the back of my horse shall be my resting-place, and my sword and mail my pillow, till I trample down the lands of Irak, and destroy their deserts and their cities.

When the market for the sale of lives is established, and they cry out, and the criers proclaim the goods, and I behold the troops stirring up the war-dust with the thrusts of spears and sharp scimitars

Then will I disperse their horsemen, and the foe shall be cut down, deprived of their hands.

The eyes of the envious shall watch; but the eyes of the pure and the faithful shall sleep.

And I will return with numerous Asafeer camels that my love shall procure, and Shiboob be my guide.

Thus Antar and Shiboob journeyed until they came to the land of Hirah, where they discovered "populous towns, plains abounding in flowing streams, date-trees, warbling birds, and sweet-smelling flowers; and the country appeared like a blessing to enliven the sorrowing heart; and the camels were grazing and straying about the land." Here was every sign of wealth and power; but, nothing dismayed, Antar despatched his brother to look after the Asafeer camels while he rested Abjer.

Shiboob, disguised as a slave, proceeded to the tents of the slaves who had charge of the camels, and telling them a plausible story of his having run away from his master, and feigning sickness, he spent all the day with them; and when the slaves were all fast asleep, he stole away, and rejoined Antar, to whom he communicated the results of his observations regarding the numbers of the camels and of the slaves who guarded them. Antar stations Shiboob with his bow on the road to Hirah; he then cuts off a thousand of the Asafeer camels, and compels some of the slaves to drive them towards his own country. He is overtaken by King Monzar and his hunting party, and defends himself manfully against them all, until Abjer stumbles and brings him to the ground. Shiboob, seeing his brother fall, and supposing him to be slain, gives his feet to the wind, and speeding homeward through the deserts, thus laments the fate of Antar:

O KNIGHT of the Horse! why, alas! has the steed to mourn thee?--why, alas! has the barb of the spear to announce thy death in wailings?

O that the day had never been, that I saw thee felled to the earth, cut down--stretched out--and the points of the lances aimed at thee!

Could the vicissitudes of fortune accept of any ransom--O, I would have redeemed thee from the calamities of fortune!

Thine uncle has in his wiles and frauds made thee drink of the cup;--but may thy cup-bearer, O son of my mother, ne'er taste of the moisture of dew!

And thy cousin will mourn thee; and she belongs to thy foe, whose slave thou wouldst never consent to be.

O Knight of the Horse! I have no strength of mind--I have not a heart that can ever feel consolation for thee in my sorrows!

And the war-steed among the troopers as he neighs will turn towards thee, mourning for thee, like a childless woman in despair!

Antar, however, was not dead, though taken prisoner, and brought bound into the presence of King Monzar, who demanded to know whence he came. Antar replied that he was of the tribe of noble Abs.

"One of its warriors, or one of its slaves?" inquired the King. "Nobility, my lord," said Antar, "amongst liberal men, is the thrust of the spear, the blow of the sword, and patience beneath the battle-dust. I am the physician of the tribe of Abs when they are in sickness; their protector in disgrace; the defender of their wives when they are in trouble; and their horseman when they are in glory, and their sword when they rush to arms."

He then relates the occasion of his enterprise which had thus miscarried. The King expresses his astonishment that he should have exposed himself to such dangers for the sake of an Arab girl.

"Yes," replied Antar, "it is love that emboldens man to encounter dangers and horrors; and there is no peril to be apprehended but from a look from beneath the corner of a veil"; and thinking of Abla's charms, and his present condition, he continued, in verse:

THE eyelashes of the songstress from the corner of the veil are more cutting than the edge of the cleaving scimitars;

[155]

And when they wound the brave are humbled, and the corners of their eyes are flooded with tears.

May God cause my uncle to drink of the draught of death at my hand!--may his hand be withered, and his fingers palsied!

For how could he drive one like me to destruction by his arts, and make my hopes depend on the completion of his avaricious projects?

Truly Abla, on the day of departure, bade me adieu, and said I should never return!

O lightnings! waft my salutation to her, and to all the places and pastures where she dwells!

O ye dwellers in the forests of tamarisks! if I die, mourn for me when my eyes are plucked out by the hungry fowls of the air.

O ye steeds! mourn for a knight who could engage the lions of death in the field of battle.

Alas! I am an outcast, and in sorrow;--I am humbled into galling fetters--fetters that cut to my soul!

The King was expressing his surprise at the eloquence and fortitude of the prisoner, when there arose a great commotion among his followers, caused by a savage lion that had rushed from the desert, and was busy mangling the boldest of the king's warriors. Antar offers to slay the lion, if only his hands are set free, leaving his legs still fettered, and he was given a sword and a shield. This feat he performs to the admiration of all; and Monzar sees in the hero one well qualified to aid his ambitious design of rendering himself independent of Nushirvan, the King of Persia.

Monzar had been made the subject of a practical joke, which he little relished, at the court of Persia--by eating dates, stones and all, at dinner, in imitation of the King and his courtiers, who he supposed were also eating dates, but in reality simply almonds and sugar-plums prepared to resemble dates. On returning to his own country he resolved to revenge this insult, and secretly incited several Arab tribes to plunder Persian towns. Chosroe commanded him to punish these marauders; but Monzar had the hardihood to send back the royal messenger with a letter, stating that, in consequence of the insult that had been offered him at the Persian court, he had now little or no influence with the Arab tribes, and that Chosroe must look after his own kingdom. And Monzar was awaiting the result of his answer to Chosroe when Antar fell into his power.

THE SATRAP KHOSREWAN SENT TO CHASTISE MONZAR.

[156]

Immediately on receiving Monzar's audacious message, the King of Persia despatched his satrap Khosrewan (the original cause of all the trouble), with a large army, to chastise his Arabian vassal. On the approach of the Persians, Monzar collected all the clans of the tribe of Shiban, and all the Arab hordes, and, giving battle to Khosrewan, was signally defeated. In his extremity he thought of his prisoner, the lion-slayer. Antar was freed from his fetters, and brought before Monzar.

"I am now in your power," said the hero; "and I demand of you the marriage dower of Abla, my uncle's daughter: restore my sword, my cuirass, my arms, and my horse, and give me a thousand men to defend my rear; and you shall see what my courage and force will effect against your foes."

Monzar swore, by the sacred Kaaba, that if Antar proved successful in destroying the Persian army, all his camels should be at his disposal, and ordered the hero's horse and arms to be restored to him.

Early on the morrow the Arabs went forth against the Persians, and at their head was Antar, who, exclaiming, "By thine eyes, O Abla!" received the attack of the enemy "as the parched ground the first of the rain." The Persians were mowed down by the irresistible Dhami: terror seized upon their hearts at the sound of his voice, "like the thunder's peal"; and his sword-strokes were more rapid than the flashes of lightning: the army of Monzar was victorious.

COMBAT BETWEEN ANTAR AND KHOSREWAN.

Next morning both parties prepared to renew the contest; and Antar, having engaged to challenge Khosrewan to decide matters by single combat, mounted on a mare ("for his horse Abjer, wounded the day before, was still unfit for the day of encounter"), rushed between the two armies, and thus spoke:

SALLY forth--ay, every lion warrior! Taste a draught at the edge of my sword, more bitter than the cups of absinthe.

When Death appears in the crowded ranks, then challenge me to the meeting of armies;-- ye Persians, I heed ye not--I heed ye not!

Where is he who wishes to fight me, and wants to make me drink the liquor of death?

Bring him forth!--let him see what he will meet from my spear under the shades of the war-dust;--I swear, O Abla! he shall eat of death!

By thy teeth, luscious to the kiss, and by thine eyes, and all the pangs of their enchantment, and their beauty--were thy nightly visionary form not to appear to me, never should I taste of sleep!

[157]

O thou, my hope!--O may the western breeze tell thee of my ardent wish to return home!

May it waft thee my salutation, when the sparkling dawn bursts the veil of night!

May God moisten thy nights, and bedew thee with his rain-charged clouds!

May peace dwell with thee as long as the western and northern breeze shall blow!

No sooner had Antar concluded than Khosrewan appeared on the plain, "mounted on a long-tailed steed, marked with the new moon on his forehead, and on his body was a strong coat of mail well knit together, the workmanship of David; and armed with an imperial casque and a glittering sword; and under his thighs were four small darts, each like a blazing flame.

"And when he came forth on the field of battle he roared aloud, and contemptuously of the Arabs. Antar assailed him: high arose the dust about them, so that they were hid from the sight. They exhibited most extraordinary prowess; they separated, they clung to each other; now they sported, now they were in earnest; they gave and took; they were close; they were apart; until it was mid-day, and both had severely toiled. But whenever Khosrewan attempted to assail Antar and strike him with his mace, he ever found him vigilant and on his guard, and aware of his intent. So he darted away from him in order to gallop over the field, and would exhibit all his manoeuvres and stratagems.

"But Antar kept him employed, and wearied him, and prevented his executing his designs, so that the chieftain's wrath became intense. He snatched up one of his darts, and shook it and hurled it at him--it flew from his hand like the blinding lightning, or descending fate. Antar stood firm; and when it came near him he met it, and dexterously turning it off with his shield, it bounded away, and fell upon the ground far off. Khosrewan snatched out a second dart and levelled it at him; but Antar sprang out of its way, and it passed harmless. He aimed a third; but Antar rendered it fruitless by his dexterity and his persevering activity. He hurled the fourth; but it shared the same fate as the others.

"When Khosrewan saw how Antar had parried the darts, his indignation was extreme. Again he took up his mace, and he roared even as a lion roars;--then stretching himself out with it he hurled it, backing it with a howl that made the plains and the air rebellow. Antar threw away his spear, and met the mace, and caught it with his right hand in the air; then, aiming it at Khosrewan, he cried out: 'Take that, thou son of a two thousand-horned cuckold!--I am the lover of Abla, and am alone--the Phoenix of the world!' Khosrewan saw him grasp the mace in the air, and was horrified, for his strength and force were exhausted. He retreated, and attempted to fly from his antagonist, for he was now convinced of his destruction. He moved round his shield between his shoulders; but he felt that his fate was nigh at hand, for the mace fell upon his shield more forcibly than the stone of a sling: furiously it rattled on the Persian chief, and hurled him off his saddle to the distance of twelve cubits, and broke his ribs and snapped his spine.

"Every warrior was intensely agitated at this surprising deed; and when the Persians saw it they were bewildered: they rushed upon Antar, agonized as they were at this calamity, and exposed their lives to certain death. The Arabs received them with undaunted courage at the points of their spears, and their spirit was exhilarated by the acts of Antar. The two armies assailed, and the earth was pounded under the trampling of the horses. The horsemen and the clans encountered: clouds of dust thickened over their heads. And their fury increased till they were like the waves of the boisterous ocean. Spears penetrated through hearts and waists; heads were flying off; blood was boiling; cowards were scared; the courageous full of fire: the King of Death circled round the cup of mortality; and the commands of the Most High were executed upon them."

ANTAR AT THE COURT OF CHOSROE.

Encouraged by his success, Monzar now resolved to formally declare war against Chosroe; but he was induced to defer his purpose by the counsel of his sagacious old vizier, Amru, who undertook to proceed to the Persian capital, and ascertain how the tidings of Khosrewan's death had been received. Amru finds the courtiers of Chosroe in a state of great excitement, in consequence of the arrival of a renowned knight, called Badhramoot, who had recently come thither, as the champion of the Emperor of Greece, to do battle for the Christian faith against the knights of Persia. The Emperor was preparing to send his yearly tribute of treasure to Chosroe, when Badhramoot arrived at his court, from Syria, where he had long been distinguished for his warlike prowess; and the indignation of the Christian champion was roused at the sight of so much wealth intended for a prince who was not of the true faith. Badhramoot proposed to convey the tribute, and deliver it only if he was vanquished in single combat by a Persian knight. The Emperor accepted his offer, and the champion accordingly departed for Persia with 500 horsemen in his suite. Monzar's vizier learns that Badhramoot had been engaged during fifteen days in single combat with the flower of Persian chivalry, and had overthrown all his antagonists. Chosroe was almost in despair: should none of his knights be able to vanquish the champion of the Emperor, his supremacy was gone. Amru contrives to acquaint him, through a friend at court, of the lion-hero Antar, who had lately slain his satrap Khosrewan, and routed his warriors, sent to chastise Monzar; and he sends to Hirah for Antar.

In the meantime Bahram, the famed knight of Deelem, encounters Badhramoot, and holds his own against the Greek for two successive days. On the morning of the third day, when the champions were about to renew the combat, King Monzar and Antar, accompanied by a hundred Arab horsemen, appeared on the plain.

The Arabian prince and the Absian hero having been ushered into the presence of Chosroe, after Monzar had duly saluted him, Antar stepped forward, and thus addressed the Persian monarch in verse:

MAY God avert from thee the evils of fortune, and may thou live secure from calamities!

May thy star be ever brilliant in progressive prosperity, and increase in glory!

May thy sword be ever sharp, and cleave the necks of thy foes, O thou King of the age!

May thy renown be ever celebrated in every land; for thou art just and beneficent!

So mayst thou ever live a sovereign in glory, as long as the dove pours forth its plaintive note!

Chosroe was filled with admiration at the hero's eloquence, and was astonished to perceive his prodigious form: here, at last, thought he, was come the destined conqueror of Badhramoot. The king then gave orders that Monzar and Antar should be treated with all kindness and hospitality. But when it was proposed to pitch the tents, in order that they might repose till the next day, Antar declared that he would not rest until he had slain the Greek chief, and at once prepared for the combat. Badhramoot, having been apprised of the new champion who was come to oppose him, eagerly entered the lists, and Antar, as he advanced towards him, exclaimed:

THIS day will I aid King Monzar, and I will exhibit my powers and my prowess before Chosroe:

I will break down the support of Greece from its foundations, and I will sever Badhramoot's head with my scimitar.

I will exterminate every lion-hero with my sword;--let him vaunt, let him boast, let him scoff!

Is it not known that my power is sublime on high?--is it not among the stars in the vicinity of Jupiter?

I am he whose might is uncontrollable in battle;--I am of the race of Abs--the valiant lion of the cavern!

If thou art Badhramoot, I am called Antar among men!

It was easy for me to vanquish the armies of Chosroe in the contest; and soon will I overthrow Caesar's self with my spear.

Hear the words of an intrepid lion--resolute, undaunted, all-conquering:

[160]

I am he of whom warriors can bear witness in the combat under the turbid battle-dust.

My sword is my companion in the night-shades, as are also my Abjer and my lance and my spear in the conflicts.

Night is my complexion, but Day is my emblem: the sun is unquestionably the mirror of my deeds.

This day thou shalt feel the truth of what I have said; and I will prove that I am the Phoenix of the age!

He then rushed down upon the Greek, and wonderful was the combat that ensued. Badhramoot soon found that in the Absian hero he had met with no common warrior;--all his skill and prowess were of no avail when opposed to the agility and strength of Antar, who evaded his most deadly spear-thrusts with the utmost ease. Bahram, the knight of Deelem, an envious spectator of the combat, foreseeing that Antar should achieve a victory which had been denied to himself, basely threw a dart at him while both combatants were obscured in a cloud of dust. But Antar's ever-watchful eyes saw the action, and catching the missile as it approached him, he hurled it against Badhramoot with such force that it pierced his chest and issued out at his back, and the Greek fell lifeless from his horse.

Antar would then have taken a terrible revenge on the treacherous Bahram, had not Chosroe prevented him by despatching his satraps to conduct the hero before him; when, having presented Antar with an imperial robe, he commanded that all the gold and jewels and beautiful slave-girls that came with Badhramoot should be delivered to him.

Next day, at a magnificent feast, the slave-girls employed all their blandishments to divert Antar, but in vain; for his heart was filled with the image of Abla; which his friend Monzar observing, he rallied the hero on his attachment to an absent Arab girl, reminding him that he was now raised to a station of glory which all the chiefs of Arabia would envy. Antar replied that even the grandeur which surrounded him had no charm in his eyes: nothing could cause him to forget his own land, and his beloved Abla; and thus he continued in verse:

THE fresh breeze comes in the morn, and when it blows on me with its refreshing essence, it is more grateful to me than all which my power has obtained in nightly depredations--than all my property and wealth.

The realms of Chosroe I would not covet, were the phantom of my love to vanish from my sight.

May the showers of rain ever bedew the lands and mounds of Shurebah!--lands, where the brilliancy of the veiled full moons may be seen in the obscurity of their sable ringlets-

-where my heart chases among them a damsel whose eyes are painted with antimony, more lovely than the Houri.

Thou mayst see in her teeth a liquor when she smiles, where the wine-cup is studded with pearls.

The fawn has borrowed the magic of her eye, and it is the lion of the earth that chases its prey for her beauty.

Lovely maid--delicately formed--beauteous--enchanting! and at her charms is the brightness of the moon abashed.

O Abla! the anguish of absence is in my heart--thou mayst see the shafts of Death driven through my soul!

O Abla! did not thy visionary form visit me by night, I should pass the night in sorrows and restlessness.

O Abla! how many calamities have I endured, and have plunged into them with my highly-tempered falchion, whilst the charging steeds and undaunted warriors dive into the ever perilous ocean of death!

The hero's return to his own land, for which he so eagerly longed, was delayed from day to day by the grateful hospitality of Chosroe. He accompanies the king on a hunting expedition, and narrowly escapes being foully slain by Bahram, still envious of his good fortune in having vanquished the Greek champion. Antar eludes his stroke, and dashes him senseless to the earth. Bahram's myrmidons rush upon the hero, who defends himself against them all, until Chosroe comes up, and orders his satraps to seize the dastards and strike off their heads. They were accordingly taken and pinioned. "But Antar, seeing Bahram's attendants thus disgraced, dismounted from Abjer, and advanced towards the great King, and kissing the earth before him, begged him to pardon them, saying:--'O my lord, pardon is becoming in you, and most suitable for such as you--here I kiss your noble hands, praying you to forgive them this crime, for to-morrow I intend to return home: my objects and wishes with respect to you are accomplished, and I do not wish to be mentioned after my departure, but for virtuous deeds; and let it not be said of me, I went unto a tribe, and left it in disgrace, and clothed with shame.'" The king, admiring Antar's magnanimity, granted his request, and set Bahram's followers at liberty.

The same day Antar was present at a great feast given by Chosroe in a splendid pavilion erected in the royal gardens: "It was a superb palace, like a fairy pavilion, ninety cubits in length, and seventy cubits wide, built of marble and red cornelian. In the centre was a fountain filled with rose-water and purest musk; in the middle of it was a column of emerald, and on its summit a hawk of burnished gold; its eyes were topazes and its beak jasper; around it were various birds, scattering from their bills, upon Chosroe and all that were present, musk and ambergris. The whole edifice was scented with perfumes, and the

[162]

ceilings of the palace glittered with gold and silver. It was one of the wonders of the period, and the miracle of the age."

Chosroe pressed the hero to drink freely of wine, and to take pleasure in the strains of the singing-girls; but amidst all this regal splendour Antar's heart was far away, in the land of Shurebah, and thus he recited:

WINE cannot calm my heart; sickness will not quit my body; my eyelids are ever sore-- tears ever stream in torrents from them.

The songstress would soothe my heart with her voice; but my love-sick heart loathes it.

The remembrances of Abla draw off my mind from her song, and I would say to my friend: This is all a dream!

In the land of Hejaz are the tents of my tribe, and to meet them again is forbidden me.

Amongst the tents of that people is a plump-hipped damsel, that never removes her veil; and under her veil are eyes that inspire sickness, and the pupils of her eyes strike with disease.

Between her lips is the purest musk, and camphor diluted with wine.

My love and madness are dear to me; for to him who loves, sweet is the pang of love.

O daughter of Malik! let my foes triumph in my absence--let them watch or sleep!

But in my journey I have encountered events that would turn children gray in their cradles.

Pleasures have succeeded to difficulties; and I have met a monarch whom no words can describe: A King to whom all the creation is a slave, and to whom Fortune is a vassal; whose hand distributes bounties, so that I know not whether it is the sea or a cloud.

The sun has invested him with a crown, so that the world need not fear darkness.

The stars are his jewels, in which there is a moon, brilliant and luminous, as at its full.

Mankind is corporeal, and he is spiritual;--let every joint and every member laud his name! Live for ever! Prince of the horsemen!--long as the dove pours its plaintive note, live for ever!

Delighted with these beautiful verses, Chosroe took the tiara from his brow and presented it to Antar, as a gift to Abla on her

[163]

bridal day; he also gave him a canopy of pure silver, richly adorned with the rarest gems. And Antar took the opportunity of interceding for his friend king Monzar, who was graciously pardoned, and reinstated in power.

Rostam, the king's famous wrestler, envious of these princely honours bestowed upon a stranger, challenges Antar to wrestle with him before Chosroe. But Antar is reluctant to accept his challenge, lest it should be said of him that, after being the recipient of Chosroe's bounties, he had slain one of his subjects in his own presence--for, if he did wrestle with Rostam, who sought his life, assuredly he would kill him. The king advises Rostam to withdraw his challenge, but the wrestler insists upon the contest, and Nushirvan at length grants his permission. Rostam then stripped off his clothes, but Antar merely tucked his skirts into his waistband, and advanced to his antagonist.

"Rostam bent himself like an arch, and appeared like a burning flame. He rushed upon Antar with all his force, for he looked on him as a common man, and he did not know that Antar, even in his youth, used to wrestle with he and she camels in the plains and the rocks. They grasped each other with their hands, they butted with their heads, they assaulted with their whole might, like two lions, or two elephants. Then Rostam stretched out his hand at Antar's waistband, and clung to it, and attempted to lift him up in his arms, but he found him like a stone fixed in a tower, and he tottered before him. Then he repented of what he had done, and of having provoked Antar. He slackened his hold, and he ran round him for an hour, in the presence of Chosroe and his attendants. He then sprang behind him, and thrust his head between his legs, and attempted to raise him on the back of his neck and to dash him on the ground; but Antar knew what were his intentions and his secret designs; so he closed his knees on Rostam's neck, and almost made his eyeballs start from their sockets, and nearly deprived him of life. Rostam was terrified, and wished to escape from between his legs, but he could not; every attempt failed: Antar was like a block of stone growing on a desert or a mountain. Antar seized him and clung to him, and raised him up in his hands like a sparrow in the claws of a bird of prey, and walked away with him among the multitude, wishing to wrestle quietly before the king. But Rostam, when he saw his life was in Antar's hands, like a young child, was abashed and mortified before the warriors and satraps and the great King. He clenched his fist, and struck Antar on the ear. Antar soon recovered from the blow,--he returned to the threshold of the palace, and dashed him on the ground, and smashed him to atoms."

The king then announced that Rostam had been justly slain for having transgressed the laws of fair battle, and assigned to Antar all the wrestler's property and wealth.

Shortly afterwards, the eventful day being spent, Monzar and Antar retired to their lodgings, where they were presently joined by Mubidan, the chief-priest of the Fire-worshippers, who, in compliance with the hero's urgent request, introduced him to the Temple of Fire.

[164]

"There he beheld a magnificent building, of yellow brass, raised on pillars of steel, with precious stones in the interstices,--the wonder of the age, to astonish the wisest of men. It had three storeys, and to each storey were three portals, and to each portal were slaves and servants, stationed over the edifice. Antar gazed at these men with glittering forms; and round the waists of each were leather coverings in the form of short breeches; and they were standing at the doors of the Temple, some near, and some at a distance. In their hands were pokers of steel, with which they raised the flame, heedless of the God of the two worlds, and uttering Magian words that ravished the soul; whilst their sheikh, seated on a bench of skin, chanted in his own tongue. The fire blazed before him; the fuel was of aloe-wood; towards which they all addressed their prostrations, saying: 'I and you, we laud the adored God!'"

On their quitting the Temple, and the fragrant odours, more exquisite than ambergris, Antar, thinking of his beloved Abla and his own distant land, thus exclaimed in verse:

THE logs of aloe sparkle in the fire, and the flames blaze high in the air; the sweetness of its vapour refreshes my heart when it is wafted with a northerly wind:

Its brilliancy and flame are like the face of my beauteous Abla.

But, O Fire, blaze not--burn not--for in my heart is a flame more furious than thee!

Sleep has abandoned my eyes by night, when I behold my friends in the wings of darkness.

Delightful to me would be the abode of my tribe, were I even poor, and not worth a halter;--in a distant land I should feel no more anxiety for the song, though all its cities were in my possession.

The smoke of the herbs at home, when it is scented even with camels dung, is sweeter to me than the aloe-wood, and more brilliant to my eyes in the obscurity of night.

O my lord, my anxiety increases to see my friends, so permit me to depart: thou art my stay and my support; be merciful, and compassionate my situation.

I have no succour in the world but thee, towards the success of my projects.

So grant me my request; and may thou ever live happy: may thou live long, and glorious, and great, in every felicity and every honour!

At length Antar obtains permission of Nushirvan to return to his own country; and the king bestowed on the hero, as his parting gifts, a vast quantity of treasures, in gold and silver, and precious jewels; a thousand embroidered velvet robes, and a thousand rich silk vests; four hundred white male slaves and four hundred strong black slaves, fit for battle, with all their horses and accoutrements; four hundred Georgian female slaves, four

[165]

hundred Copht and four hundred Persian slaves, and four hundred slaves of Tibah, each slave mounted on a mule, and under each were two chests of rich silk.

"Thus Antar departed with boundless wealth. The great king also mounted, with Mubidan and all the satraps, to take leave of Antar. And when they were at some distance from Modayin, and had plunged into the barren desert, Antar dismounted from Abjer, and, moving towards the king, kissed his feet in the stirrup, and begged him to return with his attendants, thus addressing him:

O THOU, whose station is sublime--in thy beneficence above the height of Sirius and Aries!--

Thou art the King like whom there is no king, and whose munificence is renowned over hill and dale!

O thou, my hope!--thou hast overwhelmed me with favours!

O thou, whose largesses resemble the bounteous rain-cloud!--thou hast bestowed gifts on me whose extent I cannot count:

So liberal is thy hand, O thou, my life and my hope!

Thou art he to whom all kings must submit; and in thy justice thou hast surpassed all thy predecessors!

"'Do not imagine,' exclaimed the King, with augmented delight, 'that we have been able duly to recompense you. What we have given you is perishable, as every thing human is; but your praises will endure for ages.'

"He then kissed Antar between the eyes, and bade him adieu, giving him as a last token a rich robe; and begging him to visit him frequently, he departed."

King Monzar and Antar journeyed on till they reached Hirah, where the hero was sumptuously entertained for some time; and when he was about to depart for his own land, Monzar gave him a thousand Asafeer camels, besides many other valuable gifts. Antar then began his journey homeward, attended by the troops of slaves presented to him by Nushirvan and Monzar. As he traversed the deserts, he reflected on all the adventures and perils he had encountered for the sake of Abla, and on approaching the land of Hejaz, he gave way to his feelings in verse:

IS it the breeze from the heights of the land of Shurebah that revives me and resuscitates my heart, or is it the gale from the tamarisks?

Is it the flame that consumes me for Abla, or is it the lightning flash from her dwelling that deprives me of my senses?

[166]

O thou spot where she resides! may thy hillocks be ever inhabited by the families, and may thy plains be ever crowded with friends!

Have thine eyelids been seen to watch at night, as my eyelids have watched ever since I quitted thee?

And has the turtle-dove's moan filled thee with sorrow in thy sleeplessness, as the turtle-dove's moan has distressed me?

I departed from thee not uneasy, or much in anguish; but my uncle has outraged me, and coveted my death.

He has exposed me to a sea of dangers, but I plunged into it with my glittering two-edged blade.

I have cut through the neck of Fortune, and the nocturnal vicissitudes and the nightly calamities have trembled.

My good fortune has seated me in a mansion of glory, man and genii could never attain.

I have encountered in Irak horsemen that may be accounted as whole tribes when the battle rages.

I am returning with the wealth of Chosroe and Caesar--with he and she camels, horses, and slaves;

And when I reach home, my enemies shall weep, as one day they laughed, when Shiboob announced my death.

They indeed sought my destruction in a distant land; but they knew not that Death was-- my sword and my spear!

ABLA'S TRIALS DURING ANTAR'S ABSENCE.

After it was spread abroad that old Malik had maliciously despatched Antar on the desperate enterprise to procure the Asafeer camels for Abla's dowry, he soon found himself the object of scorn and contempt among his tribe, and resolved to depart secretly, with fifteen horsemen, on a marauding expedition, and not to return until the scandal had been forgotten. But instead of plundering others, Malik and his party were taken prisoners by Vachid, a famous horseman of the tribe of Kenanah. This chief being informed by his mother that Malik had a beautiful daughter called Abla, he demands her in marriage, to which Malik readily consents, and offers to go and bring her to him as his bride. On this condition Vachid releases Malik and his son Amru, who at once depart for the land of Shurebah; and on approaching the habitations of their tribe, they find all the people in grief on account of the reported death of Antar. They skulk along until they reach their own tents, where they discover Abla, clothed in black, and seated in the deepest affliction, beside a newly-made grave. Tears flowed down the maiden's cheeks, and she gave vent to her despair and sorrow in these verses:

O GRAVE! my tears shall ever bedew thy earth!--my eyes have renounced sweet sleep!

O grave! is there any one but my cousin Antar in thee? or is his sepulchre in my heart?

Alas!--alas for thee!--felled to the ground art thou, and the groans of a distracted mourner survive!

They slew him barbarously; and his foes exult when they see my agony and misery on his account!

O never will I surrender myself to another, were he to come with a thousand charms!

Malik then enters the tent of his wife, who informs him that Shiboob had brought tidings of Antar's death, adding that all the tribe execrated himself as the cause; and after attempting to soothe the anguish of Abla, who refuses to be comforted, and calls him the murderer of her cousin, he next visits his brother Shedad, and hears him thus bitterly lamenting the loss of his heroic son:

O MY eyelids, let your tears flow abundantly--weep for the generous, noble horseman!--

A knight in whom I took refuge when my efforts failed, at my up-risings and my down-sittings!

My brother exposed him to a sea of death in his malice, and the hearts of the envious exult!

He planned his murder, and he has abandoned me: no more will my honour and my engagements be respected!

He behaved cruelly to him in exacting the marriage dower, and he now refuses to do him justice.

He was the drawn sword of the race of Abs, cleaving through armour above the skin.

He used to fell the foe in every land, till the warriors cried out for succour.

Prostrate--fallen--bowed to the earth is he now, beneath the shadow of lances and the waving of banners!

[168]

Now he is gone, the Absian dames are in sorrow, dashing their hands against their cheeks, in fear of slavery.

Dishevelled is their hair, streaming are their tears over their fair necks decorated with chains.

Sighing they mourn the hero of Abs in sobs of sorrow, that give pleasure to the envious.

Grieve they must ever in tears from their eyes for him who was the illustrious knight!

May God destroy Malik, son of Carad, and make him suffer what the tribe of Themood endured!

Altogether the wretched Malik found matters very unpleasant, to say the least, and there was nothing for it but to emigrate with his family;--meanwhile concealing himself, lest Amarah, to whom he had also betrothed Abla, should suspect his design, and prevent his departure. But presently Amarah, now that his formidable rival was dead, resolves to lose no time in claiming his bride; and, accompanied by Oorwah the son of Wird, and ten other horsemen, he departs for the land of Yemen, to procure the dowry (by plunder, of course); and Malik resolves to take advantage of his absence and remove with his family. But when he acquainted Abla of how he had promised her in marriage to Vachid, she protested that she would never become the bride of either Amarah or Vachid, since her heart was buried in the grave of Antar, exclaiming:

O HEART! be patient under the agonies I endure!--But how can my tears cease to flow?--no balm is there to soothe them!

How can my tears be soothed away?--ever must they flow for the loss of him who shamed the brilliancy of the loveliest!

High exalted are his glory and his exploits: noble is his birth, permanent in the pinnacle of honour!

He who dwells in every life--he, the Eternal Cupbearer--has made him drink of the cups of Death!

O I shall weep for him for ever, as long as the dove pours forth its lament on the boughs and the leaves!

In spite of Abla's tears and agonies, however, Malik caused the tents to be struck, and at midnight he quitted the tribe, and proceeded with his family to the Springs of Zeba, where Vachid lay concealed with Malik's companions, whom he held as hostages. On Malik's arrival, Vachid released his prisoners, who returned home; and the party of Vachid, including Malik's family, commenced their journey back to their own land.

[169]

On the fourth day of their march they were attacked by a party of brigands, led by a chief who rejoiced in the name of the "Nocturnal Evil." Eager to display his prowess in presence of Abla, Vachid encounters this formidable robber, and is slain. Malik and his son Amru are taken prisoners and securely bound; but while the brigands are engaged with Vachid's followers, Abla and her mother release them, and they all escape into the desert, where they meet with Amarah and his party, returning, exulting and victorious, with plunder, from the land of Yemen. Malik was giving Amarah an account of their misfortunes when they were surprised by the appearance of the Nocturnal Evil and his gang, who, having defeated the Kenanians, and turned back in quest of the howdah containing Abla, and finding it empty, had hastened to overtake the fugitives. Amarah and Oorwah prepare to resist the brigands, but are speedily overpowered and pinioned; and once more the fair Abla and her family are in the power of the dreaded "Evil." Having rested in that spot for the night, at daybreak the Nocturnal Evil sent before him five slaves in charge of Abla, with orders to proceed to a place called Zatool Menahil, and there pitch the tents--"for there," said the foul wretch, "I intend to remain three days with this lovely damsel."

ABLA AND HER FAMILY RESCUED BY ANTAR.

Now it happened that Antar, pursuing his journey homeward, reached the Zatool Menahil shortly after the five slaves in charge of Abla's litter had pitched the tents there; and he was not a little surprised to hear the voice of a woman within the litter, calling upon his own name in her distress, saying, "Woe to these dastard slaves! O Antar! where are thine eyes, that they might behold me?" and thus she continued her lament:

WHERE are thine eyes, O Knight of men and genii?

O that thou couldst see me in the infamy of despair, with wretches who respect no protection: no, no--and have no mercy!

O that I had never lived in this age of traitors, who only see in thee my misery and dishonour!

Why has God prolonged my existence, now the lion is gone, who ever protected the country and the women?

May God ever bedew his grave with plenteous showers that fail not!

For, in truth, he was a knight and a hero that could vanquish with his fingers the beasts of the desert, and destroy the warriors in the day of battle, whenever he appeared in the plains of contention!

Antar was now assured that the distressed damsel could be none but his own beloved Abla; and furiously assailing the slaves with his spear, he slew three of them, while the two others fled, to carry the news to their chief.

[170]

Abla was naturally overcome by the sudden apparition of her brave lover, whom she had long regarded as dead, but at length her spirits revived, and she expressed her feelings in these verses:

ALL my misery--all my grief--is past, now that we have met after so long an absence!

Time now happily announces the existence of one who had been trampled beneath the dumb grave!

Now the eyes of the age are illumined, after a period of darkness; and I am returned to life after my death!

O Knight of men and genii!--O thou that excellest every warrior in glory! mine eyes gladden at beholding thy liberality, and the beauty of thy truth!

I will implore God ever to exalt thy glories, both morning and evening!

She then told Antar how Shiboob had brought the doleful news of his death, and of all that had occurred to her during his long absence; and Antar, in his turn, briefly recounted his own adventures, and the perils he had been exposed to since he quitted the land of Shurebah to procure the Asafeer camels for her dowry.

Thus the lovers were conversing when the Nocturnal Evil was seen rapidly approaching, having heard, from the two slaves that escaped Antar's spear-thrusts, of the irresistible champion who had come to the rescue of their fair charge. Antar, mounted on Abjer, impetuously assailed the brigand with his spear, and, crying "O by Abs! O by Adnan!--I am the lover of Abla!

Forced it through his breast, so that he fell lifeless to the earth. The hero then hastened to disperse the followers of the Nocturnal Evil and release the prisoners; and while expressing his gratification at meeting his uncle Malik, he reminded him that all his late sufferings were but a just punishment for his past conduct.

Then were the tents pitched, and a grand feast prepared by Antar's slaves; and the hero entertained his friends with his adventures in Irak and the honours and princely gifts bestowed on him by king Nushirvan. After the feast was over, Antar rejoined Abla, who threw herself into his arms, and kissed him repeatedly; and when he told her of all the riches he had brought home with him, "Truly," she replied, "thy safety is more acceptable to me than all thou hast described: I have felt no pleasure but in thy presence." Antar smiled, and his bosom expanded with joy at the purity of her love.

THE HERO'S RECEPTION BY HIS TRIBE.

At daybreak the hero ordered the camels to be loaded and preparations made for continuing their journey home. Decorating Abla with magnificent robes studded with jewels, and placing on her head the diadem of Chosroe, he raised her into the silver litter, with her mother, and commanded the slaves to proceed with them in advance and guard them on the journey. "When Abla was seated in the litter, her countenance became radiant and illumined; she smiled in the loveliest manner: every charm was heightened, and from her eyelashes she shot arrows that penetrated the slayer of men and heroes." It was therefore no wonder that the coxcomb Amarah should be tortured with envy and rage at thus beholding the bride of Antar!

When the party were within one day's journey of the tribe of Abs, Malik, with his son Amru and Abla's mother, went in advance to apprise King Zoheir of Antar's return. All the warriors of Abs, with the King at their head, came forth to meet the hero,--and never was there such another meeting--such a glorious day! "The noble Absians all surrounded him, whilst, in reply to King Zoheir, he related his adventures. His mother and his brothers wept, and clamoured at the ecstasy of meeting, and in the excess of their happiness after all past alarms and afflictions." Antar then distributed rich presents to Zoheir and his sons, and to all the noble horsemen of Abs; to his father Shedad he gave abundance of gold and silver, and many stout slaves; and the remainder, with the Asafeer camels, he delivered to his uncle Malik. After this every one sought his own tent. "But Amru, Abla's brother, made the camels that conveyed his sister kneel down; he lifted up the curtain of the litter--but Abla was not there!"

ANTAR'S GRIEF FOR THE LOSS OF ABLA.

"Fortune builds up, and throws down!"--Antar's cup of happiness, filled to overflowing, was in an instant dashed from his lips, by the mysterious disappearance of his beloved Abla, for whose sake he had braved the perils of the deserts and the wastes, and fought with savage lions, and with warriors all but invincible. This was a calamity for which the heroic son of Shedad was totally unprepared; it fell upon him with a force that threatened to deprive him of his reason. In vain the kindhearted King Zoheir tried to soothe him with the assurance that he would soon clear up the mystery. The grief-stricken lover bitterly accused himself of having, in his anxiety to meet the King, carelessly left his heart's idol in charge of slaves who knew not her worth. The King sent forth parties to scour the country in every direction, but they all returned without having obtained tidings of the beautiful daughter of Malik. As to Antar himself, the calamity had quite unmanned him: his "native hue of resolution was sicklied o'er with the pale cast of thought;" and the slayer of heroes was for the time being unfit for "enterprises of great pith and moment." He despatched his brother Shiboob, however, in quest of his lost bride, and awaited his return with anxious expectation, that banished sleep from his eyelids. The heart of the hero was completely subdued; and thus, with many a sob and sigh, he expressed his sorrow:

MY tears stand in drops on my eyelids, and short is the sleep of my eyes.

[172]

For love there is no rest--no comfort when the railers advise.

We met, but our meeting quenched not the flame;--no, it did not cool the boiling heat!

How long shall I mourn for the mate that grieves me?--tears and lamentations avail not.

I have implored a peaceable life from Fortune, but her favours to me are like the boons of a miser.

I am dying; and the most extraordinary forbearance aids me not in my calamities.

SHIBOOB BRINGS TIDINGS OF ABLA.

Antar endured many days and weeks of torturing suspense, his only source of consolation being the society of King Zoheir, until at length Shiboob returned--with news of Abla.

"After I had passed through various cities of Yemen," said Shiboob, "I came to Sana and Aden, and encountered numerous difficulties until I reached the tribe of Tey. It was there I found Abla, in the power of Moofrij: there she attends on the camels and the sheep. He has clothed her in garments of raw leather, and makes her serve in the meanest offices day and night. His mother too threatens her, and treats her harshly in her speech; so that she weeps both when she rises and lies down. She calls on your name, and seeks her wonted succour from you both night and day."

"Well, Shiboob," said Antar, while the tears gushed from his eyes; "but what was the cause of her falling into the power of Moofrij?--How came he, of all people, to obtain possession of her?"

"Son of my mother," replied Shiboob, "the cause of all this is Amarah, in whose mind are ever harboured evil and deceit. His envy at last overpowered him, at the sight of the vast wealth you had with you. He turned aside into the desert; but his love for Abla was so violent, that he followed your traces, and watched her after you had quitted her in the morning. Fate and destiny overcame her. He seized her; and, though he was desirous to vanquish her, Moofrij overtook him in the desert. He tore her away from him, and reduced him to a most pitiable state."

"Brother," said Antar, whose heart was almost bursting as he listened to this narrative, "how did you obtain this information?"

"Know," continued Shiboob, "that, when I quitted you, I made the circuit of every tribe and horde, and made inquiries of every one I met, whether on horseback or on foot, until I came to Aja and Selma, and the waters of the tribe of Tey. With every family I passed one night, saying to myself, peradventure I may learn something. On the last night of my

[173]

stay I slept in the dwelling of Moofrij, and my place of rest was close to that of one of his slaves, called Moobshir. He invited me to converse with him, and was very kind to me; and to his questions about my connections, 'Son of my aunt,' I replied, 'I am of the tribe of Jalhema, of the family of Saad, son of Khoozrej--and this is the family of Hatim Tey.' So he complimented me.

"But when all was still and quiet, and every one asleep, the voice of Abla struck upon my ears. She was loudly wailing, and exclaiming through the calmness of the night--'O for the joys of Mount Saadi and the land of Shurebah!' and she was expressing her regret at being separated from her native soil, and her loss of friends; adding--'O protector of the tribe of Abs, how often have I called on thee! Where is the path by which I can give thee news of myself and meet thee? O son of my uncle! for torments distract me. My eyes are ulcered with weeping, O son of my uncle! Thy foes triumph, and watchful are the eyes of thy enemies. It was the very moment of meeting, when separation closely followed its traces; and thou hadst but just arrived from Irak, when we were again scattered over the globe! Woe to me! my lot is nothing but tears and sighs. What a misery it is to put on raw leather for a garment! Cruel is this grievous state! Hasten, then, thy arrival, son of my uncle;--rescue me by thy exertions, that laid low the lions of the caverns. Let me hear thy shouts in the tumults of spearsmen and swordsmen.'

"After this doleful effusion, my brother, she sobbed and sighed so bitterly, it might almost be said that she was dead, and that her soul had departed. Again she sighed from her sorrowing heart, and thus spoke:

MY anxious love is vehement, and my tears flow profusely, and they ease the anguish of my pains in my frame.

Ask my burning sighs that mount on high: they will tell you of the flaming passion in my liver.

By your violence you overpower my weakness: I have not forbearance or resignation to endure it.

O bird of the tamarisk!--all the livelong night, drooping, he mourns for his mate that is gone and returns not;--

This is thy sorrow, and to-morrow thou art relieved: but alas! what is the state of the captive of love and-anguish?

O western breeze! blow to my country, and give information of me to the fierce lion--the hero of Abs, and their champion when start forth the foreheads of the horse and warriors in multitudes!

How oft has he protected me with the edge of his sword!--he, the refuge of mothers, fearful of being bereft of their children!

Here I dwell, hoping for a relief from my agonies at his hand: to no other will I complain.

(As Shiboob repeated these verses, streams flowed from the eyes of Antar.)

"I immediately turned," continued Shiboob, "towards the slave near whom I was lying: 'Son of my aunt,' said I, 'why is this damsel grieving? Does she not sleep? Does she pass her nights generally thus?'--'Young man,' replied the slave, 'she is a foreigner, and she is a captive; it is thus she passes her mornings and evenings. Her name is Abla, daughter of Malik, the Absian.'

"I soon contrived to draw from him the whole story: how Moofrij happened to meet Amarah and her; how he took Amarah prisoner, and carried him home; and when he demanded of her what man demands of woman, how she used the most opprobrious expressions towards him--threatening him with her cousin, a fierce lion, who had raised himself from the state of a slave to that of a chief; how Moofrij upon this treated her most vilely--stripping her of her clothes, and overwhelming her with cruelties; how also he behaved in the same manner to Amarah--handcuffing and fettering him, until he should ransom himself with money and camels; and that he had sent to Rebia to rescue him from misery.

"At hearing this, O son of my mother, sweet sleep abandoned my eyes, and I anxiously waited for the dawn of day, that I might hasten to you, and return with my intelligence. But on my way I met the family of Zeead, travelling towards that tribe. I turned out of the road, so that they did not see me: and this is what I have seen and heard during my absence."

ANTAR RESCUES HIS BELOVED.

When Shiboob had concluded his story, Antar appeared to be stupefied with rage and grief; but recovering himself, he cried, "I must be revenged on that family of Zeead!--I will deprive them of their sweet slumbers!" He hastened to his friend Prince Malik, who conducted him to the King, to whom he related Amarah's ungrateful return for his services in liberating him from the Nocturnal Evil. Zoheir was greatly exasperated at the infamous conduct of Amarah, and vowed vengeance upon the whole family of Zeead. But Antar tells Prince Malik that he will not put the king to any trouble on his account, for he will alone undertake the rescue of Abla. His friend, however, insists upon going with him; and, taking advantage of the king's absence at the chase, he musters his father's horsemen, while Antar summons Shedad and his brother Malik, with his son Amru; and the sun was not yet high when the warriors, to the number of two hundred, set out to revenge the insult that had been offered to the family of Carad, and to the whole tribe of Abs. On the way, Antar, turning to Prince Malik, thus addressed him:

"Truly, my lord, it is very absurd in me to set out to the assistance of my foes. This is the most grievous circumstance of all; for I am aware that, though they become victorious by my means, they will not let me be quiet. But it is on Abla's account that I act thus. Some poet has observed:

HAD I a heart of pity and compassion for myself, I would not pass the night grieving in the agony of love.

It is extraordinary, that from thine eyes I feel no arrow, but still my heart is pierced with shafts.

I am kind to thy friends in my love, though they are my foes; and on account of two eyes a thousand eyes are respected."

And again addressing the Prince, he said, "On Abla's account I will submit to these pains;" adding--

I ENDURE torments from my relations that fatigue me; and I conceal from them my passion and my transports.

When they question me, I say: Kill me; for I am an oppressive tyrant.

They insult me, and seek to separate me from my beloved; and she is my hope and my object.

They long for my death:--it is their sole wish to see me felled to the ground in the day of battle.

But when the foe comes upon them, they entreat my aid, and are inclined to love me.

I will have patience till I obtain my desire; and I will punish the enemy by my resignation to insults.

Meanwhile Rebia, with two hundred horsemen of his family, is advancing to the rescue of his brother Amarah. But Moofrij has timely warning, and, assailing them, routs the party and takes thirty prisoners; and Rebia, with the remnant of his followers, retreats into the sand-hills. There they are in distress from want of water, and Rebia sends a messenger to Moofrij, asking his protection in order that they might surrender themselves and procure their ransom; or, if he will not consent to forego the further shedding of blood, at least supply them with water. To this message Moofrij returns the grim answer, that he would furnish them with water only on the condition that they throw away their arms, and come dismounted before him; when he would shave off their beards, and cut off their noses and their ears; after which--by Lat and Uzza!--he would hang them all. In desperation Rebia and his followers descend and commence another attack; but, being weakened by thirst, the Teyans easily make prisoners of them all.

[176]

"The night was not far spent when Moofrij became intoxicated. The people had departed to their respective tents, and every one was asleep, when Moofrij happened to think of Abla; and as he was considering how he should complete his gratification, he repaired to his mother, and said: 'I wish you would bring me that Absian damsel. If she will not consent, I will use her most cruelly; I will multiply her distresses, and slay her countrymen.' Away hastened his mother to Abla.--'Go to your master instantly,' said she, that he may show some kindness to you and your countrymen; but if you still obstinately refuse to yield to him, dread his violence.'--'Vile hag!' exclaimed Abla, 'were your son even to hack my limbs with the sword, or to massacre the whole tribe of Abs, and all that the sun rises upon, never would he see me his property--never see me yield or submit to him. Wishes he my death? I will kill myself with my own hand.'--'Accursed wretch!' cried the old woman. She struck her with her fist, and ordered the slave-girls to drag her forth, as she screamed out, 'O by Abs! O by Adnan! who can now save me? who can assist me? who can redeem me from this captivity? Alas! is there any one to deliver me from this distress?'"

That same night the Teyans were surprised in their tents by the renowned Antar and his warriors, crying, 'O by Abs! O by Adnan!' and sparing neither old nor young. While the horsemen were engaged in slaying or capturing the Teyans, Shiboob released Rebia and his companions; then roamed among the tents in search of Abla, whom he at length found covered with the bodies of the slain, and groaning like a woman bereft of her children; and while she listened for the voice of Antar, thus she exclaimed:

O MY COUSIN! ease my heart, and lead me home by the hand, for my body is worn out and my strength fails!

For the black hero I have encountered disgrace.

My frame--the zephyr would overwhelm it, so greatly have they exhausted me with eternal pains: my resignation, it is at an end.

My foes exult over me, and I have endured endless horrors.

Convey me to the protection of Antar: no one but the lion can defend the fawn.

Tell him I am in dismay, and my heart wanders gild in its fears.

My eyelids--no sleep have they; but they mourn for eternal sleep.

Shiboob took Abla in his arms, and brought her to Antar, who pressed her to his breast, and kissed her between the eyes, saying, "Grievous indeed it is to me that you should suffer such calamities, and I be alive in the world! But it is the misfortune of the times, against which no human being can find refuge." He then desired his brother to convey her to the tent of Moofrij (who had escaped to the sand-hills); and here Shiboob has the

[177]

satisfaction of discovering all Abla's property--her rich robes and strings of jewels--which he restores to her. "Thus all her distresses and afflictions vanished, and her hopes and wishes were realised."

As the Absians are about to set out for their own country, Rebia and Amarah come up to Antar, and in the most abject manner implore his forgiveness for their infamous deeds "Antar pitied them; and, feeling favourably inclined towards them on account of his relationship, he embraced them, saying: 'Although I am abused for being black, my acts are the acts of the noble born.'"

Returning from the land of Cahtan, they encounter the tribes of Jadeelah and Nibhan, and, after a dreadful battle, are victorious. When they had collected all the spoil, they returned to their tents, preceded by Antar.

"Abla rejoiced at his prowess and intrepidity, and smiled; and as Antar saw her smile,-- 'Daughter of my uncle,' said he, 'are you smiling at what you saw me perform this day in the carnage and combat?'--'By the faith of an Arab,' she replied, 'my sight was bewildered at your slaughter among these wretches!'--Her words descended into his heart sweeter than the purest water to the thirsty spirit."

At midnight, the Absians, having first divided the spoil, mounted their horses and resumed their march home. When the sun's rays began to dispel the darkness they discovered the Teyans, headed by King Maljem, son of Handhala, and his brother, the Blood-drinker, in pursuit of them. On seeing the number of the enemy, they were disposed for flight, but Antar inspired them with courage, by rushing impetuously among the Teyans, dealing death and destruction with his irresistible sword Dhami. At this juncture the Absians are reinforced by troops which King Zoheir had despatched to Antar's assistance, and the Teyans are defeated with great slaughter.

The next day, Abla's father, acting upon Rebia's suggestion, begs Prince Shas to take Abla under his protection, to prevent Antar from marrying her, to which he consents; and sending for Antar, he intimates to him that henceforth Abla shall be under the protection of his wife; at the same time reproaching him for lusting after a woman to whom he has no claim. Tears filled the eyes of the hero as he replied, saying that it was his uncle Malik who had excited his passion;--for whenever Abla is a prisoner, he entreats him to liberate her; but when she is in safety, he calls him a slave, and the son of a slave-woman.

Antar then goes to his friend Prince Malik, and acquaints him of his uncle's new device to thwart his union with Abla. The Prince promises to carry her off for him--only let him wait until they return to King Zoheir, and he should obtain justice. But the hero, unwilling to burden his friend with his distresses, or to be the cause of dissensions in his tribe, resolves to set out secretly for Mecca, and there make his complaints to the Lord of mankind.

[178]

ANTAR GOES TO MECCA.

At night, when all was still, Antar, mounted on Abjer, and accompanied by his brother Shiboob, departs for the Holy Shrine. As they travelled through the deserts, the hero's reflections found expression in these verses:

IF, O tear! thou canst not relieve me in my sorrow, perhaps thou mayst quench the flame that consumes me.

O heart! if thou wilt not wait patiently for a meeting--die, then, the death of a woe-begone, wandering stranger!

How long must I defy the evils of Fortune, and encounter the vicissitudes of night with the Indian blade?

I serve a tribe, whose hearts are the reverse of what they exhibit in their fondness for me.

I am, in the field, the prince of their tribe; but, the battle over, I am more despised than a slave.

O that I could annihilate this affection of a lover! how it humiliates me!--it agonizes my heart--it enfeebles my courage.

But soon will I seek the Sacred Shrine, and complain of my ill-usage to the Judge against whose decrees there lies no appeal.

I will renounce the days when my tears deceived me; and I will aid the widowed and plaintive dove.

On thee, O daughter of Malik! be the peace of God!--the blessing of a sorrowing, heart-grieved lover!

I will depart; but my soul is firm in its love for thee;--have pity, then, on the cauterised heart of one far away!

Soon will my tribe remember me when the horse advance--every noble warrior trampling and stamping over them:

Then, O daughter of Malik! will agony be plainly evident, when the coward gnaws his hands in death!

Their journey was marked with no particular incident until they drew near Mecca, when Shiboob observed to his brother that it was strange they had met with no adventure on the way. Antar replied that he was harassed with encountering dangers, and his heart was disgusted at fighting; and he quoted these verses:

[179]

RETIRE within yourself, and be familiar with solitude:

When you are alone, you are in the right road.

Wild beasts are tamed by gentle treatment;

But men are never to be induced to abandon their iniquity.

But presently they hear, in the calmness of the night, a female voice crying out, evidently in sore distress; upon which Antar slackens his bridle, and gallops in the direction whence proceeded the cries. He discovers a lady, who informs him that she is of the noble tribe of Kendeh; her husband, As-hath, the son of Obad; that a famine having visited their land, they were proceeding, with their family, to the country of Harith, where they intended to settle, having a daughter married there, when they were attacked by a horseman of the desert, called Sudam, the son of Salheb, with forty plundering Arabs, who had slain her three sons, wounded her husband, and taken herself and her three daughters captive; and that the brigands were about to convey them to the mountains of Toweila, there to sell them as slaves. Consigning the ladies to the care of his brother, Antar grasped his spear, and turned to meet Sudam and his followers, whom he now saw hastily advancing towards him. The hero is assailed by several of the brigands at once, but he cuts them down on either side, and at length encounters Sudam, and, striking him on the breast with his cleaving Dhami, the chief falls to the ground dead, weltering in his blood.

The three damsels and their mother crowd round their deliverer, kissing his hands and thanking him for having saved them from dishonour; and Antar, desiring the damsels to veil themselves, and having bound up the old sheikh's wounds, sat down to rest himself after the fatigues of his conflict. The old sheikh, grateful for the good service rendered his family by Antar, offers him his choice of his three daughters, but Antar courteously declines the compliment, saying to the damsels:

WERE my heart my own, I should desire nothing beyond you--it would covet nothing but you.

But it loves what tortures it; where no word, no deed encourages it.

Having escorted the old sheikh and his family to the land of Harith, Antar took leave of them, and, in company with Shiboob, proceeded to Mecca. "He alighted in the Sacred Valley, and there he resided; passing his days in hunting, to relieve his sorrows and afflictions, and his nights with Shiboob, in talking over old stories and past events."

PRINCE SHAS IN CAPTIVITY.

The friends of Antar were much troubled at his departure, and searched for him in all directions; but his uncle was especially gratified, since it left him free, as he thought, to dispose of Abla; and accordingly she is again betrothed to Amarah--the contract being formed by Abla's father and Amarah shaking hands. But Prince Malik, grieved at this great injustice to his absent friend, vows that he will never permit Amarah to marry Abla, while he lives to thwart his wicked plans, and those of the maiden's sordid and crafty father; and he predicts that evil will befal his brother Shas for his share in the infamous transaction.

When the Absians reached the lake of Zatul-irsad, Prince Shas with ten horsemen went into the desert in pursuit of the antelope. There they are met by a troop of warriors led by Maisoor, son of Zeead, of the clan of Hazrej, a branch of Harith, and the little band of Absians are all slain, with the exception of Shas, who is taken prisoner, and barbarously treated by Maisoor, whose brother the Prince had killed in the conflict.

Prince Malik and the others arrive in safety at the dwellings of their tribe, and the King is indignant when he learns how the noble Antar has been again deceived by Abla's father. He severely rebukes him for his scandalous conduct, and causes Amarah to be scourged as a punishment for espousing Abla, when he knew that she was already betrothed to Antar, and that her father was in possession of the rich dowry which the hero had brought from Irak. The absence of Prince Shas causes the King great uneasiness. Having sent horsemen into the desert in quest of him without success, his affliction increases, and he declares that if Shas is slain, he will strike off the head of Amarah, and hang Malik, the son of Carad, because they had incited his son to act basely towards Antar.

In the meantime Shas is a prisoner in the land of Harith, and daily tortured by Maisoor, who "enclosed him between four bars of iron, and stationed a guard of slaves over him; and whenever he went out he kicked him, and whenever he entered he thumped him with his fists." The chief of the clan, however, hearing of this shameful treatment of a noble Arab, sends for Maisoor, and advises him to relax his severities towards his prisoner, which he does, in this manner: he hastens back to Shas and unties his hands, but binds his feet; then he kicks him in the rear, and places a slave over him.

ANTAR SUMMONED FROM MECCA TO RESCUE SHAS.

The unhappy Prince, however, finds a friend in need in the old lady of Kendeh, who, with her family, had been rescued from the brigand Sudam, by Antar, on his way to Mecca. Misfortune had taught Shas a salutary lesson, and he now bitterly repented of his conduct towards the noble hero: he assured the old lady that if ever he gained his freedom he would henceforth befriend Antar, and further his union with Abla. Perceiving the advantages which Antar would derive from the friendship of Shas, the good old lady despatches her husband, As-hath, to Mecca, to acquaint the hero of Shas' condition.

[181]

"With all haste he traversed the plains till he reached Mecca, where he inquired for Antar; and being directed to his residence, he introduced himself, and told what had happened to Shas, and how he had left him in despair.--'May God never deliver him from peril or death!' cried Shiboob; 'for my brother has no such enemy among the Absians as he.'--'Brother,' said Antar, bear malice against no man;' and he repeated these verses:

DO not bear malice, O Shiboob!--renounce it, for no good ever came of malice.

Violence is infamous: its result is ever uncertain, and no one can act justly when actuated by hatred.

Let my heart support every evil, and let my patience endure till I have subdued all my foes.

"When Antar had finished, the old man was amazed at such clemency towards his enemies, strong and powerful as he was. That night they reposed; but early next morning Antar said to As-hath, 'Let us depart, O Sheikh, before my lord Shas be reduced to the last extremity and be killed.' The sheikh and Antar were soon mounted, and Shiboob started in front of them, making the wild beasts and antelopes fly before him."

But before Antar can come to his deliverance, Maisoor has determined to hang Prince Shas without further delay, and the old lady of Kendeh therefore enables him to escape, in the disguise of a slave, directing him to take the road to Mecca. Having rested during the night in a mountain-cave, the Prince resumes his flight at daybreak, and meets with a party of the tribe of Riyan, one of whom mistakes him for a slave who lately stole his horse. He tells them that he is Shas, the son of Zoheir; but unfortunately his captors are enemies of his tribe; and they are about to put him to death, when they discover a man running towards them with the speed of the wind, and close behind him two horsemen. These are Shiboob and the noble Antar and As-hath. The hero, with his sword Dhami, and Shiboob, with his arrows, soon make all the warriors to bite the dust, save one, who escapes on a swift camel.

Prince Shas expresses his contrition to Antar, and promises to make him ample amends for the past. Antar having presented to As-hath all the horses and plunder, the old sheikh takes his leave, and departs for his own country; while the hero and Prince Shas begin their journey to the land of Hejaz, with the trusty Shiboob for their guide. On the fifth day they reached the waters of the tribe of Akhram, where they rested for the night.

Antar had a delightful dream of his beloved Abla, and in the morning, when he awoke, he thus recited:--

THE dear image of Abla visited in sleep the victim of love, intoxicated with affliction.

I arose to complain of my sufferings from love, and the tears from my eyes bedewed the earth.

[182]

I kissed her teeth--I smelled the fragrance of musk and the purest ambergris.

I raised up her veil, and her countenance was brilliant, so that Night became unveiled.

She deigned to smile, and looked most lovely; and I saw in her eye the lustre of the frill moon.

She is environed with swords and calamitous spears, and about her dwelling prowls the lion of the land.

O Abla! love for thee lives in my bones, with my blood; as long as life animates my frame, there will it flow.

O Shas! I am persecuted with a deadly passion, and the flame of the fire blazes still fiercer.

O Shas! Were not the influence of love overpowering every resolution, thou wouldst not thus have subdued Antar!

THE HERO ENCOUNTERS ROUDHA, A GALLANT HORSEMAN, GOING A-WOOING TO ABLA.

Shiboob continued to guide his brother and Prince Shas in safety past many hostile tribes, and on the eleventh day they reached the country called Zat-ul-ialam. "In the middle of the plain they met six howdahs, upon six camels; and over each howdah was a crescent of polished gold, with hangings of magnificent velvet; and round the howdahs rode a troop of sturdy slaves, armed with shields and sharp swords. The whole cavalcade was preceded by a knight in whom fortitude and intrepidity shone conspicuous. He was close-vizored and broad-shouldered; over his body was a corslet that enveloped his limbs; upon his head was an Aadite helmet, like a raised canopy; he was girt with a well-watered scimitar, and a well-proportioned spear was slung round him; and beneath him was a white horse, of the noblest breed; and, like a ferocious lion, he marched in front of the howdahs and the camels."

This horseman was Roudha, the son of Meneea, who, like Amarah, had fallen in love with the daughter of Malik, from descriptions he had heard of her beauty; and he was now on the way to the tribe of Abs, with rich presents for Abla, and accompanied by his mother and his five sisters--eager to encounter Antar, or any other famed knight who would oppose him, for Abla's sake.

A combat, of course, ensues between Antar and Roudha, in which the Absian hero unhorses his antagonist, but spares his life and grants his liberty on the intercession of his

[183]

mother and sisters; and Roudha, full of admiration and gratitude for his clemency, begs Antar's acceptance of the presents he had intended for Abla, and returns home.

Prince Shas and Antar at length reach the land of their tribe, and are heartily welcomed by the King and all the noble warriors of Abs. The hero's time-serving uncle congratulates him on his return, and declares that Antar shall be married to Abla that very night. "Shedad thought the world too narrow for the extent of his joy on the arrival of his son: his mother, Zebeebah, kissed him, as she said, 'If you would but stay and tend the camels with me, my heart would be relieved from the pain of all these terrible events.' Antar smiled, and composed her." The King celebrates the return of Shas and Antar with a grand feast, at which all the sons of Zoheir warmly profess their friendship for the hero.

ANTAR UNDERTAKES ANOTHER ENTERPRISE FOR ABLA'S SAKE.

Thus, once more, every obstacle to Antar's marriage appears to be removed; but in reality his treacherous uncle is as much averse as ever to his union with Abla, and he soon devises another stratagem to bring about the hero's death. Artfully instructed by her father, Abla demands of Antar that at her marriage she should be as exalted as was Jaida, the daughter of Zahir: when she was married to her cousin Khalid, the son of Moharib, the bridle of her camel was held by the daughter of Moawiyah, son of Nizal. The hero boldly promises that at Abla's marriage Jaida herself shall hold her bridle, with Khalid's head slung round her neck. To this wild proposal the father of Abla pretends opposition; but, as he had anticipated, Antar is resolute; and that same night the hero, eager to gratify the wishes of his darling Abla, set out on his perilous enterprise, exclaiming:

I TRAVERSE the wastes, and the night is gloomy: I stray over the wilds, and the sands are parching; I desire no other companion but the sword, whether, on the day of horrors, the foe be few or numerous.

Ye beasts of the desert! beware of the warrior; for when he brandishes his scimitar, caution avails not.

Accompany me: ye will behold prostrate carcasses, and the birds darting at them as they hover and look on.

Now that I am going in quest of him, no eternity is there for Khalid.

No, no; let Jaida no longer boast;--short will be the happiness of their country--soon will the tiger come!

O Abla! may the riches that come for thee rejoice thee, when Fortune casts me among thy enemies!

O thou, who, with one glance of the eye, hast exposed my life to deadly arrows, whose wounds are frightful--it is well; for thy embrace is an unadulterated paradise, and the flames of separation from thee cannot be endured.

O Mount Saadi! may showers from the rain-cloud ever moisten thee, and may the dew ever refresh thy lands!

How many nights have I travelled in thy society, and lived in happiness, unalloyed by pain, with the damsel who circles the goblets, and whose form shines among them like the flame of wine!

The maiden who passes them round is of the daughters of Arabia, elegantly formed, and Paradise is in her eye.

If I live, it is she whom I will ever remember: if I die, a night in death with her will be existence!

STORY OF JAIDA AND KHALID.

Moharib and Zahir, the fathers respectively of Khalid and Jaida, were brothers. Moharib was chief of the tribe of Zebeed, and Zahir was his counsellor. The brothers quarrelled, and Zahir struck his tents, and cast his lot with the kindred tribe of Saad. Zahir's wife becoming pregnant, he said to her that if a son were born, he would be most welcome; but if a girl, then she was to conceal the fact, and let it appear to the world that they had a male child, in order that his brother should not exult over him. In due course a daughter was born, and was called, in private, Jaida, but Jooder in public, that it might appear she was a boy. About the same time Moharib had a son born to him, whom he called Khalid. The daughter of Zahir was brought up as a boy, and taught to ride on horseback; and soon she became famous in all the exercises befitting a noble warrior--accompanying her father to battle, in which she ever took a prominent part. Khalid was also one of the most illustrious horsemen of the age, universally acknowledged as an intrepid warrior and a valiant hero.

The fame of his cousin Jooder (Jaida) having reached him, Khalid, after his father's death, visited his uncle, and spent ten days in jousting with the horsemen of the family. Jaida became deeply enamoured of him, and her mother, on learning this, revealed the secret of her sex to Khalid's mother, and suggested that their children should be united in marriage. But when Khalid was told by his mother that his cousin was a woman, he was greatly chagrined, slighted her love for him, and hastened back to his own tribe.

Jaida, enraged at finding herself thus scorned, resolved to be revenged on her cousin, and disguising herself, she set out for the land of Zebeed. Arrived there, she entered a tent of public entertainment, close-vizored, like a horseman of Hejaz. After proving her superiority over the best horsemen in the course, she encountered Khalid for three days in

[185]

succession, without either of them obtaining any advantage; when she discovered herself to her cousin, whose hatred was now suddenly converted into love. But Jaida rejected him, and returned home.

Khalid hastened to his uncle and demanded Jaida in marriage. His cousin at length consents, on condition that he provide for slaughter at her wedding-feast a thousand camels belonging to Gheshm, son of Malik, surnamed the Brandisher of Spears. These Khalid procured by plundering the tribe of Aamir; but on his return, Jaida imposed a further condition--that her camel should be led by the captive daughter of a prince. Khalid again set out with his horsemen, and, assailing the family tribe of Moawiyah, son of Nizal, took captive his daughter Amimah; and his marriage with Jaida took place immediately after his return; when the daughter of Moawiyah held the bridle of her camel, "and the glory of Jaida was exalted among women and among men."

ANTAR IN THE LAND OF ZEBEED.

On reaching the country of the Zebeedians, Antar finds Khalid absent on a plundering expedition, but he is met by Jaida on horseback, armed as a knight. The warlike lady boldly encounters Antar: she is vanquished, and taken prisoner. Zoheir having summoned his warriors and set out to join Antar, the father of Abla avails himself of this opportunity of again quitting the tribe, and accordingly Malik emigrates with his family, and accompanied by Rebia, to the tribe of Aamir. But here his usual ill-fortune follows him; for the Aamirites are presently attacked by Khalid and his warriors, and Malik and Rebia are taken captive. Returning home, Khalid meets the Absians, and a desperate battle ensues, with great slaughter on both sides. During the following night Antar and Khalid keep watch over their respective tribes: the two chiefs meet; Khalid is slain by the all-conquering hero, and Shiboob cuts off his head as a trophy to grace Abla's wedding. Meantime a general battle takes place, in which the Absians are completely victorious. After the horsemen of Abs had returned from pursuing the enemy and collected the spoil, Antar inquired for Jaida, but she had escaped; Malik and his daughter too were nowhere to be found; and the hero passed a sleepless night, lamenting the loss, once more, of his darling Abla.

At daybreak the noble Absian warriors set out for home, and as they drew near the tents of their tribe, "high and low came out to meet them, and it was a grand day for them all." When friends had greeted friends, all retired to their tents; but Antar remained gazing sorrowfully upon the abandoned and ruined dwelling of Abla; and leaning on his spear, in a voice expressive of his poignant grief, he recited these verses, which form the opening of his famous Moallacah:

HAVE the poets left aught to be repaired in song? Canst thou recollect the abode of thy love, after long meditation?

[186]

O dwelling of my Abla! Speak to me from Jiwa! Hail to thee, dwelling of my Abla! secure and safe be thou!

ADDRESS TO THE TURTLE-DOVE.

Soon after his return from the land of Zebeed, Antar was present at a feast, given by the tribe of Fazarah to the Absians, in a spacious meadow, abounding in springs and fountains, trees and flowers. The wine cups went merrily round, and beautiful maidens sang the most enchanting melodies. But Antar thought only of his lost darling; and going out of the tent, he heard the melancholy voice of the turtle-dove, and thus he expressed his feelings:

O BIRD of the tamarisk! thou hast rendered my sorrows more poignant--thou hast redoubled my griefs.

O bird of the tamarisk! if thou invokest an absent friend for whom thou art mourning-- even then, O Bird, is thy affliction like the distress I also feel?

Augment my sorrows and my lamentations; aid me to weep till thou seest wonders from the discharge of my eyelids!

Weep, too, from the excesses that I endure;--fear not--only guard the trees from the breath of my burning sighs.

Quit me not till I die of love--the victim of passion, of absence, and separation!

Fly!--perhaps in the Hejaz thou mayst see some one riding from Aalij to Nomani, wandering with a damsel, she traversing wilds, and drowned in tears, anxious for her native land.

May God inspire thee, O Dove! when thou truly seest her loaded camels.

Announce my death: say, thou hast left him stretched on the earth, and that his tears are exhausted, but that he weeps in blood.

Should the breeze ask thee whence thou art, say: He is deprived of his heart and stupefied; he is in a strange land, weeping for our departure; for the God of heaven has struck him with affliction on account of his beloved.

He is lying down like a tender bird, that vultures and eagles have bereft of its young; that grieves in unceasing plaints, whilst its offspring are scattered over the plain and the desert.

[187]

THE MATRIMONIAL SCHEMES OF ABLA'S FATHER AGAIN COME TO NAUGHT.

Shiboob having been despatched by the sorrowing hero to obtain tidings of Abla, after many days he returns with a message of love from her to Antar; but also with the unpleasant intelligence that her father, now dwelling in the tribe of Shiban, had promised Abla in marriage to Bostam, the son of Prince Kais, on condition that he brought him Antar's head as her dowry.

Bostam accordingly sets out for the land of Abs, meets Antar, and is vanquished in combat with the hero. Shiboob comes to report the capture of all the women of Shiban by the tribe of Temeen. Bostam offers his assistance in rescuing Abla; Antar releases him; and together they proceed to take vengeance on the despoilers. Again the hero rescues Abla from captivity; and as he gazed upon her, bathed in tears of joy, thus he addressed his darling:

HAIL! I greet thee, branch of the tamarisk!--welcome to the new moon of the desert and the city!

O Abla! thy form during my absence was ever in the core of my heart and my eye.

Since thou hast been absent, all my joys have been absent--all my pleasures closed; and my blood-shot eyes have passed the nights in sleeplessness:

Never has slumber visited me since I quitted thy form.

O thou full moon of obscurity, in truth, thou face of the moon itself! were I to complain of what I have endured in sorrow, I should fail to describe--by the truth of the Shrine and the Stone 1--what I suffered in the horrors of my journey, and the jealousies I have been subject to from my relations.

How many horsemen, whom I have encountered in the barren waste, have been laid low on the earth, and in the tombs!

Keshaab, son of Ghayath, lies prostrate--on the day of horrors felled by my Indian blade!

These shall ever be my deeds with the foe as long as the sun shines, and as long as the morning star glitters at the dawn.

I am the son of Shedad, and the lion to whom every one that dwells in the desert or in towns bows in submission.

His uncle Malik also wept (crocodile's tears), and once more renewed to him his promise of Abla's hand. The crafty old fellow, however, persuades Antar to return home, on a vain errand, and as soon as he is gone, again flees with his daughter but Antar gets word of

[188]

this, and pursues him. Malik places himself and his family under the protection of King Amru, of Kendeh, and espouses Abla to Mas-hil, the king's nephew.

SHIBOOB IN MASQUERADE AT THE TENTS OF KENDEH.

Shortly before the appointed day of Abla's bridal, Antar arrived in the neighbourhood of the tribe. Shiboob disguised himself as a woman, and, with a water-bag slung over his shoulders, sought the tents of Kendeh.

"He perceived the tents destitute of horsemen, for they were gone out to the plain, and the families were occupied in festivities. The unmarried girls were playing about, and beating the cymbals and musical instruments, and the slaves were brandishing their swords and shields, and their countenances appeared glistening with joy. When Shiboob saw this, he advanced towards them, and mixing with them, looked towards a tent, on the outside of which was a brilliant illumination of lamps and candles. Being convinced that this must be the nuptial pavilion, he made a great noise, and began to play, and mingled with the women and slave-girls, and danced till he attracted the attention of all present, and they all crowded round him, staring at him whilst he sang, for he knew his voice would reach Abla:

FAWN of the huntsman, thy captor is come: say not he is not come; to! here he is-- certain are all thy hopes!--rejoice in the aid of the sword of thy hero!

Understand the tale I tell thee: how long wilt thou delay? Joy is now descending on thy home, and will ever endure, summer and winter.

"Now Abla was at that moment listening to the music from the tent. She signified her wish to sing and play with the other damsels, and thus addressed Shiboob:

O WANDERER of the desert, dancer of the tent!--the lion is the noble animal that affords refuge after excess of pain--this is indeed a period of my joy in thee!

All my sorrows and griefs have vanished. My joy depends on thee, O Chief! Approach, for I am here as one dead!

"When Shiboob heard these words, he pretended being tired, and sat down near the tent. Just at that time Abla also appeared and looked at him, and, as he was dressed in woman's clothes--'This damsel cannot be a Kendeyan maid,' she said: 'she must be a damsel of Shedad's." Then went pit-a-pat Shiboob's heart; but he turned towards her, and calmed her mind, and uncovered his face. She recognised him. 'O Shiboob!' said she, 'where is my cousin Antar?'--'Here he is,' replied Shiboob, 'hard by; and with him his friend Oorwah, and a hundred horsemen. We arrived here last night, and I am come to procure intelligence of you: I shall return and inform him.'--'Shiboob,' said she, 'there are still three days for the marriage with Mas-hil, son of Tarak; but let that rather be the means of

[189]

separation. Return immediately and tell him my situation; but let him not think of assaulting the tribe; he must lie in wait for me till I set out: then let him rush forth, and slay all that are with me. Do you seize the bridle of my camel, and we will return to our native land. All--all must taste of death; bid Antar not to spare even my father.'

"Shiboob, having heard this, returned to Antar, and related to him all that Abla had told him."

Antar forms his plans accordingly; and, waylaying the bridal party, slays Mas-hil, and seizes his uncle Malik. The Kendeyans are attacked by Bostam, and the Absians, led by Zoheir's sons, arrive to the aid of Antar. The Princes reproach Antar for leaving them, and abuse his uncle for his infamous conduct. Antar magnanimously offers to make no demand upon his uncle, if he will go back to the land of Abs with his daughter; but he must marry her to no one else. Malik is thus compelled to return with Abla to his own tribe; while Antar determines to reside for some time with his friend Bostam in Shiban. But his passion for the daughter of Malik soon sends him forth again in quest of her, and as he traversed the wastes he recited:

WHEN the zephyr gently blows, its breath relieves the sickened heart, and brings me news of the damsel and of those I love, who are travelling on their journey.

Regardless are they of whom they have left behind, cast down and dead in the land of love;--one who has quitted their country, and roams anxious about them, wheresoever they drive their baggage-camels.

Indeed, O Abla! they have betrayed my vows;--it is thy father that is ungrateful for favours.

I have borne sorrows and absence patiently, even in my weak state; and I have defied the railers.

I am accustomed to grief, so that my body, were it to lose its pains, would sigh after its emaciated state.

The raven taunts it, as if it had been one that had destroyed its plundered young:

It weeps, and the torrents of my tears sympathise with it;--it sighs, and my woes cruelly increase;--it passes the night in anguish for the loss of its mate, for whose absence it mourns the live-long night.

I said to it: Thou hast wounded the inmost recesses of my heart: ever is thy grief a mental disease.

I have shed tears from my eyes, and my native home and country excite all my interest.

[190]

Absence has left me no soul, no body, in which, miserable as I am, I can live.

Wert thou to take off the armour from it, thou wouldst see beneath it only a ruined vestige; and on those worn-out remains is a coffin-sword, whose edge would notch the bright-polished scimitar.

I am so accustomed to the calamities of Fortune, that all their vastness appears but trifling to me.

Antar finds his uncle lying in the desert, desperately wounded, his party having been attacked by Anis, son of Madraka, the Kitaamite, and Abla and her brother taken prisoners. He pursues this chief, rescues Abla and Amru, and returns to the land of Abs with his uncle's family.

ATTEMPTED MURDER OF ABLA.

A fresh plot is formed by Rebia, the brother of Amarah, to thwart Antar's marriage. Rebia employs a female slave to decoy Abla to the lake, one evening, on pretence of her meeting with Antar, when she is carried off, and concealed in the land of Shiban. The slave-girl soon afterwards discovers the iniquitous affair, and Rebia is compelled to leave the tribe. He proceeds to Shiban, where he finds Mooferrij, the friend who had charge of Abla, in terror lest Antar should come to know of his share in the transaction. They determine to have Abla murdered and buried in the sand-hills, so as to leave no trace of her. A slave, named Basharah, accordingly carries Abla into the desert, and is about to deal her a fatal blow with his poniard, when a man suddenly pounces upon him, strikes him with a dagger between the shoulders, and the assassin falls to the earth, bathed in blood.

The deliverer of Abla was Shiboob, who chanced to pass that way in quest of her. Basharah, however, was not killed, though badly hurt. He disclosed the chief actors in the murderous plot, and, with Shiboob's consent, he placed Abla under the care of his own mother, living at a distant place; and there she remained until Antar found an opportunity of exposing Rebia's guilt to the King.

THE HERO QUITS HIS TRIBE.

But at length Antar's love for Abla is the cause of so many dissensions in the tribe that King Zoheir requests him to depart. The noble hero, with his father and uncles, accordingly quits the land of Abs. After plundering the tribe of Fazarah, the warriors of Carad, led by Antar, invade the land of Shiban; and this was the hero's spirited war-song, before assailing Mooferrij, who had concealed Abla from him, and whom he took prisoner:

THE morning of thrusts in the field of battle (where wine is not put round in glasses) is dearer to me than the varied amusements with the cup, and the ewer, and the flowers;--

My wine is indeed that which gushes about the spear's point, when the war-steeds trample.

I am the slave of whom it shall be reported that I encountered a thousand free-born heroes: my heart was created harder than steel; how, then, can I fear sword or spear?

I have met the chargers, and I cared not: I am raised above Arcturus, and the Lyre, or the Eagle: when the warrior beholds me, he avoids me, his courage fails, and he flies.

Ye have indulged a thought, ye people of Shiban, but my horse and my perseverance have thwarted your imagination.

Ask Rebia of me, when he came against me with the chiefs of Beder:

I took their chiefs prisoners, and only quitted them when I had dispersed them over every desert.

Here, now, again I come forth, and in you will I appease my heart, and allay my bosom:

I will seize the property of Abla with my sword, and the Lord of the Balcony shall acknowledge my power.

NUMAN, KING OF HIRAH, MAKES WAR AGAINST KING ZOHEIR--THE HERO SAVES HIS COUNTRY.

King Zoheir had soon cause to wish for the presence of the champion of Abs and Adnan. Having refused to give his daughter in marriage to Numan, King of Hirah, the latter sends his brother, Prince Aswad, with a large army to lay waste the land of Abs; and Antar patriotically resolves to assist his sovereign and old friend in repelling the invaders. The army of Prince Aswad was destroyed by a stratagem of Shiboob, who contrived to obtain access to their water-bags, and, cutting them open, allowed all the water to escape. Weakened by thirst, they were easily vanquished by a very small force of Absians, and, among others, Prince Aswad was taken prisoner.

Meanwhile the renowned female warrior, Jaida, who had been captured by Antar and afterwards escaped, set out from her own country to take vengeance on the hero for the death of Khalid. She did not meet Antar, however, but, attacking a party of Absians, she took Malik and Abla prisoners; then she went to Irak, and delivered them to Numan, who declared that he would hang Abla beside Antar, and would not leave a single Absian alive. But when he heard of Antar's great victory over his brother's army, he despatched a satrap to the hero, offering to exchange Abla and the other Absian women for Prince

Aswad and his companions. The royal messenger returned with the answer, that Abla and all her jewels must be restored before he would release Prince Aswad; and Numan, hearing from his satrap a fearful account of Antar's exploits and prodigious courage, at once complied with the hero's demand. As soon as Abla and her father were restored to their tribe, Antar proceeded to release his prisoners, among whom was Maadi Kereb, a cousin of Jaida.

"Having now entered the mountains, Antar ordered Shiboob to set at liberty Prince Aswad and his people. And Shiboob released them. But Antar cut off Maadi Kereb's hair with his own hand, saying: 'O Maadi Kereb, I have cut off your hair in revenge for Jaida's insults towards my cousin Abla'; and he ordered the slaves and attendants to turn out the prisoners bare-footed, and naked, and bareheaded. And as they were executing Antar's commands,--'Art thou not ashamed, O son of Shedad,' cried Aswad, 'to drive us away in this condition? We have not a horse to ride on! We have nothing to eat or drink!'--'By the faith of an Arab,' said Antar, 'reproach me not for my conduct towards any one of you; for you are all going to assemble in a body against me, and you will return a second time to fight me, and the horses I should give you, verily I shall have to fight you for them. As to eatables, you will find on your way green weeds that you may graze on, and drink out of the puddles; but we at all events are a tribe entrenched within the mountains, and in the day of battle a small supply will feed us. Ay, and most of you say of me that Antar is a black slave and a bastard;--these are the expressions you and others make use of towards me, and would do so were I to release you a thousand times: my best plan would be to kill you all at once--thank God you are alive.'--'Do not act thus, O Aboolfawaris,' said Aswad; 'for indeed I cannot walk on foot, no, not a quarter of a mile; so do give me something to carry me, or put me instantly to death, and deliver me from this ignominy.'--'Hola, Ebe Reah!' said Antar to Shiboob, 'bring here a she-camel; let him mount it and quit my presence, or I shall never be able to keep my sword off his neck.' So Shiboob ran off, and, with his usual ingenuity and sagacity, he chose out a she-camel, foundered and quite worn out--horn lame and blind--weasy and broken-winded--grunting, loose-lipped, and toothless--crop-eared and spavined. When it was presented to the Prince his soul was most indignant.--'Come, Prince,' cried Shiboob, 'mount, whilst I hold the bridle, for I am terribly afraid she will fly away; for indeed she is one of that celebrated breed of Asafeer camels!'--'May God curse the bowels that bore thee!' cried the Prince; 'away with it, for I want it not'; and he rushed out from the mountains, blaspheming the fire."

Nushirvan, King of Persia, hearing of Antar's exploits against his vassal, Numan, of Hirah, sends his satrap, Wirdishan, with a large army, to humble the champion of Abs. A fearful battle takes place between the Persians and the Absians, in the Valley of Torrents, in which Wirdishan (like his renowned predecessor, Khosrewan) is slain by the irresistible Antar, and the Persians are completely routed.

The hero's fair enemy, Jaida, still burning to avenge the death of her husband, Khalid, again takes the field at the head of the warriors of Zebeed; and having brought them face to face with the Absians, thus she addressed them:

[193]

O BY my tribe! tears have festered my cheeks, and in the greatness of my agony sleep has abandoned me.

These mourning garments have debilitated my energies, and sickness has weakened my bones and my skin;

For I had a hero whom a black slave by his oppression and violence made to drink of death:

The full moon indeed fell to the earth when the arrow was aimed at him, sped from the hand of the slave.

Now he is gone, I am left to my afflictions and griefs, and I endure my distresses in solitude. The sword mourns him, now he is gone, and in the sheath it bewails its condition.

O thou dead!--mourners have wept him in the mountains of Fala and the land of Nejd!

He was like a branch in form--the revolutions of Fortune cut him off--alas! how cut him off!

O by my tribe! who will assuage my sorrows, and will regard his engagements with me, now Khalid is gone?

When she had finished, "the tribe of Zebeed sent forth one general shout that made the mountains tremble--they remembered the death of their chief Khalid--they poured down upon Antar, uncovering their heads, and lightening their garments, to the number of five thousand, and about two thousand of the tribes of Lakhm and Juzam followed them; they all attacked, led by Maadi Kereb, bellowing like a lion." But Antar, with only three hundred horsemen, resolutely received their attack, and defeated the whole seven thousand--Jaida and Maadi Kereb flying for their lives.

King Numan, having sent another army against Abs, which was driven back by the noble Antar and his lion-warriors, now became anxious for peace, and renewed his proposal for the hand of Zoheir's daughter. Antar, grateful to Numan for having released his father Shedad, who had fallen into his power, strongly advised Zoheir to consent, and peace was proclaimed, and Numan duly married to Zoheir's daughter.

But Prince Aswad misrepresents his brother Numan's conduct in the late war to Nushirvan, who deposes him, confers his kingdom on Aswad, and sends his son Khodawend with fifty thousand Persians to destroy the Absians. At the same time the chief Hijar and the warriors of Kendeh advance to lay waste their lands. Antar obtains information of their movements from the ubiquitous Shiboob, and, putting himself at the head of three thousand horsemen of Abs (leaving Prince Cais with a party to protect the women and property of the tribe in the mountains), goes forth to give the enemy a warm reception. The noble hero's reflections on the march found expression in these verses:--

OUR country is laid waste, and our lands despoiled: our homes are ravaged, and our plains are devastated!

Let us halt; let us mourn for them: for there is no friend in that quarter, and the country is ruined.

Fate has fallen upon our companions, and they are dispersed as if they had never alighted at their tents.

In sportive merriment they tucked up the garments of joy, and their spears were spread along their tents.

The wand of happiness was waving over us, as if Fortune had been favourable, and our enemies thought not of us.

O Abla! my heart is rent with anguish on thy account: my patience is fled to the wastes!

O Hijar!--hey! I will teach thee my station: thou shalt not dare to fight me, disgraced as thou art!

Hast thou forgotten in the Vale of Torrents the deeds of my valour, and how I overthrew the armies, undaunted as they were?

I precipitated them with the thrust, and I abandoned them and their carcasses to be trampled on by the wild beasts!

Shall I not behold thee in anguish to-morrow?--ay!--thou shalt not escape from me to the arms of thy beloved!

I will leave the brutes of the desert to stamp over thee, and the eagles and the ghouls shall mangle thee!

I am Antar, the most valiant of knights--ay, of them all; and every warrior can prove my words.

If you have a milch-camel, milk her; for thou knowest not to whom her young may belong.

Antar takes Hijar prisoner, and his little army is victorious. But now Khodawend has come with his legions, and in the battles between the Persians and Absians, Antar performs many marvellous exploits. Khodawend, thinking the Absians would willingly surrender on almost any terms, causes his vizier to write a letter to King Zoheir, offering peace if he would give up to him that vile slave Antar. This letter he sends by a satrap, escorted by twenty Persian horsemen, and accompanied by an interpreter called Ocab, the son of Terjem. On reaching the Absian encampment, it chanced that only Antar and another chief were mounted.

"They were in conversation when the satrap came up to them; he did not salute them, but asked for King Zoheir. 'He inquires for King Zoheir,' said the interpreter, 'for he has a letter from Khodawend for him.'--'We, O Arab,' said Antar, 'have read your letter before its arrival: in it your Prince orders us to surrender ourselves without fighting.--Pull that satrap off the back of his horse,' said he to Shiboob; 'ay, and the rest, too: seize all their property; and if any one dares to struggle with you, treat him thus,'--and at the word he extended his arm, and pierced the satrap through the chest, forcing the spear out quivering through his back, and he hurled him down dead. When his comrades saw what Antar had done, they cried out for quarter, and surrendered themselves to Shiboob, who bound them fast by the shoulders. As to the interpreter, he shuddered. 'May God requite you well,' said he; 'for you have answered us before even reading the letter! If this indeed is the honorary robe for a satrap, let it not be so for an interpreter; for I have children and a family, and I am but a poor fellow. I only followed these Persians but with the prospect of gaining some miserable trifle. I never calculated on being hung; and my children when I am gone will remain orphans.' So he wept and groaned, thus expressing himself:

O KNIGHT of the horses of warriors that overthrow; their lion, resembling the roaring ocean!

By your awful appearance you have disgraced heroes, and reduced them to despair.

As soon as the Persian sees you he is dishonoured: if they approach you, and extend their spears against your glory, they must retreat, or there is no security.

Have compassion, then, on your victim, a person of little worth, whose family will be in misery when he is gone!

Not the thrust of the spear or battle is among my qualifications;--I profess no fighting--I have no cleaving scimitar.

My name is Ocab: but indeed I am no fighting man; and the sword in the palm of my hand only chases pelicans.

"Antar laughed at Ocab's verses, and let him go. 'Return to your family,' said he, 'and go no more to the Persian, or you will be in danger; for when they see you safe they will accuse you, and perhaps put you to death.'--'You are very right, my lord,' said he; 'by the faith of an Arab, had I known these Persians would have been thus worsted I would not have quitted you; and probably I might have managed to secure some of their goods, and return with it to my family.'--'Sheikh,' said Antar's companion, 'this business has failed; but come, take the spoils of this satrap, and return to your family, and pass not your evening a dead man.'--'Ay, my lord,' said Ocab, 'he is a wise fellow who returns safe to his friends.'--So he ran up to the satrap and despoiled him. Round his waist was a girdle and a sword, and when Ocab saw all that wealth he was bewildered; and having completely rifled him,--'O my lord,' said he to Antar, 'I will never separate from you again. I wish you would present me to your king, that I may kiss his hand and offer him my services: then indeed I will for ever cleave to your party, and whenever you slay a satrap I will plunder him.' Antar laughed heartily."

A battle of seven days' duration ensued, which, despite of the heroic exertions of Antar, ended in the discomfiture of the Absians, who, however, still continued to contend with the enemy among the sand-hills and the defiles. Antar himself was wounded in three places, but his spirit remained undaunted, albeit afflictions were multiplied around him. At this crisis King Numan obtains an interview with Khodawend, and clears himself of the false charges brought against him by his brother: Aswad is degraded; Numan restored to power; and peace being proclaimed between the belligerents, the Absians return in joy to their homes. Antar and a select number of his comrades accompany King Numan to Hirah, where they are splendidly entertained for some time; and before they return to their own country, Chosroes Nushirvan, having heard, from his son Khodawend, how the Absians had been saved by Antar's indomitable prowess, sends the hero a robe of honour and many other rich presents, in token of his renewed friendship.

PRINCE HARITH IN LOVE.

Prince Harith, one of Zoheir's sons, while hunting, one day chanced to stray into a valley, at some distance from the land of Shurebah. There he saw a party of women of the tribe of Zohran, and conspicuous among them was the chief's beautiful daughter, Labna. They fell in love with each other at first sight. Shiboob contrived to carry off the damsel to her lover; but her father, breathing vengeance, pursued them, with his warriors. Harith was taken prisoner, but was soon afterwards released by Shiboob, who, however, in his turn, was captured. At this juncture, Antar, returning from Hirah, reached the place, and rescued his brother; and Labna and Harith were restored to each other. The hero then continued his journey home; and as his passion for Abla burst upon him, thus he recited:

OH! is it the fragrance of musk, or is it itr?

Is it a voice, or the breeze, warbling over the desert, that sings of her?

Is it a flash of lightning? or is it her teeth in the wastes, resembling the full moon when it rises?

Is it the branch of the tamarisk, that sweetly waves in the wilds?

Is it the stem of the spear, or her form?

[197]

Is it the narcissus of the gardens, endued with visual powers, or her cheek, like the untouched apple?

I rave through love of her; but let my railers see the torrents of my tears, to which there is no end!

O Abla! my heart for love of thee suffers tortures: this frequent separation and these echoes fill me with grief.

O Abla! fear not thy enemies; for against the destiny of God there is no opposition.

KING ZOHEIR AND HIS BROTHER, ASYED.

While Prince Harith was absent and in trouble on account of his love-affair, King Zoheir went to meet his brother Asyed, "a learned man in that age of ignorance, who generally passed his time at the Sacred Shrine and the Zemzem. He was full of virtue and liberality, loving justice and equity, and detesting violence and oppression." Asyed visited the tribe of Abs once every year, and on this occasion Zoheir, accompanied by three hundred horsemen, met him, by appointment, at a place called the Valley of 'tamarisks. When the brothers had affectionately greeted each other, Asyed suddenly exclaimed, in a voice choked with emotion:

O TREES of the tamarisk! where do ye behold them? Do the people of my vows dwell in your neighbourhood?

I look all around, but the hand of ravage has destroyed them; yet never have I broken my former protestations--I have not betrayed them.

My vows were made to one like the full moon, resembling the branches and boughs of the tamarisk;--

But I am alone and solitary, though once we met, and here, now they are gone, are only the owl and the raven!

O trees of the tamarisk! whither are they gone? They are gone, and in my heart passion has left a burning flame!

If ye ever, after being watered, complain of drought, my tears to-day shall form a lake around you!

The King was not a little surprised to hear his grave and learned brother thus refer, apparently, to some secret love-episode of his youth, and earnestly desiring to know the particulars, Asyed thereupon related the following tale:--

[198]

"Know, then, my brother, that the year our father, King Jazeema, made his pilgrimage, I accompanied him; and when our pilgrimage was expired, as we were on our way home, we happened to pass by this place, in which I saw a vast quantity of wild beasts and deer. My father rode on and went home, but I remained for the sake of the chase. Thus occupied, I stayed till the meridian heat overpowered me, and the sultry air became so excessive, I returned also, seeking the track of my father. I chanced to pass by this tree, and when I reached it, I saw a very old sheikh beneath it, and with him an immense quantity of camels, and also his daughter, who was tending them at the pasture--she was the most beautiful and most elegant of forms; and as soon as I came up to him I saluted him. 'What do you want, young man?' said he.--I only said, 'Will you accept of a guest when he comes?'--'Welcome, to me,' said he, 'in winter and in summer. But, young man, every one, according to his means.'

"On hearing this, I resolved on alighting at the lake, in order to drink, and water my horse. But the sheikh prevented me, and called out to his daughter, who brought me some fresh camel's milk and gave me to drink, and also watered my horse. I remarked the beauty of the maiden, and I perceived her moving in the plains of loveliness. Her father, too, observing the symmetry of my horse, and my rich garments, brought me some victuals. 'Excuse my scanty offering,' said he, 'for I am a poor man, and the liberal pardon, when they see the apology is sincere.'--'O Sheikh!' said I, 'this is the greatest charity; but if you will accede to my wishes, I would request you to accept my proposal, and gratify my desire with regard to your daughter, and you shall then go with me to my tribe. I am anxious you would receive me as her husband, and I will take you to my land and family; speak to me and bestow her. By Him who has created her and fashioned her,' I added, 'take all I have about me as part of her marriage dower'; and I took off my sword-belt and my horse-trappings, which were all of gold.

"The sheikh at the sight of this was much surprised and delighted, and came towards me without hesitation, and, giving me his hand for the marriage, drove away the camels and cattle, and went to his own dwelling, and I accompanied him; and on our arrival he slaughtered all the sheep he possessed, and some she-camels, and rejoiced in me as no one ever rejoiced before, and married his daughter to me that night. I tarried with them three days, and afterwards I informed them who I was. I stayed some time longer, and quitted them, bearing in my heart the greatest attachment for them, and intending to return to them with abundant wealth.

"Having reached home and joined my family, I despatched a slave to conduct my wife to me, and sent with him a great quantity of camels and sheep to this valley and desert. I remained anxiously expecting them, till my slave returned in despair, and brought back all my property. I asked him what was the matter. 'I have seen no one there, my lord,' said he. I stayed some time quiet, and despatched emissaries to all the Arab tribes, and expended amongst them much gold and silver, but I never could obtain any intelligence of her. And even now, my brother, I bear her in my memory. It was on her account I attached myself to Mecca and the Sacred Shrine, till I this day beheld these remembrances of her, and now all my sorrows come upon me anew; and whilst I

[199]

meditated on the past, I was anxious that you should come with me to this spot, that I might renew the vows made so many years ago."

Asyed having thus ended the recital of his pathetic story, the King caused the slaves to spread carpets beneath the tamarisk trees, and, the hunters presently returning with abundance of hares and deer, a sumptuous feast was quickly prepared. They passed the night in the same spot, but at break of day the party were surprised and taken prisoners by a troop of horsemen of Cahtan, led by a young chief called Nazih, who was returning in triumph to his own tribe, with his distinguished captives, when he was met by Antar. The noble champion of Abs impetuously assailed Nazih, and unhorsed him. Shiboob bound him securely, and then hastened to release the King and his brother. Antar proposed to put Nazih and his companions to death; and proceeding to strip off the young chief's clothes, he discovered on his wrist a bracelet of cornelian, on which were engraved images of Lat and Uzza. Asyed recognises the trinket as being identical with one which he had given to his bride in the Valley of Tamarisks: he questions the young chief regarding his parentage, and discovers in Nazih his own son. Ultimately Asyed has the felicity of being re-united to his long-lost bride.

DEATH OF PRINCE SHAS AND KING ZOHEIR.

About this time Prince Shas, while journeying through the land of Aamir, was foully murdered by a huntsman, called Thalaba. The Prince's attendant escaped to carry the tidings to King Zoheir, who immediately placed himself at the head of his warriors, and set out to avenge his son's death. Khalid, the chief of the tribe, being absent in Irak, the Aamirites feared to oppose the Absians, and offered to pay King Zoheir ten times the usual price of blood. The King refused to compound with them for the murder of his son, but after assailing the tribe, he was duped into granting a truce, of which the Aamirites availed themselves to occupy a strong position in the mountains, where they continued in safety during the few days that remained before the sacred month of Rejeb, when war ceased among the Arabs. Hostilities are renewed as soon as the sacred month is past; and Khalid, having in the interim returned from Irak, encounters King Zoheir, who is slain by a foul stroke from Jandah, one of Khalid's followers; and the Absians, being discomfited, return to their own land.

KING CAIS AVENGES HIS FATHER'S DEATH.

Cais, the eldest surviving son of King Zoheir, having acceded to the supreme power, goes forth with his warriors to avenge the death of his father. But, acting on the advice of Antar's enemies, he leaves the hero behind. The Absians attack the tribe of Aamir, and are defeated. King Cais then sends a letter to Antar, begging him to come to their assistance. Meantime a fierce combat takes place between the young chief Nazih, on the part of the Absians, and Harith the son of Zalim, a renegade knight, on the part of the Aamirites. Just as Nazih is about to succumb to his antagonist, a strange knight makes his appearance, mounted on a meagre, foundered horse, and poorly armed. This Bedouin wanderer assails Harith and takes him prisoner; then he overcomes Jandah--who gave Zoheir his death-blow; and King Cais is the first to recognise in the person of the uncouth champion Antar himself. The King strikes off the head of Jandah with the assassin's own sword. After a period of repose, the Absians again made war upon the Aamirites, who were ultimately vanquished.

ABLA'S FATHER AND BROTHER AGAIN RESCUED BY ANTAR.

Notwithstanding the great respect entertained for Antar by King Cais and the noble warriors of Abs, his uncle Malik was yet far from being reconciled to his proposed union with Abla. On one occasion the ungrateful wretch planned a murderous attack upon Antar by a party of the tribe of Fazarah, while the hero was carousing with himself in his own tent. But Antar, having been warned of the plot by Abla's maid, defeated his uncle's inhospitable designs. Enraged at his failure, and perhaps also a little ashamed, Malik resolves again to emigrate; but this time Abla firmly refuses to accompany her father and brother, and these two worthies have no help but to leave Abla behind, in the care of Shedad, the father of Antar.

A few days after Malik and his son had quitted the tribe, Antar determined to go in quest of them, and induce them to return. Accompanied by Shiboob and two trusty comrades, he sets out accordingly; and learning that Malik and Amru are prisoners of Ramih, chief of the tribe of Jibhan, they proceed thither with all haste. When they reached the tents of Ramih, Shiboob and Antar disguised themselves, and, each carrying a bundle of wood on his head, they approached the dwelling of the chief.

"It was almost dark when they entered the tents, through which they continued to pass, attentively observing everything, till they came to the tents of Ramih, where they saw Malik and his son, in extreme misery, tied up with the dogs. 'Behold your uncle,' said Shiboob; 'let your grief be now assuaged.' Antar threw his bundle of wood off his head, and Shiboob did the same; but they did not stop till Ramih, who was the chief of the Jibhanians, came out, attended by a troop of slaves, who laid out a sofa for him to sit on. He then began to talk to his shepherds, who were parading before him his horses and his cattle; and he inquired of them about the pastures and the grain.

"'O my lord,' said one of the slaves, 'I beheld a most extraordinary sight this day: for whilst I was in the Valley of Meadows, tending the flocks, I cane upon the high road, where, behold! was a knight hunting the fawns. He was mounted on a black steed, and in front of the knight was a man on foot, girded with an Arabian bow, and round his waist was a quiver full of arrows, and both were in pursuit of a fawn, endeavouring to catch it. I stopped to look at them, when, to! the man on foot outstripped the knight. He seized the fawn by the left horn, and the knight, catching it by its right horn and gazing in its face, thus in poetry exclaimed:

DEPART, and, ever in the protection of God, may no evil e'er overtake thee! for thou resemblest my love in her eyes, and her beauty; so depart in security.

Although thy form resembles the damsel, no imagination can comprehend the virtues of her mind.

"As soon as the knight had finished his verses, my lord, he let the fawn go out of his hand, and it went off skipping over the barren waste, when soon two more knights joined them.'--'And what is there so wonderful in all this?' said Ramih. I suppose they are of the tribe of Cahtan, and that the evening has surprised them, and consequently they must repose in my land, and will quit it in the morning.'"

Malik, however, who had overheard this conversation, was convinced that the man on foot, spoken of by the slave, must be Shiboob, while the humane knight could only be Antar, on the way to rescue them; and he was right. Immediately there was great confusion in the tents;--the lion-hero struck off the chief's head with his sword Dhami, and having released Malik and his son, they all returned to the land of Abs.

A HORSE RACE, AND ITS CONSEQUENCES.

King Cais having despatched some of his slaves to obtain tidings of Antar, one of them returned with a glowing account of a wonderful colt, called Dahis, which he had seen in the course of his journey. In beauty and in speed this colt had no equal in all Arabia. The King bargained for Dahis with the owner, and was delighted when he came to terms for his purchase. Soon after this Carwash, a cousin of King Cais, was present at a grand feast given by Hadifah; and the conversation turning upon horses, Carwash boasted of the racing qualities of Dahis. Hadifah offers to back his mare Ghabra for twenty camels, to run against Dahis, and a match is made accordingly. But the King takes the matter in his own hands, and visits Hadifah, to arrange the conditions of the race.

"'As to the first bet, Hadifah,' said Cais, 'I dissolve it, and I will lay you another, and let the wager be thirty.' 'Forty,' said Hadifah. 'Fifty,' said Cais. 'Sixty,' said Hadifah; and they continued rising till they made the bet a hundred she-camels, and consigned the contract into the hands of a man called Sabik, son of Wahab, whilst a crowd of old and young collected about them.--'What distance shall we run?' said Hadifah to Cais.--'Forty arrow-shots,' said Cais; 'and we have an archer called Ayas, son of Mansoor'--for there was no Arab at that day could shoot like him, and the Arabs had made him quite a proverb. King Cais was anxious indeed for a longer race on account of the strength of his horse's muscles; for the greater distance he went, the more his spirit and animation increased in his movements. 'Determine, then,' said Cais to Hadifah, when the match shall take place.'--'Forty days, I think,' said Hadifah, will be required to train the horses.'--'Very well,' said Cais; and the affair was mutually settled, that the horses should be trained forty days, and the race-ground should be near the lake of Zat-ul-irsad; and the horse that should arrive first should be the winner. Cais having given his consent, he returned to the tents."

[202]

The race between Dahis and Ghabra came off at the place appointed, and Dahis would have won, but for foul play on the part of Hadifah, who caused the colt to be injured before reaching the goal; the consequence of which was the famous Forty Years' War between the tribes of Abs and Dhobyan, known as the War of Dahis.

PRINCE MALIK'S MARRIAGE AND DEATH.

Prince Malik, while hunting, like his brother Harith, fell in love with a beauteous damsel of the tribe of Ghorab, and straightway asked her in marriage of her father, an old sheikh, who consented, after some little demur on the ground of his own poverty, and they shook hands for the nuptials.

"On the next day Prince Malik sent to the sheikh he and she-camels, and variegated robes, and cattle, and precious jewels, and howdahs, brilliant with magnificent velvet, and servants and slaves, and with them horses and sheep, ordering them to be expeditious, on account of the passion that was in his heart; and he appointed a certain hour on the seventh day. When all these presents reached the tribe of Ghorab, the old and the young rejoiced; they passed those days in the greatest delight, and slaughtered the sheep and the camels, and filled the goblets with wine; and they were perfectly happy, to the exclusion of every sorrow.

"Soon after, Prince Malik clad himself in the robes of noble-born kings, and his beauty was more dazzling than the new moon. On this expedition Antar accompanied him, fearful lest some enemy should waylay him; and he took ten horsemen and five of his brothers. They wandered through the Arab dwellings till they reached the tribe of Ghorab, and Prince Malik dismounted at the marriage canopy, his brothers also alighting round the tent. The feast immediately commenced; the damsels waved the cymbals, and the horsemen flourished their swords; exclamations of joy arose, and the cups went round; and thus they continued till the laughing day was spent, when the nymph was married to Malik."

But who could guess that "upon night so sweet an awful morn would rise?"--that the nuptial night of the good Prince Malik should be his last!--"By morning their joys were converted into sorrows, and shots were precipitated at them from arrows for which there is no surgeon;--for Fortune never gives, but it pillages; is never stationary, but it revolves; is never merry, but it sorrows; never bestows, but it takes back; never joys, but it grieves; never sweetens, but it embitters."

Early next morning, Hadifah, with a party of his kinsmen, attacked the marriage-guests. Antar was the first to start up on the alarm being given by the slaves; springing upon his horse Abjer, he hastened to meet the enemy, and soon the whole tribe of Ghorab were in motion. Hadifah advanced towards the nuptial tent. Prince Malik, half asleep, and his garments scented with musk and saffron, rushed out, and mounting his horse, cried, "I am

[203]

Malik, the son of Zoheir!" But his horse stumbled and threw him. As he was attempting to rise, Hadifah dealt him a deadly blow on the head with his sword; then, fearing the vengeance of Antar, he rejoined his companions, and they all hastened away. When Antar returned from the conflict he found his friend in the agonies of death, lying bathed in blood beside his horse. The dying Prince opened his eyes and attempted to speak to Antar, but could not; and with a sigh his gentle spirit departed. "Antar wrapped him up in his clothes, and tying him on the back of his horse, took him away, and sought the land of Abs." As he journeyed sadly homeward his grief found expression in these verses:

ALAS! O raven, hastening in thy flight, send me thy wings, for I have lost my support!

Is it true that I have seen the day of Malik's death and murder, or has it befallen me in a dream?

The light of day is darkened in grief for the youth, the hero of Abs and of Ghiftan!

O woe is me! how fell he from his horse, and my sword and my spear were not near him?

The fated arrow of the all-bounteous Archer cast him down!--O that, when it cast him down, it had cast me down too!

O that my soul had bade farewell, and that his hands had not beckoned to me a double adieu!

Alas! his kindnesses, were I to comment on them, my tongue would fail ere I could repeat them!

I swear I will not sleep from taking vengeance: I will not repose, but on the back of my stallion.

Never shall my sword cease to cleave those Fazareans, till the desert be converted into a sea of crimson blood!

The shade of Prince Malik appeared to Antar one night in a dream;--beckoning with his fingers, he said: "O Aboolfawaris! dost thou sleep, and I unrevenged? Hast thou forgotten our former friendship? Before thee many have been faithful to their friends: be thou faithful also to him who was slain but yesterday;" and then the apparition vanished. In the darkness of the night, then and there, the hero mounted Abjer, and taking his brother Shiboob in front of him, he sought the land of Fazarah. There he slew Awef, the brother of Hadifah, as a first sacrifice to the manes of his murdered friend.

AMARAH LAMPOONED BY THE GIRLS.

Antar returned to his tribe, and lived secluded in his tent, sorrowing for the loss of his first and ever steadfast friend. One day Khemisa, Abla's handmaiden, came to him with a message from his darling, who desired him to watch over the safety of herself and her female companions while they passed some time at the lake during the evening. The hero was delighted with the duty, and readily promised Abla his protection against the wanderers of the night.

The girls set out for the lake at the hour appointed, and Amarah, disguised in women's clothes, followed them. When they reached the lake he pounced upon Abla like a voracious. vulture. But help was at hand. Antar, concealed behind the sand-hills, heard Abla's screams. He rushed forth like a furious lion, grasped Amarah, and almost heat the life out of him; then he let him go, followed by the taunts and jeers of the girls.

"This circumstance with Abla soon spread abroad, and all the women, and men, and girls, and boys, and slaves, and slave-girls joined in the laugh against Amarah, singing these verses, whilst Amarah heard them:--the women and shepherdesses sang them at their spindles; for there was a girl among the Absians who could compose verses; she was very eloquent, so she repeated these verses on Amarah the cuckold, and they were recollected by all the women and girls:"

AMARAH, leave alone the beautiful, full-hipped damsels;--let alone all disputes about the lovely girls!

For thou canst not plunge into the sea of deaths, and thou art no horseman in the day of battle.

Aspire no more to Abla: if thou dost but look at her, thou wilt see horrors from the lion of the forests!

As to the thin quivering spear, touch not its strength, nor the cleaving scimitar.

Abla is a fawn chased by a lion, with eyes that afflict with disorder the stoutest in health.

Let alone all contest about her, or the unflinching Antar will make thee drink of death.

Thou didst not cease thy obstinacy, till thy foul condition gave evidence against thee!

All the girls laughed at thee: thou vast the carrion of the plains and deserts; thou wast the common talk of the merry, and the laughing-stock for every passenger!

Thou camest to us in the robes of dyed silk, thou black greasy kettle!

As thou didst meet us, a lion met thee, whom all the lion-heroes acknowledge in the carnage:

[205]

Then fear trembled in thy heart--intoxication quitted thee, and thou wast restored to thy senses. Nothing but contempt remained for thee, when thou didst retire like a dunghill.

Abla beheld thee laid low, stretched out; and all the beautiful high-hipped damsels with her.

We held our noses at thee, as we laughed at thee and quizzed thee.

The Antar of Knights, the lion of the cave, came--he, who in generosity is a sea of liberality:

And thou art the vilest of all those that ever crossed a horse--the noblest of those who are tenacious of their lives!

We are like the sweetest flowerets, scented like the violets and the camomile; and Abla amongst us is like the branch of the tamarisk: her beauty is the full moon, and the sun of the desert.

Thou wouldst possess her by violence and outrage--thou!--the vilest of all the dogs that bark!

Die in grief, otherwise live in contempt; for never, never will there be an end of our lampoons upon thee!

MARRIAGE OF ANTAR AND ABLA.

Many more wonderful exploits were performed by Antar in opposing the enemies of Abs--many illustrious warriors fell beneath the stroke of his irresistible sword Dhami, before he attained the chief desire of his heart. At length King Cais, grateful for his services, resolved that Antar should be married to his darling Abla without further delay, and his uncle Malik freely gave his consent. And never was there such another glorious wedding! From the most distant lands came famous knights to honour the nuptials of the renowned son of Shedad and the beauteous daughter of Malik, and rich and rare were the presents they brought with them. Each of these illustrious chiefs addressed verses to Antar, in praise of his prowess, and congratulating him on his marriage. "It was now the season of spring, and the land was enamelled with the lustre of new-born flowers." For several days the horsemen jousted with each other, with blunted spears. And then came the wedding night.

"Now there was a curious custom current among the Arabs at that period. The night on which a bridegroom should wed his wife, they brought a quantity of camel pack-saddles, and heaped them one upon the other, decorating them with magnificent garments. Here they conducted the bride, and having seated her on high, they said to the bridegroom: 'Come on--now for thy bride!' And the bridegroom rushed forward to carry her off; whilst

[206]

the youths of the tribe, drawn up in line, right and left, with staves and stones in their hands, as soon as the bridegroom dashed forward, began beating and pelting him, and doing their utmost to prevent his reaching his bride. If a rib or so were broken in the affair, it was well for him; were he killed, it was his destiny. But should he reach his bride in safety, the people quitted him, and no one attempted to approach him."

This singular custom was, however, waived in the case of Antar, by order of the King, who feared lest some enemy of the hero might do him a mortal injury in the melee.

"And now, when the Arabs assembled for Antar's marriage had eaten their dinner, the cups of wine were brought round to them. The men and the women were promiscuously moving together; the girls came forth, and the slave-women were amusing themselves, enjoying the happy moments. 'Hola!' cried the matrons and the virgins, 'we will not remain covered on Antar's marriage.' They threw aside their veils, and the full moons appeared in all their lustre; and they flaunted the branches of their forms in the excess of their delight; and it was a famous day for them. 'By the faith of an Arab,' said the matrons and virgins, 'we will not remain thus concealed behind these curtains--the doors shall not be shut upon us; we will see Abla in her magnificence, and we will walk in her train, and make our offerings to her and Antar, and we will not keep a dirhem or a dinar to ourselves; for a happier night than this can never be, and no one but a madman would miss it.'

"When the women of Carad heard this, they were alarmed for the scandal and censure that would thus be occasioned: so they resolved to finish Abla's ceremony. They clothed her in most magnificent robes and superb necklaces; they placed the coronet of Chosroe on her head, and tiaras round her forehead: Abla was remarkable for her beauty and loveliness: the tire-women surrounded her, and they requested Antar to let her come forth in state. He gave them permission, whilst his brothers and slaves stood round the pavilion with their swords, and javelins, and weapons. He ordered them to place a lofty throne for Abla in front of the pavilion. They executed his commands: they lighted brilliant and scented candles before her, and spread afar the odour of aloes and camphor, and scattered the perfumes of ambergris and musk; the lights were fixed in candlesticks of gold and silver--the torches blazed--and whilst the women shouted and raised their voices to whistles and screams, Abla came forth in state. In her hand she bore a drawn sword, whose lustre dazzled the eyesight. All present gave a shout; whilst the malicious and ill-natured cried: 'What a pity that one so beautiful and fair should be wedded to one so black!'"

Thus, after all his trials and perils, the renowned son of Shedad was duly married to his darling Abla, and thus he expressed his satisfaction at the consummation of his wishes:

MY heart is at rest: it is recovered from its intoxication. Sleep has calmed my eyelids, and relieved them.

Fortune has aided me, and my prosperity cleaves the veil of night, and the seven orders of heaven.

THE DEATH OF ANTAR.

IN the course of his exploits as chief of his tribe, Antar had conquered a horseman, called Jezar, who was a famous archer; and, to punish his aggressions upon his people, he had blinded him by causing a red-hot sabre to be passed before his eyes; then he granted him life, liberty, and even the supreme rank in his own tribe.

I.

FROM that time Jezar, son of Jaber, meditated in silence on vengeance. Although his eyes were deprived of sight, he had in no way lost his skill in archery. His ear, practised in following the movements of wild animals by the sound of their steps, was sufficient to guide his hand: never did the arrow miss the mark. His hatred, always alert, listened eagerly for the news which fame spread about his enemy. He learned that Antar, after a distant and fortunate expedition against the frontiers of Persia, was returned to Yemen, laden with as much glory and booty as he had formerly brought from the court of Chosroe, and that he is about to pass into the desert adjoining his encampment. At this story Jezar weeps for envy and rage. He calls Nejim, his faithful slave:

"Ten years are passed," says he to him, "since a burning iron destroyed, by Antar's order, the light of my eyes, and I am not yet revenged! But at last the moment has come when to quench in his blood the fire which burns in my heart. Antar is encamped, they say, on the banks of the Euphrates. Thither I wish to go to seek him. I shall live hidden in the reeds of the river till Heaven delivers his life into my hands."

Jezar orders his slave to bring him his she-camel which rivals the ostrich in the race: he arms himself with his quiver of poisoned arrows. Nejim makes the camel kneel, helps his master to mount upon her back, and takes the end of the halter of the animal, to direct her steps toward the distant bed of the Euphrates. The blind warrior fills the desert with his wailings and his threats.

After a long day's march through a waterless space, Jezar and his slave reach the banks of the Euphrates, whose course is marked by the verdure of the trees and the herbs along its bed.

"What seest thou on the other bank?" asks Jezar of his slave.

Nejim casts a glance to the other bank. He sees tents richly adorned; numerous flocks; camels wandering in groups on the plain; spears planted in the ground at the doors of the tents; harnessed horses, fastened by the feet, before the dwellings of their masters. A tent

[208]

more splendid than the rest is erected at a little distance from the river. Before the door arises, like a mast, a long spear of steel, beside which is a horse blacker than ebony. Nejim recognises the noble courser of Antar, the famous Abjer, and his terrible spear. He halts his master's camel behind the shrubs and reeds, which conceal them from all eyes; and they await the hour of darkness.

II.

WHEN night had covered with its shadows the two banks of the Euphrates--

"Let us quit this place," says the blind Jezar to his slave; "the voices which I hear from the other side seem to me too far off for the range of my arrows. Bring me nearer the edge: my heart tells me that a glorious stroke is about to immortalise my name and my revenge!"

Nejim takes the blind man by the hand; brings him close to the water; makes him sit upon the bank opposite the tent of Antar, and gives him his bow and quiver. Jezar chooses the keenest of his arrows, places it upon the string, and with listening ear awaits the hour of vengeance.

Meanwhile Antar, in the arms of Abla, his beloved wife, for whom ten years of possession have in no wise diminished his love, was forgetting within his tent his fatigue and exploits, when the dismal howling of the dogs--faithful guardians of the camp--cast a prophetic unquiet into his soul.

He rises and goes out of his tent. The sky is dark and cloudy. He wanders, feeling his way in the darkness. The louder voices of the dogs attract him to the river. Impelled by his fate, he goes forward, right up to the bed of the water; and, suspecting the presence of some enemy on the opposite hank, he calls to his brother in a loud voice to search the other side.

Scarcely does his resounding voice echo in the hollow bed of the valley of the Euphrates, reverberating in the rocks and mountains, when an arrow pierces his right side, and penetrates to his entrails. No cry--no groan unworthy of a hero--escapes him through his pain. He withdraws the iron with a firm hand.

"Traitor, who has not dared to attack me in the light of day!" cries he in a loud voice to his invisible enemy--"thou shalt not escape my vengeance!--thou shalt not enjoy the fruit of thy perfidy!"

At that voice, which makes him think that his arrow has missed its mark, the blind Jezar, struck by terror at the thought of the vengeance of Antar, swoons upon the bank, and his slave, thinking him dead, flies upon his camel, leaving his inanimate master where he lay.

[209]

Antar's brother swims across the river, stumbles against a body which he takes for a corpse, and bears it upon his shoulders, with the bow and arrows, to the camp.

III.

ANTAR, stretched in his tent amidst his despairing friends, is suffering horrible torments: the tender Abla is stanching his blood, bathing the wound with her tears.

They bring the body of the assassin, the bow and the arrows, into the tent. Antar recognises the mutilated countenance of his enemy: he no longer doubts that the arrow discharged by such a hand was poisoned. Hope leaves his heart: death inevitable presents itself before his eyes.

"Son of my uncle!" says Abla tenderly to him, "why abandon hope? Ought a slight arrow-wound to alarm him who has confronted without fear so many swords and spears, the wounds from which cover his body?"

"Abla," replies Antar, "my hours are numbered. Look at the features of that face;--it is Jezar: the traitor's arrow was poisoned!"

At these words Abla fills the night with her sobs; she rends her garments; she tears her long hair, and picks up dust, which she scatters on her head. All the women of the encampment re-echo her lamentations.

"Dear wife!" says Antar to Abla, "who will defend thy honour and thy life after the death of Antar, in that long journey which remains for thee to make through our enemies before reaching thy father's land? A second husband, another I, can alone save thee from the horrors of slavery. Of all the warriors of the desert, Zeid and Amnem are those whose courage will best protect thy life and thy liberty: choose one of those, and go and promise him thy hand."

Abla replies not but by her tears to a thought which is to her horrible.

"To return to the land where dwell the children of Abs--to assure thy passage through the desert which separates thee from it--clothe thyself with my arms and mount my courser Abjer. In this disguise, which will make our enemies think that I still live, fear not of being attacked. Reply nothing to those who

salute thee upon the road: the sight of the arms and the horse of Antar will suffice to intimidate the boldest."

IV.

[210]

ANTAR after these words orders the departure. They strike the tents, fold them, and place them upon the camels. Abla, bathed in her tears, constrains herself, through obedience, to don the heavy armour of Antar. Girt with his sword, holding his straight spear in her hand, she mounts his courser Abjer, whilst the slaves lay the dying Antar in the litter in which Abla used to travel in happier days, when she crossed, like a queen, the desert.

Scarce have they lost sight of the verdant banks of the Euphrates to plunge into the immensity of the desert, when they perceive in the distance tents, like dark dots on the horizon, or a black fringe on the blue mantle of heaven. It is a numerous and powerful tribe. Three hundred horsemen advance to fall upon the caravan; but, on approaching, they recognise the litter and the horse.

"'Tis Antar and Abla!" they say to one another in a low voice--"see, there, his arms, his horse Abjer, and Abla's splendid litter. Let us return to our tents, and not expose ourselves to the anger of these invincible warriors."

Already they are turning the rein, when an old sheikh, more reflective and more sagacious than the young men, says:

"My cousins, that is indeed the spear of Antar, that is indeed his helmet, his armour, and his courser, whose colour resembles a dark night;--but that is neither his lofty figure nor his manly bearing. It is the figure and the deportment of a timid woman, borne down by the weight of the iron which galls her frail limbs. Believe my surmises--Antar is dead, or else a mortal illness hinders him from mounting his horse; and this false warrior whom Abjer bears is Abla, who, to frighten us, has clad herself with her husband's arms, whilst the real Antar is perchance laid dying in the women's litter."

The horsemen, recognising something probable in the old man's words, retrace their steps and follow at a distance the caravan, without daring to attack it.

V.

NOW the feeble arm of Abla is bending beneath the weight of the iron spear: she is obliged to hand it to her husband's brother, who walks beside her. Soon, when the sun, arrived half-way in his course, had made the sand of the desert glow like fire, Abla, worn out with suffering and fatigue, raises the vizor of her helmet, to wipe off the sweat which bathed her forehead. The eyes of the hostile Arabs who are watching her catch a glimpse of the whiteness of her face:

"It is not the Black!" they cry; and they dash with all the speed of their horses upon the tracks of Antar's little troop.

[211]

At the gallop of their horses behind him--at the neighing of their steeds--at the voice of Abla, which calls him--Antar, who is lying half dead in the litter, rises, shows his head from between the curtains, and utters, for the last time, his terrible war-cry, known of all the desert. The manes of the horses stand erect: the horses bear their riders rigid with terror.

"Woe to us!" say the Arabs, enemies of Abs,--"Antar still lives! It is a snare which he has laid: he has wished to know which is the tribe so bold as after him to aspire to capture his wife and his possessions."

Only a small number, still trusting the voice of the old sheikh, continue to follow afar the caravan.

VI.

ANTAR, spite of his weakness, places Abla in the litter, and mounted upon Abjer, clad in his arms, he marches slowly beside her.

At the close of the day, they reach a valley not far front the tribe of Abs. This place was called the "Valley of Gazelles." Surrounded by inaccessible mountains, one could only enter it from the desert side by a narrow and tortuous pass, where three horsemen could scarcely march abreast. Antar, stopping at the opening of this defile, causes first to enter his flocks, his slaves, and the camel which bears the litter of his dear Abla. When the whole caravan is in safety in the valley, he comes back, to stand alone as sentinel at the end of the gorge, opposite the plain and the Arabs who are following him afar. At this moment his agonies increase; his entrails are torn; each step of his courser makes him suffer torments like to the fire of hell. Death invades his limbs, and yet reveres his dauntless soul. He faces the Arabs; he stops Abjer; he plants the point of his spear in the ground, and leaning against the stem, like a resting warrior allowing his horse to breathe, he stands motionless at the entrance of the pass.

VII.

AT that sight, the thirty warriors who have hitherto followed the tracks of his caravan halt, hesitating, a few hundred steps from the hero.

"Antar," say they to one another, "has noticed that we were following his march; he awaits us there to slay us all;--let us profit by the shades of night which fall, to escape his sword and rejoin our brothers."

But the old sheikh, steadfast in his opinion, keeps them still.

"My cousins," says he to them in a low voice, "heed not the counsels of fear. The immobility of Antar is the sleep of death!--What! do you not know his fiery courage? Has Antar ever waited for his enemy? Were he living, would not he fall upon us, as the vulture falls upon his prey?--Come on, then, bravely; or, if you refuse to risk your lives against his sword, at least wait till dawn arises, and clears away your doubts."

Half persuaded by the old man, the thirty horsemen resolve to remain where they are; but, always troubled and alarmed at the least cloud of dust which the wind raises about the feet of Abjer, they pass the whole night on horseback, allowing not their eyes to close in sleep.

VIII.

AT length the day begins to lighten the sky, and to clear away the shades which cover the desert. Antar is still in the same attitude at the entrance of the pass: his courser, obedient to his thought, is motionless as his master.

At this strange spectacle the astounded warriors consult long before coming to a decision. All appearances say to their hearts that Antar has ceased to live; and yet not one of them dares advance to make sure: so strong is the habitude of fear which the hero inspires! . . . The old sheikh wishes to convince himself and them by a proof before flying or advancing. He descends from his mare, lets go the bridle, and pricking her haunch with the point of his spear, he drives her towards the entrance of the pass. Scarcely has she reached in her course the border of the desert next the gorge, when the fiery stallion Abjer darts neighing after the riderless mare. At the first bound of the courser, Antar, supported only by the stem of his spear, which slips away from under him, falls like a tower, and the clang of his armour resounds in the pass.

At that fall--the sound of a lifeless body falling upon the earth--the thirty horsemen flock round the corpse stretched at their horses' feet. They marvel to see lying motionless in the desert him who made Arabia tremble. They cannot resist measuring with their eyes his gigantic limbs and stature. Foregoing the attack upon the caravan of Abla--to which the stratagem of Antar had given an entire night to reach the tents of the tribe of Abs--the warriors content themselves with robbing the hero of his arms, to carry them to their tribe as a trophy conquered by death. In vain they endeavour to capture his courser. The faithful Abjer, having scented his master dead, feels that there is no longer a rider worthy of him: fleeter than the lightning, he escapes them, disappears from their eyes, and plunges into the freedom of the desert. They say that the old sheikh, softened by the fate of the hero who had made himself illustrious by so many exploits, wept over his corpse, covered it with sand, and addressed to it these words:

GLORY TO THEE, BRAVE WARRIOR! WHO, DURING THY LIFE, HAST BEEN THE DEFENDER OF THY TRIBE, AND WHO, EVEN AFTER THY DEATH, HAST SAVED THY BRETHREN BY THE TERROR OF THY CORPSE AND OF THY

[213]

NAME! MAY THY SOUL LIVE FOR EVER! MAY THE REFRESHING DEWS MOISTEN THE GROUND OF THIS THY LAST EXPLOIT!

THE "BURDA,"
i.e.,
THE POEM OF THE MANTLE,
BY
KA'B, SON OF ZUHAYR, SON OF ABU SULMA
RECITED BY HIM BEFORE MUHAMMAD, AT MADINA.
IN THE NINTH YEAR OF THE HIJRA,
AFTER THE CONQUEST OF MAKKA.
TRANSLATED, WITH PREFACE AND NOTES,
BY
J. W. REDHOUSE, ESQ., M.R.A.S.,
HON. MEMB. R.S.L., ETC.

Nec omittendum est Caab Ebni Zoheir carmen, cujus hoc est initium admirabile:
 "Abiit (amica mea) Soada, et cor meum hodie dolore percitum (relinquitur),
 "Amore confectum, et vinculis constrictum, a quibus nulla est redemptio."
 --Poeseos Asiaticae commentariorum libri sex; auctore Gulielmo Jones, A.M.   Lipsiae, 1777.

PREFACE.

KA'B, the Poet, and MUHAMMAD, the Lawgiver, were issued, each by seventeen and fifteen degrees of descent respectively, from a common ancestor, Ilyas, son of Mudhar, son of Nizar, son of 'Adnan. This last, 'Adnan, was himself a descendant, in some very uncertain degree and line, of Ishmael, the son of Abraham, forefather of the Children of Israel by his other son Isaac. Most, but not all, Arabians trace their pedigrees to this 'Adnan. Muhammad was descended from Mudrika, son of Ilyas, while Ka'b claimed descent from Tabikha, a brother of Mudrika.

Ka'b was a son of Zuhayr, son of Abu Sulma. He had a brother named Bujayr; and, like their father, both these brothers were poets in an eminent degree. Ka'b had two sons, also lyrists.

Zuhayr is the author of one of the pre-Islamite poems known as the Mu'allaqat, translations of which, by Sir William Jones, form part of the present volume. That poem was a production of his old age. He is said to have frequented the society of men learned in the various religions then extant, and thus to have become aware of a general expectancy, at that period, by the most pious and best informed, of the appearance of a great apostle, who should reconcile all divergences and unite mankind in a pure worship of the one sole God, who had revealed the truth to the prophets of old. He is said to have seen in a vision, shortly before his death, a rope let down from heaven, which he essayed

[214]

to grasp, but which he found to be beyond his reach. This he interpreted to himself as a revelation that the advent of the long-expected apostle was at hand, but that the poet would not himself live long enough to see and hear him. He recounted his vision, and his interpretation of the same, to his two sons, whom he advised to be on the outlook, and to accept the teachings of the new apostle, if he should appear in their time. Zuhayr then died.

Accordingly, when the fame of the teachings of Muhammad became noised abroad among the cities of Arabia and the children of its deserts, and also the news of his various victories, culminating in the submission of his native city, Makka, and its confederates, to his sway, it happened that Ka'b and his brother Bujayr were led, in conducting their flocks and herds to the summer pasturages, into the neighbourhood of the newly-conquered districts. Naturally, the two poet-brothers conversed together, and with their neighbours, about the new doctrine and dominion. These consultations ended in Bujayr's proposing to go to Muhammad and learn for himself what was the truth of the matter. He sought the Apostle, in consequence, and soon embraced the faith of Islam.

Tidings of the lapse of his brother from the religion of their forefathers reached Ka'b, who thereupon became very much incensed. He composed a lampoon on his brother and the Prophet, together with their new religion. This he sent to his brother by the mouth of a messenger. Bujayr thought it his duty to lay the circumstance before Muhammad, who had now returned to Madina. He recited the lampoon to the conqueror, who commented on its words, turning them all to the praise of the new faith and himself, to the condemnation of Ka'b. Then, as appears to have been a rule with him towards all his waspish satirists, Muhammad passed a sentence of death upon his new assailant, who was to receive no quarter, should he fall into the hands of any future expeditionary Muslims.

Bujayr--knowing how several lampoonists of the Quraysh, Formerly denounced, had been slaughtered by the incensed victors, in the first moments of the occupation of Makka, while others had only saved their lives by flight and exile, and others again had been most generously pardoned by the Prophet himself, on their seeking his personal protection and adopting the faith--became deeply alarmed at the danger in which he had placed his brother. He therefore, in his turn, composed a poem, which he sent orally to Ka'b, and advised him to do what the most eminent were doing--renounce his errors, and come in to the Prophet repentant; warning him of what would otherwise be his certain fate.

It appears that the circumstances became noised abroad. Enemies of Ka'b assailed him in verse, blackening him in every way, as is usual in like cases. He probably heard also that some of them were preparing to attack him with more lethal weapons. He therefore had recourse to one of the Arabian customs, and fled for protection to a powerful neighbour and old friend. Here he was told that his friend could not venture to shield him against the all-powerful foe whose wrath had been excited; while everywhere he was greeted with jibes as to his being already virtually a dead man.

Ka'b now formed the resolution of a desperate, but wise and brave man. He set out secretly for Madina, found there an old friend, claimed his protection, and was by him, the next morning at dawn, conducted to the then most simple meeting-house where Muhammad and his chief followers performed their devotions of worship and praise (not prayer). His friend indicated the Prophet to Ka'b, who recognised the person and features he had heard described. The service ended, Ka'b approached Muhammad, and the two sat down together. Ka'b placed his own right hand in that of the Prophet, whom he addressed in the words: "Apostle of God, were I to bring to you Ka'b the son of Zuhayr, penitent and professing the faith of Islam, wouldst thou receive and accept him?"--The Prophet answered: "I would."--"Then," said the Poet, "I am he."

Immediately on this intelligence being heard by the bystanders, one of the men of Madina seized Ka'b, and demanded the Prophet's permission to put him to death. Muhammad commanded his zealous partisan to desist; but the incident raised in the Poet a feeling of resentment, to which he gave vent immediately afterwards. For he now improvised, probably with more or less premeditation, the Poem of which a translation is here given, in which, Arab fashion at the period, after an exordium in praise of some real or imaginary beauty, and of the camel on which alone she could be reached in her distant abode, he passes to a cursory mention of what had happened to himself since his denunciation by the Prophet, ending, at the thirty-eighth verse, with a description of his present interview, his hope of pardon, his awe at the dread vengeance he had evoked, a cleverly introduced eulogium on the "Emigrants" from Makka, and a scathing cut at the "dwarfish tawny [Madina] men" who "ran away." It is said that when Ka'b reached the fifty-first verse: "Verily the Apostle is a Light from which illumination is sought: a drawn Indian blade--one of the Swords of God," Muhammad took from his own shoulders the mantle he wore, and threw it over the shoulders of the Poet, as an honour, and as a mark of protection. This incident has been the cause of the title given henceforth to the effusion: THE POEM OF THE MANTLE.

It is said that after Mu'awiya, the first Caliph of the house of 'Umayya, had firmly established his sway over Syria and Egypt, he sent a messenger to Ka'b, and offered him ten thousand pieces of silver for the deceased Prophet's sacred mantle; but that Ka'b refused to part with the relic to any one. When the Poet died, the Caliph sent another messenger to his heirs, and offered them twenty thousand pieces for the mantle, which now passed into his possession. It has, ever since, been reverently preserved by the head of the realm of Islam. In the treasury of the Sultan-Caliph of the Ottomans, at Constantinople, there is an apartment, named the "Room of the Sacred Mantle," in which this robe is religiously preserved, together with a few other relics of the great Lawgiver.

As an instance of the surpassing richness of the Arabian tongue, it may be mentioned that Ka'b's "Poem of the Mantle," now nearly thirteen hundred years old, is found recorded in manuscripts with variant words in great number, though still preserving the one sense. A collector, curious in the matter, is recorded, who knew by heart seven hundred variations of the Poem; but, not long after, a more successful hunter raised the number to nine hundred. With such variety of expression, commentators have had a glorious task; and it may easily be understood that volumes would be required to give the whole detail. In the present translation, that version has been followed which is given in Westerfeld's edition of "The Life of Muhammed, based on Mohammed Ibn Ishak, by Abd El-Malik Ibn Hisham," published by Messrs. N. Trubner & Co., London, 1867. I have made but one alteration to it, of a single word in verse 56, authorised by two commentaries, and without which the clause appears to me untranslatable.

J. W. REDHOUSE.
LONDON, July, 1880.

KA'B'S POEM OF THE MANTLE.

BEATRICE [Su'ad] hath departed. Therefore was my heart that day distracted, raving after her, irredeemably enchained.

2. On the morrow of our separation, when she went forth, Beatrice was no other than a bleating antelope, with downcast glance, and eyes set off with collyrium.

3. When she smiles, she displays [a row of] teeth of glancing whiteness, as though it had been a damaskeened sword-blade, once tempered, and then dipped a second time in wine,

4. Dashed, on a cold day, with water from a meandering stream, clear, and flowing in a wide, pebbly channel, fanned by a north wind when the day is high;

5. From which the winds banish all sticks and straws, and on which the silvery bubbles raised by a morning rain appear in great numbers.

6. God bless her mother! for the darling she would have been, had she kept true to her promise, and if advice had been acceptable [to her]!

7. But she is a darling, in the very blood of whom are blended pain, anxiety, disappointment, and change!

8. She remains not constant to any state she may have assumed, even as the demon of the wilds varies in its costume!

9. She does not hold to any promise she has spoken, save as sieves hold water!

10. [The proverbial expression,] "the promises of 'Urqub" is [as it were] a parable concerning her; and his promises were naught but lies!

11. I wish and desire that they would become present in an eternity: but what ails them, then? I feel the whole duration of time an impatience!

[217]

12. Let not, then, that deceive thee which she has bestowed, or which she has promised. Verily, desires and dreams are a delusion!

13. Beatrice is to-day in a land where naught can enable one to reach her, save the noble, generous, free-going she-camels.

14. And certainly nothing could carry one to her, save a huge and dauntless she-camel, possessed, against fatigue, of speed and endurance;

15. Of those which drench the roots of their ears when they sweat; whose unknown energy blurs all the road-marks;

16. Who looks at the highlands with the eyes of an isolated white addax, when the rocky flats and sand-hills are [as it were] on fire;

17. Whose neck is thick where her collar sits; whose pastern is plump; in whose build there is a superiority over the daughters of the stallion-camel;

18. Large-headed, large-jawed, strongly formed; in whose side is capaciousness; whose neck is an obelisk;

19. Whose hide is that of a sea-turtle, on which tikes, slim in the loins and meagre, can make no impression;--

20. A graceful creature; whose brother is her father out of a full-blooded dam, and whose paternal uncle is also her maternal uncle; who is long in the back, and agile;

21. Upon whom the tikes crawl; which are then dropped off by a chest and by flanks that are sleek;--

22. A very wild-ass; who, from plumpness, might be accused of too much flesh; whose elbow is twisted out from her chest-ribs;

23. Aquiline of nose; in whose ears, to an observer, there is manifest nobility; in whose cheeks is a smoothness;

24. As though what stands out in front of her two eyes and of the stabbing-place of her throat, as her muzzle and jaw-sides, were a millstone-pick;

25. Who whisks [a tail] the like of a palm-branch, set with tufts of hair, against a flat udder, which the teats have never made to shrink;

26. Who, as she plays, alights on agile, slender legs, the fall of which on the earth is a mere pat;

[218]

27. Dusky in their tendinous parts, which leave the pebbles scattered; and which no [leather] shoeing protects from the black [basaltic] stones of the hills,

28. On which, by day, the chameleon remains on the outlook, as though his back, exposed to the sun, were turned to ashes in the fire,

29. When the leader of a party has said to them--the piebald locusts having already begun to kick the pebbles--"Make your siesta;"

30. The alternating play of whose fore-legs [they having already sweated, and the mirages having already shone on the rocks]

31. Is [as it were] the alternating movement of the hands of a bereaved, grizzly, howling woman, standing up, and answered by [other] bereaved ones suffering from unsucked milk;

32. Lamenting, her arms drooping, deprived of reason when the bringers of bad news announced the [menaced] death of her first-born;

33. Who tears her breast with her two hands, her corset being burst into tatters away from her chest-ribs;

34. By whose side walk the misinformers, their words being: "O thou son of Abu Sulma, verily thou art already slain!"

35. And each faithful friend, from whom I had entertained hope [of protection from Muhammad's emissaries], said to me: "I will not deceive thee; I am busy with other things than thee."

36. Then I spoke out: "Make ye way for me;--may your fathers perish! For all that the Most Merciful [God] hath forewilled will be accomplished:

37. "Every son of a female, long though his safety may be, is one day borne upon a ridged implement [a bier with a ridged lid]."

38. I have been informed that the Apostle of God hath threatened me; but pardon is hoped for from the Apostle of God.

39. "Respite!--May He guide thee [O Apostle!) aright, who hath given thee the free gift of the Qur'an, in which are exhortations and detail!--

40. "Punish me not, then, at the words of calumniators: for I have not offended, though stories have multiplied concerning me."

41. Verily, I occupy a position, such that, were the elephant [of Abraha] to occupy it, and were to see and hear what I hear [and see],

42. Out of distraction would his shoulders tremble, unless generosity were shown by the Apostle of God.

43. I ceased not to traverse the wilderness, penetrating the folds of darkness, the skirts of night having dropped over all,

44. Until I have placed my right hand, which I will not remove, in the palm of him who had a claim to vengeance,--whose word is the word.

45. A mere plaything unto me was the most terrible object, when I spoke to him, and it was said [unto me]: "Thou art accused and responsible!"

46. By a lion, whose den is in a level spot of the land, in the marshy hollow of 'Aththar, surrounded by jungle upon jungle;

47. Who goes forth in the morning and provides with food two cubs, that feed on the flesh of men soiled in the dust and torn into fragments;

48. Who, when he attacks his equal, is not permitted to leave that equal otherwise than mortified;

49. From whom the wild asses of the desert take flight, and in whose valley bands of men cannot march;

50. In whose valley there never lacks a man of courage, whose weapons are soiled with blood, his garments in shreds, and [himself] eaten!

51. Verily the Apostle of God is a Light from which illumination is sought: a drawn Indian blade--one of the Swords of God;

52. Among a small band of the Quraysh, whose spokesman said, in the Vale of Makka, when they had embraced Islam: "Depart ye!"

53. And they did depart. But there departed not [among them] the poltroons, the dastards in time of the encounter, the puny, and the unarmed.

54. They walk with the gait of light-coloured camels;--a blow protects them; while the dwarfish tawny men [of Madina] run away:

55. Aquiline-nosed heroes; whose clothing, in combat, is of shirts of the tissue of David--

56. Bright and ample, interlaced with links like the tendrils of the Qaf'a plant, firmly wove together;

57. Who are not boisterously joyful if their lances wound a foe; and who piteously bewail not when wounded;

58. Whom the spear-thrusts hit not, save on the front of their throats: for whom there is no shrinking back from the [battle-] pools of death!

THE "BURDA,"
i.e.
THE POEM OF THE MANTLE,
IN PRAISE OF MUHAMMAD,
BY
EL-BUSIRI.
TRANSLATED, WITH PREFACE AND NOTES,
BY
J. W. REDHOUSE, ESQ., M.R.A.S.,
HON. MEMB. R.S.L., ETC.

BORDAH.--Manteau des Arabes contre la pluye, et habit grossier des Religieux et des pauvres. C'est ainsi qu'on appelle aussi un excellent Poeme compose par Scherefeddin al Busiri a la louange de Mahomet, duquel il se vantait d'avoir ete gueri en songe.

Cet ouvrage est si fort estime parmi les Mahometans, que plusieurs l'apprennent par coeur, et en citent les vers comme autant de sentences. Plusieurs aussi l'ont paraphrase et commente; et on en trouve un grand nombre de versions Persiennes et Turquesques, tant en prose, qu'en vers.--D'Herbelot: Bibliotheque Orientale.

PREFACE.

THIS Poem was composed by Abu-'Abdi-'llah Muhammad, son of Sa'id, of Busir, in Upper Egypt (whence his surname of "Busiri"), whose cognomen was Sherefu-'d-Din (Honour of Religion). His praenomen of Abu-'Abdi-'llah merely states, as is usual with Arabians, that he had a son named 'Abdu-'llah (Abdallah), and would seldom be used by any but very intimate friends. Generally, he is known as Sherefu-'d-Din Muhammad, El-Busiri. He is said to have been born A.H. 608 (A.D. 1211), and to have died between 691 and 700 (A.D. 1291-1300).

The exact date of the Poem is not known; but it would appear to have acquired celebrity while a certain Baha'u-'d-Din was the Vazir of El-Maliku-'t-Tahir, one of the Mamluk (slave) Kings of Egypt, successors to the dynasty of the great Salahu-'d-Din (Saladin).

[221]

Various reasons have been assigned by commentators, without any better foundation than surmise or tradition, for the composition of the Poem. The author himself, however, in verse 140, gives the most satisfactory account of what prompted him to undertake the task: "by which I seek pardon for the sins of a lifetime passed in poetry and services." It was a doxology and a prayer composed in old age by a pious man who repented and regretted the futilities in which his years had been spent.

With regard to the title of the panegyric, "The Mantle Poem," as many opinions have been expressed as separate commentaries have been written. This title legitimately belongs solely to the eulogy pronounced on Muhammad, the great Arabian reformer and lawgiver, in his presence, by Ka'b, the son of Zuhayr, which was recompensed by the bestowal of the great teacher's mantle on the eulogist then and there, as is detailed in the Preface to the translation of that Poem, as given in the present volume. But the title has been also conferred by the public voice on the Poem of Busiri; and commentators have sought to account for this more or less reasonably. One relates that the Poet was stricken with palsy, and obtained his recovery of God through the Prophet's intercession at the invocation contained in the Poem. Seine have thought that the Poem was thence named the "Bur'a Poem," the word bur'a signifying "a cure," "a recovery;" afterwards corrupted, by ignorance or design, into the well-known name of the "Burda Poem"--the word burda signifying "a plaid wrapper." Another commentator relates that the Prophet appeared to the sick man in a dream, assured him of his recovery, and threw over him his own plaid or mantle, which the Poet saw spread upon his bed when he awoke and found himself whole.

The entire Poem, and also selected portions of it, are much used as chanted recitations in cases of sickness; and even when a corpse is being prepared by ablution for interment, as is mentioned in Lane's "Modern Egyptians" (p. 513, l. 12. edition of 1860, Murray, London); also during the funeral procession (p. 517, l. 12). They are used, too, as charms or amulets, to avert evil and to secure blessings, by being written out and suspended, in frames, in rooms, &c., or, in cases, on the person. The Poem is known everywhere in the world of Islam, and enjoys a much greater veneration than the original eulogy by Ka'b, since it recites in detail most of the chief acts of Muhammad's life, and of his highest titles.

J. W. REDHOUSE.
LONDON, August, 1880.
EL-BUSIRI'S POEM OF THE MANTLE.

IS it from a recollection of neighbours at Dhu-Salam that thou hast mixed with blood the tears flowing from an eyeball?

2. "Or, has the wind blown from the direction of Kadzima, and has the lightning gleamed in the darkness from Itzam?

[222]

3. "What ails thy two eyes? If thou sayest, 'Leave off,' they fill. And what ails thy heart? If thou sayest, 'Be tranquil,' it is perplexed.

4. "Does the deeply-entangled lover suppose that affection can be concealed, when it is being partly wept for, and partly suffered for?

5. "Were it not for fondness, thou hadst not shed tears over projecting ruins, neither hadst thou remained sleepless with the memory of the moringa-tree and the long hill.

6. "And how wilt thou deny love, when the truth-speaking witnesses, tears and wasting, have testified to it against thee,

7. "And ardour hath fixed upon thy cheeks the two lines of grief and woe, like unto the corn-marigold and the 'anam?"

8. "Yea! The phantom of her I love passed before me, and made me sleepless. For love doth dash delights with pain.

9. "O my chider for an excusable affection! [receive] an excuse from me to thee: and if thou wert just, thou wouldst not have reproached me.

10. "My condition hath become manifest unto thee; my secret is not concealed from the traducers; nor is my disease cut off.

11. "Thou hast given unto me sincere advice; but I listen not thereto. Verily a lover is in a state of surdity to all blamers!"

12. In truth, I have suspected my sincere gray hairs of being among my blamers; but my gray hairs are very far from blamings in giving advice.

13. For, indeed, the dominating spirit that commands me to do evil has not accepted admonition, through its ignorance, from the warning voice of gray hairs and decrepitude;

14. Neither has it made ready, out of good actions, a feast for the guest that has settled tenaciously on my head unabashed.

15. Had I known that I should not treat it with respect, I would have concealed with woad a secret that became revealed to me.

16. Who is for me in checking perversity in its erratic movements, as the perversity of horses is checked with bits?

17. Propose not, therefore, to crush its inclination in its acts of rebellion; for food invigorates desire in the insatiate.

18. The Flesh is like a child: if thou leavest him alone, he grows up with a love for suckling; and if thou weanest him, he is weaned.

19. Turn, then, away its desire; and take heed lest thou make it thy master: for whomsoever desire masters, it kills, or binds fast.

20. And watch thou over it, while it grazes in the [field of] actions. Then, if it find the pasturage sweet to its taste, leave it not to pasture.

21. How often hath it made a lethal thing appear pleasant of taste unto a man, while he knew not that poison was in the gravy!

22. And beware of artifices devised by hunger and satiety. For many an emptiness of stomach is more detrimental than indigestion.

23. And dash out the tears from thine eye that has filled from [a desire for] forbidden things; and strictly observe the diet of penitence.

24. And withstand thou the Flesh and the Devil, and rebel against them. Even when they offer thee sincere advice, doubt it.

25. And be not thou obedient to them, either as adversary or arbiter; for thou art aware of the devices of the adversary and of the arbiter.

26. I ask forgiveness of God for my spoken words unaccompanied by deeds; for therewith have I accused a spouse of barren wives of having posterity.

27. I have commanded thee [to do] good; but I have not [myself] conformed thereto. I have not been upright;--what, then, is my word to thee: Be upright?

28. I have not provisioned myself, before death, with a [store of] supererogatory good works; I have not worshipped, save as is incumbent; nor have I fasted [otherwise].

29. I have swerved from the practice of him who made the darkness [of night] alive [with his devotions], until his two feet complained of injury from tumefaction;

30. And bound up his entrails from hunger, and girded beneath stones a tender-skinned hypochondriac region;

31. Whom the towering mountains sought to entice from his self-possession by talking about gold; but to which he exhibited a surprising loftiness;

32. Whose necessity confirmed his disinclination towards them; for, verily, necessity doth not invade continences.

[224]

33. Then, how could his necessity invite to [the things of] the world, him, without whom the world would not have come forth from naught?--

34. MUHAMMAD, the Prince of the two universes [material and spiritual], of the two ponderable classes [men and demons], and of the two sections [of mankind], of the Arabians and of the Non-Arabians;

35. Our Annunciator, who commands and who prohibits; than whom no one is more righteous in the word "No!" or in [the word] "Yea!"

36. Who is also the "Beloved One [of God];" whose intercession is hoped for in every terror, of the terrors that beset;

37. Who called [men and demons] to [obedience to] God; so that they who lay hold on him have hold of a cable that will not break;

38. Who surpassed [all] the prophets in manly form and in moral qualities; whom they do not approach in knowledge or in generosity;

39. All of them supplicate the "Apostle of God" for a handful of [his] sea [of knowledge], or for a sip of [his] steady rain [of exposition];

40. Compared with whom, they, in their degree, are cognisant of a [mere] dot of the [divine] knowledge, or a [bare] suspicion of [God's] wisdoms;

41. Whose outward form and inner significance the Creator of the soul perfected, and whom He then selected [as His] "Beloved One;"

42. Who is unassociated with any partner in his beauties; in whom the essence of loveliness is undivided.

43. Put aside that which the Nazarenes have laid claim to for their prophet; pronounce what thou wilt in his praise, and decide;

44. Attribute to his personality what thou wilt of nobility; and ascribe to his worth what thou wilt of vastness;

45. For verily the superiority of the Apostle of God hath no limit, that a speaker can clearly enunciate with his mouth concerning it.

46. If his miracles had equalled his worth, his [very] name, when called upon, would have brought back to life mouldering bones fallen to pieces.

47. But, out of anxious solicitude towards us, he hath not tried us with anything at which men's reasons break down; we therefore doubt not, nor vainly surmise.

[225]

48. The comprehension of his spiritual mystery outwearies the human race; thou wilt, therefore, not see, far or near, any not out of breath [thereat];--

49. Even as the sun at a distance appears small to our eyes, but fatigues the sight with over-closeness.

50. And how should a sleeping people comprehend his reality in this lower world? They console themselves with dreams in lieu thereof.

51. The utmost scope of [their] knowledge concerning him [is], that he was a man, and that he is the best of God's creatures--of the whole of them.

52. And all the signs that the noble apostles wrought [in former days] pertained unto them merely through his glory.

53. For verily he is the sun of superiority, of which they are the stars. They exhibit their lights to the people in the darknesses [but the sun is visible by day].

54. How noble was the manly form of the Prophet; whom moral qualities adorned; whom beauty enveloped; and whom beauty of features distinguished!

55. Like the flowers in softness, and the full moon in splendour, and the sea in liberality, and time in endeavours!

56. Through his majesty, when thou meetest him, in an army, or in a body of attendants, it is as though he were a solitary individual!--

57. As though the pearl enclosed in the shell were [composed] of the two ores--speech from him, and smiling!

58. There is no perfume to equal the earth that has enclosed his bones;--blessed is he that sniffs therefrom, and he who kisses [it]!

59. His birth made manifest the sweet-smelling goodness of his substance. How fragrant was the commencement thereof, and the conclusion!

60. [It was] a day in which the Persians sagaciously opined that they were warned of the happening of evil and of vengeance;

61. And the pavilion of the Chosroes became, being fissured, like unto the courtiers of the Chosroes, irremediably disarrayed;

62. And the [Sacred] Fire, through sorrowfulness thereat, became extinct in its respirations [of flame], and the river [of the Tigris] dry at fount, through choking;

[226]

63. And it afflicted [the town of] Sawa that its lake should sink into the earth, and that the corner thereto for water should be angrily repelled when he thirsted;--

64. As though in the Fire [there was], through sadness, the wetness that is in water; and in the water, the [heart-] burning that is in fire;--

65. Then the genii make their voices heard; and the meteors are flashing, and the truth becomes manifest in sense and in words;

66. [But men] were blind and deaf; so the proclamation of the good news was not heard; nor were the flaming admonitions heeded;

67. Although their soothsayers had informed the peoples that their crooked religions would not stand;

68. And though they had seen in the horizon blazing stars fallen, in like manner with what [took place] on earth with idols;

69. Until it happened, by means of revelation, that one discomfited individual of the demons followed the footmarks of [another] discomfited one;

70. As though they were, in [their] flight, the cowards of Abraha, or the army lapidated with pebbles from his [Muhammad's] two hands,

71. In a throw, after a recitation of doxology within their two palms; even as the casting forth of the doxologist [Jonah] from the entrails of the swallowing fish;

72. At his [Muhammad's] call the trees came prostrating themselves, walking towards him on legs [trunks] without feet;

73. As though they were tracing lines for what their branches wrote, of a beautiful handwriting, in the main track of the path:

74. Like the cloud, which followed wherever he went, shielding him from the oven-like heat of noontide waxed sultry.

75. I swear by the cloven moon,--verily, it hath a relation, through his heart, which makes an oath thereby sacred to fulfil,--

76. And by what the Cave enclosed of good and generous, while all the eyes of the misbelievers were blind thereto,

77. And "Honesty," in the Cave, and the "Vouching Friend" [Abu-Bekr], budged not, while they [their pursuers] were saying: "No soul is in the Cave:

78. They imagined that the Dove would not circle, and they supposed that the Spider would not weave, around the "Best of Mortals;"

79. The protection of God rendered [them] independent of twofold coats of mail, and of high towers.

80. Time has not offered me an injury [against which] I have had recourse for protection unto him [Muhammad], but I received a protection from him that is not to be infringed;

81. And I have not craved from his hand the riches of this world, or the next, but that I received a bounty from the best of [bestowing hands] respectfully kissed [as their bounty is accepted] .

82. Deny thou not the revelation from his vision. Verily he had a heart that did not sleep when the two eyes slept;

83. For this [happened] in the time of the fulness of the prophetship; therefore the state of the dreamer is not denied regarding him.

84. God be sanctified! No revelation can be acquired by effort; and no prophet is suspected without his privity.

85. How many hath his [Muhammad's] hand cured by the touch who were diseased; and hath skilfully set free from the halter of insanity!

86. And his prayer hath made the year of drought to be alive--so that it hath been told of as a chief [year] among the times of rich vegetation--

87. By a cloud-bank that rained copiously, so that thou wouldst thence have imagined the pebbly torrent-channels were dikes cut from the ocean, or an inundation from a mountain-reservoir broken loose!

88. Let me alone, and my description of some of his miracles, which were as manifest as is the conspicuousness of the hospitality-fire. by night on the mountain-top;--

89. For pearls increase in beauty when they are in regular strings, while they lose no value when unstrung;--

90. And what [signifies] the aspiringness of the yearnings of the panegyrist toward that which is in him [Muhammad] of noble qualities and habits?

91. [And that volume of] Miracles of the Truth, brought into new existence by the All-Merciful, though [itself] an attribute of Him who is qualified with eternity, and [itself also] eternal;

92. It is not in conjunction with any one time [alone]; but it reminds us of the Resurrection, and of [the people of] 'Ad, and of [the garden of] Iram;

93. It remains perpetual with us; therefore it hath surpassed every miracle of the prophets [of old], since they came forth and endured not;

94. [Its miracles, i.e., verses, are] self-evident, so that they remain not matters of doubt to the caviller, neither do they excite a desire for [another] arbiter;

95. It has never been contested, but that the most aggressive of its attackers has returned to it proposing peace;

96. Its eloquence repels the pretensions of its disputer, with the repulsion of the jealous one [who repels] the hand of the criminal from the things held sacred [to virtue];

97. Its miracles [verses] have significations like the waves of the ocean at full tide, and above the pearls thereof in beauty and in values;

98. Its wonders are not to be told or counted, neither does it verge, through over-abundance, on tediousness;

99. The eye of its reader is made to sparkle; therefore have I said to him [the reader]: "Thou hast found the stay [cable] of God; keep fast hold [thereon];

100. "If thou recite it out of fear of the heat of the fire of hell's lowest pit, thou hast extinguished the heat of the pit with its refreshing recitation."

101. It is, as it were, the Tank, at which the faces of transgressors become whitened, who have approached it black as charcoal;

102. And as the [strait] Path and the Balance, in equity; for justice, by any other than it, is not established among the people.

103. Wonder thou not at envious ones who deny it through ignorance, whereas it is [as] the [very] eye [-sight] of the perspicacious and intelligent:--

104. The eye, through ophthalmia, has, ere now, denied the light of the sun; and the mouth, through disease, has denied the taste of water.

105. O [Muhammad] thou Best of those whose court the guests seek, trudging on foot, or [seated] upon the loins of easy-paced she-camels;

106. And who art the greatest sign for one who takes admonition; and who art the greatest blessing to him who avails [thereof]!

107. Thou travelledst by night from one sacred site to [another] sacred site, as the full moon journeys in the deepest of darkness;

108. And thou continuedst to mount, until thou reachedst the stage of Two Bow-shots, not reached [by another], and not attempted;

109. And all the prophets and messengers gave thee the precedency--the precedency of the served one over the servants;

110. And thou traversedst with them the seven strata [of the heavens] in a procession, in which thou wast the standard-bearer;

111. Until thou leftedst not a further limit for any to go beyond thee in propinquity [to God's throne], nor a stair of ascent for any one mounting;

112. Thou debasedst every degree by comparison, when thou wast invited to go up higher, like the sole distinguished guest;

113. That thou mightest have an interview with One curtained in how special a manner from the eyes [of mankind] and [the communication of] a secret concealed in how profound a degree;

114. Thou gainedst every subject of [legitimate] boasting, without a co-participator; and thou passedst through every stage [of progress] free from the throng;

115. And illustrious was the worth of the grades thou acquiredst; difficult is the comprehension of the favours thou receivedst!

116. Glad tidings unto us, the host of Islam! For verily we have, through [God's] grace, a corner pilaster undemolishable!

117. Inasmuch as God has named him [Muhammad] "the Most Noble of the Apostles," who called us to obedience unto Him [God], we are the noblest of peoples.

118. The tidings of his mission scared the hearts of the enemies, as a cry that puts to flight an unminded flock of sheep and goats;

119. Neither did he cease to meet them on every battle-field, until, through his lances, they put [men] in mind of flesh on a tray;

120. They preferred flight; and therein they had well-nigh envied the [torn] limbs rising [into the air] with the eagles and the vultures;

[230]

521. The nights went by, and they knew not the count thereof, when these were not nights of the months when warfare is unlawful.

122. As though the religion [of Islam] were a guest that had alighted in their court with all noble brood camels, eager to devour the flesh of his enemies,

123. Who led a flood of an army [mounted] upon fleet horses, that threw up dashing waves of brave warriors,

124. [Composed] of all ready answerers to his call, confiding in God, and attacking with an exterminating weapon--extirpator of blasphemy;

125. Until, through them, the religious community of Islam, after its exile, became united to its blood-kindred;

126. For ever guaranteed, through them, with the best of fathers, and the best of husbands; so that it shall not become an orphan, nor a widow.

127. They were [immovable as] mountains. Ask, then, concerning them, of him who encountered with them: what was it he experienced from them in every place of encounter?

128. And ask Hunayn, and ask Badr, and ask 'Uhud: seasons of death more dire to them than the pest!

129. They sent forth the bright swords red, after these had reached every black hanging ear-curl of the hair of their enemies;

130. And they wrote with brown lances of Khatt, whose pens did not leave one body of a letter unpunctuated;

131. Whose weapons are keen; who have a mark that distinguishes them; for the rose is distinguished from the acacia by its mark.

132. The winds of victory guide unto thee their odour; so that thou deemest each armour-clad warrior a flower in its calyx.

133. They are, on the backs of their steeds, as it were, trees on hills, by reason of the firmness of courage, not through stringency of girths.

134. The hearts of the enemies sank with dismay at their onset; so that thou couldst not distinguish whether they were a flock of lambs or an army of warriors.

135. For whoso hath his stay in the Apostle of God, if lions meet him in their thickets, they are struck mute and motionless.

[231]

136. Thou wilt never see one of his friends unsuccoured by him, nor one enemy unbroken!

137. He hath caused his people to camp in the protection of his religion, even as the lion lays him down with his whelps in the thickets!

138. How many disputants concerning him have the words of God confounded; and how many adversaries has the Demonstration overcome in argument!

139. Let science in the "Illiterate One," in a time of universal ignorance [of God], and education in the "Orphan," suffice thee as a miracle!

140. I have given him my service in a panegyric, by which I seek pardon for the sins of a lifetime passed in poetry and services,

141. Which have placed on my neck that of which the results are to be feared; as though I were, through them, a victim from among cattle.

142. In both those occupations I have obeyed the seductions of youth; and I have earned nothing, save through sins and regret.

143. O what loss to a soul, in its traffic, that has not purchased religion with the world [as its price], and has not made a bid [for future happiness]!

144. And whoso selleth his future for the present, there becomes manifest for him a being cheated in the sale, and in the prepayment!

145. If I have committed a sin, my compact is not broken away from the Prophet, nor my cable sundered;

146. For verily I hold a safeguard from him through my being named Muhammad; and he is the most true of men to his bond.

147. If, in my resurrection, there be not one to take me by the hand out of goodness, then, otherwise, say thou [of me]: "Alas, the footslip!"

148. Be it not imagined of him that he will frustrate of his generosities the expectant one, or that the refugee will return from him other than treated with honour.

149. And ever since I have devoted my thoughts to his praiseworthy qualities, I have found him the best of sureties for my salvation.

150. Wealth from him will never fail a hand pinched with poverty: verily the rain maketh the flowers to grow on the hills!

151. And I have not desired the glory of the world, which the hands of Zuhayr [the poet] grasped through what he sang in praise of Harim.

152. O thou most noble of the creation! I have not any one [beside thee] to whom to betake me, on the occurrence of the universal event [of death and resurrection].

153. And thy dignity, O Apostle of God! will not be narrowed through me when the All-Generous God shall manifest Himself in His name of an Avenger.

154. For the world and its fellow [future life] exist out of thy bounty; and out of thy science exists the science of the Tablet and of the Pen!

155. O Flesh! despair thou not by reason of a footslip that was great: verily deadly sins, in the divine forgiveness, are as venial offences.

156. Maybe that the grace of my Lord, when He shall share it out, will come, in the shares, in proportion to the transgressions.

157. O my Lord [God], let not my hope be reversed in Thy counsel; and judge Thou not my reckoning deficient!

158. And deal Thou graciously with Thy servant: verily he hath a fortitude, which, when terrors call for it, is put to flight.

159. And grant Thou that showers of benedictions from Thee [may be] perpetual upon the Prophet, copious and continuous;

160. And upon the family and the companions; then upon the successors of these, the men of piety, and virtue, and forbearance, and generosity;

161. While the breath of the zephyr waves the branches of the moringa, and the camel-leader enlivens the camels with chants.

APPENDIX.

When the Arabians became the only   learned people, and their empire extended over the greater part of the known   world, they impressed their own genius on those nations with whom they were   allied as friends, or reverenced as masters.--Isaac D'Israeli: Curiosities of Literature.

APPENDIX.

[233]

EXTRACTS FROM
THE LAY OF THE HIMYARITES,
BY THE
KADHI NESHWAN IBN SA'ID, EL-HIMYARY.
TRANSLATED AND EDITED
BY MAJOR W. F. PRIDEAUX, F.R.G.S., &C.

["PTOLEMY mentions the Homerites as a nation seated in the southern parts of Arabia Felix, and bounded on the east by the Adramitae, or province of Hadramaut. His Arabiae Emporium he likewise places in their country, as Pliny does his Massala. Some authors make them the same people with the Sabaeans, whilst others consider them in a different light. For our part, we look upon Sabaei and Homeritae to have been different names of the same nation, and are countenanced herein by the Oriental historians. For these inform us that the Sabaeans were called Hamyarites from Hamyar the son of their great ancestor Saba; and that they ruled over almost the whole country of Yaman. Though the kingdom of the Hamyarites, or Homerites, was at length translated from the princes of Hamyar to the descendants of Cahlan his brother, yet they all retained the title of King of Hamyar. . . . They made a great figure amongst the ancient Arabs before the time of Mohammed."-- Ancient Universal History, vol. xviii. p, 352.

MAJOR W. F. PRIDEAUX has employed some of the few leisure hours afforded by his official duties at Sehore, Central India, in rendering into English the excellent didactic Poem, the "Lay of the Himyarites," composed in the 12th century A.D., by Neshwan ibn Sa'id. His work--printed, for private circulation, at the School Press of Sehore, in 1879, and the impression limited to 25 copies--presents the original text together with the prose translation; also Notes, giving the more important variants found in the texts previously published, and collated with the Miles and Rich MSS. in the British Museum; to which is added a series of genealogical tables, "designed to exhibit, at one comprehensive glance, the various degrees of relationship in which the chiefs and heroes who are commemorated in the Poem stood to one another."

The "Lay of the Himyarites" is chiefly valuable, as Major Prideaux remarks, for the light it throws upon the ancient history of that nation. The opening and closing verses, which are here reproduced, with the translator's kind permission, will perhaps enable the general reader to form a tolerably clear notion of the design and character of this fine Poem, written by a learned and pious descendant of the renowned princes of Himyar.--ED.]

FROM THE TRANSLATOR'S PREFACE.

BEYOND his pedigree, we know but little of Neshwan ibn Sa'id. He tells us himself in his great work, the Shems el-'Ulum, that his mother, like his father, was of noble Himyaritic descent, and that his residence was at Huth, a little village in the district of

Hamdan. Here we may imagine him to have lived and worked until his death, which took place in A.H. 573 [A.D. 1177]. The knowledge which is so copiously displayed in his works was probably derived, not only from the writings of more ancient authors, such as Wahb ibn Munebbih and 'Ubaid ibn Shariyah, but from the oral traditions of the peasantry. His principal work, the Shems el-'Ulum, is in lexicographical form, and, according to Dr. D. H. Muller, is of the highest value from a historical and geographical point of view. A manuscript of this book is in the Royal Library at Berlin, and it is much to be wished that Dr. Muller, who has already turned its contents to considerable use, should complete his task by giving to the world the work in its entirety. Neshwan ibn Sa'id was also the author of several other works, chiefly, it would appear from their titles, of an exegetical nature, and of a few scattered poetical pieces, which the searcher amongst Arabic manuscripts may here and there light upon.

The work, however, which has been chiefly associated with his name is the Lay of the Himyarites. The motif of this Poem is clearly ethical: it deals with the most commonplace and yet the newest of themes, the decay of glory, the vanity of human power. Not less vain perhaps are the efforts of poet or moralist to persuade man that he is but a sharer in the common lot, and that he, even he, like every one else, "cometh in with vanity, and departeth in darkness, and his name shall be covered with darkness;" for that which strikes him as only natural in the case of the rest of the world, appears something strange and novel when his own turn comes to endure it. The Poet of Himyar takes as his text the fallen fortunes of his own illustrious race. "Where," asks he, "are the kings and nobles of Himyar? They have been ground down as the kernel of the date beneath the millstone: they have become as dust in the earth!"

But reflections which are merely the echo of the voice of the Preacher may be thought too trite to merit much attention. This is true; the writer's claims to a hearing rest on other grounds. The Poem is a terse epitome of the ancient history of El-Yemen: if it does little more than record the names of kings and princes, still these names are rarely to be found else where, and, when read with the Commentary and with the Shems el-'Ulum of the same author, the work affords valuable testimony in support of the theory that the interminable genealogies which we find scattered throughout the works of the early Arab writers are not the mere figments of their imagination, but are actually founded upon evidence which is more or less of a historical character.

OPENING VERSES OF THE POEM.

THE purpose of GOD is a serious matter, and not a subject for jesting; employ thyself; therefore, my comrade, in religious works.

2. How is stability possible with diversities of temperaments, and the everlasting recurrence of night and morning!

[235]

3. Time is the best of counsellors to admonish a young man; and its ad vice surpasses that of the most friendly monitors.

4. Direct thine eyes to what is certain; and inquire not, oh thou drunken one, from him who is recovering from intoxication.

5. The world runs away with us towards peril, like as the boat of the seaman hastens to it;

6. It runs away with us into a sea of waters, in which there is neither shore nor shallows.

7. The occupations of mankind divert them from the worship of their LORD; the seductions of their world and its contentions,

8. And the love of the world which enters ever with the souls into bodies.

9. All mankind are drinkers of the cup of Death; by natural means or by bloodshed.

10. Do not despair at evil accidents, and be not too joyful over happy events.

11. Where is Hud, the man who feared GOD, and his testamentary injunctions? or Kahtan, of the seed of the Prophet and of holiness?

12. Where is Ya'rub, who was the first to speak Arabic, and who introduced articulate language among man?

13. Where is Yashjub, whom his fate betrayed; and for whom sorrow was ordained by the decree of destiny?

14. And Saba, the son of Yashjub, who in foray was the first to lead into captivity the women who wore girdles?

15. Or Himyar and his brother Kahlan, who perished through the accidents of all-destroying Time?

16. And the Kings of Himyar?--a thousand kings have betaken themselves to the dust, to rest in graves beneath slabs of stones.

17. Their monuments in the land give us information of them: and the books in their stories record the truth.

18. Their generations are made manifest in them, and their renown is fragrant as the perfume of ambergris.

19. They reigned over the East and the West; and obtained possession of all the country between Ankarah and Nejd-el-jah.

[236]

20. Thamud and the latter 'Ad reigned together; from them proceeded noble princes in whom was no covetousness.

21. Where is El-Humaisa', and Aiman after him, and Zuhair, a king brilliant in splendour?

22. In course of time Thamud came to destruction through a she-camel, and met with great grief on her account.

23. And 'Arib and Katan and Haidan together?--They were smitten as though they were date-stones in the crusher.

[Of the next 105 verses, in which the Poet continues his recital, begun as above, of the names of famous princes and heroes of Himyar, the five following, referring to the visit of the celebrated "Queen of Sheba" to King Solomon, are selected as being of general interest.]

45. Where is Bilkis, the mighty-throned one, or her palace, lofty above all palaces?

46. She visited Solomon the prophet in Tadmor, coming from Marib on an errand of faith, without thoughts of marriage,

47. With thousands upon thousands of the armed men of her people; she did not approach him with jaded camels.

48. She came to acknowledge Islam, at the season when his writing came, with which he invited her with a loud-voiced Hoopoe.

49. She bowed in worship to her mighty Creator, and humbly became a Muslim; and formerly her adoration was to the Sun.

[Having reviewed the long line of Himyarite princes, who were, each in his day, "possessed of power for evil or for good," the Poet thus moralises in conclusion.]

CLOSING VERSES.

129. The chiefs of Himyar, and their kings, are buried in the dust, to rest in graves beneath slabs of stones.

130. They have become dust, they are trodden on like as Death treads upon the mounds of earth and the pebbles of the watercourse.

131. The world they lived in submitted to them, then turned away and smote them with its kicking hoof.

[237]

132. There rained upon them, after the clouds of their prosperity, the clouds of misfortune in heavy-pouring showers.

133. The accidents of Time had no regard for them, nor could they defend themselves from them with swords or lances;

134. No, not with troops and with palaces; nor with armies, and fortresses, and weapons.

135. They have their dwelling in the earth, after living in castles, and delighting themselves with eating and drinking, and the pleasures of wedlock.

136. Their castles, which were built on supports of wide-spreading stone, have become as smouldering wood.

137. Time mingles its misfortunes with its favours, and affects its children with misery in the midst of joy.

138. Praise be to GOD, whose beneficence is to be hoped for! may He remain an object of praise in the morning and the evening!

139. And may blessings he upon the Prophet and his followers, as long as the winged pigeon may coo!

NOTES.

As Major Prideaux' brochure is designed chiefly for scholars, the Notes appended to his translation treat only of the original text and variants: the Editor of the present volume ventures to offer explanatory notes on a few of the verses given above, which may not be, otherwise, very intelligible or interesting to some readers.

v. 11. "Hud, the man who feared GOD." The prophet who, according to the received story of the Muslims, was sent to warn the tribe of 'Ad of the punishment in store for them if they did not abandon their idolatry, and return to the worship of the true GOD. The people of 'Ad rejected the prophet's message, and were utterly destroyed because of their unbelief. (Kur'an, sur. vii.) According to some authors, a few of the 'Adites, being at Mecca praying for rain, escaped the fate of their brethren; and these survivors gave rise to a tribe called "the latter 'Ad"--mentioned in v. 20. The Arabs employ the phrase, "as old as King 'Ad" to signify the great antiquity of anything.

"Kahtan, of the seed of the prophet and of holiness." Joktan the son of Eher, whom the Arabs call Kahtan, had thirteen sons, one of whom, Sheba, or Saba, was the ancestor of the Sabaeans, or Himyarites.

v. 12. Ya'rub, the son of Kahtan, succeeded his father in the kingdom of Yemen, giving name, if we may credit the Arab historians, both to their country and language.

v. 14. Abd Shems, "the Servant of the Sun," surnamed Saba, the son of Yashab, the Arab historians tell us, was successful in his expeditions against his enemies, carried off great spoils, and took many of them prisoners. He is said to have built the city of Saba, or Marib, as likewise the stupendous mound or building which formed the vast reservoir above that city. By means of this reservoir, which received all the water that came down from the mountains, the Kings of Yemen did not only supply the inhabitants of Saba and their lands with water, but likewise kept the territories they had subdued in greater awe; since by cutting them off from a communication with it they could at any time greatly distress them.--Ancient Universal History, vol. xviii. p. 419. The water [in this reservoir] rose to the height of almost twenty fathoms, and was kept in on every side by a work so solid, that many had their houses built upon it. But at length GOD, being highly displeased at their pride and insolence, and resolving to humble and disperse them, sent a mighty flood, which broke down the mound by night, while the inhabitants were asleep, and carried away the whole city, with the neighbouring towns and people. This inundation is styled in the Koran, "the inundation of al-Arem," and occasioned so terrible a destruction that from thence it became a proverbial saying, to express a total dispersion, that "they were gone and scattered like Saba." No less than eight tribes were forced to abandon their dwellings on this occasion, some of which gave rise to the kingdoms of Hira and Ghassan.--Ibid., p. 428.

v. 55. Himyar, the son of Abd Shems, or Saba, according to Oriental authors, was so called from the red clothes he wore. This seems a plain indication that Himyar was only a surname. He expelled the Thamud from Yemen, who took refuge in Hejaz. From this prince the tribe or kingdom of Himyar deduced its name. Some assert that Himyar, not Kahtan, was the first king of Yemen that wore a diadem.--An. Univ. Hist., vol. xviii. p. 419.

v. 22. "Thamud came to destruction through a she-camel."

As the prophet Hud (see note on verse 11) had been sent to warn the tribe of 'Ad of their wickedness, so the prophet Salih was sent with a similar message to the people of Thamud. (Kur'an, sur. vii.) "The Thamudites," says Sale, "insisting on a miracle, proposed to Salih that he should go with them to their festival, and that they should call on their gods, and he on his, promising to follow that deity which should answer. But after they had called on their idols a long time to no purpose, Jonda Ebn Amru, their prince, pointed to a rock standing by itself, and bade Salih cause a she-camel big with young to come forth from it, solemnly engaging that, if he did, he would believe, and his people promised the same. Whereupon Salih asked it of GOD, and presently the rock, after several throes as if in labour, was delivered of a she-camel answering the description of Jonda, which immediately brought forth a young one, ready weaned, and, as some say, as big as herself. Jonda, seeing this miracle, believed on the prophet, and some few with him; but the greater part of the Thamudites remained, notwithstanding, incredulous."--"Those who were elated with pride said: 'Verily we believe not in that wherein ye believe.' And they slew the camel, and insolently transgressed the command of their LORD, and said: O Salih, cause that to come upon us with which thou hast threatened us, if thou art one of those who have been sent by GOD.' Whereupon a terrible noise from heaven assailed them; and in the morning they were found in their dwellings prostrate on their faces, dead." (Kur'an, sur. vii.)--The tribe of Thamud dwelt first in the country of the Adites, but their numbers increasing, they removed to the territory of Hejr [Petra] for the sake of the mountains, where they cut themselves habitations in the rocks, to be seen at this day.--Sale. This dreadful punishment of the Thamudites would appear to have passed into a proverb. For example: Sheddad, lamenting the supposed loss of his heroic son 'Antar, calls down a hearty curse upon the cause of his misery in these words: "May GOD destroy Malik, son of Carad, and make him suffer what the tribe of Thamud endured!" (Romance of Antar, <page 237> of the present volume.) And Hafiz, the Persian poet, in one of his odes, advises his friend to "drink wine and dismiss the story of 'Ad and Thamud."--Zuhayr (Mo'allaqah, v. 32) compares the deformed offspring of War to "the dun camel of 'Ad," not of Thamud, as the legend runs in the Kur'an.

vv. 45-49. Queen Bilkis, according to the genealogical tables compiled by Major Prideaux, and appended to his translation of this poem, was the daughter of El-Hadhad ibn Sharahbil; and she is placed twenty-second in Pocock's list of the sovereigns of El-Yemen. The Arabs this princess with the famous "Queen of Sheba," or Saba, who went to see King Solomon in all his glory.

King Solomon, as Eastern legends inform us, among his wonderful accomplishments, was versed in the language of birds. One day a hoopoe (called by the Arabs "al-Hudhud") brought him an account of the city of Saba, and of the great Queen Bilkis, who, with all her subjects, worshipped the sun. Shocked at such wickedness, Solomon wrote a letter to the Queen, commanding her to relinquish her errors and embrace the true religion; and having perfumed the letter with musk and sealed it with his signet, he despatched the hoopoe to deliver it to Queen Bilkis. The feathered messenger, having arrived at her palace, and finding the doors all shut, as El-Beidawi opines, flew in at a window and dropped the letter on the Queen's lap; but Jelalu-'d-Din says that she was surrounded by her army when the lapwing threw it into her bosom. All agree, however, that the letter was duly delivered, and that Queen Bilkis, taking with her, as the Poet of Himyar states, "thousands upon thousands of the armed men of her people," immediately set forth to visit King Solomon, and ascertain the truth of the reports which were spread abroad regarding his wisdom and piety. The result was her profession of Islam--for according to the Muhammadan theology, Solomon and the other venerated Biblical personages were all good Muslims: Muhammad professed, not to introduce a new religion, but to restore the original and only true faith.

They say that Solomon afterwards married Queen Bilkis of Saba. This forms the subject of a curious legend related by commentators on the Kur'an. A version of this story is given by Mrs. Godfrey Clerk, in her entertaining little book of Oriental tales and anecdotes, entitled, 'Ilam-en-Nis. In a prefatory note to her translation of the legend, Mrs.

Clerk remarks that the reign of Queen Bilkis very nearly coincided with the commencement of the Christian era. According to M. Caussin de Perceval, this princess killed her husband by means of poison.

vv. 138, 139. A benediction on the Prophet often concludes a Kasideh of an ethical or devotional character (see verses 159-161 of Mr. Redhouse's translation of El-Busiri's Poem of the Mantle, page <page 341> of the present volume). The poetical exclamations of pilgrims when they first behold El-Madina are expressed in a similar strain: "O Allah! bless the last of prophets, the seal of prophecy, with blessings in number as the stars of heaven, and the waves of the sea, and the sands of the waste! bless him, O Lord of Might and Majesty, as long as the corn-field and the date-grove continue to feed mankind!"-- "Live for ever, O most excellent of prophets! live in the shadow of happiness during the hours of night and the times of day, whilst the bird of the tamarisk [the dove] moaneth like the childless mother; whilst the west wind bloweth gently over the hills of Nejd, and, the lightning flasheth bright in the firmament of El-Hejaz!" (Burton's Pilgrimage to El-Medina and Meccah, vol. ii. pp. 25, 26). In the Romance of Antar the same form of benediction frequently occurs; for example: "Live for ever, Prince of the horsemen! long as the dove pours its plaintive note, live for ever!"--"May peace dwell with thee as long as the western and the northern breeze shall blow!"

*** An error in one of the preceding notes, discovered after the sheet was printed, may be corrected here. (v. 11.) Sheba, or Saba, the ancestor of the Sabaeans, was not one of the sons of Kahtan--although it is said he had a son of the same name--but a great grandson; being ['Abd-Shems, surnamed] Saba, the son of Yashjub, the son of Ya'rub, the son of Kahtan.

THE POET 'OMAR.

[THE Editor is indebted to the courtesy of Messrs. Macmillan and Company, publishers, of London and Cambridge, for liberty to make the following extracts from the interesting account of the life and poetry of 'Omar the Mogheeree, by Mr. William Gifford Palgrave (author of "Central and Eastern Arabia"), in his "Essays on Eastern Questions"--a volume at once highly instructive and entertaining. Mr. Palgrave's graceful renderings of 'Omar's verse must induce the wish on the part of every reader that he would give us more Arabic poetry in the same pleasing English dress.]

"POVERTY of means," says Mr. Palgrave, "isolation of circumstance, and insecurity of life had, during the long ante-Islamitic period, cramped the energy, narrowed the ideas, and marred the taste of almost all, indeed in some degree of all, Arab poets. The circle they moved in was rough, barren, and contracted: their genius dwarfed itself into proportion with the limits which it could not overpass. The high rank and noble birth of the pre-Islamitic 'Amroo-ben-Kelthoom and 'Amroo-l-Keys had not exempted them from ever-recurring personal dangers and privations on the road and in the field; while the vigorous spirit of Shanfara', Ta'abbet Shurran, and their like, was distorted by the physical misery and the savage loneliness to which their writings bear such frequent witness. All this had now passed away. Union had given security, conquest riches; while intercourse and Islam had developed the intellect of the nation. Two entirely new classes of society henceforth came into existence--the men of pleasure and the men of literature: the former heirs of a wealth they cared rather to enjoy than to increase; the latter seekers after wealth, fame, and name, but by intellectual, not by physical distinction. Love and song tissued the career of the former; poetry and eloquence, but chiefly poetry, were the business of the latter. Meanwhile a select few, the spoilt children of destiny--the Mirandolas or Byrons of their land and day--combined the advantages of birth and fortune with those of genius. Foremost among these stands the nobleman, the warrior, the libertine, but above all, the poet--the Don Juan of Mecca, the Ovid of Arabia and the East--'Omar the Mogheeree, the grandson of Aboo-Rabee'ah."

Mogheerah, the great-grandfather of the poet 'Omar, had, by a wealthy marriage, re-united two important divisions of Koreysh, and thus founded a powerful clan, known as the Children of Mogheerah. His son, Hodeykah Aboo-Rabee'ah, the grandfather of 'Omar--called, from his gigantic stature, "Two Spears," or Longshanks, as we should phrase it--distinguished himself at the battle of Okatz, shortly before the birth of the Prophet. Aboo-Rabee'ah's son, Bojeyr, the father of the poet, was converted to Islam by Mohammed himself, who on the occasion bestowed on him the honourable appellation of 'Abd-Allah, "Servant of God." He was enormously wealthy, having almost the monopoly of the trade in metals, cloth, and spices with Abyssinia and Yemen.

'Omar's mother was an Arab woman of Hadramaut, a province ever famed for its female beauty; and it happened that he was born on the same day that his renowned namesake the Caliph 'Omar was murdered by the fanatic Persian slave Firooz (A.H. 23, A.D. 643). 'Abd-Allah had a second son, called Hirth, by his other wife, an Abyssinian woman. The half-blood Hirth, an austere Muslim, passed his life in government employment; while 'Omar idled and made love-songs, and got himself into trouble through his amours, from which it was often his brother's painful task to extricate him.

"One year," says Mr. Palgrave, on the authority of the poet's best biographer Aboo-l-Faraj, "on the very high day of the great annual festival, when the pilgrims, assembled from all quarters of the Mohammedan world at Mecca, were engaged in the evening performance of their solemn traditionary rite, pacing seven times in prayer round the sacred Ka'abeh, Zeynab, a young girl of noble birth, happened to be present among the crowd of worshippers, from whom, however, she was easily to be distinguished by her surpassing beauty and the gay dresses of her numerous attendants. What next followed 'Omar may best recite after his own fashion, and in his own metre, which we have as far as possible preserved in the translation; though the rhyme, which if rendered would have necessitated too frequent divergence from the original style and imagery, has been omitted:

Ah for the throes of a heart sorely wounded!
  Ah for the throes of a heart sorely wounded!
  Ah for the eyes that have smit me with madness!

[242]

Gently she moved in the calmness of beauty,
Moved as the bough to the light breeze of morning.
Dazzled my eyes as they gazed, till before me
All was a mist and confusion of figures.
Ne'er had I sought her, and ne'er had she sought me;
Fated the love, and the hour, and the meeting!
There I beheld her, as she and her damsels
Paced 'twixt the temple and outer enclosure:
Damsels the fairest, the loveliest, the gentlest,
Passing like slow-wending heifers at evening,
Ever surrounding with courtly observance
Her whom they honour, the peerless of women.
Then to a handmaid, the youngest, she whispered:
"'Omar is near; let us mar his devotions.
Cross on his path that he needs may observe us;
Give him a signal, my sister, demurely."
"Signals I gave, but he marked not or heeded,"
Answered the damsel, and hasted to meet me. [p. 359]
Ah for that night by the vale of the sand-hills!
Ah for the dawn when in silence we parted!
He who the morn may awake to her kisses
Drinks from the cup of the blessed in heaven!

"The last four lines of this lyric seem, however, to have been written under the influence of poetical anticipation; for many weeks and even months passed without any closer intercourse than that of love-messages and glances at a distance. Zeynab, with her father Moosa, and her two elder sisters, prolonged their visit at Mecca. 'Omar was now in the prime of youth and personal beauty, advantageously set off by rank, wealth, and idleness. No wonder that his reputation as a lady-killer was already pretty well established; and that Zeynab, young herself, and only too susceptible of attentions like 'Omar's, should have received from her alarmed relatives much prudent cautioning Spring and summer passed thus, but 'Omar's suit advanced little; thanks to the coyness of the lady, and still more, it may be well believed, to the vigilance of her guardians. . . .

"Love, however, at last prevailed; and a rendezvous was given at some distance from the town, in one of the valleys that lie south-east of Mecca, bordered by high abrupt rocks, and green in its winding course below with thick gardens and palm-groves: the very place for a stolen interview. Thither Zeynab was to betake herself for an afternoon stroll with a few chosen attendants; while 'Omar was to meet her 'quite promiscuous,' as if returning from a journey. The plan succeeded; its opening scene is thus described by 'Omar in verses which long remained the envy and despair of rival poets:

Late and early, Love between us idle messenger had gone,
Till his fatal ambush in the valley of Khedab was laid:
There we met; nor, sign, nor token, needed but a glance--no more; [p. 360]

[243]

All my heart and all its passion mirrored in her heart I saw;
And I said: "'Tis evening cool; the gardened houses are not far;
Why unsocial bide we seated weary on the weary beasts?"
Turned she to her damsels with "What say ye?" They replied, "Alight;
Better far the cool earth's footing than the uneasy saddle perch."
Down they glided, clustering starlike round the perfect queen of night,
Calmly wending in her beauty, as to music's measured beat.
Shyly drew I near and greeted, fearful lest some jealous eye
Should behold us, or the palm-trees tell the story of our loves.
Half-withdrawn her veil, she whispered: "Fear not, freely speak your mind.
Kinsmen none are here to watch us; thou and I may claim our own."
Bold I answered: "Were there thousands, fearless would I bide their worst:
But the secret of my bosom brooks no ear, no eye but thine."
Then the maidens--ah, the maidens!--noted how apart we drew;
Well they guessed unspoken wishes, and the inmost thoughts of love.
Said they: "Give us leave to wander; bide thou here alone awhile;
We will stroll a little onwards, 'neath the pleasant evening star."
"Be not long, she answered; said they: "Fear not, we will straight return--
Straight be with thee; "and at once like trooping fawns they slipped away.
Little need to ask their meaning; if they came or if they went--
Known to her, to me, the purpose: yet we had not said a word.

"It may be easily imagined that Zeynab's attendants were too discreet to return in a hurry; and the lovers, regardless of time, prolonged their meeting till evening had passed into night, when there came on a sudden storm of rain, such as is not uncommon among the hills of the Hejaz coast. 'Omar, gallantly fearful lest the light dress of his fair companion should suffer, took off his cloak, one of red embroidered silk and wool, such as still may be often seen worn by the upper classes in the peninsula, and cast it over her shoulders; while she playfully refused to accept the shelter unless on condition that he should keep a part of it over himself; and in this amiable proximity they remained awhile till the shower had blown over, and the approach of dawn warned them to separate.

"Thus far all was well, and might perhaps have continued so but for the vanity of 'Omar himself, who a few days afterwards published the whole adventure, not forgetting the circumstance of the shower and the cloak, in verses that expressed much and suggested more. In spite of the thin disguise of fictitious personages, Zeynab's name, joined with that of 'Omar, was soon in every mouth; and Moosa, the father of the young lady, began to have serious fears as to the consequences of so compromising a courtship. Young 'Omar, wealthy and powerful, not only in the popularity of rising genius, but in the near relationship of princes and caliphs, was beyond the reach of his anger; and Moosa determined accordingly to seek for his daughter in flight the security which he could not hope from open contest. Silently and secretly he prepared his departure from the Hejaz; but 'Omar had notice of it in time to obtain yet one more interview with the young lady. Zeynab, however, took her precautions, and brought with her this time, not her own attendants only, but several others of her Meccan female friends, easily induced to

[244]

accompany her by their curiosity to make a nearer acquaintance with the first poet of the day. The rendezvous was in a valley at some distance out of town; and there the whole party remained from evening to sunrise: the result was a serious proposal of marriage on 'Omar's part, accepted by Zeynab; but on condition that, after her own and her father's removal to their projected establishment in the neighbourhood of the Persian Gulf, 'Omar should follow them thither, and there make his offer in due form. In the meantime he was neither to see her nor speak with her, either in public or in private."

'Omar, however, soon broke his promise, and attempted, but without success, to obtain another interview with Zeynab before her departure. His half-brother Hirth, alarmed at the possible consequences of his levity, "giving him a large supply of money for the road, sent him off to look after some family estates in the extreme south of Yemen, after a serious warning and a solemn promise exacted that he would amend his doings in future. 'Omar obeyed; but once alone, a male Mariana in the south, separation and solitude proved too much for him; and before many weeks of his banishment were over, he had begun to solace his loneliness with several pathetic effusions, to all of which Zeynab was the keynote. The following may serve as a specimen:

Ah! where have they made my dwelling? Far, how far, from her, the loved one,
 Since they drove me lone and parted to the sad sea-shore of 'Aden!
 Thou art mid the distant mountains; and to each, the loved and lover,
 Nought is left but sad remembrance, and a share of aching sorrow.
 Hadst thou seen thy lover weeping by the sand-hills of the ocean,
 Thou hadst deemed him struck by madness: was it madness? was it love?
 I may forget all else, but never shall forget her as she stood,
 As I stood, that hour of parting: heart to heart in speechless anguish;
 Then she turned her to Thoreyya, to her sister, sadly weeping;
 Coursed the tears down cheek and bosom, till her passion found an utterance:
 "Tell him, sister, tell him; yet be not as one that chides or murmurs--
 'Why so long thy distant tarrying on the unlovely shores of Yemen? [p. 363]
 Is it sated ease detains thee, or the quest of wealth that lures thee?
 Tell me what the price they paid thee, that from Mecca bought thy absence?'"

At length 'Omar returns to Mecca; and for the next six years he continued, in exquisite poetry, to lament the absent Zeynab--and to make love to other girls. In the meantime Zeynab's two elder sisters had married, but she remained single; and on the death of her father Moosa she returned to Mecca, accompanied by an old negress who had formerly been her nurse. It happened that 'Omar, splendidly dressed, mounted on his best horse, and with numerous attendants, was riding about the neighbourhood of the city when Zeynab's litter approached. Questioning the old negress, he soon elicited the news of Zeynab's return. The courtship was renewed, and this time in earnest; for 'Omar married Zeynab, who bore him a son and a daughter.

"'Omar is twice mentioned as taking part in the numerous military expeditions of the time; one, against the restless inhabitants of Hasa, then fermenting into the rebellion

[245]

which ultimately separated them from the body of the empire; the other, when he was already over seventy, if dates be exact, against the Byzantine capital itself during the reign of Suleyman, the seventh Caliph of the Omeyyah family. In this latter expedition the Poet, according to Ebn-Khallikan, found a soldier's, and, in Mohammedan estimation, a martyr's death; perishing with countless others by the Greek fire that consumed the beleaguering Arab fleet. On the other hand, the Isphahanee chronicler Aboo-l-Faraj brings him back to die some years later in his bed, at the advanced age of eighty. The former account is probably the more correct one; but in no case has the charge of military incapacity been laid against 'Omar; and personal cowardice, a fault rare among Arabs, whatever their tribe or clan, would have been indeed a prodigy in one descended from Koreysh."

ON THE PROSODY OF THE ARABS;
WITH SPECIMENS OF THE POETRY OF "THE THOUSAND AND ONE NIGHTS."

[In the New Quarterly Magazine, for January and April, 1879, there appeared two excellent papers on "The Thousand and One Nights," from the pen of Mr. John Payne-- author of "The Masque of Shadows," "The Poems of Francis Villon," and other well-known poetical works--who has been for some time engaged on a new translation (the first complete one) of the fascinating romances and tales comprised in that work. The following outline of the general principles of Arabian Prosody--including specimens of the charming poetry of "The Thousand and One Nights," in which the various forms of metre and rhyme are admirably preserved in English verse--taken from the second of these articles by permission of the author, will doubtless prove very acceptable to the class of readers for whom the present volume is mainly designed; while to scholars Mr. Payne's versified translations must be peculiarly interesting, as showing the adaptability of our language, in some degree, to the peculiarities of Oriental prosody. Mr. Payne's translation of Elf Leyleh wa Leyleh, or "The Thousand and One Nights," is looked for, both by Arabists and men of general literary culture, with considerable interest; and judging by the specimens of the tales which are given in the articles above mentioned, his work, when published, is likely to attain an immediate and a lasting popularity.--ED.]

BEFORE proceeding to cite specimens of the verse of "The Thousand and One Nights," it is perhaps well to give a rough outline of the principles upon which the prosody of the Arabs is founded. The invariable unit, upon which Arabic (and Persian) verse is built, is the beit or line, usually but improperly translated "couplet." The word beit signifies literally "a house," but by analogy "a tent" (and from this we may fairly conclude at least this fundamental part of Arabic prosody to have originated with the Bedouins or Arabs of the desert, as it is only they who would be likely to call a tent a house), the verse being whimsically regarded by the Arabs as an edifice; and this simile is carried out in the nomenclature of the different parts of the line, one foot being called "a tent-pole," another "a tent-peg," and the two hemistichs of the verse being known as the folds or leaves of the double-door of the tent. Each beit is divided into two hemistichs of equal length, each containing two, three, or four feet, of two, three, or four syllables, and the whole verse is known as a tetrameter, hexameter, or octameter, according as it contains four, six, or eight feet, or from sixteen to thirty-two syllables.

A peculiarity of Arabic verse is the excess of long syllables over short and the absence of the dactyl and other swift feet in use among Europeans: a characteristic which produces a graver and more stately movement of the rhythm than is common in European poetry. I should perhaps, however, observe that the qualifications "long" and "short" are somewhat empirically applied to the syllables of Arabic feet, as their quantities appear to be hardly appreciable to a European ear--the "long," in particular, being of a shifting character, so much so indeed that certain readers of the Koran are said to have been known to make use of no less than seven varieties of this quantity. This being the case, it has been suggested by the eminent French orientalist, M. Stanislas Guiraud, that musical notation should be applied to the determining of the Arabic rhythms; but notwithstanding the ingenuity and ability of his treatise on the subject, his tentatives do not as yet appear to have brought about any very definite result. The distinguished scholar Professor E. H. Palmer (who adds to his high scholastic attainments a literary faculty and a gift of graceful and polished versification rare among scholars) has indeed endeavoured to reproduce in English the precise rhythm and accent of Arabic verse; but he himself acknowledges the experiment to be an unsuccessful one, and pronounces against the feasibility of representing Oriental metres by a similar arrangement of feet and accents in English verse. The genius of the two languages, belonging as they do to opposite groups of speech-forms, presents no point of union; and it seems to me therefore that the only satisfactory way of rendering Arabic poetry into English verse is to content oneself generally with observing the exterior form of the stanza, the movement of the rhyme and (as far as possible) the identity in number of the syllables composing the beits.

The principal Arabic metres are sixteen in number, each subdivided by numerous variations; and it may, perhaps, be interesting to note here the somewhat whimsical names given to them in the East. The generic name given to them is Behr, literally "sea," but by analogy the space comprised within the walls of a tent--thus continuing the metaphor before mentioned; and they are distinguished individually as the long, the extended, the open, the copious, the perfect, the trilling, the tremulous, the running, the swift, the flowing, the light, the analogous, the improvised, the curtailed, the approximative, and the consecutive. I should perhaps mention here that the system of Arabic prosody is said to have been invented by one Khalil, a grammarian, and to have been suggested to him by the strokes of a blacksmith's hammer upon an anvil: not the most promising combination of circumstance for the birth of so important a branch of art.

The principal form used in Arabic Poetry is the Kesideh, practically identical with the better-known form of the Ghazel or love-song par excellence, with the exception that the latter is limited to eighteen beits or verses, and must contain the name of the poet in the last beit. The Kesideh may be either tetrametric, hexametric, or octametric, and is built upon a single rhyme, the two hemistichs of the first beit rhyming with each other and with the second hemistich of each succeeding beit to the end of the poem, however long it may be. It is a curious fact, that the same prohibition of enjambement or the carrying on of the sense from one verse (or pair of hemistichs) to another obtains in Arabic as in French classic verse, it being considered a fault not to complete the sense in the one verse. It is allowable to repeat the same rhyming word, but (according to the strict laws of prosody) not unless seven verses intervene between the repetitions. However, this and the preceding rule are constantly violated by Arabic poets, who appear to have little scruple in repeating the rhyming word whenever it suits them, and in Persian verse (whose laws are essentially the same as those of Arabic prosody) the license is still greater, the same word in the same sense being allowed to form the rhyme throughout a whole Ghazel. The Kesideh is the form which most frequently occurs in "The Thousand and One Nights." The following is a specimen:

LADY of beauty, that dost take all hearts with thy disdain,
 And slay'st with stress of love the souls that sigh for thee in vain,
 If thou recall me not to mind beyond our parting day,
 God knows the thought of thee with me for ever shall remain.
 Thou smitest me with cruel words, that yet are dear to me;
 Wilt thou one day vouchsafe to me thy sweetest sight again?
 I had not thought the ways of Love were languishment and woe
 And stress of soul, before, alas! to love thee I was fain.
 Even my foes have ruth on me and pity my distress;
 But thou, O heart of steel, wilt ne'er have mercy on my pain!
 By God, although I die, I'll ne'er be comforted for thee!
 Though Love itself should fail, my love shall never pass or wane!

Another form which is of frequent occurrence in the collection is the Kitat or Fragment. It is formed in precisely the same manner as the Kesideh, with the exception that the two hemistichs of the first beit do not rhyme with each other. Here is a specimen of this form:

THOU madest fair thy thought of fate, when that the days were fair,
   And fearedst not the coming ills that they to thee should bring;
 The nights were calm and safe to thee; thou wast deceived by them,
   For in the peace of night is born full many a troublous thing. [p. 368]
 Lo! in the skies are many stars, no one can tell their tale;
   But to the sun and moon alone eclipse brings darkening.
 The earth bears many a pleasant herb, and many a plant and tree;
   But none are stoned save only those to which the fair fruits cling.
 Look on the sea, and how the waifs float high upon the foam;
   But in its deepest depths of blue the pearls have sojourning.

The only other verse-form that occurs with any frequency is the Mukhemmes or Cinquain, a succession of stanzas, each formed of two beits and a hemistich, the five hemistichs of the first strophe having the same rhyme, the first four hemistichs of the succeeding stanzas taking a new rhyme independently of the first, and the fifth hemistich rhyming with the first strophe to the end of the poem. Another form of the Mukhemmes also occurs, which differs only from the first in that the last hemistichs of the stanzas

[248]

rhyme with each other only, independently of the first stanza. Here is a specimen of the first form:

I STROVE to hide the load that Love on me did lay:
 In vain; and sleep from me for aye is fled away.
 Since that wanhope doth press my heart both night and day,
 I cry aloud: "O Fate, hold back thy hand, I pray!
 For all my soul is sick for anguish and dismay."

If that the Lord of Love were just indeed to me,
 Sleep had not fled my eyes by his unkind decree.
 Have pity, sweet, on one that is for love of thee
 Worn out and wasted sore, that once was rich and free,
 Now humbled and cast down by Love from his array.

Thy foes cease not to speak thee ill; I heed not, I;
 But stop my ear to them and give them back the lie:
 I'll keep my troth with her I love, until I die.
 "Thou lovest one estranged," they say; and I reply:
 Enough. Fate blinds the eyes of those that are its prey.

The following is a specimen of the second form of the Mukhemmes:

WHO says to thee, "The first of love is free,"
 Tell him, "Not so;" but on the contrary:
 'Tis all constraint, wherein no blame can be.
 History indeed attests this verity;
 It does not style the good coin falsified.

Say, if thou wilt, "The taste of pain is sweet,
 Or to be spurned by Fortune's flying feet;"
 Talk of whatever makes the heart to beat
 For grief or gladness, fortune or defeat;
 'Twixt hope and fear I tarry stupefied.

But as for him whose happy days are light,
 Fair maids whose lips with smiles are ever bright,
 Sweet with the fragrant breath of their delight,
 Who has his will, unhindered of despite,
 'Tis not with him that craven fear should bide.

The Muweshih or Ballad is another form which occurs in the "Thousand and One Nights." It is, perhaps, the most complicated verse-form in the language, and is said to have been invented by the Muslim poets of Spain, shortly after the conquest, and to have been adopted from them by their brethren of Egypt and Syria. It consists of a succession

[249]

of three-line stanzas, in the first of which all six hemistichs end with the same rhyme. In the second and succeeding stanzas, the first line and the first hemistich of the second line take a new rhyme; but the second hemistich of the second line resumes the rhyme of the first stanza, and is followed by the third line of the latter, which serves as a refrain to each stanza of the poem, which is often of considerable length. Here is a specimen of this elegant form:

O CENSOR OF LOVE! thou that art bright as the day,
 Fortunate, clad with delight as the trees in May! [p. 370]
 If Fate with its cruel hand should thee assay,
    Then wilt thou taste of its bitter cup and say,
    Alas for Love, and out on his whole array!

My heart with his flaming fires is burnt away.
 But to-day thou art safe as yet from his fell commands,
 And his perfidy holds thee not in its iron bands;
 So scoff not at those that languish beneath his hands
 And cry, for excess of passion that doth them slay,
    Alas for Love, and out on his whole array!
    My heart with his flaming fires is burnt away.

Be not of those that look on Love with disdain,
 But rather excuse and pity the lovers' pain,
 Lest thou be bound one day in the self-same chain,
 And drink of the self-same bitter draught as they.
    Alas for Love, and out on his whole array!
    My heart with his flaming fires is burnt away.

There is none that can tell of Love and its bitterness
 But he that is sick and weak for its long excess,
 He who has lost his reason for love-distress,
 Whose drink is the bitter dregs of his own dismay.
    Alas for Love, and out on his whole array!
    My heart with his flaming fires is burnt away.

How many a lover watches the darksome night,
 His eyes forbidden the taste of sleep's delight!
 How many whose tears, like rivers adown a height,
 Course down their cheeks! How many are they that say,
    Alas for Love, and out on his whole array!
    My heart with his flaming fires is burnt away.

How many a lover wasteth for sheer despair,
 Wakeful, for void of sleep is the dusky air!
 Languor and pain are the clothes that he doth wear,

[250]

And even his pleasant dreams have gone astray.
    Alas for Love, and out on his whole array!
    My heart with his flaming fires is burnt away.

I, too, of old was empty of heart and free,
 And lay down to rest in peace till I met with thee:
 The taste of the sleepless nights was strange to me,
 Till Love did beckon, and I must needs obey.
    Alas for Love, and out on his whole array!
    My heart with his flaming fires is burnt away.

How often my patience fails and my bones do waste,
 And my tears, like a fount of blood, stream down in haste!
 For my life, that of old was pleasant and sweet of taste,
 A slender maiden hath bittered this many a day.
    Alas for Love, and out on his whole array!
    My heart with his flaming fires is burnt away.

Alack for the man among men that loves like me,
 And watches the wings of night through the shadows flee!
 Who drowns in his own despair as it were a sea,
 Who cries, in the stress of an anguish without allay,
    Alas for Love, and out on his whole array!
    My heart with his flaming fires is burnt away.

Whom hath not Love stricken and wounded indeed?
 Who has been aye from his easy fetters freed?
 Whose life is empty of Love, and who succeed
 In winning their hearts' delight without affray?
    Alas for Love, and out on his whole array!
    My heart with his flaming fires is burnt away.

Other forms of the Muweshih exist, but the above is the only one to be found in "The Thousand and One Nights." Single lines are of frequent occurrence, which are apparently "blank" (that is to say, the two hemistichs of which do not rhyme with each other), but this is only apparent, as the verses in question are nothing more than the commencing lines of a Kitat or an extract from that form of poem or from a Kesideh, blank verse having no existence in Arabic poetry.

NOTES ON THE MOALLAKAT.

BESIDES Professor E. H. Palmer's elegant translation of Antara's Mo'allaqah, included in a small volume entitled "The Song of the Reed, and Other Pieces," published by Messrs. Trubner and Co., of London, the only attempts that have been made to render passages of the "Seven Arabian Poems" into English verse are--the first sixteen verses of Lebid by Carlyle, and a few of the more striking passages of the other Poems by the anonymous writer of an article on the Mo'allaqat in vol. v. of the Retrospective Review, 1822. Carlyle's "learned translation" of Lebid's opening couplets, as Burton terms it half-scornfully in his "Pilgrimage to El-Medina and Meccah," forms the first of his "Specimens of Arabian Poetry," but was omitted in the reprint of his translations in the present volume, in order that it might be more appropriately placed, with the other versified passages of the Mo'allaqat, among the following Notes.

A new translation of the Mo'allaqat, done with the light of the Commentaries, will probably appear shortly, by Mr. C. J. Lyall, of the Indian Civil Service, who has already published, by way of specimens, in the Journal of the Bengal Asiatic Society, the Poems of Lebid and Zuhayr, with Introductions and copious Notes. In these translations Mr Lyall has preserved the external form of the original verses, though he has not attempted to reproduce the Qasida rhyme. When Mr Lyall's complete translation is published, it will doubtless supersede that of Sir William Jones; which, however, with all its imperfections, must continue to be respectfully regarded as being the first attempt to translate these remarkable compositions into any of the modern European languages.

The following Notes are designed simply for the general reader, to whom they may perhaps serve to render certain obscure passages and expressions in the English text somewhat more intelligible. It is perhaps hardly necessary to state that the words printed in italic letters in the text are explanatory interpolations of the translator, and are not in the original. Those verses which are distinguished by asterisks are not given in the original texts which, printed in Roman characters, are appended to the translation as given in Sir W. Jones' collected Works.

THE POEM OF AMRIOLKAIS.

vv. 1-6.

Stay! let us weep, while memory tries to trace
 The long-lost fair one's sand-girt dwelling-place;
 Though the rude winds have swept the sandy plain,
 Still some faint traces of that spot remain.
 My comrades reined their coursers by my side,
 And "Yield not--yield not to despair!" they cried.
 (Tears were my sole reply; yet what avail
 Tears shed on sands, or sighs upon the gale?)
 "The same thy fortune, and thy tears the same,
 When bright Howaira and Rebaba came
 To say farewell on Mosel's swelling brow,
 And left thee mourning, as thou mournest now!"

"Think ye--ah, think ye I forget the day
That tore those damsels from my soul away,
Who breathed a farewell, as they left these bowers,
Sweet as an eastern gale on fields of flowers?"--Ret. Rev.

v. 18. The word thiyab (clothes) in this couplet is taken by some commentators to mean "heart"; and in this sense it is used in the Kur'an: "thy clothes [i.e. heart] cleanse." Among the pagan Arabs a divorce consisted in the man's withdrawing his clothes from his wife, and the wife's withdrawing her clothes from him. The poet therefore, in effect, says: "If there be aught in me that offends thee, then withdraw thy clothes from my clothes--thy heart from mine."

v. 23. The Pleiads.--It is very usual in all countries to make frequent allusions to the brightness of the celestial luminaries, which give their light to all; but the metaphors taken from them have an additional beauty if we consider them as made by a nation who pass most of their nights in the open air, or in tents, and consequently see the moon and the stars in their greatest splendour.--Sir W. Jones: Essay on the Poetry of Eastern Nations.

v. 31. Wejrah is a stage on the road from Mecca to El-Basrah, 40 miles, or 3 stages, from the former, and much frequented by wild-kine. The mention of the look which a wild cow or deer casts on her young one, at which time her eyes are most beautiful and tender, as a comparison for the eyes of a beautiful woman, is common in old Arab poetry.--Lyall. (See Lebid's. Mo'all. v. 14, and Tarafa's Mo'all. v. 32.)

vv. 22-33.

Once through the ranks, at midnight's gloomy hour,
 Of hostile tribes, I sought the maiden's bower,
 When shone the Pleiads in the starry globe,
 Like golden spangles on an azure robe.
 Soon as I came, I saw her figure bent
 In eager gazing from the opening tent.
 "By heaven!" she whispered, as her hand she gave,
 "Secure I'll trust me to a heart so brave;"
 We rose, and gliding o'er the silent plain,
 She swept our footsteps with her flowing train.
 A plain we reached beneath the cloud of night,
 Whose sandy hillocks hid our onward flight
 Safe from the foeman. By her waving hair
 To my fond heart I drew the trembling fair:
 Raptured I gazed upon her polished breast,
 Smooth as a mirror set within her vest;
 Or like an ostrich-egg, of pearly white,
 Left in the sands and half exposed to sight.

The timid maiden turned away her face,
With eyes averted shunned my rude embrace,
Raised her arched neck in conscious virtue's pride,
Then like the wild fawn gazed from side to side.
Her jet-black tresses down her shoulder strayed,
Like clustering dates amid the palm-trees' shade.--R. R.

v. 33. "Her hair, like bunches of dates clustering on the palm-tree"--a favourite of the old poets of Arabia; also that of a pretty girl's tresses to the branches of the vine: see verses from the Romance of Antar, <page 191> of the present volume.

v. 56. "Like henna on gray flowing locks"--see v. 15 of El-Busiri's Poem of the Mantle, where the poet says that had he known that his gray hairs would reproach him he would have dyed them with woad.--The leaves of the henna-tree (Lawsonia inermis, also called the Egyptian privet) are used by the women of Cairo to stain certain parts of the hands and feet.--Lane.

v. 58. The commentary of Zauzani says that wild heifers are compared to bead-pearls of Yemen because their extremities are black, while the rest of them is white. The onyxes on the neck of a youth. who had many uncles on both sides of his family to caress and bedeck him would be of a superior quality.

v. 73. The comparison of a cloud unloading its freight on the desert to a merchant displaying his rich bales, must be considered as peculiarly appropriate in a climate where rain falls like a blessing on the parched soil.

v. 74. "Early draught of generous wine." The morning draught of wine is praised above all others by the ancient poets. In the work entitled El-Marj-en-nadir ("the green meadow") Mohammed ibn Abi Bekr el-Usyuti says of the sabuh or morning potation: "The poets make mention of the morning draught in preference to wine drunk at other times, because in ancient times Kings and others used to prefer drinking in the morning, and because of the freedom of the heart at that time from care or thought of the obstacles and calamities of Fortune; also because those that arose early to drink anticipated those who blamed their wantonnesss: for it is the custom of the blamer to blame a reveller in the morning for what he has done the night before, because that is the time when he becomes sober and recovers from his drunken fit."--Lyall: Notes on Lebid's Mo'all. (quoted from Kosegarten: Mo'all. of 'Amr Kulth. p. 49).--See Tarafa, vv. 46 and 58; Lebid, vv. 60, 61; and Note on Amru, v. 1.

THE POEM OF TARAFA.

v. 6. The Bedouins feed their camels with the leaves of the erak-tree.

vv. 8, 9. Lane, n his "Modern Egyptians," describing the composition of the black powder, called kohl, with which ladies of Cairo paint the edge of their eyelids, both above and below the eye, mentions the powder of various kinds of lead-ore (kohl el-hagar) as being employed for this purpose. He also states that "some women, to make their teeth glisten, tattoo their lips." It would appear from these verses that the Arab women in like manner employed a preparation of lead-ore in order to render their teeth more sparkling by contrast with their "dark-coloured bases."

v. 30. El-Yemen was famous for the production of red leather.

v. 41. This verse resembles a couplet in the song of Beshameh son of Hazn of Nahshal, thus rendered by Mr Lyall in his "Songs from the Hamaseh and Aghani:"

If there should be among a thousand but one of us,
   and men should call--"Ho! a knight!" he would think that they meant him.

vv. 41-48.

'Tis mine, whene'er the tribes to glory call,
 In deeds of daring to outstrip them all.
 High waves the lash above my camel's head;
 Though sultry vapours o'er the mountains spread,
 Onward she rushes, and her flowing tail
 Floats, like the dancer's garment, on the gale.
 Me you will find, or at the council board,
 Or where the taverns maddening draughts afford:
 Come in the morning, and I'll give a bowl
 Shall warm the prudence of thy chilly soul.
 Come to the council of our tribe, and see
 Its brightest honours showered down on me:
 But, above all, come join the merry ring
 Where gay youths laugh and blooming maidens sing.--RR.

vv. 48-51. The singing-girls who sang at the drinking-parties of the ancient Arabs were Greeks, Syrians, or Persians. Until after El-Islam the Arabs, though masters of rhythm and metre, had no indigenous system of singing except the rude song (originally of the camel-driver) called rajez. These girls probably sang for the most part in their own tongue, and played the music which they had learned in Persian 'Irak or Syria; but in the life of En-Nabigha of Dubyan, as given in the Aghani (ix. 164), a singing girl of Yethrib (afterwards El-Madina) is mentioned, who sang one of that poet's pieces in Arabic, and so enabled him to detect a fault of prosody.--Lyall: Notes on vv. 60, 61, Lebid's Mo'all.

v. 49. In Lane's "Modern Egyptians," Ed. 1860, p. 378, is an illustration of two Ghawazee, or public dancing-girls of Cairo, in which the costume exactly corresponds with Tarafa's description of the singing-girls' vests.

[255]

v. 56. This sentiment of the old Arab poet finds a parallel in the following verse, from the Persian of Omar Khayyam:

What boots it to repeat
How time is slipping underneath our feet?
Unborn To-Morrow, and dead Yesterday--
Why fret about them if To-Day be sweet?

"Poets of all ages," remarks Nott, in his "Select Odes of Hafiz," "and particularly those who were voluptuaries, urge the advice of making the best use of the present moment. The carpe diem of Horace is a frequently-quoted maxim."

In a very different strain does a modern English poet endeavour to inculcate the lesson of life:

Know'st thou Yesterday, its aim and reason?
  Work'st thou well To-Day for worthy things?
Then calmly wait the Morrow's hidden season,
  And fear not thou what hap soe'er it brings.

[paragraph continues] The great American, Longfellow, too, in one of his beautiful prose-poems: "Look not mournfully into the Past: it comes not back again. Wisely improve the Present: it is thine. Go boldly forth into the shadowy Future, without fear, and with a manly heart."

v. 58. The Arabs, like the Greeks and the Romans, commonly drank their wine diluted with water; and only on extraordinary occasions drank the lighter kinds pure, and the more heavy wines mixed with a very little water. (See Mo'all. of Amru, v. 2. and Note.)

vv. 62-68.

If Death be near me, let me quaff the bowl,
  That none to-morrow mourn a thirsty soul.
The same dark mansions, by an equal fate,
The noble spirit and the mean await;
Their mother-Earth impartial seals their doom,
And one broad stone protects their common tomb.
Death, the all-conquering, seizes on the bold,
His proudest prey--then claims the miser's gold.
Though short my life, I've seen the age of man
Dwindling, still dwindling, in its narrow span
The camel-riders, when they loose the rein,
With firmer grasp the slackened cord retain:
So, though he spare them for a little space,

Death holds dominion over all our race.
Let me then quaff the goblets while I live,
Nor die unconscious of the joys they give. --Ret. Rev.

vv. 64, 65. Thus Horace, in his well-known ode (Sir Theodore Martin's translation):

It recks not whether thou
 Be opulent and trace
 Thy birth from Kings, or bear upon thy brow
 Stamp of a beggar's race:
 In rags or splendour, Death at thee alikc,
 That no compassion hath for aught of earth, will strike.

And our English poet Young:

What though we wade in wealth or soar in fame?
 Earth's highest station ends in "Here he lies!"
 And "dust to dust" concludes the noblest song.

And the Persian Sa'di: "When the pure and spotless soul is about to depart, of what importance is it whether we expire upon a throne or upon the bare ground?"

THE POEM OF ZOHAIR.

*** The following Notes are adapted from those appended to Mr. Lyall's translation of this Mo'allaqah.

v. 2. "Blue stains renewed," &c. The second hemistich of this verse gives concisely a simile for the water-worn traces of the tents which is found in a more expanded form in Lebid's Mo'allaqah, vv. 8, 9, q.v. The tattooing over the veins of the inner wrist is said to be renewed, because the torrents have scored deeply certain of the trenches dug round the tents, while others that did not lie in the path of the flood have become only faintly marked, like the veins beneath the tracery.

v. 5. "Canal": round the tent a trench is dug to receive the rain from the roof and prevent the water from flooding the interior.

v. 6. "May thy morning be fair and auspicious!" The morning was the time when raids were made. To wish peace in the morning to a place was therefore an appropriate greeting. [See Antara's Mo'all., v. 2.]

v. 52. Tassels of scarlet wool decorated the haudaj in which ladies rode.

v. 17. The "Sacred Edifice" is the Ka'beh. The mention of its building by the Qureysh and the men of Jurhum must not be understood of the same time. Jurhum was the name of two Arab stocks: the first, the ancient race who peopled the lower Hijaz and the Tihameh at the time of the legendary settlement of Ishmael among them, with whom he is said to have intermarried; the second (whom M. de Perceval regards as alone having had a historical existence), a tribe who ruled in Mekkeh from about 70 B. C. to 200 A.D. They were expelled from Mekkeh and dispersed so that no memorial of them remained by an

Azdite stock from el-Yemen, called the Khuza'ah. (C. de Perceval, Essai, i., 218. Aghani, xiii, 108-111.) The second Jurhum are said (Agh. id. p. 109) to have rebuilt the Ka'beh on the foundations laid by Abraham after it had been overthrown by a flood: the architect was one 'Omar el-Jarud, whose descendants were known as the Jedarah, or masons. The Qureysh settled in Mekkeh during its occupation by the Khuza'ah, and gained possession of the Ka'beh in the time of Qusayy, whose mother was of the race of the Jedarah, about 440, A.D. (C. de Perceval.) Qusayy, in the year 450 A.D. or thereabout, caused the building erected by the Jurhum to be demolished, and rebuilt the Ka'beh on a grander scale. It was rebuilt a third time in the year 605 A.D., very shortly before the Mo'allaqah was composed. Mohammed, then thirty-five years old, assisted in the work. These three occasions are probably those to which Zuhayr refers.

"Make devout processions": the tawaf, or going round seven times, was one of the most ancient rites of the religion of the Arabs; it was the mode of worship used not only for the Ka'beh, but also for the other objects of reverence among the pagan Arabs: see Lane, s.v. Duwar.

v. 19. The literal translation of this verse is

Ye two repaired the condition of 'Abs and Dubyan (by peace), after that
 they had shared one with another in destruction, and had brayed between them the perfume of Menshim. The second hemistich is said to refer to a custom which existed among the Arabs of plunging their hands into a bowl of perfume as they took an oath together to fight for a cause until the last of them was slain. Menshim, the commentators say, was a woman in Mekkeh who sold perfume. Such an oath was followed by war to the bitter end; and so "he brayed the perfume of Menshim" became a proverb for entering on deadly strife.

v. 22. Ma'add was the forefather of all those Arabs (generally called musta'ribeh, or insititious) who traced their descent from 'Adnan, whose son he was. [See Genealogical Table prefixed to the Mo'allaqat in this volume.] The name is thus used to denote the Central stocks settled for the most part in Nejd and El-Hijaz, as opposed to the Arabs of El-Yemen or of Yemenic origin by whom they were bordered on the north and south.

v. 29. War, el-Harb, is feminine in Arabic.

[258]

v. 31. The comparison of War to a mill and the slain to ground grain is common in the old poetry. [See vv. 31, 32, Poem of Amru, and Note.]

v. 32. ["Deformed as the dun camel of Aad: "see notes on vv. 11 and 22 of the "Lay of the Himyarites," pp. <page 351>-<page 354> of the present volume. Some of the genealogists say that Thailand was a cousin of 'Ad, and after the destruction of the ancient race of 'Ad, the people of Thamud inherited their possessions and were called "the latter 'Ad," which would account for Zuhayr's saying "camel of 'Ad" instead of "camel of Thamud."]

v. 36. This verse appears to refer to the breaking out again of strife which followed the deed of Hoseyn. The camels are the warriors, and the pools the pools of death. The image seems intended to figure the senselessness of the strife and its want of object and aim.

v. 37. The grazing on pernicious and noxious weeds is the brooding over wrong in the intervals of combat. Thus Qeys son of Zuhayr [the Prince Cais of the Romance of Antar] says, of the bitter results of wrong in this same War of Dahis (Hamaseh p. 210, Aghani, xvi, 32)

But the stout warrior Hamal son of Bedr
    wrought wrong; and wrong is a surfeiting pasturage.

[El-Busiri, in v. 27 of his Mantle Poem, employs the same phrase, with reference to impure thoughts: "If Desire find the pasturage sweet to its taste, leave it not to pasture."]

v. 47. Among the Arabs, when two parties of men met, if they meant peace, they turned towards each other the feet of their spears; if they meant war, they turned towards each other the points.

v. 53. The "cistern" (haud) is a man's home and family.

v. 56. Zuhayr was eighty years old when he composed his Mo'allaqah--608 or 610 A.D., according to M. de Perceval.

v. 57. Mr. Lyall's note on this verse will be better understood if read with his own rendering of the passage--v. 49 of his text:

I have seen the Dooms trample men as a blind beast at random treads
    --whom they smote, he died; whom they missed, he lived on to strengthless eld.

"Blind beast" ('ashwa): literally "a weak-eyed she-camel"--one that sees not well where she is going, and therefore strikes everything with her forefeet, not paying attention to the places where she sets down her feet.--Lane. The word is used proverbially: you say, Rekiba fulanuni-l-'ashwa, "such a one rides the weak-eyed she-camel," that is, he prosecutes his affair without due deliberation; and Khabata Khabta-l-'ashwa, "he trod with the careless tread of a weak-eyed she-camel"--he acted at random.

vv. 47-64. The different order in which these maxims occur in different recensions of the poem, and the fact that some recensions omit several of them which others supply, make it doubtful, Mr. Lyall thinks, whether they properly belong to the Mo'allaqah. "No other poem of those by Zuhayr that remain has the same metre and rhyme as his Mo'allaqah, and it is most likely that fragments of other poems, now lost, in this measure and rhyme, that have survived have been included in it, because there was no other piece into which they could be put."--In Mr. Lyall's text these maxims are placed in a very different order from that in which they stand in Sir William Jones' translation.

THE POEM OF LEBEID.

THE beautiful elegiac verses with which this masterpiece of ancient Arabic poetry opens have been compared, by Dr. Carlyle, to Goldsmith's Deserted Village. "But the Arab," remarks Burton, "with equal simplicity and pathos, has a fire, a force of language, and a depth of feeling, which the Irishman, admirable as his verse is, could never rival." (, vol. iii., p. 54.) Carlyle's translation, as follows, of these verses, however inadequately it may represent the beauties of the original, can hardly fail of pleasing the English reader, from the grace and smoothness of the rhythm:

THOSE dear abodes which once contained the fair
   Amidst Mitata's wilds I seek in vain;
Nor towers, nor tents, nor cottages are there,
   But scattered ruins and a silent plain!

The proud canals that once Rayana graced,
   Their course neglected and their waters gone,
Among the levelled sands are dimly traced,
   Like moss-grown letters on a mouldering stone.

Rayana, say, how many a tedious year
   Its hallowed circle o'er our heads hath rolled,
Since to my vows thy tender maids gave ear,
   And fondly listened to the tale I told?

How oft, since then, the star of spring, that pours
   A never-failing stream, hath drenched thy head?
How oft, the summer-cloud, in copious showers,
   Or gentle drops, its genial influence shed?

How oft, since then, the hovering mist of morn
   Hath caused thy locks with glittering gems to glow?

How oft hath eve her dewy treasures borne
   To fall responsive to the breeze below?

The matted thistles, bending to the gale,
   Now clothe those meadows once with verdure gay;
Amidst the windings of that lonely vale
   The teeming antelope and ostrich stray:

The large-eyed mother of the herd, that flies
   Man's noisy haunts, here finds a sure retreat,
Here watches o'er her young, till age supplies
   Strength to their limbs and swiftness to their feet.

Save where the swelling stream hath swept those walls
   And given their deep foundations to the light
(As the retouching pencil that recalls
   A long-lost picture to the raptured sight);--

Save where the rains have washed the gathered sand,
   And bared the scanty fragments to our view
(As the dust sprinkled on a punctured hand
   Bids the faint tints resume their azure hue);--

No mossy record of those once-loved seats
   Points out the mansion to inquiring eyes:
No tottering wall, in echoing sounds, repeats
   Our mournful questions and our bursting sighs.

Yet, midst those ruined heaps, that naked plain,
   Can faithful memory former scenes restore--
Recall the busy throng, the jocund train,
   And picture all that charmed us there before.

Ne'er shall my heart the fatal morn forget
   That bore the fair ones from these seats so dear--
I see--I see the crowding litters yet,
   And yet the tent-poles rattle in my ear.

I see the maids with timid steps ascend,
   The streamers wave in all their painted pride,
The floating curtains every fold extend,
   And vainly strive the charms within to hide.

What graceful forms those envious folds enclose!
   What melting glances through those curtains play!

Sure Weira's antelopes or Tudah's roes
    Through yonder veils their sportive young survey!

The band moved on--to trace their steps I strove;
    I saw them urge the camels' hastening flight,
Till the white vapour, like a rising grove,
    Snatched them for ever from my aching sight!

Nor since that morn have I Nawara seen--
    The bands are burst which held us once so fast:
Memory but tells me that such things have been,
    And sad Reflection adds, that they are past!

This is Mr. Lyall's rendering of the same passage, from his translation of Lebid's Mo'allaqah, previously mentioned:

1. Effaced are her resting-places--where she stayed but a while and where she dwelt long
    in Mina: desolate are her camps in Ghaul and er-Rijam,

2. And by the torrents of er-Rayyan: the traces thereof are laid bare
    and old and worn, as the rocks still keep their graving:

3. Tent-traces over which have passed, since the time that one dwelt there,
    long years, with their rolling months of war and peace.

4. The showers of the signs of Spring have fallen on them, and there have swept
    over them the rains of the thundering clouds, torrents and drizzle both--

5. The clouds that came by night, those of the morning that hid the sky,
    and the clouds of even-tide, with their antiphons of thunder;

6. There have sprung up over them the shoots of the rocket, and in the sides
    of the valley the deer and the ostriches rear their young;

7. The large-eyed wild-kine lie down there by their young ones
    just born, and their calves roam in herds over the plain.

8. The torrents have scored afresh the traces of the tents, as though
    they were lines of writing in a book which the pens make new again,

9. Or the tracery which a woman draws afresh as she sprinkles the blue
    over the rings, and the lines shine forth anew thereon.

10. And I stood there asking them for tidings--and wherefore did I ask
    aught of deaf stones that have no voice to answer?

11. Bare was the place where the whole tribe had rested: they passed away
    therefrom at dawn, leaving behind them the tent-trenches and the thatch.

12. The camel-litters of the tribe stirred thy longing, what time they moved away
    and crept into the litters hung with cotton, as the wooden framework creaked--

13. The litters hung all round, over their frame of wood,
    with hangings, thin veils and pictured curtains of wool.

14. They began their journey in bands, wide-eyed as the wild-cows of Tudih,
    or deer of Wejrah as they watch their fawns lying around.

15. They were started on their way, and the sun-mist fell off them, as though
    they were low rocky ridges of Bisheh, its tamarisks, and its boulders.

16. Nay--why dost thou dwell on the thought of Nawar? for she is gone,
    and severed is all that bound her to thee, whether strong or weak.

*** The subjoined notes on Lebid's Poem are, for the most part, adapted from those appended to Mr. Lyall's translation.

vv. 1, 2. Minia [Mina], a place in Dariyyeh, a province of Nejd, on the route from Mecca to el-Basrah. There is a valley of the same name near Mecca. Ghaul, er-Rijam, and er-Rayyan, hills in the neighbourhood. [Captain Burton renders these couplets as follows:

Deserted is the village--waste the halting-place and home
 At Mina, o'er Rijam and Ghul wild beasts unheeded roam;
 On Rayyan hill the channel lines have left a naked trace,
 Time-worn, as primal writ that dints the mountain's flinty face.

"This passage," he remarks in a foot-note, "made me suspect that inscriptions would be found among the rocks, as the scholiast informs us that 'men used to write upon rocks in order that their writing might remain.' (De Sacy's Moallaka de Lebid, p. 289.) I neither saw nor heard of any. But some months afterwards I was delighted to hear from the Abbe Hamilton that he had discovered in one of the rock-monuments a 'lithographed proof' of the presence of Sesostres (Rhameses II.)."--Pilgrimage, vol. iii., pp. 136, 137.]
v. 3. "Many a month, holy and unhallowed." Four months of the year--the first, Muharrem; the seventh, Rejeb; the eleventh, Dhulkaade and the twelfth, Dhulhajje--were esteemed sacred in Arabia from the oldest times; and, excepting by one or two tribes, were so religiously observed, that if a man met during that time the murderer of his father, he durst not offer him any violence. The history or traditions of the old Arabs do not mention above six transgressions of this law; and these are styled "impious wars."--Richardson.

vv. 4, 5. "The rainy constellations of Spring:" marabiu-n-nujum. Mirba' is rain that comes in the beginning of the season called Rabi' or Spring; en-Nujum are the constellations called anwa', that is, the twenty-eight Mansions of the Moon, which, by their rising or setting at dawn, were supposed to bring rain or wind, heat or cold.--Lane. Rabi' is not strictly Spring; for it includes the whole time from September to March, during which rain falls in Arabia: it is that season when the pastures are fresh and grazing abundant. The commentator on verse 5 divides the year into three seasons, viz., Shita', Rabi', and Seyf, or Winter, Spring, and Summer; and he says that in the different words used for clouds in verse 5 the rains of the whole year are described: those of Winter fall generally by night, those of spring in the morning, and those of Summer in the evening.

v. 8. The comparison of the almost effaced traces of a spring encampment, washed by the rain and worn by the winds, to lines of writing which have faded by long use is common in old Arabic poetry. Zuheyr says (the lines are quoted in the notice of him in the Aghani)--

Worn are they: thou wouldst think their lines
    over which two years have passed were a parchment old and faded.

From this it is evident that writing and books were not so strange to the Arabs of the time immediately preceding el-Islam as has sometimes been asserted.

v. 9. The reference here is to the weshm or tracery pricked into the skin of a woman's hands and arms. The pattern is pricked out with a needle, and there is sprinkled over the skin and rubbed into it a preparation called na'ur, which may either mean powdered indigo or powdered lamp-black. As the rains which deepened and broadened the traces of the tents are in v. 8 compared to a writer who goes over lines of writing again with a pen, so in v. 9 they are likened to a woman who renews the tattooing by sprinkling fresh pigment over the old lines; which being rubbed in, the lines appear afresh. [Lane ("Modern Egyptians") states that the females of the lower orders in Cairo tattoo upon the face, front of the chin, back of right hand, and arms. The operation is generally performed at the age of about five or six years, by gipsy women.]

v. 11. ["Canals" see rite on v. 5, Zuheyr's Mo'all.] "Thumam," i.e. panic grass. Forskal (p. 20) says that the name is used for Panicum Dichotomum; but it is applied by the Arabs to many species of panicum. The grass is used for thatching and for stuffing holes in the tents so as to keep out the weather.

v. 12. "Hid themselves in carriages": the word used (takannus) is appropriate to the action of a hare or a fox creeping into its hole (kinas).

v. 14. "Roes of Wegera" (Wejrah): see note on v. 31, Amriolkais.

v. 15. Beisha (Bisheh) is the name of a valley in el-Yemen which is thickly populated; also of a village in Tihameh: so the Marasid; the commentary says that it is a valley on

[264]

the road to el-Yemameh. The long line of camels with their litters in which the ladies ride is compared to the ridges of rock of this valley in the part where its ridges are low and sink into the plain. These, in the noon-tide, stand out from the midst of the mirage, with their rocks and tamarisks (athl, Tamarix Orientalis), even as the tall camel-litters make their way through the mists of morn which cling round them like a skirt.

[The vapour here alluded to, called by the Arabians Serab, is not unlike in appearance (and probably proceeding from a similar cause) to those white mists which we often see hovering over the surface of a river in a summer's evening after a hot day. They are very frequent in the sultry plains of Arabia, and, when seen at a distance, resemble an expanded lake; but upon a nearer approach, the thirsty traveller perceives the deception. Hence the Serab in Arabian poetry is a common emblem of disappointed expectation.-- Carlyle.]

v. 23. "The thong of her shoe is broken:" camels frequently have their soft feet protected by a leather shoe, which is tied by a strap round the pastern. [See Mr. Redhouse's translation of Ka'b's Poem of the Mantle, v. 27.]

v. 43. Mr. Lyall renders this couplet:

And she shone in the face of the mirk with a white glimmering light
    like a pearl born in a sea-shell that has dropped from its string,

The restless roaming of the cow is compared to the pearl rolling about on the ground.

v. 50. "Javelins made by the skilful hand of Samhar." According to the commentary and other authorities quoted by Lane, Semhar was the name of a famous maker of spears, who dwelt in the town of el-Khatt, in el-Bahreyn, where the best bamboos from India were landed and fashioned into lances, which are thence frequently called khattiy. [See Amru, v. 40: "our dark javelins, exquisitely wrought of Khathaian reeds;" also El-Busiri, v. 130: "brown lances of Khatt."] Semhar is said to have been the husband of Rudeyneh, who also used to straighten spears. ["Spears of Khatt," and "Rudeyhnian lances" are often mentioned in the Romance of Antar.] Other authorities say that Semhar was the name of a town in Abyssinia, where good spears were made.

vv. 57-61. Sir W. Jones gives the following imitation of these verses in his "Essay on the Poetry of Eastern Nations":

But ah! thou know'st not in what youthful play
 Our nights, beguiled with pleasure, swam away:
 Gay songs and cheerful tales deceived the time,
 And circling goblets made a tuneful chime.
 Sweet was the draught, and sweet the blooming maid,
 Who touched her lyre beneath the fragrant shade.
 We sipped till morning purpled every plain,

[265]

The damsels slumbered, but we sipped again.
The waking birds, that sung on every tree,
Their early notes were not so blithe as we.

v. 58. "The flag of the wine-merchant." Wine-shops were distinguished by flags hung outside of them: when the wine was all sold, or the shop was closed, the flag was taken down. [See Antara's Mo'all., v. 54.] In this verse and the next Lebid vaunts his liberality in buying wine for his fellows when it was at its dearest.

vv, 60, 61. Morning draught: singing-girls--see Amriolkais, v. 74; Tarafa, vv. 46, 48-51; Amru, v. 1, and Notes.

v. 63. "A swift horse, whose girths resemble my sash adorned with gems." Mr. Lyall translates this hemistich: "a swift mare, my girdle its reins as I went forth at dawn;" and explains that the poet "threw the bridle over his shoulders so that it became a girdle to him, in order that he might have his hands free for his weapons."

v. 70-72. In these verses the poet refers to the controversy which took place between himself and er-Rabi' son of Ziyad at the court of en-No'man son of el-Munzir, king of el-Hireh. (See the Argument prefixed to translation of Lebid's Poem in this volume.)

v. 73. The custom of the Arabs in gambling with arrows was to require those who lost to pay for the camel which was the prize of those who won: Lebid's liberality consisted in his furnishing the prize himself from his herds, and thus those who lost had not to pay.

v. 74. A barren camel, says the commentary, is the fattest, while one with young is the most delicate of flesh.

v. 76. "A camel doomed to die at her master's tomb." It was customary among the pagan Arabs when a warrior died, to tie his camel near his grave, where she was left to perish of hunger and thirst in order that she should accompany him to the next world, and that he should ride on her at the Resurrection: to go on foot on that occasion was considered very disgraceful.

v. 88. "An enlivening Spring." As the season of Spring was the pleasantest of the year, rich with fertilizing rains and green pasture, so men of bountiful and kindly nature were likewise called by that name. Lebid's own father Rabi'ah, as the Aghani informs us, was known as Rabi'at-el-Mo'tarrin--"a spring for those who came to seek his bounty." [See v. 77, Hareth's Mo'all., where a certain chief is styled "a vernal season of beneficence."]

"The year of widowhood." A commentator says that in the time of Ignorance it was the custom for widows, on the death of their husbands, to undergo a period of separation ('iddeh) extending to one year. During this period they could not marry again, nor go forth from their houses, and were thus "disconsolate."

[266]

THE POEM OF ANTARA.

*** The learned Von Hammer-Purgstall says that Antara's Mo'allaqah is contained twice in the complete copies of the Romance of Antar: once in fragments, as the hero delivers them extempore on divers occasions in the ardour of the moment, in praise of his darling Abla, of his matchless horse, of his irresistible sword and spear, &c.; and again on the occasion of the poetic contest before the assembly of the tribes at Okatz, when the poet united the hitherto scattered pearls of his genius by a golden thread and suspended them on the Ka'beh.

vv. 1, 2. Hamilton's rendering of the opening verses of Antara's Mo'allaqah are given on page <page 264> of the present volume. This is how Professor E. H. Palmer has turned the same into English verse, in his translation entitled, "An Ancient Arabic Prize Poem":

Have then the Poets left a theme unsung?
Dost thou, then, recognise thy love's abode?
Home of my Abla! dear for her sake!
Would that thy stones, Jewa could speak to me!

According to the Romance of Antar, Abla was in Arabian 'Irak when, on the hero's return home from the land of Zebeid, he beheld her deserted dwelling, and, leaning sadly upon his spear, gave vent to his feelings in these two couplets.

vv. 13-19. There is a charm in Professor Palmer's graceful metrical rendering of this beautiful passage which is not to be expected in a literal translation:

'Twas then her beauties first enslaved my heart--
Those glittering pearls and ruby lips, whose kiss
Was sweeter far than honey to the taste. [p. 393]
As when the merchant opes a precious box
Of perfume, such an odour from her breath
Came towards thee, harbinger of her approach;
Or like an untouched meadow, where the rain
Hath fallen freshly on the fragrant herbs
That carpet all its pure untrodden soil:
A meadow where the frequent rain-drops fall
Like coins of silver in the quiet pools,
And irrigate it with perpetual streams;
A meadow where the sportive insects hum,
Like listless topers singing o'er their cups,
And ply their fore-legs, like a man who tries
With maimed hand to use the flint and steel.

vv. 22-25.

[267]

I'll choose a camel of surpassing speed,
 Patient of thirst, from Shaden's generous breed:
 Proudly she'll bear me to my fair one's home,
 Nor stay her vigorous strides though evening come.
 Proud as the earless ostrich, and as fleet,
 Who strikes the sands with many-sounding feet,
 While round her steps the gathering brood rejoice,
 Like thirsty camels at their keeper's voice.--Ret. Rev.

v. 27. It seems somewhat odd that the poet should compare an ostrich to a slave dressed in a long fur garment, yet such is the sense of the original, which Mr. Redhouse renders as follows:

"Of a small-headed [male ostrich] that visits his [female's] eggs at Dhu-'l-'ushayra, like the slave in a long furred garment, whose ears [and nose] are close cut off." Mr. Redhouse remarks that "we can only conjecture why the poet likened the ostrich's feathers to a long fur garment. Slaves were then negroes; and perhaps, being from Africa and sensitive to cold, wore furs (of sheepskin?). The exact length understood by the poet's 'long' would depend on the kind of fur jacket, or robe, worn by slaves in the desert camps. Twenty inches is long where twelve is usual."

v. 42. The comparison in the second hemistich is thus rendered by Professor Palmer:

Where'er descending falls my flashing blade,
 Low lies the husband of some noble dame,
 And like the whistling of a cloven lip,
 The life-blood gurgles from his ghastly wound,
 And sparkles round him in a crimson shower.

v. 54. "Skilful in casting lots": see Tarafa's Mo'all., v. 102, and Lebid's Mo'all., vv. 73, 74, and Nate.--The arrows used for casting lots were without heads and feathers, like those employed in divination.

"Causing the wine-merchant to strike his flag ": see note on v. 58, Lebid's Mo'all.

vv. 60-62. In Professor Palmer's translation the little maiden whom the Poet sends to bring him news of his "sweet lamb" is represented as saying on her return:

I saw the foemen lulled by treacherous ease,
 And whoso wills it his that lamb shall be.
 Her neck is comelier than the graceful fawn's,
 Her form is fairer than the young gazelle's! According to Sir William Jones' rendering, the girl simply informs Antara that she found "the hostile guards negligent of their watch," and that the lady might therefore be easily visited; and we are to suppose that Antara, on thus learning that "the coast was clear," so to say, at once proceeded to visit

[268]

the lady, who, on seeing him, "turned towards him with the neck of a young roe."--Mr Redhouse thinks that "the variant positions which these verses occupy in different editions make it almost impossible to judge whether his sweetheart turned to Antara, or to the maiden sent. The words read as though the maid turned to Antara; but that is not the probable sense."--The Bedouin coxcomb Amarah, in the Romance of Antar, sends a female slave on a similar errand--to bring him an account of Abla's personal charms: see page <page 209> of the present volume.

v. 70. "Make the perched birds of the brain fly quickly from every skull." Among the old Arabs the belief was prevalent that of the blood near a dead person's brain was formed a bird, called Hamah (Carlyle calls it Manah, but this was the name of a stone-idol worshipped by the pagan Arabs), that sat upon the grave of the deceased, and uttered doleful cries. This seems alluded to in Job, xxi., 32, which Carlyle thus translates:

He shall be brought to the grave,
 And shall watch upon the raised-up heap.

Others say that the soul of a man who was murdered or slain in battle animated this bird and continually cried, Oscuni! Oscuni!--"give me to drink," i.e. of the slayer's blood.

vv. 72-77.

"On! Antar, on!" the exulting warriors cry--
 'Gainst my black steed a thousand lances fly.
 Onward to stem the coming tide I prest,
 Till streams of blood o'erflowed my courser's chest;
 Silent and sad he turned--his rider eyed,
 And though the words of utterance were denied,
 Looks of reproach his inward feelings spoke,
 While sobs of anguish from his heart-strings broke;
 Rallying, again his fiery head he rears,
 And proudly charges 'mid his proud compeers,
 While, as War's terrors I again defy,
 "On! Antar, on!" the exulting warriors cry.--Ret. Rev.

v.v. 79-81.

Damdam was slain by Antara on the Day of El-Mureyqib, one of the earliest battles of the War of Dahis. Herim, a son of Damdam, was afterwards slain by Ward son of Habis; and Hoseyn, in retaliation for his brother's death, basely violated the laws of hospitality by killing a kinsman of Ward (whose name is given by El-Meydani as Tijan) who was his guest: see Argument to the Poem of Zohair.

Oh may I live till justice on the heads
 Of Damdam's sons the cup of vengeance sheds! [p. 396]

[269]

To blight my hard-earned fame they basely sought,
Who ne'er in word had wronged them, or in thought:
They sought my blood, who ne'er had wrought them harm,
But I, at least, have known the rapt'rous charm
Of sweet revenge--I've left their father dead,
And ravenous vultures hovering o'er his head.--Ret. Rev.

THE POEM OF AMRU.

v. 1. "Our morning draught:" see note on v. 74, Amriolkais--"A cheerful cup of wine in the morning," says Nott, "was a favourite indulgence with the more luxurious Persians. And it was not uncommon among the Easterns, to salute a friend by saying: 'May your morning potation be agreeable to you!'" Thus Hafiz (Nott's translation):

    While the soft lyre and cymbals sound,
      Pour cheerful melody around;
    Quaff thy enlivening draught of morning wine;
      And as the melting notes inspire
      Thy soul with amorous desire,
    Kiss thy fair handmaid, kiss her neck divine.

v. 2. "Wine diluted with water:" see note on v. 58, Tarafa's Mo'all.--In the Romance of Antar, the hero is represented as exclaiming:

Give me pure wine to drink, or let it be mixed;
 Give it me old, that I may imagine it was made before the world:
 Give me to drink, and let me hear the song that delights me!

Amru, in v. 1, and Lebid, v. 59, also refer to the Arab custom of hoarding the best wines.--Hafiz, in one of his odes, calls for a draught of pure or unmixed wine: mi nab, wine not diluted with water.

vv. 1-4.

Wake, damsel! wake! and bring yon generous wine,
 The joyous soul of Enderina's vine;
 Fill, fill the crimson goblet to the brim,
 Till the wine totters o'er the circling rim: [p. 397]
 Cheered by its smiles, the youth forgets his care,
 His fair one's coldness, and his own despair:
 Cheered by its smiles the doting miser rests
 From the fond worship of his well-filled chests.--Ret. Rev.

[270]

v. 17. It must not be supposed that the poet's special reference to the well-developed haunches of his fair one in this verse tends to confirm the notion still generally entertained by Europeans that the Orientals like large, fat women--a notion utterly erroneous. (See Lane's translation of "The Thousand and One Nights," Ed. 1859, vol. i, p. 25, note 19.) It is true that Arabian and other Eastern poets often mention in terms of admiration the "large and wide hips" of the maidens whose charms they celebrate; for example, in the poetry of the Romance of Antar contained in the present volume: p. 229, l. 3; p. 292, l. 1; p. 293, l. 6;--but their slender waists are also invariably praised, as in this same verse of Amru. And in the following couplet, cited in the Anvari Suhaili of Husain Va'iz (a modern Persian version of the Hindoo Fables of Vishnusarman, better known to general readers as the Fables of Bidpai, or Pilpay, the original of the Kalilah wa Damnah) the large haunches and slender waist of a maiden are described by an amusing play upon words:

How shall I describe her hips and her waist?
 Who has seen a mountain (Kuh) suspended by a straw (KIM)?

It is slender women only who are celebrated in Arabic poetry. The hero-poet Antar describes his beloved Abla as being "delicately formed"--"like the branch of the tamarisk"; while the palm-tree, the cypress, and the well-proportioned spear are common similitudes in Eastern poetry for the gracefully slender form of a beautiful woman.

v. 26. Mr Lyall, in a note on one of his translations of Songs from the Hamaseh and the Agahni (published in the Bengal Asiatic Society's Journal), thus renders the couplet:

Many the Days are ours, long blazed with glory,
   when we withstood the King and would not serve him.

 "Days" (Ayyam), he explains, is the word used in Arab legend for battles: one says, "the Day of el-Kualb," "the Day of Shi'b Jebeleh," &c., although the fight may (as it did at el-Kulab) have lasted longer than one day. (See note on vv. 25, 26, Hareth's Mo'all.)

vv. 31, 32. In a note on v. 31 of Zohair's Mo'all., Mr Lyall gives these couplets of Amru as follows:

When our war-mill is set against a people,
   As grain they fall thereunder ground to powder;
 Eastward in Nejd is set the skin beneath it,
   And the grain cast therein is all Quda'ah;

and he explains that thifal (rendered "cloth" by Sir W. Jones) is the mat of skin that is placed beneath the mill to receive the flour.--In the introductory part of the Romance of Antar, King Jazimah (the father of King Zoheir, the hero's friend) thus threatens a hostile tribe: "I shall command these warriors, numerous as locusts, to assault you, and to grind you like grain." Akin to this comparison of War to a mill is the similitude in 2 Kings,

[271]

xiii., 7: "The King of Syria had destroyed them, and had made them like the dust by threshing." (See Poem of Zohair, v. 31, and Note.)

v. 40. "Our javelins exquisitely wrought of Khathaian reeds," i.e. lances of Khatt: see note on v. 50, Lebeid's Mo'all.

v. 45. The syringa-flower.--The tree of Judas, on which the arch-traitor hung himself after betraying his Master: the tree in consequence is said to have wept blood, with which its blossoms still remain deeply dyed.--Nott: Odes of Hafiz.--In the Romance of Antar, warriors whose armour is stained with blood are frequently compared to the flowers of the Judas-tree; and the hero himself describes cups of wine as mantling like the Judas-flower. It is the Cercis Siliquastrum of botanists, according to Hamilton, "the flowers of which are of a very bright purple colour, coming out from the branches and stem on every side in large clusters and on short peduncles."

v. 66. Colaib Ebn Rabiah governed the Bani Maad (the Saraceni Maadeni of Procopius), and was so proud that he would not suffer any one to hunt in his neighbourhood, nor any camels to be watered with his, nor any fire to be lighted near that which he himself used. He was at last slain by one Jassas, for shooting a camel, named Sarab, that he found grazing on a prohibited spot of ground. This camel belonged to an Arab, who had been entertained by Basus, a near relation of Jassas. The murder of Colaib Ebn Rebiah occasioned a forty years' war [see Argument prefixed to the Poem of Amru, page <page 65>], whence came the Arab proverbs: "a worse omen than Sarab;" "more ominous than Basus."--It may not be improper here to observe that the kings and chiefs of the Arabs generally forbade others to bring their flocks upon those places and pastures which they chose for themselves. In order to ascertain the limits of these pastures, when they came to a fruitful valley or plain, they caused a dog to bark, and the whole extent of ground over which he could be heard they appropriated to themselves.--Ancient Universal History, vol. xviii., p. [440].

v. 97. "They walk with graceful motions, and wave their bodies," &c. The gait of Arab women is very remarkable: they incline the lower part of the body from side to side as they step, and with hands raised to the level of the bosom they hold the edges of their outer covering. Their pace is slow, and they look not about them, but keep their eyes towards the ground in the direction to which they are going.--Lane: Thousand and One Nights: Notes.

vv. 92-100. The following passage, from Richardson's "Dissertation on the Languages, Literature, and Manners of Eastern Nations," will serve as an interesting commentary on these verses: "The military ideas which prevailed in old Arabia seem to have been peculiarly calculated to promote a romantic attention to the fair sex. A long cessation of hostilities was painful to the Arabs: their arms were often turned against the neighbouring countries, and caravans of travellers; but oftener against each other. Captives and plunder were the chief objects; and the women were considered as most valuable spoils. To protect them became in consequence a great point of honour. Those predal wars, in whatever light we may view them, were considered as highly honourable in Arabia, and no man was thought in any way accomplished, who could not boast, in them, some feat of arms. Their expeditions were in general short. If they found the enemy too powerful, they retired; if unprepared, they suprised them; if of equal or inferior force, they attacked them: and one battle was for the most part decisive. A young warrior returning after a short absence, and laying his laurels, his captives, and his spoils at the feet of his mistress, would in general woo with success: and he whose gallant intrepidity had saved his tribe from rapine and captivity would ever be a favourite of the fair. When the flower of any tribe were absent upon a distant enterprise, some hostile neighbours would often attack those they had left behind: and hence perhaps arose the custom of the Arabian women, even of the highest rank, attending their husbands, fathers, and brothers in their military expeditions; and of fighting often with a degree of heroism not inferior to the fabled achievements of the ancient Amazons."

vv. 103-108.

Ours is the world, and all its riches ours;
 None dares resist us 'midst Arabia's powers;
 None dares control--if any vainly try
 To chain our freedom, from the yoke we fly:
 None dares rebuke our valour as unjust,
 Else the rash slanderer should repent in dust;
 One chief we own, and when that chieftain's son
 Swears to maintain the name his sire has won,
 In such frank fealty as becomes the free,
 We bend, and make the nations bend the knee.
 Still will we pour our warriors o'er the plain,
 And still our ships shall rule the boundless main.

Ret. Rev.

The concluding verses of Amru's oration in praise of his tribe furnish a fair specimen of the unbounded boasting in which the old Arabs were fond of indulging on such occasions as that which gave rise to this Poem and the following one, in which the venerable poetical champion of the tribe of Bekr answers the vain Taglebite.

THE POEM OF HARETH.

v. 1. It was as incumbent on the old Arab poets that they should begin their compositions with a lament for the departure of a beloved fair one as it was once the fashion among European poets to affect, in their songs, sonnets, &c., an all-absorbing passion for some real or imaginary lady of beauty. Thus, Petrarch had his Laura; Dante his Beatrice; Surrey his Geraldine; Lovelace his Althea and his Lucasta; Waller his Sacharissa. But among the desert Arabs there was often good reason for such doleful lamentations as those with which their poems usually open. Young men fell in love with damsels of a tribe stationed in the neighbourhood of their own tents; and when at length the two tribes separated, to seek "fresh fields and pastures new," the distress of the forlorn youths at the sight of the camel-litters bearing away their sweethearts frequently found expression in such verses as the following (translated by Mr. Payne), which are quoted in the "Thousand and One Nights":

WHEN they mount their female camels just before the break of day,
 And the male ones hurry after with the ardour of desire,
 And my eyes perceive my loved one through the crannies of the wall,
 I exclaim with streaming eyelids and a heart for love on fire,
 "Turn, thou leader of the camels, let me bid my love farewell!"
 In her absence and desertion life and hope in me expire.
 Never, never have I broken troth and plighted love with her:
 O that troth-plight! would I knew that she had kept her faith entire!

vv. 6-8. As a token of their hospitality, the desert Arabs were wont to kindle fires at night on the tops of hills, which guided belated travellers to their tents, and assured them of a hearty welcome. A fire of this kind was called "the hospitality-fire," and the larger and more brilliant it was, the greater the honour reflected on him who lighted it. So Hareth, in v. 7, praises Hinda for her hospitable disposition, in kindling such a fire on the hills that it "blazed like the splendour of the sun."--El-Khansa, the celebrated poetess of the tribe of Sulaim (who was one of the early converts to el-Islam, and greatly esteemed by the Prophet), thus praises the hospitality of her brother:

Sakhra is a beacon to the leaders of caravans,
 As were he a mountain crowned with fire.

And El-Busiri, in v. 88 of his Mantle Poem, says that the miracles performed by the Prophet were "as manifest as is the conspicuousness of the hospitality-fire by night on the mountain-top."

v. 19. "As soon as dawn appeared." The early morning was the time when a hostile tribe were generally attacked and plundered. Prince Malik lost his life in one of these morning raids, when his wedding-party were attacked by Hodifah and his kinsmen: see pp. 289, 290; also Zohair's Mo'all., v. 6 and Note, and Antara's Mo'all., v. 2.

vv. 21-26.

Oh thou adorner of a slanderer's tale,
 What can thy lies in Amru's court prevail?
 Think not thy varnished falsehood can do more
 Than envious hosts have vainly tried before.
 Still have we flourished, spite of Slander's aim,
 While glory crowned our pantings after Fame;
 Long have the tribes, through Envy's shades of night,

Seen and been dazzled by our glory's light.
Fate on a lofty rock has fixed our seat,
Where sunshine settles, and whence clouds retreat;
Firm is its base, its summit seeks the skies,
O'erlooks the storm, and all its rage defies.--Ret. Rev.

vv. 25, 26. The "dark rock" is the glory and great name of the tribe, says Mr Lyall, in a note on the following parallel verses, from the spirited song of 'Abd-el-Melik, son of 'Abd-er-Rahim, of the Benu-d-Dayyan ("Songs from the Hamaseh," &c.):

A mountain we have where dwells he whom we shelter there,
  lofty, before whose height the eye falls back blunted:
Deep-based is its root below ground, and overhead there soars
  its peak to the stars of heaven whereto no man reaches.

In the same note Mr Lyall thus renders vv. 23-26:

And we have stood, spite of their hate, and high towers
  and firm-based glory lift us aloft;

Before to-day has it blinded the eyes
  of men in which were wrath and denial.

As though the Fates beating against us met
  a black mountain cleaving the topmost clouds,

Mighty and strong above the changes of things,
  which no shock of the Days can soften or shake.

In the second hemistich of the last verse, as above, we find "Days" employed for "battles" as in v. 26 of Amru's Mo'all., on which see Note.

v. 30. "Concealing hatred in our bosoms, as the mote is concealed in the closed eyelid"-- rankling, though unseen.

v 34. "The sacred month": see note on v. 3, Lebid.

v. 37. Al Mondar, the son of Amriolkais the son of Numan, and of Maiwiah, the daughter of Aus, a lady of such transcendent beauty that she was called Maissamai, i.e. "water of heaven," governed after his father in Hira. From his mother he and his posterity were likewise surnamed Al Mondar Ebn Maissamai, which appellation they had in common with the Kings of Ghassan, according to Al Jauharius. For these last princes were so denominated from Abu Amer, of the tribe of Azd, the father of Amru Mazikia, who, by his surprising liberality and beneficence, supplied the want of rain, furnishing his people with corn when an extreme drought had rendered it so dear that they were incapable of

[275]

buying it. This prince was deposed by Khosru Kobad, King of Persia.--Ancient Universal History, vol. xviii., p. 432.

v. 38. "The Day of Hayarin": see note on vv. 25, 26.

v. 42. "Contracts written on tablets": see note on v. 8, Lebid's Mo'all.

v. 58. "Whose blood has flowed unrevenged"--a bitter taunt: meaning that the Taglebites had not the courage, or the power, to exact blood for that of their slain kinsmen. Vengeful as the old Arabs were, however, it was optional for the next of kin to the man who was foully slain (called the "avenger of blood") to compound with the slayer or his family by accepting ten camels as satisfaction for the blood of his kinsman. The Prophet raised the mulct to one hundred camels.

v. 64. "The sultry vapour of noon increased their magnitude": i.e., the mirage: see note on v. 15, Lebid's Mo'all.

v. 77. "A vernal season of beneficence in every barren year": see v. 88, Lebid's Mo'all. and Note.

V. 79. Amrio'l Kais was the name of several of the princes of Hira, who were under the protection of the Kings of Persia, whose lieutenants they were over the Arabs of 'Irak. It does not appear from Dr. Pocock's list which is the one here referred to. The kingdom of Hira was founded by Malek, a descendant of Cahlan, son of the famous 'Abd-Shems, surnamed Saba, prince of El-Yemen: see note on v. 14 of the "Lay of the Himyarites," <page 352>.

v. 80. Mondir, King of Ghassan. The kingdom of Ghassan, like that of Hira, owed its origin to the inundation of El-Arem see note, v. 14, <page 352>. El-Mondar, or Mundhir, was the general name of the princes of this kingdom, also of those of Hira. The Kings of Ghassan were the lieutenants of the Roman Emperors over the Arabs of Syria. Perhaps the 27th of Dr. Pocock's catalogue is the prince here mentioned.

v. 82. The sons of Aus: a tribe descended from Cahlan, son of 'Abd-Shems of Yemen.

NOTES ON SHORTER POEMS.

*** Of the biographical, historical, and critical Notes prefixed to Carlyle's translations, the more lengthy ones are, with a few exceptions, here presented in an abridged form. Additional Notes are placed within brackets.

ON THE TOMB OF MANO--<page 95>.

THE simile at the conclusion of this little piece will appear elegant to every reader, but to an inhabitant of the East, where vegetation and fertility are in many places almost entirely dependent upon the overflowing of the rivers, it must have been peculiarly striking.

ON THE TOMB OF SAYID--<page 97>.

THE figure in the last stanza is undoubtedly somewhat bold, but we have many in our own language almost equally so; and while we admire the "darkness visible" of Milton, we ought not to find fault with the "speaking silence" of the Arabian poet.

ON THE DEATH OF HIS MISTRESS--<page 98>.

[THE allusion to the superstition of the pagan Arabs that a bird issued from the brain at a man's death and screeched over his grave (see note on v. 70, Poem of Antara) determines, as the translator remarks, the antiquity of this poem. The idea contained in the four last lines is also found in one of the odes of Hafiz--thus paraphrased by Atkinson, in the Notes on his epitome of the Shah Nameh of Firdausi:

Zephyr through thy locks is straying,
 Stealing fragrance, charms displaying;
 Should it pass where Hafiz lies,
 From his conscious dust would rise
 Flow'rets of a thousand dyes.]

HATIM TAI, THE GENEROUS ARAB CHIEF--<page 99>.

HATIM TAI was an Arabian chief who lived a short time prior to the promulgation of Mohammedanism. He has been so much celebrated through the East for his generosity, that even at the present day the greatest encomium which can be given to a generous man is to say that he is "as liberal as Hatim." He was also a poet; but his talents were principally exerted in recommending his favourite virtue. An Arabian author thus emphatically describes Hatim's character: "His poems expressed the charms of beneficence; and his practice evinced that he wrote from the heart." The instances related of Hatim's generosity are innumerable; and the following are selected as affording a lively picture of Arabian manners.

The Emperor of Constantinople having heard much of Hatim's liberality, resolved to make trial of it. For this purpose he despatched a person from his court to request a particular horse which he knew the Arabian Prince valued above all his other possessions. The officer arrived at Hatim's abode in a Clark tempestuous night, at a season when all the horses were at pasture in the meadows. He was received in a manner suitable to the dignity of the imperial envoy, and treated that night with the utmost hospitality. The next day the officer delivered to Hatim his message from the Emperor, at which Hatim appeared greatly concerned. "If," said he, "you had yesterday apprised me of your errand, I should instantly have complied with the Emperor's request, but the horse he asks is now no more: being surprised by your sudden arrival, and having nothing else to regale you with, I ordered that particular horse to be killed, and served up to you last night for supper." (The Arabians prefer the flesh of horses to any other food.) Hatim immediately ordered the finest horses to be brought, and begged the ambassador to present them to his master. The Emperor could not but admire this mark of Hatim's generosity, and confessed that he truly deserved the title of the most liberal among men.

It was the fate of Hatim to give umbrage to other monarchs. Numan, King of Yemen, conceived a violent jealousy against him, on account of his reputation; and thinking it easier to destroy than surpass him, the envious prince commissioned one of his sycophants to rid him of his rival. The courtier hastened to the desert where the Arabs were encamped. Discovering their tents at a distance, he reflected that he had never seen Hatim, and was contriving means to obtain a knowledge of his person, without exposing himself to suspicion. As he advanced, deep in meditation, he was accosted by a man of an amiable figure, who invited him to his tent. He accepted the invitation, and was charmed with the politeness of his reception. After a splendid repast, he offered to take leave, but the Arab requested him to prolong his visit.

"Generous stranger," answered the officer, "I am confounded by your civilities; but an affair of the utmost importance obliges me to depart."

"Might it be possible for you," replied the Arab, "to communicate to me this affair, which seems so much to interest you? You are a stranger in this place; if I can be of any assistance to you, freely command me."

The courtier resolved to avail himself of the offer of his host, and accordingly imparted to him the commission he had received from Numan. "But how," continued he, "shall I, who have never seen Hatim, execute my orders? Bring me to the knowledge of him, and add this to your other favours."

"I have promised you my service," answered the Arab. "Behold, I am a slave to my word. Strike!" said he, uncovering his bosom--"spill the blood of Hatim, and may my death gratify the wish of your prince, and procure you the reward you hope for. But the moments are precious; defer not the execution of your king's command, and depart with all possible expedition; the darkness will aid your escape from the revenge of my friends: if to-morrow you be found here, you are inevitably undone."

These words were as a thunderbolt to the courtier. Struck with a sense of his crime and the magnanimity of Hatim, he fell down on his knees, exclaiming: "God forbid that I should lay a sacrilegious hand on you! Nothing shall ever urge me to such baseness." He then quitted the tent and took the road again to Yemen.

[278]

The cruel monarch, at the sight of his favourite, demanding the head of Hatim, the officer gave him a faithful account of what had passed. Numan in astonishment cried out: "It is with justice, O Hatim! that the world reveres you as a kind of divinity. Men instigated by a sentiment of generosity may bestow their whole fortune; but to sacrifice life is are action above humanity!"

After the decease of Hatim, the Arabs over whom he presided refused to embrace Islam. For this disobedience Mohammed condemned them all to death, except the daughter of Hatim, whom he spared on account of her father's memory. This generous woman, seeing the executioners ready to perform the cruel command, threw herself at the Prophet's feet, and conjured him either to take away her life or pardon her countrymen. Mohammed, moved with such nobleness of sentiment, revoked the decree he had pronounced, and, for the sake of Hatim's daughter, granted pardon to the whole tribe.

[It is related that Hatim, the poet En-Nabigha of Dubyan, and a man of the tribe of Nabit were at the same time suitors for the hand of Mawia, the daughter of Afsar. Mawia, disguised as a poor woman, visited each of her three lovers, to partake of their hospitality. Each killed a camel on the occasion: the man of Nabit and the poet En-Nabigha placed before her the tail of the camel each had killed; but Hatim gave her the fattest pieces of the hind part, of the hunch, and of the part between the shoulders, which are esteemed the greatest dainties. It so happened that when Hatim came to woo Mawia he found both his rivals there on the same business. Mawia desired each of them to describe his way of life in verses, promising to give her hand to him who excelled in poetical talent. En-Nabigha and the man of Nabit in their verses boasted of the good use which they made of their riches; and when it came to Hatim's turn he recited the poem, beginning: "O Mawia! riches come in the morning and depart in the evening," which Carlyle has freely rendered into English (pp. <page 99>, <page 100> of this volume). When the table was spread, the servants put before each of the wooers that portion of camel's flesh which he had given Mawia when she visited them in disguise. En-Nabigha and the man of Nabit thereupon slunk away ashamed. Hatim at this time had already one wife, whom Mawia required him to divorce before she would give him her hand in marriage. "Never," said Hatim, "never shall I put away the mother of my daughter," and he departed home. But on the death of his wife, shortly after this, he renewed his wooing, and married Mawia, who bore him the spirited daughter that saved her tribe from destruction by her intercession with the Prophet, as above mentioned.--A number of Hatim's poetical effusions are preserved by Oriental writers; among these is the following little piece (paraphrased, by Miss Louise Zoller, a young lady of considerable literary culture, from the German version of Von Hammer-Purgstall):

How many are sordid slaves to their pelf!
 Little doth Avarice give, and evil its gifts.
 Praise be to God! riches serve as my slaves,
 Freeing captives forlorn, helping the needful.
 Mean minds are contented with that which is mean;
 But he who truly is great aspires to deeds which are noble.

Hatim is the hero of a modern Persian romance, of which an English translation, by Mr. Duncan Forbes, was published in 1830. This work professes to recount Hatim's marvellous adventures in distant lands--going about relieving the distressed and removing obstacles to the union of fond lovers. The Romance of Hatim Tai appears to be mainly compiled from ancient Sanskrit fables and tales; and the adventures ascribed to the generous Arab chief are purely fictitious, but very entertaining.--Like Zuhayr the poet, Hatim is said by Muslim writers to have predicted the advent of Muhammad.

"Hatim Tai no longer exists," says the celebrated Persian poet Sa'di, in his Gulistan, or Rose-Garden; "but his exalted name will remain famous for virtue to eternity. Distribute the tithe of your wealth in alms; for when the husbandman lops off the exuberant branches from the vine, it produces an increase of grapes."]

THE BATTLE OF SABLA--<page 101>.

THE antitheses contained in the second and last stanzas of this poem are much admired by the Arabian commentators. Both this poem and the one following [<page 102>] are taken from the Hamasa; and afford curious instances of the animosity which prevailed amongst the several Arabian clans, and of the rancour with which they pursued each other, when once at variance.

NABEGAT BENI JAID--p. I04.

THERE have been several poets of the name of Nabegat: the author of these verses was descended from the family of Jaid. As he died in the 40th year of the Hijra [A.D. 660], aged one hundred and twenty, he must have been fourscore at the promulgation of Islam; he however declared himself an early convert to the new faith. The Arabian historians give us a curious instance of Mohammed's affection for him. Nabegat, being one day introduced to the Prophet, was received by him with a salutation usual enough amongst the Arabians: "May God preserve thy mouth!" This benediction, proceeding from lips so sacred, had such an effect, that in an instant the poet's teeth, which were loosened by his great age, became firm in his head, and continued sound and beautiful as long as he lived. The Mohammedan doctors however are much divided in opinion upon the important point, whether Nabegat actually retained all his original teeth, or whether, having lost them, he got a new set.

THE SONG OF MAISUNA--<page 105>.

[THIS song is still popular in Arabia, especially among the desert tribes. Mrs. Godfrey Clerk, in her 'Ilam-en-Nas, p. 108, gives the following translation:

A hut that the winds make tremble
  Is dearer to me than a noble palace;

[280]

And a dish of crumbs on the floor of my home
  Is dearer to me than a varied feast;
And the soughing of the breeze through every crevice
  Is dearer to me than the beating of drums;
And a camel's-wool abah which gladdens my eye
  Is dearer to me than filmy robes;
And a dog barking around my path
  Is dearer to me than a coaxing cat;
And a restive young camel, following the litter,
  Is dearer to me than a pacing mule;
And a feeble boor from midst my cousinhood
  Is dearer to me than a rampant ass.

And this is Captain Burton's version (Pilgrimage, iii. p. 262):

O take these purple robes away,
  Give back my cloak of camel's hair,
And bear me from this tow'ring pile
  To where the black tents flap i' the air.
The camel's colt with falt'ring tread,
  The dog that bays at all but me,
Delight me more than ambling mules--
  Than every art of minstrelsy.
And any cousin, poor but free,
  Might take me, fatted ass! from thee.

The differences observable in these two translations and in that by Carlyle probably arise
from each having been made from distinct variants of the original.

Mu'awiya was the fifth Khalif in succession from Muhammad, and the founder of the
house of 'Umayya.]

THE IMAM SHAFAY--<page 108>.

SHAFAY, the founder of one of the four orthodox sects into which the Mohammedans
are divided, was a disciple of Malek Ben Ans, and the master to Ahmed Ebn Hanbal;
each of whom, like himself, founded a sect which is still denominated from the name of
its author. The fourth sect is that of Abu Hanifah. This differs in tenets considerably from
the three others; for whilst the Malekites, the Shafaites, and the Hanbalites are invariably
bigoted to tradition in their interpretations of the Koran, the Hanifites consider
themselves as at liberty in any difficulty to make use of their own reason.--The reputation
Shafay acquired was not entirely the consequence of his theological writings: he
published many poems, which have been much admired. This specimen seems intended
to recommend the doctrine of fatalism--a doctrine which has always been favoured by the
orthodox Mohammedans.

["It is eminently erroneous and unjust," says Mr. Redhouse, in a valuable paper on "The Most Comely Names, i.e., the Titles of Praise bestowed on GOD in the Qur'an," &c., which appeared in a recent number of the Journal of the Royal Asiatic Society,--"as well as inconsequent and inconsistent, for professing Christians, writers and speakers, to cast upon Muslims, their scriptures, and their prophet, the unfounded accusation of fatalism. That is a pagan idea, with which Islam has no more in common than Christianity has. What Muhammad taught, what the Qur'an so eloquently and so persistently sets forth, and what real faithful Muslims believe, conformably with what is contained in the Gospels and accepted by devout Christians, is, that God's Providence pre-ordains, as His Omniscience foreknows, all events, and overrules the designs of men, to the sure fulfilment of His all-wise purposes."]

IBRAHIM BEN ADHAM--p. 109.

IBRAHIM BEN ADHAM was a hermit of Syria, equally celebrated for his talents and piety. He was the son of a prince of Khorassan, and was born about the 97th year of the Hijra [A.D. 715]. The reason of his betaking himself to a religious life is related by Ibrahim Ben Yesar, from the holy man's own mouth. "I once requested him," says this author, "to inform me by what means he arrived at his exalted sanctity, and by what motives he was first induced to take leave of the world. For a while he continued silent, but upon my repeatedly urging him, he answered, that being one day eagerly engaged in the chase, he was surprised with hearing a voice behind him utter these words: 'Ibrahim! it was not for this purpose thou wast created.' He immediately stopped his horse, and turned about to see from whence the voice came, but discovering no one near, he fancied it to be an illusion, and returned to his sport. In a short time he heard the same words pronounced still more loudly, Ibrahim! it was not for this purpose thou wast created.' He now no longer doubted the reality of the admonition, and falling down in a transport of devotion, cried out: 'It is the LORD who speaks; his servant will obey.' Immediately he desisted from his amusement, and changing clothes with an attendant, bade adieu to Khorassan, took the road towards Syria, and from thenceforward devoted himself entirely to a life of piety and labour." Ben Adham performed the stated pilgrimage to Mecca without companions, and without having provided any necessaries for his journey. He obliged himself also to make eleven hundred genuflexions in every mile, by which means twelve years elapsed before he completed his pilgrimage. As he was returning from Mecca he met the Khalif Haroun Alrashid, who was going thither, accompanied by a magnificent train; and it was upon this occasion that he addressed these verses to the Commander of the Faithful, as a reproach for his ostentatious devotion.

ISAAC ALMOUSELY--<page 110>.

ISAAC ALMOUSELY is considered by the Orientals as the most celebrated musician that ever flourished. He was born in Persia, but having resided almost entirely at Mousel, he is generally supposed to have been a native of that place. Mahadi, the

father of Haroun Alrashid, having accidentally heard Almousely sing one of his compositions, accompanied by a lute, was so charmed with the performance that he carried him to Bagdad, and appointed him principal musician to the court; an office which Almousely filled with universal applause during the reigns of five successive Khalifs of the house of Abbas, viz., Mahadi, Hadi, Haroun, Amin, and Mamoun.--Haroun Alrashid, whose inauguration is commemorated in these verses [<page 110>], was the fifth of the Abbasside Khalifs, and the second son of Mahadi. He succeeded to the throne upon the demise of his elder brother Hadi, in the 170th year of the Hijra [A.D. 786]. Haroun, who was passionately fond of music, could not but be charmed with the talents of Almousely. At every party of amusement given by the Khalif, Almousely made one; and he is represented, like another Timotheus, to have been able at pleasure, by the touches of his lute, to raise or depress the passions of his master. Ebn Khalican relates the following remarkable instance of the effect of his musical powers upon the Khalif:

Haroun Alrashid having quarrelled with his favourite mistress, Meridah, left her in a rage, and refused to see her again. The lady was in despair, and knew not in what manner to bring about a reconciliation. In the mean time the vizier, Jaafer, who had always been a friend to Meridah, sent for Almousely, and giving him a song, composed for the purpose, requested him to perform it before the Khalif with all the pathos he was master of. Almousely obeyed; and such were the powers of his execution, that Haroun, immediately bidding adieu to his anger, rushed into the presence of Meridah, and taking all the blame of the quarrel upon himself, entreated his mistress to forgive his indiscretion, and bury what was past in an eternal oblivion. The historian adds (for such must always be the catastrophe of an Eastern story when it terminates happily), that the lady, overjoyed with this sudden alteration in the Khalif's disposition, ordered ten thousand dirhems to be given to Jaafer, and as much to Almousely; while Haroun, on his part, not less pleased with their reconciliation than the lady, doubled the present to each.

THE RUIN OF THE BARMECIDES--<page 111>.

THE family of Barmec was one of the most illustrious in the East: they were descended from the ancient Kings of Persia, and possessed immense property in various countries; they derived still more consequence from the favour which they enjoyed at the court of Bagdad, where for many years they filled the highest offices of the state with universal approbation. The first of this family who distinguished himself at Bagdad was Yahia Ben Khaled, a person endowed with every virtue and talent that could render a character complete: He had four sons, Fadhel, Jaafer, Mohammed, and Musa, all of whom showed themselves worthy of such a father. Yahia was chosen by the Khalif Mahadi to be governor to his son Haroun Alrashid, and when Haroun succeeded to the Khalifate, he appointed Yahia to be his grand vizier, an event alluded to in the preceding composition.

[283]

This dignity Yahia held for some years, and when increasing infirmities obliged him to resign it, the Khalif conferred it upon his second son, Jaafer.

Jaafer's abilities were formed to adorn every situation: independent of his hereditary virtues, he was the most admired writer and the most eloquent speaker of his age; and during the time he was in office, he displayed at once the accuracy of a man of business and the comprehensive ideas of a statesman. But the brilliancy of Jaafer's talents rendered him more acceptable to his master in the capacity of a companion than in that of a minister. Haroun resolved, therefore, that state affairs should no longer deprive him of the pleasure he derived from Jaafer's society; and accordingly made him relinquish his post, and appointed his brother Fadhel, a man of severer manners, grand vizier in his room. For seventeen years the two brothers were all-powerful in Bagdad and throughout the empire; but, as often happens in the East, their authority was overturned in a moment, and their whole house involved in ruin.

The disgrace and consequent ill-treatment of the Barmecides throw an eternal stain upon the memory of Alrashid; and the causes to which they are commonly attributed seem so vague and romantic that we can scarce imagine a prince like Haroun could ever have been actuated by such motives to commit such enormities. The reason for their disgrace most generally received is as follows:

The Khalif had a sister called Abassa, of whom he was passionately fond, and whose company he preferred to everything but the conversation of Jaafer. These two pleasures he would fain have joined together, by carrying Jaafer with him in his visits to Abassa; but the laws of the Harem, which forbade anyone except a near relation being introduced there, made that impossible; and he was obliged to be absent either from his sister or from his favourite. At length he discovered a method which he hoped would enable him to enjoy at the same time the society of these two persons who were so dear to him: This was to unite Jaafer and Abassa in marriage. They were married accordingly; but with this express condition, that they should never meet except in the presence of the Khalif. Their interviews, however, were very frequent; and as neither could be insensible of the amiable qualities which the other possessed, a mutual affection took place between them. Blinded by their passion, they forgot the Khalif's injunction, and the consequences of their intercourse were but too apparent. Abassa was delivered of a son, whom they privately sent to be educated at Mecca. For some time their amour was concealed from Alrashid; but the Khalif having at length received intelligence of it, he gave way to his rage, and determined to take the most severe revenge. In consequence of this cruel resolve, he immediately commanded Jaafer to be put to death, and the whole race of Barmec to be deprived of their possessions and thrown into prison. These orders were obeyed: Jaafer was beheaded in the antechamber of the royal apartment, whither he had come to request an interview with the implacable Haroun; and his father and brothers perished in confinement.

Some of the consolatory words which Yahia delivered to his unfortunate family, whilst they were in prison, are preserved by Ben Shonah: "Power and wealth," said the venerable old man, "were but a loan with which fortune entrusted us: we ought to be thankful that we have enjoyed these blessings so long; and we ought to console ourselves for their loss by the reflection that our fate will afford a perpetual example to others of their instability."--The fall of the house of Barmec was considered as a general calamity. By their courtesy, their abilities, and their virtues, they had endeared themselves to everyone; and, according to an Oriental writer, "they enjoyed the singular felicity of being loved as much when in the plenitude of their power as in a private station; and of being praised as much after their disgrace as when they were at the summit of their prosperity."

TAHER BEN HOSEIN--<page 112>.

TAHER BEN HOSEIN appears to have been the most celebrated general of his time. He commanded the forces of Mamun, the second son of Haroun Alrashid, and it was chiefly owing to his abilities that Mamun arrived at the throne.

This epigram on Taher reminds us of the following well-known lines, upon a brother and sister, both extremely beautiful, but who had each lost an eye; and it is curious to observe how easily the same idea is modified by a different poet into a satire or a panegyric:

Lumine dextro Acon, capta est Leonilla sinistro,
    Sed potis est forma vincere uterque deos:
 Alme puer, lumen quod habes concede sorrori,
    Sic tu caecus Amor, sic erit illa Venus.

An eye both Lycidas and Julia want,
    Yet each is fairer than the gods above;
 Couldst thou, sweet youth, thine eye to Julia grant,
    Thou wouldst be Cupid, she the Queen of Love.

THE ADIEU--

THIS beautiful little composition, which hears a striking resemblance to one of Sappho's odes, was sung before the Khalif Wathek, by Abu Mohammed, a musician of Bagdad, as a specimen of his musical talents; and such were its effects upon the Khalif, that he immediately testified his approbation of the performance by throwing his own robe over the shoulders of Abu Mohammed, and ordering him a present of a hundred thousand dirhems.--Wathek was the ninth Khalif of the house of Abbas, and a son of Motassem, the youngest of Haroun Alrashid's children. He succeeded his father A.D. 841, and died after a short reign of five years. Wathek was not deficient either in virtue or abilities: he not only admired and countenanced literature and science, but in several branches of them, particularly poetry and music, was himself a proficient. His last words were.: "King of heaven, whose dominion is everlasting, have mercy on a wretched prince, whose reign is transitory!"

[285]

[This prince is the hero of Beckford's "Arabian" tale of Vathek, which Byron has highly praised for "correctness of costume, beauty of description, and power of imagination;" but, though certainly a remarkable work of fancy, it is far from meriting the encomiums which were at one time so lavishly bestowed upon it.]

ABU TEMAN HABIB

ABU TEMAN is reckoned the most excellent of all the Arabian poets; and I regret that I have not been able to give a more adequate specimen of his talents. He was born near Damascus, A.H. 190 [A.D. 805], and educated in Egypt; but the principal part of his life was spent at Bagdad, under the patronage of the Abbaside Khalifs. The presents he is reported to have received from these princes, and the respect with which he was treated by them, are so extravagant that one can scarce give credit to the accounts of historians. For a single poem which he presented to one of them, he was rewarded with fifty thousand pieces of gold, and at the same time assured that this pecuniary favour was infinitely below the obligation he had conferred; and upon reciting an elegy he had composed on the death of some great man, he was told that no one could be said to die who had been celebrated by Abu Teman. This poet expired at Mousel, before he had quite reached his fortieth year. His early death had been already predicted by a contemporary writer, in these words: "The mind of Abu Teman must soon wear out his body, as the blade of an Indian scimitar destroys its scabbard."

[Lord Byron, in his Letters, employs the same expression, with reference to himself, that "the sword wears out the sheath."--Abu Temmam was the compiler of the Hamasa, a collection of ancient Arabic poetry, consisting of epigrams, odes, elegies, &c. It was a saying of Abu Temmam that fine sentiments delivered in prose were like gems scattered at random, but when they were confined in a poetical measure, they resembled bracelets and strings of pearls.]

ABD ALSALEM BEN RAGBAN

ABD ALSALEM was a poet more remarkable for abilities than morality. We may form an idea of the nature of his compositions from the nickname he acquired amongst his contemporaries of "Cock of the evil Genii." He died A.H. 236 [A.D. 850], aged near eighty.

EBN ALRUMI--

EBN ALRUMI is reckoned by Arabian writers as one of the most excellent of all their poets. He was by birth a Syrian, and passed the greatest part of his life at Emessa, where he died, A.H. 283 [A.D. 896]. Alrumi attempted every species of poetry, and he attempted none in which he did not succeed. But he requires no further encomium when we say that he was the favourite author of the celebrated Avicenna, who employed a great portion of his leisure hours in writing a commentary upon the works of Ebn Alrumi.

[The beautiful epigram of Ibnu 'r-Rumi, which our translator has expanded into the verses, "To a Lady Weeping" is thus rendered into Latin verse by Sir W. Jones, in his Poeseos Asiaticae Commentarii:

Vidi in hortulo violam,
    Cujus folia rore splendebant;
 Similis erat flos illi (puellae) coeruleos habenti oculos,
    Quorum cilia lacrymas stillant.

Professor John W. Hales, of King's College, London, has directed the Editor's attention to the close resemblance which a verse of one of Lord Byron's "Hebrew Melodies" bears to the first stanza of Carlyle's paraphrase of Ibnu 'r-Rumi's epigram:

I saw thee weep--the big bright tear
    Came o'er that eye of blue;
 And then methought it did appear
    A violet dropping dew.--Byron.

When I beheld thy blue eye shine
    Through the bright drop that Pity drew,
 I saw beneath those tears of thine
    A blue-eyed violet bathed in dew.--Carlyle's Trans.

Byron's "Hebrew Melodies" were published, with music arranged by Braham and Nathan, in 1814; the second edition of Carlyle's "Specimens of Arabian Poetry" was issued in 1810: Byron had, doubtless, read the volume, and boldly appropriated the Arab poet's fine simile.]

ALI BEN AHMED BEN MANSOUR

ALI BEN AHMED distinguished himself in prose as well as in poetry; and a historical work of considerable reputation of which he was the author is still extant. But he principally excelled in satire; and so fond was he of indulging this dangerous talent, that no one escaped his lash: if he could only bring out a sarcasm, it was matter of indifference to him whether an enemy or a brother smarted under its severity. He died at Bagdad, A.H. 302 [A.D. 9141--The person to whom this epigram is addressed, Cassim Obid Allah, was successively vizier to Motadhed and Moctafi his son, the sixteenth and seventeenth Khalifs of the house of Abbas; the latter of whom was principally indebted to the activity of Obid Allah for his exaltation to the throne. This vizier died A.H. 294 [A.D. 906], having been entrusted with the chief direction of affairs at Bagdad for nearly fifteen years.

TO A FRIEND, ON HIS BIRTHDAY

THE thought contained in these lines appears so natural and so obvious, that one wonders it did not occur to all who have attempted to write upon a birthday or a death. To me, however, it was perfectly novel.--The Persian verses given in the Asiatic Miscellany, vol. ii., p. 374, seem to be a translation from our Arabian author.

[The verses to which Carlyle refers, translated from the Persian by Sir W. Jones, are as follows:

On parent knees, a naked new-born child,
 Weeping thou sat'st, while all around thee smiled:
 So live, that, sinking to thy last long sleep,
 Calm thou mayst smile, while all around thee weep.

Strange as it may appear, the original of these lines has been ascribed to the Rev. Charles Wesley. In Notes and Queries, May 10, 1879 (5th Series, vol. xi., p. 365), a correspondent quotes the following passage, from page 399 of Mr. George J. Stevenson's Memorials of the Wesley Family, London, 1876: "On the last day of January, 1750, a clap of thunder unusually loud and terrible aroused Mr. and Mrs. [Charles] Wesley at two in the morning. Greatly alarmed, Mrs. Wesley went with her husband to consult a physician. Overtaken by a shower of rain, they made too great haste home, and the consequence was the premature birth of their first child. The mother recovered, not the child. The occasion awakened the muse of the father, who wrote the following lines:

ON AN INFANT.

The man that ushered thee to light, my child,
 Saw thee in tears while all around thee smiled:
 When summoned hence to thine eternal sleep,
 Oh! may'st thou smile, while all around thee weep."

The writer in Notes and Queries then cites the supposed "imitation" of these lines by Sir W. Jones, and while shrewdly remarking that the resemblance was too great to be a mere coincidence, he allows that the Orientalist "has greatly improved the language, taking the rough gold of the original and moulding it into a form of beauty that will live for ever." As may be readily supposed, replies to this charge of plagiarism against Jones quickly followed in the same useful and entertaining miscellany: one writer observing that the lines ascribed to Wesley in Mr. Stevenson's book appear to be an ill-remembered citation from the beautiful and almost perfect quatrain of Sir W. Jones; another remarking that it would indeed be something strange to find such a man as Jones borrowing ideas of Charles Wesley; and both pointing out the original as given in Carlyle's volume, together with his English rendering. Other correspondents quoted a French translation of verses, identical with the Arabic original, by the Persian poet Hatif, and an apothegm, similar in sentiment and even in language, from Galland's Maximes, &c., des Orientaux.-- Altogether, the idea of Charles Wesley's having written the original of this beautiful little piece is simply absurd. Moreover, the story bears upon the face of it the stamp of improbability. Ladies in an "interesting condition" do not leave their houses at two o'clock in the morning to go and consult the family doctor.]

IBN ALALAF ALNAHARWANY

THIS author was a native of Naharwan, but he lived principally at Bagdad, where he expired, A.H. 318 [A.D. 930], at the advanced age of a hundred. He is represented to have had a most voracious appetite, and as little delicacy in the choice of his food. Of this Nuvari relates the following ludicrous instance. The poet one day mounted his ass, in order to pay a visit to a nobleman in Bagdad. He was introduced into the saloon, and in the meantime the attendants conducted his ass into the kitchen, where it was killed and dressed, and at the proper time served up to him at table. The poet relished his dinner so much that he devoured every morsel which was set before him, declaring that he had never tasted such excellent veal in his life. When evening approached, he called for his ass, that he might return home; but the animal was nowhere to be found; and at length they confessed the trick which had been put upon him. The nobleman, however, made him a present which amply compensated for his loss, and he took leave, perfectly satisfied with his entertainment.

The occasion of this odd composition and its real intent are variously related. Some say that it means no more than it pretends to do, and that it was actually composed on the death of a favourite Cat. Others tell us that the poet here laments the misfortunes of Abdallah Ebn Motaz, who was raised to the Khalifate by a popular tumult, A.H. 296 [A.D. 908], and, after enjoying his dignity a single day, put to death by his rival Moctader. As the poet durst not show his grief for Abdallah in a more open manner, he invented, according to these authors, this allegory, in which the fate of Abdallah is represented under that of a cat. But the opinion most generally received is that these verses were composed as an elegy upon the death of a private friend, whose name is not known, but who, like Abdallah, owed his ruin to the rash gratification of a headstrong passion. This young man entertained an affection for a favourite female slave belonging to the vizier Ali Ben Isa, and was equally beloved by her in return. Their amour had been concealed for some time, but the lovers being one day unfortunately surprised in each other's company by the jealous vizier, he sacrificed them both to his fury upon the spot.

EBN NAPHTA-WAH

MOHAMMED BEN ARFA, here called Naphta-wah, was descended from a noble family in Khorassan. He applied himself to study with indefatigable perseverance, and was a very voluminous author in several branches of literature; but he is chiefly distinguished as a grammarian. He died A.H. 323 [A.D. 9341

THE KHALIF RADHI. BILLAH--pp.

RADHI BILLAH, the son of Moctader, was the twentieth Khalif of the house of Abbas, and the last of these princes who possessed any substantial power. He is universally represented to have been a man of talents, and these compositions will show that he was not deficient in poetical merit. He died A.H. 329 [A.D. 940]

SAIF ADDAULET

THE Court of Aleppo, during the reign of Saif Addaulet IA.D. 944-966], was the most polished in the East: the Sultan and his brothers were all eminent for poetical talents, and whoever excelled, either in literature or in science, was sure of obtaining their patronage; so that at a time when not only Europe, but great part of Asia, was sunk in the profoundest ignorance, the Sultan of Aleppo could boast of such an assemblage of genius at his court as few sovereigns have ever been able to bring together.--Elmacin relates that Saif Addaulet, having conceived a passion for a princess of the blood royal, gave such public marks of the preference he entertained for her, that the ladies of his harem took alarm, and resolved to rid themselves of the object of their jealousy by means of poison. The Sultan, however, obtained intelligence of their design, and determined to prevent it, by transporting the princess to a castle at some distance from Aleppo; and whilst she remained in this solitude he addressed to her these verses.

THE CRUCIFIXION OF EBN BAKIAH

EBN BAKIAH was vizier to Azzad Addaulet or Bachteir, Emir Alomra of Bagdad, under the Khalifs Moti Lillah and Tay Lillah: but Azzad Addaulet being deprived of his office and driven from Bagdad by Adhed Addaulet, Sultan of Persia, Ebn Bakiah was seized upon and crucified at the gates of the city by order of the conqueror.--The mode of punishment inflicted on the vizier gave occasion to this quibbling composition, which appears to a European more remarkable for its unfeelingness than for its ingenuity. Amongst the Orientals, however, who prefer this kind of jeu de mots to every other species of wit, it has always been so much admired, that there is scarce any historian of those times who has not inserted in his work a copy of the verses upon Ebn Bakiah.

SHEMS ALMAALI CABUS

HISTORY can show few princes so amiable and few so unfortunate as Shems Almaali Cabus. He is described as possessed of almost every virtue and every accomplishment: his piety, justice, generosity, and humanity are universally celebrated; nor was he less for intellectual powers: his genius was at once penetrating, solid, and brilliant, and he distinguished himself equally as an orator, a philosopher, and a poet. In such estimation were his writings held that the most careless productions of his pen were preserved as models of composition; and we are told that a famous vizier of Persia could never open even an official despatch from Shems Almaali without exclaiming: "This is written with the feather of a celestial bird!"

Shems Almaali ascended the throne of Georgia on the death of his brother, A.H. 366 [A.D. 976]; and during a reign of thirty-five years made the Georgians happy by his administration. His ruin was at length occasioned by an unfortunate piece of generosity. In a contest between Mowid Addaulet and Faker Addaulet, two rival princes of the house of Bowiah, the latter had been overcome by his brother, and with difficulty escaped into Georgia, where Shems Almaali afforded him an asylum. Mowid Addaulet considered the kindness shown to his brother as an insult to himself, and in revenge he overran Georgia with a numerous army, and obliged Faker Addaulet and Shems Almaali to fly for refuge to the mountains of Khorassan. For three years the exiled princes led a wandering and uncomfortable life, surrounded by danger and harassed by necessity; but at the end of that period Mowid Addaulet died, and Faker Addaulet, without opposition, assumed the sceptre of Persia. With unparalleled ingratitude, Faker Addaulet refused to restore Shems Almaali to his hereditary dominions, and the unfortunate prince remained fourteen years longer in exile. At length Faker Addaulet died, and Shems Almaali reassumed the government of Georgia. He found many abuses had crept into the state, which he determined to correct; but the great men who profited by them conspired to deprive him once more of power, and during the absence of his son he was seized and thrown into prison, where the aged monarch perished of cold on the bare ground.

After the character given of Shems Almaali, it is almost superfluous to add that he was a patron of literature. His court abounded with men of genius from all parts of the East, amongst whom was the celebrated Avicenna, who lived many years under his protection.

[This little poem of Shamsu-'l-Ma'ali (i.e., "Sun of the Higher Regions") Qabus was probably composed during his exile in Khorassan.--The ideas expressed in the last six lines of Carlyle's translation, which fairly represents the original, are identical with some of those contained in the second of Mr. Payne's specimens of the Poetry of the "Thousand and One Nights," as given in pp. <page 367>, <page 368> of the present volume, which, there can be little doubt, is a variant of the Georgian monarch's poem.]

ON LIFE

[A PARALLEL to the sentiment contained in these verses--but far less elegantly expressed--is found in an old Greek epigram, which Major Robert Guthrie Macgregor has thus translated: ("Greek Anthology, with Notes Critical and Explanatory," Sect, vii., 148, p. 567)

Death dogs us all: we're fattened as a flock

[291]

Of swine, in turn, for slaughter on the block.

In Buddha's Dammapada, or Path of Virtue, rendered into English by Professor F. Max Muller, and prefixed to Captain Rogers' translation of Buddhaghosha's Parables, is the following apothegm: "Death carries off a man who is gathering flowers, and whose mind is distracted, as a flood carries off a sleeping village."]

EXTEMPORE VERSES, BY EBN ALRAMACRAM

THE occasion of this jeu d'esprit is thus related by Abulfeda: Carawash, Sultan of Mousel, being one wintry evening engaged in a party of pleasure along with Barkaidy, Ebn Fadhi, Abu Jaber, and the improvisatore poet Ebn Alramacram, resolved to divert himself at the expense of his companions. He therefore ordered the poet to give a specimen of his talents, which at the same time should convey a satire upon the three courtiers, and a compliment to himself. Ebn Alramacram took his subject from the stormy appearance of the night, and immediately produced these verses.

ALI BEN MOHAMMED ALTAHMANY

ALI BEN MOHAMMED was a native of that part of Arabia called Hijaz, and is celebrated not only as a poet but as a politician. In the latter of these characters he undertook a commission at the request of the Emir Alomra of Bagdad, the object of which was to excite an insurrection at Cairo, against the Egyptian Khalif Taher Liazaz; but being detected in his intrigues, he was thrown into prison, about A.H. 416 [A.D. 1025], and soon after suffered death.

ABU ALCASSIM EBN TABATABA

TABATABA deduced his pedigree from Ali Ben Abu Taleb, and Fatima, the daughter of Mohammed. He was born at Ispahan, but passed the principal part of his life in Egypt, where he was appointed chief of the schereffs--i.e., descendants of the Prophet, a dignity held in the highest veneration by every Muslim. He died A.H. 418 [A.D. 1027], with the reputation of being one of the most excellent poets of his time.

AHMED BEN YOUSEF ALMENAZY

BEN YOUSEF for many years acted as vizier to Abu Nasser, Sultan of Diarbeker. His political talents are much praised; and he is particularly celebrated for the address he displayed while upon an embassy to the Greek emperor at Constantinople. His passion for literature appears to have been extreme. The greater part of his leisure hours were devoted to study; and such was his assiduity in collecting books, that he was able to form two very large libraries, the one at Miaferakin and the other at Amid, which for some centuries after his death were considered as the great fountains of instruction for all Asia.

THE SULTAN CARAWASH

THE life of this prince was chequered with various adventures: he was perpetually engaged in contests either with neighbouring sovereigns or with the princes of his own family. For several years, however, he maintained himself in the possession of his little kingdom, and during this period rendered Mousel the seat of science and literature. But in the year of the Hijra 442 [A.D. 1050] he was obliged to submit to his brother Abu Camel, who caused him to be conveyed to a place of security, where, however, he was treated with every consideration for his rank and years until after his brother's death, when it is said he was murdered by the inhuman hands of his own nephew.

ABU ALOLA

ABU ALOLA is esteemed one of the most excellent of the Arabian poets. He was born blind, or at least lost his sight at a very early age; but this did not deter him from the pursuit of literature. To prosecute his studies with more advantage, he travelled from Maara, the place of his nativity, to Bagdad, where he spent a few months in attending the lectures of the different professors at the academy of that city, and in conversing with the learned men who resorted thither from all parts of the East. After this short stay in Bagdad, he returned to his native cottage, which he never again quitted. But notwithstanding the difficulties he laboured under, and the few advantages he had received from education, "he lived," according to Abulfeda, "to know that his celebrity spread from the sequestered village which he inhabited to the utmost confines of the globe."--Abu Alola died at Maara A.H. 449 [A.D. 10571, aged 86. He attempted every species of poetry, and succeeded in all.

NEDHAM ALMOLK

THE character and fate of this illustrious statesman are thus described by Gibbon: "In a period when Europe was plunged in the deepest barbarism, the light and splendour of Asia may be ascribed to the docility rather than the knowledge of the Turkish conquerors. An ample share of their wisdom and virtue is due to a Persian vizier who ruled the empire under Alp Arslan and his son. Nedham, one of the most illustrious ministers of the East, was honoured by the Khalif as an oracle of religion and science; he was trusted by the Sultan as the faithful vicegerent of his power and justice. After an administration of thirty years, the fame of the vizier, his wealth, and even his services were transformed into crimes. He was overthrown by the insidious arts of a woman and a rival; and his fall was hastened by a rash declaration that his cap and inkhorn, the badges of his office, were connected by the divine decree with the throne and diadem of the Sultan. At the age of ninety-three years the venerable statesman was dismissed by his master, accused by his

[293]

enemies, and murdered by a fanatic. The last words of Nedham attested his innocence, and the remainder of Malec's life was short and inglorious."

Malec died in the year of the Hijra 465 [A.D. 1072], and with him expired the greatness and union of the Seljuk empire.

THE PRINCESS WALADATA

WALADATA, the daughter of a Spanish king named Mohammed Almostakfi Billah, was born at Cordova. She was a woman no less beautiful than talented. She was devoted to the study of rhetoric and poetry; she cultivated the friendship of the distinguished poets of her age, and frequently indulged in the pleasure of their conversation. In writing she had a great deal of wit and acumen, as may be seen from this distich.--Cassiri: Bib. Hisp.

Almostakfi was the last Khalif of the house of 'Umayya who reigned in Spain.

THE SULTAN MOTAMMED BEN ABAD

SEVILLE was one of those small sovereignties into which Spain had been divided after the extinction of the house of 'Umayya. It did not long retain its independence, and the only prince who ever presided over it as a separate kingdom seems to have been Motammed Ben Abad, the author of these verses. For thirty-three years he reigned over Seville and the neighbouring districts with considerable reputation, but being attacked by Joseph, son of the emperor of Morocco, at the head of a numerous army of Africans, was defeated, taken prisoner, and thrown into a dungeon, where he died, A.H. 488 [A.D. 10951.

ALI BEN ABD ALGANY, OF CORDOVA

THIS author was by birth an African, but having passed over to Spain, he was much patronised by Motammed, Sultan of Seville. After the fall of his master, Ben Abd returned into Africa, and died at Tangier, A.H. 488 [A.D. 1095].--Ben Abd wrote at a time when Arabic literature was upon the decline in Spain, and his verses are not very unlike the compositions of our own metaphysical poets of the 17th century.

[The Arabian conquerors of Spain introduced the gallant custom of serenading their mistresses, on which occasion, not only the words of their songs, but the airs, and even the colour of their habits, were expressive of the triumph of the fortunate, or the despair of the rejected lover. The Kitar--whence our guitar, from the Spanish guitarra--was their favourite instrument.--Richardson.

The idea expressed in the first stanza of this serenade--the comparison of the eye of his sleeping mistress to a sheathed sword--is identical with a verse of Antara's beautiful poem beginning: "When the breezes blow from Mount Sa'di," &c., where the poet says of his darling Abla (p. 198, l. 4, et seq.):

"She draws her sword from the glances of her eyelashes, sharp and penetrating as the blade of her forefathers, and with it her eyes kill, though it be sheathed."

Again, in the verses recited by Antara before King Mundhir (foot of page <page 217>):

"The eyelashes of the songstress from the corner of the veil are more cutting than the edge of cleaving scimitars."

The Persian poet Hafiz employs the same comparison:

"The glance of the cup-bearer is an unsheathed sword for the destruction of the understanding."

And the Afghan poet, Khushhal Khan, Khattak ("Selections from the Poetry of the Afghans," by Major Raverty, page 188):

I am intoxicated with that countenance, which hath sleepy, languid eyes:
 By them I become all cut and gashed--thou wouldst say those eyes sharp swords contain.

Other illustrations of this similitude are given in Notes on the Poetry of the Romance of Antar.]

ISAAC BEN KHALIF

[CARLYLE furnishes no particulars regarding this author, nor does he state whence the jeu d'esprit which he translates was taken. Mr. Lyall, in his "Translations from the Hamasa and Aghani," gives a fragment by Ishaq son of Khalaf, who was probably the same with our author. This fragment is of a very different cast from the amusing epigram paraphrased by Carlyle: it expresses the author's anxiety as to the possible fate of his daughter when he is dead. Mr. Lyall infuses into his translations so much of the real spirit of Arabic poetry, and the verses in question are so peculiarly interesting, that the temptation to reproduce his rendering of them in this connection is simply irresistible:

1. If no Umeymeh were there, no want would trouble my soul--
    no labour call me to toil for bread through pitchiest night;

2. What moves my longing to live is but that well do I know
    how low the fatherless lies--how hard the kindness of kin.

3. I quake before loss of wealth lest lacking fall upon her,
    and leave her shieldless and bare as flesh set forth on a board.

[295]

4. My life she prays for, and I from mere love pray for her death--
   yea, Death, the gentlest and kindest guest to visit a maid.

5. I fear an uncle's rebuke, a brother's harshness for her:
   my chiefest end was to spare her heart the grief of a word.

These explanatory Notes on the above are also by Mr. Lyall:

v. 3. "Meat on a butcher's board" is a proverbial expression for that which is utterly defenceless and helpless.

v. 4. The scholiast compares the proverbs (both current in the Ignorance)--"An excellent son-in-law is the Grave," and "To bury daughters is an act of mercy;" the reference in the latter is to the practice of burying female children alive immediately after birth, which was still prevalent (though not widely spread) among the pagan Arabs at the time of the Prophet's mission. The lot of women among the Arabs of the Ignorance was a hard one; and it is most probable that the practice in question was perpetuated, if it did not begin, in the desire to save the family the shame of seeing its women ill-used or otherwise disgraced.

v. 5. He looks forward to the time when his daughter will be 'left fatherless, and find no love such as that which she found in him.

Of the author, Mr. Lyall has been able to ascertain nothing. The fragment, as shown in rhyme of the first hemistich of the original, is the beginning of a qasida. By his name (Ishaq), Mr. Lyall thinks the author should be a Muslim, since but one authentic instance is known of a biblical name being borne by an Arab, who was not a Jew; yet the sentiment of v. 4 is rather pagan than Islamic.]

LAMIAT ALAJEM

ABU ISMAEL was a native of Ispahan. He devoted himself to the service of the Seljuk Sultans of Persia, and enjoyed the confidence of Malek Shah, and his son and grandson, Mohammed and Massoud, by the last of whom he was raised to the dignity of vizier. Massoud, however, was not long in a condition to afford Abu Ismael any protection; for being attacked by his brother Mahmoud, he was defeated and driven from Mousel, and on the fall of his master the vizier was seized and thrown into prison, and at length, in the year 515 [A.D. 1121], sentenced to be put to death. This poem seems to have been composed in the interval of time between the flight of Massoud and the imprisonment of Abu Ismael; at least it breathes such sentiments as we might expect from a man in a similar situation.

This composition has obtained more general approbation than almost any poem extant in the East; it is celebrated by the historians, commented on by the critics, and quoted by the people. I have therefore given it entire from the edition of Dr. Pocock.--The extreme popularity of this production is a striking proof of the decay of all true taste amongst the Orientals: it were otherwise impossible that they could prefer the laboured conceits and tinsel ornaments of Abu Ismael to the simplicity of the bards of Yemen, and the elegance of the poets of Bagdad.

[Such is our translator's estimate of the Lamiyyatu-'l-'Ajem, to which, whatever may be its shortcomings, his own rendering into English verse has certainly not done justice. It were much to be wished that Carlyle had endeavoured to preserve in his translation the external form, at least, of the original verses; but this could hardly have been expected perhaps in an age when our own English poetry was characterised by an absurd affectation of refined "sensibility," and was, according to Lord Byron, artificial as Carlyle would have us believe this poem of Et-Tugra'i to be. And yet, in 1758, or forty years before the first edition (very inaccurately printed, by the way) of Carlyle's "Specimens" was published, the Lamiyyatu-'l-'Ajem, under the title of "The Traveller: an Arabic Poem," was "rendered into English verse, in the same iambic measure as the original," by Leonard Chappelow, BD., of Carlyle's own University of Cambridge; of which, strange to say, our translator makes no mention. And it may here be remarked as not less strange, perhaps, that in Lowndes' Bibliographer's Manual, while Dr. Pocock's Latin version of the original, with Notes, and Chappelow's English translation are both noticed, no mention is made of Carlyle's later rendering.

This poem is styled Lamiyyatu-'l-'Ajem, or the Lamiyya of the non-Arabs, from the rawi, or binding letter of the rhyme running through the piece, which is the Arabic letter called lam (our "L"); and from the author of it being a Persian, or foreigner: the Arabs distinguishing mankind into two sections--first, themselves, 'Arabs, and secondly, 'Ajem, i.e., non-Arabs; as the "Jews and Gentiles," "Greeks and Barbarians." The author is commonly styled Et-Tugra'i, from the office he held of "Cypher-writer to the King"--Abu Isma'il had to write the king's Tugra, or cypher, on all the royal edicts. This office still exists in Turkey: the holder is styled Tugra-kesh, cypher-drawer, and tevqi'i, cypherer; formerly, nishanji, marker. The Poet's full name was Mu'ayyidu-'d-Din, Hasan (or Husayn) 'bnu 'Ali, Abu Isma'il, Et-Tugra'i--which signifies: Hasan, son of 'Ali, father of Isma'il, Supporter of the Faith, Cypher-Writer to the Sultan.

A still more remarkable "L" poem is the Lamiyyatu-'l-'Arab of the renowned pre-Islamite brigand-poet Shanfara', of whose life and poetry a most fascinating account is given by Mr. W. G. Palgrave, in his "Essays on Eastern Questions." "Nowhere," says Mr. Palgrave, "is his indomitable self-reliance more savagely expressed than in this famous poem--famous so long as Arab literature shall exist; the completest utterance ever given of a mind defying its age and all around it, and reverting to, or at least idealizing, the absolute individualism of the savage. It is a monolith, complete in itself; and if ever rendered (though I doubt the possibility) into English verse, must stand alone."]

IBN ALTALMITH

ABOUT the middle of the sixth century of the Hijra there lived in the East three physicians, almost equally celebrated for their abilities. They were all surnamed Hebat Allah: the Gift of God; and each professed a different religion, one being a Christian, one a Muslim, and the other a Jew. The first of these--our author--was a native of Bagdad, and according to Abulfaraj, "the elegance of his manners equalled his learning, and the sweetness of his disposition was only exceeded by the sublimity of his genius." Ibn Altalmith was a favourite with all the princes who flourished at Bagdad during his time; but with Almoktafi he lived as a friend. He died, as he had lived, professing the Christian religion, A.H. 560 [A.D. 1164], at the advanced age of one hundred. His last words are preserved by Abulfaraj, and prove at least that his vivacity was unimpaired to the last: "Ibn Altalmith was expiring when his son approached his bed, and inquired whether there was anything he wished for. Upon which the old man in a faint voice exclaimed: 'I only wish that I could wish for anything!'"

ON THE DEATH OF ABU ALHASSAN ALI

THE young man whose death is here lamented was the favourite son and intended successor of Alnassar, the thirty-fourth Khalif of the house of Abbas. On his death the Khalif was inconsolable: he resorted frequently to the tomb of his son, where he shut himself up, and abandoned himself to the most extravagant expressions of sorrow. Nor were the inhabitants of Bagdad less affected with the death of this amiable young prince: there was scarce a house in the city, we are told by a historian, which did not resound with lamentation, nor a countenance that was not depressed by grief.--Alnassar died A.H. 622 [A.D. r225], having survived his son ten years.

NOTES ON THE ROMANCE OF ANTAR.
PUBLIC RECITERS OF ROMANCES IN THE EAST.

VON HAMMER'S statement that the recitation of the Romance of Antar fills the coffee-houses of the East must be taken with the qualification that there are several other Arabian romances of a similar character which are still more popular. Mr. Lane furnishes a very full account both of the mode of public recitation and of the romances themselves, in his charming work on the Manners &c. of the Modern Egyptians. "The reciter," he informs us, "generally seats himself upon a small stool on the mastabah, or raised seat which is built against the front of the coffee-shop; some of his auditors occupy the rest of that seat, others arrange themselves upon the mastabahs of the houses on the opposite side of the narrow street, and the rest sit upon stools or benches made of palm-sticks; most of them with the pipe in hand, some sipping their coffee, and all highly amused, not only with the story, but also with the lively and dramatic manner of the narrator. The reciter receives a trifling sum of money from the keeper of the coffee-shop for attracting customers: his hearers are not obliged to contribute anything for his remuneration; many of them give nothing, and few give more than 5 or 10 faddahs." (A faddah is the smallest Egyptian coin, value, nearly a quarter of a farthing.) The most numerous class of public

[298]

reciters in Cairo are called Sho'ara (singular Sha'er, properly, a poet), all of whom recite only the Romance of Aboo Zeyd. "The Sha'er recites without book. Poetry he chants, and after every verse plays a few notes on a viol which has but a single chord, and which is called 'the Poet's viol' from its only being used in these recitations. The reciter generally has an attendant with another instrument of the kind to accompany him." Next in point of numbers are the Mohadditeen, or Story-tellers (singular, Mohaddit), who exclusively recite the Romance of Ez-Zahir, without book. "There is in Cairo a third class of reciters of romances, who are called 'Anatireh, or 'Antereeyeh (in the singular 'Anteree), but they are much less numerous than either of the two classes before mentioned. They bear this appellation from the chief subject of their recitations, which is the Romance of 'Antar (Secret 'Antar). The reciters of it read it from the book: they chant the poetry, but the prose they read, in the popular manner; and they have not the accompaniment of the rebab [a kind of viol]. As the poetry in this book is very imperfectly understood by the vulgar, those who listen to it are mostly persons of some education." The Anatireh also recite the Romance of Delhemeh, which is contained in fifty-five volumes, or ten more than that of 'Antar.

CHARACTERS OF THE ROMANCE.

THE hero himself--ANTARA the son of Sheddad--is always the central figure,: his blackness of complexion, his homeliness, even ugliness, of feature, are forgotten in admiration of his prodigious strength of arm and his invincible courage; his lofty and impassioned verses; his greatness of soul and his tenderness of heart. A true knight, sans peur et sans reproche, is Antara: bold as a lion when face to face with his foes; magnanimous towards an inferior antagonist; soft and gentle when he thinks of his fair cousin Abla, still more so when he is in her presence. Abla, the beauteous Abla, whose dark flowing tresses at first ensnared the heart of the hero, and whose bright eyes completed the capture--a true Bedouin damsel: like Desdemona with the Moor, she saw Antara's beauty in his mind. And Antara--spite of his black complexion--spite of his base birth--"loved her with the love of a noble-born hero!" When the enemy approaches the tents of the tribe--when the time has come for sword-blows and spear-thrusts--his base origin is forgotten: his sword is then his father, and the spear in his right hand is his noble kinsman.

The other characters are of course subordinated to the hero and his achievements; yet each has an individuality which is strongly marked. Zuhayr, king of the tribes of 'Abs and 'Adnan, Fazarah and Ghiftan, &c.--a prince possessing all the virtues, and not a few of the failings, of his age and race: chivalrous himself, he was not slow to recognise in the youthful slave-son of Sheddad the future hero. Prince Sha's, naturally ill-tempered, proud and tyrannical, yet not without his good points, after adversity had tamed his spirit. Prince Malek, the brave but gentle son of Zuhayr, Antara's first friend and protector against the malice of his enemies: ever ready to plead eloquently in his favour, or to draw his sword when the hero was overwhelmed with numbers. Sheddad, the father of Antara: a bold fellow--"of a heavy-handed kin: a good smiter when help is needed"--proud of his pure blood as ever was hidalgo, yet yearning towards his brave son when his deeds were

[299]

noised abroad, and bitterly lamenting his reported death. But his simple-minded slave-mother--like mothers of great men in general--does not appreciate her son's heroic achievements--thinks he had much better stay at home and help her to tend the flocks. Malek, the father of Abla--crafty, calculating, sordid, perfidious, malicious, time-serving; withal, a great stickler for the honour of his family. Amara, the Bedouin exquisite--proud, boastful, at heart a coward. Shibub, the half-brother of Antara, and his trusty squire--fleet of foot, and hence surnamed Father of the Wind (not Son of the Wind, as stated in page <page 214>); a dexterous archer; ready with admirable expedients for every emergency--never had brave knight a more useful auxiliary.

With the noble lyric of the hero's death the curtain is appropriately dropped on the stirring drama. The moral of the story--for a moral there is to those who can read it aright--is, the triumph of a lofty mind and a resolute will over the clogging circumstances of humble birth and class prejudice.

THE HERO'S BIRTH AND EARLY YEARS

THE circumstance of Antara's birth bears some resemblance to that of Ishmael the son of Abraham, by his bondwoman Hagar. Intercourse with a captured slave was allowed in the ages before el-Islam, as a third and lowest form of marriage, but it was strictly prohibited by the Prophet.--The incident of the insolent slave who abused the poor people at the well presents a striking parallel to the story of Moses driving away the shepherds who would not allow Jethro's daughters to water their flocks.

THE MAIDENS' FESTIVAL

A CURIOUS illustration of the unchangeableness of Eastern manners is furnished in this description of a merrymaking among the women of 'Abs, which, in its circumstance,--the damsels playing on cymbals and dancing,--though not in its object, finds an exact parallel in the festival of the daughters of Shiloh, as recorded in the last chapter of the book of Judges, at which the party were also surprised and carried away captive.

The first of the songs at this festival (<page 190>), describing the charms of nature in the early springtide, and the sentiment contained in the three last verses--that the fleeting moments ought to be enjoyed--recall the beautiful ode on spring by the celebrated Turkish poet Mesihi (who died in 1512), of which Sir W. Jones' imitation in English verse has been much admired: it is, however, only an imitation, and therefore must fail of conveying to the general reader an adequate notion of the beauties of the original. Mr. E. J. W. Gibb, a young Turkish scholar (who is at present rendering into English the great work of Sa'du-'d-Din, the historian of the Ottoman Empire, Taju-'t-Tevarikh, or "The Diadem of Histories"), has made the following almost literal translation of Mesihi's ode, reproducing, as closely as possible, the original metre and rhyme (Remel-i Maqsur):

MESIHI'S ODE ON SPRING.

I.

HARK the nightingale's sweet burden: "Now have come the days of spring."
 Spread they fair in every garden feasts of joy, a maze of spring;
 There the almond-tree its blossoms, silver, scatters, sprays of spring: (a)
 Gaily live, for quick will vanish, biding not, the days of spring.

II.

Once again with many flow'rets gaily decked are mead and plain;
 Tents for pleasure have the blossoms raised in every rosy lane.
 Who can tell, when spring hath ended, who and what may whole remain?--
 Gaily live, for quick will vanish, biding not, the days of spring.

III.

All the alleys of the parterre filled with Ahmed's light appear, (b)
 Verdant herbs his Comrades, tulips like his Family bright appear:
 O ye People of Muhammad! times now of delight appear:
 Gaily live, for quick will vanish, biding not, the days of spring.

IV.

Sparkling dew-drops stud the lily's leaf like sabre broad and keen,
 Bent on merry gipsy-party, crowd they all the flow'ry green;
 List to me, if thou desirest, these beholding, joy to glean:
 Gaily live, for quick will vanish, biding not, the days of spring.

V.

Rose and tulip like to lovely maidens' cheeks all beauteous show,
 Whilst the dew-drops like the jewels in their ears resplendent glow;
 Do not think, thyself beguiling, things will aye continue so:
 Gaily live, for quick will vanish, biding not, the days of spring.

VI.

Rose, anemone, and tulip--these, the garden's noblest flowers,

[301]

Have their blood shed in the parterre under lightning-darts and showers; (c)
Thou art wise, then with thy comrades fair enjoy the fleeting hours:
Gaily live, for quick will vanish, biding not, the days of spring.

VII.

Past and gone are now the moments when the ailing herbs, opprest
 With the thought of buds, the sad head hung upon the garden's breast;
 Come is now the time when hill and rock with tulips dense are drest:
 Gaily live, for quick will vanish, biding not, the days of spring.

VIII.

Whilst each dawn the clouds are shedding jewels o'er the rosy land,
 And the breath of morning's zephyr, fraught with Tatar musk, is bland; (d)
 Whilst the world's fair time is present, do not thou unheeding stand:
 Gaily live, for quick will vanish, biding not, the days of spring.

IX.

With the fragrance of the garden so imbued the musky air,
 Every dew-drop ere it reaches earth is turned to attar rare;
 O'er the parterre spread the incense-clouds a canopy right fair:
 Gaily live, for quick will vanish, biding not, the days of spring.

X.

Whatsoe'er the garden boasted, smote the black autumnal blast,
 But, to each one justice bringing, back hath come Earth's King at last; (e)
 In his reign joyed the cup-bearer, round the call for wine is past:
 Gaily live, for quick will vanish, biding not, the days of spring

XI.

Fondly do I hope, Mesihi, fame to these quatrains may cling;
 May the worthy these four-eyebrowed beauties oft to mem'ry bring;--(f)
 Stray amidst the rosy faces, then, thou bird that sweet dost sing:
 Gaily live, for quick will vanish, biding not, the days of spring.

NOTES.

(a) The almond-blossoms are here compared to the silver coins scattered at weddings.

(b) The parterre is the world (of Islam), the garden or mead being its symbol. The "light of Ahmed" (Nur-i Ahmed) means primarily "the Glory of Muhammad"; but it seems also to be the name of some flower; and, lastly, probably refers to some Turkish victory recently gained, or peace concluded.

(c) This again may allude to some battle in which many illustrious Turks fell.

(d) The musk of Tatary, especially that of Khoten, is the most esteemed.

(e) Earth's King is in one sense the Sun, in another the Sultan.

(f) "May the worthy ", i.e., may those who appreciate these verses, &c.--A youth with new moustaches is called "four-eyebrowed." The "four-eyebrowed beauties" are the verses of four hemistichs each.--It is usual for the poet to address himself in the last verse of compositions of this kind.

Mr. J. W. Redhouse has already done somewhat to disabuse the popular mind of the utterly erroneous notion that the Ottomans have produced no men of undoubted genius-- no poets worthy of the name--by his excellent little treatise on the "History, System, and Varieties of Turkish Poetry; with illustrations in the original and in English paraphrase," published by Messrs. Trubner & Co., London. And it is to be hoped that the above pleasing translation may indicate that Mr. Gibb intends following the example of that eminent Orientalist, by giving his unlearned countrymen further specimens of the Ottoman muse.

A variant of the other song at the maidens' festival (pp. <page 190>, <page 191>) occurs in the "Thousand and One Nights," and has been translated by Mr. Payne, who reproduces the original metre and rhyme, as follows:

THE meadow glitters with the troops of lovely ones that wander there;
 Its grace and beauty doubled are by these that are so passing fair:
 Virgins that with their swimming gait the hearts of all that see ensnare;
 Upon whose necks, like trails of grapes, stream down the tresses of their hair;
 Proudly they walk, with eyes that dart the shafts and arrows of despair:
 And all the champions of the world are slain by their seductive snare.

'ADITE HELMETS

CASQUES were perhaps so called to denote their antiquity and durability--"old as the time of 'Ad" being a proverb among the Arabs. (See notes on vv. 11 and 22 of the "Lay of the Himyarites," pp. <page 351>, <page 352>.)

THE SWORD DHAMI

THIS marvellous weapon (the word Dhami signifies "subduing") is worthy of a place beside the famous Excalibar of King Arthur, and the Durindana of Orlando. There is a grim humour in the account given of the old chief Teba's mode of proving himself qualified to wield the Dhami, by striking off the head of the unfortunate smith who forged it. The incident calls to mind a story of Muley Ismael, emperor of Morocco, who died in the year 1714, after a long reign. An English shipmaster once presented this monarch with a curious hatchet, which he received very graciously, and then, asking him whether it had a good edge, he tried it upon the donor, who, adroitly stepping aside, escaped with the loss only of his right ear.--It is possible, however, that the Arab chief was not actuated by mere wantonness in thus slaying the clever artizan: his object may have been to prevent the smith from ever making a still more formidable weapon for some hostile warrior. Instances are not wanting in European tradition of ingenious men being put to death from a similar motive, after having constructed some wonderful building or piece of complicated mechanism. At all events, the man who made the Dhami having been killed immediately after he had finished his task, the weapon was necessarily unique: there could not be another Dhami in the world.

COMBAT OF ANTARA AND THE SATRAP

IT seems to have been a practice of remote antiquity for two contending armies to agree to abide by the result of a single combat between their chosen champions; though very often such a combat was followed by a general engagement. The historical books of the Bible furnish several instances of combats of this kind: that between David and Goliath (1 Sam. xvii. 38-51) is a remarkable example; and another is the battle between the men of Abner and the men of Joab (2 Sam. ii. 15, 16). In the Romance of Antar single combats are of frequent occurrence. The haughty manner in which the warriors address each other before engaging in deadly conflict was common to the heroes of antiquity. "Come to me," said Goliath to David, "and I will give thy flesh to the fowls of the air, and to the beasts of the field." In like manner exclaims a hero of the Shahnama (Book of Kings, or Heroes) of Firdausi, the Homer of Persia:

> I am myself Hujer,
> The valiant champion, come to conquer thee,
> And to lop off that towering head of thine.

From the minute descriptions of the arms and armour of the combatants, as well of their mode of attack, it would appear that chivalry, in all its essential particulars, was an institution in the East long before it was regularly established in Europe. The satrap whom Antara encounters and kills (<page 221>) is encased in a complcte suit of mail "of Davidean workmanship" (see Mr. Redhouse's note on v. 51 of Ka'b's Mantle Poem) and plumed helmet, and armed with sword, mace, shield, &c.--precisely like the European knights.

[304]

Nor was knight-errantry unknown to Asiatic chivalry. Mention is made by Oriental historians of a Persian knight who was surnamed Rezm Khah--i.e., "one who goes in quest of adventures;" and of two famous Arabian knights-errant: one named Abu Mohammed el-Batal, who wandered everywhere in search of adventures and redressing grievances, and who was killed A.H. 121 (A.D. 738); the other was a great grandson of the Khalif Abu Bekr, named Ja'far es-Sadik--eminent for his piety and extensive knowledge as well as for his feats of arms--who died in the reign of Almansor, A.H. 147 (A.D. 764).

ANTARA AT THE PERSIAN COURT

KHUSRAU, Chosroe, or Chosroes, was the general title of the Sassanides, or third dynasty of Persia: as Caesar was that of the Roman emperors; Pharaoh, of the Egyptian kings; and Tobba', of the princes of el-Yemen.--The Chosroe who occupied the Persian throne at this time was the celebrated Nushirvan the Just. Sa'di, in his Bustan, records the dying injunctions of this wise and good king to his son and successor:

"I have heard that King Nushirvan, just before his death, spoke thus to his son Hormuz: 'Be a guardian, my son, to the poor and helpless; and be not confined in the chains of thine own indolence. No one can be at ease in thy dominions while thou seekest only thy private rest, and sayest: "It is enough." A wise man will not approve the shepherd who sleeps while the wolf is in the fold. Go, my son, protect thy weak and indigent people, since through them is a king raised to the diadem. The people are the root, and the king is the tree that grows from it; and the tree, O my son, derives its strength from the root.'"

ANTARA AND THE WRESTLER

WRESTLING, says Atkinson, "is a favourite sport in the East. From Homer down to Statius, the Greek and Roman poets have introduced wrestling in their epic poems. Wrestlers, like gladiators at Rome, are exhibited in India on a variety of occasions. Prize wrestlers were formerly common in almost every European country."--Sa'di, in the first book of his Gulistan, tells a story of a professor (ustad) of wrestling who had taught a certain pupil every trick of his art except one, and who was enabled by this reservation to overcome the presumptuous young man, when, confiding in his youth and superior strength, he had insultingly challenged his master to contend before the King. "He lifted him," says Sa'di, "above his head, and dashed him down. Loud plaudits ascended from the people. The king bestowed an honourable present on the master, and upbraided the youth, who said: 'O my sovereign! one little portion of the wrestling art yet remained, which he withheld from me.'--The master replied: 'For such an occasion as this, I reserved it; because the philosophers have thus advised: Give not your friend so much power that should he become your enemy, he may be able to hurt you."

JAIDA, THE FEMALE WARRIOR

THE Romance of Delhama furnishes a counterpart to the renowned Jaida, in a damsel named El-Gunduba, who, from her warlike exploits, was styled Kattalet-esh-Shug'an, or Slayer of Heroes. And we read of another female warrior, named Gurd-afrid, in the Shahnama:

Quickly in arms magnificent arrayed,
 A foaming palfrey bore the martial maid;
 The burnished mail her tender limbs embraced;
 Beneath her helm her clustering locks she placed;
 Poised in her hand an iron javelin gleamed,
 And o'er the ground its sparkling lustre streamed:
 Accoutred thus, in manly guise, no eye,
 However piercing, could her sex descry.

It is, however, contended by a learned French Orientalist, that before the time of el-Islam Arabian women did not engage in warfare.

DEATH OF KING ZOHEIR

IT is a historical fact that Zoheir son of Jazima was slain by Khalid, who was murdered by Hareth in the private tents of King Numan; and this was the cause of many wars. It is also stated that Hareth in vain sought the protection of other tribes to secure him from Numan's vengeance.--Note by Translator.

A HORSE RACE, ETC

THE race between King Cais' [Qeys] horse Dahis and Hadifah's mare Ghabra is historically true; in consequence of which a war was kindled between the two tribes that lasted forty years; and it became a proverb amongst the Arabs, so that whenever a very serious dispute arose they would say, "the battle of Dahis and Ghabra is arisen."--Another account states that Cais was the owner of both Dahis and Ghabra, and that Hadifah was possessed of two mares which he ran against them. That Hadifah injured Dahis is also confirmed by good authorities, and that Ghabra won the race; but Hadifah, being dissatisfied, raised troubles and dissensions which lasted forty years.--Note by Translator.

Zuhayr's Mo'allaqah celebrates the termination of the War of Dahis.--It is said that to atone for so great an effusion of blood, King Qeys embraced the Christian religion, and even entered upon the monastic state.

ILLUSTRATIONS OF THE POETRY.

THE question, which of the numerous poetical fragments inserted in the Romance really belong to Antara, which are the composition of El-Asma'i, and which are interpolations of different copyists, is not likely ever to be satisfactorily answered. That some of them are the genuine reliques of Ancient Arabic Poetry is allowed by the most distinguished Orientalists of Europe.

Many of the effusions ascribed to Antara himself are of the highest poetical excellence, and, in boldness of imagery and beauty of expression, are equal if not superior to the most admired passages of his famous Mo'allaqah, which, indeed, is composed of similar fragments--"orient pearls in beauteous order strung."

Several of the similitudes employed in the Poetry of the Romance to describe the charms of a beautiful woman find both interesting and curious parallels in Eastern poetry generally, and even in the works of the best poets of Europe. The epithet "moon-faced," applied to a beautiful damsel, is commonly supposed to be peculiarly Oriental--and ridiculous. Antara, however, in common with other good poets before and since his time, very frequently compares the face of his beloved Abla to the moon and to the sun. For example:

"The brilliant moon calls out to her: 'Come forth, for thy face is like me when I am at the full, and in all my glory!'"
"The sun, as it sets, turns towards her, and says: 'Darkness obscures the land--do thou rise in my absence!'"

Solomon anticipates the poet of 'Abs: "Who is she that looketh forth in the morning, fair as the moon, clear as the sun?"

Firdausi often employs the same comparisons:

If thou wouldst make her charms appear,
 Think of the sun, so bright and clear.

____

 Love ye the moon? Behold her face,
 And there the lucid planet trace.

In the touching story of Nala and Damayanti, an episode of the Mahabharata, translated from the Sanskrit into English verse by Dean Milman, the heroine outshines the moon with her beauty:

There he saw Vidarbha's maiden, girt with all her virgin bands,
 In her glowing beauty shining, all excelling in her form;
 Every limb in smooth proportion, slender waist and lovely eyes;
 Even the moon's soft gleam disdaining in her own o'erpowering light.

And in the Nalodaya of Kalidasa, the Shakspeare of Hindustan:

[307]

"Her countenance is brighter than the moon;"

and the Persian Hafiz:

Thou nymph, whose moon-like forehead bears
  An arch as purest amber bright;

and the tenebrious Arabian el-Hariri, as Burton terms him:

The moon denotes a beautiful countenance;

and the Afghan poet 'Abdu-'r-Rahmin:

The face of the beloved, the sun, and the moon, are one.

——————

 If for once only she will show her face from her veil,
 She will take the diploma of beauty from the sun;

and the Turkish poet Belig:

Should sun and moon behold her, they'd be through envy rent in twain.

The Minnesingers of Germany, too, have the same similitudes. Thus, Vogelweid sings of
a lady, who

Walks through the throng with graceful air,
  A sun that bids the stars retire;

and Henry von Muringe thus laments the absence of his lady-love:

Where is now my morning star?
  Where now my sun?

Our Elizabethan poet Spenser:

Her spacious forehead, like the clearest moon,
  Whose full-grown orb begins now to be spent,
  Largely displayed in native silver shone,
  Giving wide room to Beauty's regiment.

And our own great Shakspeare:

The noble sister of Publicola,
  The moon of Rome!

[308]

And as the bright sun glorifies the sky,
So is her face illumined by her eye.

It is to be regretted that the authenticity of "Ossian's Poems" should be doubtful, else a Keltic bard might be added; for Ossian says (or Macpherson says it for him): "She came forth in all her beauty, like the moon rising from a cloud in the East."

But Abla's tresses--they are "like the dark shades of night":--"in the night of thy tresses darkness itself is driven away": "it is as if she were the brilliant day, and as if night had involved her in obscurity."

The Afghan poet Khushhal Khan, Khattak, has the same similitude as this last:

When the tresses become dishevelled about the fair white face,
 The bright day becometh shrouded in evening's sombre shade;

and still more beautifully does he express this in another poem:

Since in thy tresses my heart is lost, show thou thy face to me;
 For in the night's gloom lost things are with lighted lamp sought for.

In the following passage from the Megha Duta ("Cloud Messenger") of Kalidasa, the face of the demigod Yacsha's wife is likened to the moon and her tresses to the night:

Sad on her hand her pallid cheek declines,
 And half unseen through veiling tresses shines;
 As when a darkling night the moon enshrouds,
 A few faint rays break straggling through the clouds.

[paragraph continues] The Afghan poet Ashraf Khan, Khattak, compares the dark ringlets of the beloved to warriors:

When she disposeth her flowing tresses in curls about her face,
 To the Ethiop army she accordeth permission devastation to make.

Abla's eyes are like those of the fawn: see note on v. 31 of the Poem of Amriolkais, <page 374>. In Sanskrit poetry this is a very common similitude; for example: in the drama of Malati and Madhava--"her eye the deer displays;" in the Uttara Rama Cheritra, the wife of Rama is styled, "fawn-eyed Sita;" in the Megha Duta--"fawn-like eyes that tremble as they glow;" in the Naishadha of Shri Harsha--"her eyes were like the stately deer;" and in the Sakoontala of Kalidasa:

    These her cherished fawns,
 Whose eyes, in lustre vying with her own,

Return her gaze of sisterly affection.

Homer terms Juno "ox-eyed."

Abla's eyes are "full of magic." Firdausi says: "Her eyes, so full of witchery, glow like the narcissus." But the antelope has "borrowed the magic of her eyes," says Antara, as the moon has stolen her charms. So Hafiz chides the zephyr for having filched the perfume of his darling's tresses; the rose, her bloom; the narcissus, the charming brightness of her eye: in like manner Shakspeare, in one of his sonnets ("The froward violet," &c.), accuses all the garden-flowers of having each stolen some sweet or colour from his love.

The hero is slain with the arrows shot from Abla's eyes. Thus, in the Megha Duta: "wanton glances emulate the dart; our English Spenser also:

I mote perceive how in her glancing sight
 Legions of Loves with little wings did fly,
 Darting their deadly arrows fiery bright.

The eyelashes (and the glances) of the peerless Abla are like sharp scimitars. 'Abdu-'r-Rahmin, an Afghan poet, says:

Each of the eyelashes of the beloved pierceth me to this degree,
 That I declare it is the two-edged sword of 'Ali, and nought else.

(Zu-'l-fikar was the name of the famous sword of 'Ali, son-in-law of Muhammad.) 'Abdu-'l-Hamid, another Afghan poet:

Shroud well thy sight from the black eyes' glances;
 Arise not, but from drawn swords guard well thine eyes:

the Turkish poet Fuzuli also:

Where a headsman with a sabre like those lashes, where, of thine?

and Belig, another Ottoman poet:

The eye of that wanton disturber bares its sword.

 (See also "Serenade to his Sleeping Mistress," <page 146>, and Note on the same, pp. <page 430>, <page 431>.)

Abla's throat was so white that it shamed her necklace--"Alas!" exclaims the love-struck hero--"alas for that throat and that necklace!"--evidently feeling that her natural beauties were alone sufficient to disturb Isis peace of mind;--as Sir John Suckling says, or sings:

[310]

Th' adorning thee with too much art
  Is but a barbarous skill;
 'Tis like the poisoning of the dart--
  Too apt before to kill!

[paragraph continues] The same thought is expressed in the following passage from a Sanskrit writer: "Thine eyes have completely eclipsed those of the deer; then why add kajala? Is it not enough that thou destroy thy victims unless thou do it with poisoned arrows?" (Kajala--the Egyptian kohl--is a pigment used to darken the lower eyelid: see note on vv. 8, 9, Poem of Tarafa, <page 376>.) In his Mo'allaqah, v. 42, Antara speaks of certain ladies "whose beauty required no ornaments"--thus anticipating our English poet of the Seasons, in his oft-quoted lines:

        Loveliness
 Needs not the foreign aid of ornament;
 But is, when unadorned, adorned the most.

The Persian Sa'di was also an admirer of beauty unadorned: "The face of a beloved mistress requireth not the art of the tire-woman"--"The finger of a beautiful woman and the tip, of her ear are handsome without an ear-jewel or a turquoise ring."

It is interesting to remark the various comparisons employed by different poets to describe a graceful maiden. Antara likens his darling to a fawn. Solomon says: "I have compared thee, O my love, to a company of horses in Pharaoh's chariot." Theocritus, in his Epithalamium on the Marriage of Helen, says: "She resembles the horse in the chariots of Thessaly." Sophocles likens a damsel to a wild heifer; Horace, to an untamed filly; Ariosto's Angelica is like a fawn; Tasso's Erminia is like a hind; and Kalidasa, the great Hindu dramatist, compares a female divinity to--a goose! "The Rajahansa," says

Dr. H. H. Wilson, in the Notes to his translation of the Megha Duta of Kalidasa, "is described as a white gander with red legs and bill, and together with the common goose is a favourite bird in Hindu poetry. The motion of the goose is supposed to resemble the shuffling walk which they esteem graceful in a woman. Thus, in the Ritu Sanhara, or the Seasons, of our poet--

Nor with the goose, the smiling fair
 In graceful motion can compare."

(This reads as if the "fair" could not compare with the goose; but evidently the meaning of the original is that the bird in question cannot compare with the goddess in graceful motion.) Professor Monier Williams, in the Notes to his elegant translation of Kalidasa's Sakoontala, or the Lost Ring, remarks that Hamsa-gamini, "walking like a swan," was an epithet for a graceful woman. "The Indian lawgiver Manu," he adds, "recommends that a Brahman should choose for his wife a young maiden whose gait was like that of a

[311]

flamingo, or even like that of an elephant." Thus, in the drama of Malati and Madhava, we read: "the elephant has stolen her gait"; and in the Naishadha of Shri Harsha: "her stately pace was like the elephant's." In common with the Arabs and most other Oriental nations, largeness of hips was considered as a great beauty in Hindu women, and it would cause them to walk with that "waving motion" so frequently mentioned in Eastern poetry. So the King, in love with the beautiful Sakoontala, exclaims:

Here are the fresh impressions of her feet;
 Their well-known outline faintly marked in front,
 More deeply towards the heel, betokening
 The graceful undulation of her gait."

The learned Professor explains that the idea of the original is, that the weight of her haunches caused the peculiar appearance observable in her footprints. (See note on v. 17, Poem of Amru, <page 397>, and note on v. 97, same poem, <page 399>.)

Abla's tall and graceful form is very often compared to the tamarisk, and to the branch of the erak-tree: "The tamarisk trees complain of her beauty in the morn and in the eve"--an idea which also finds expression in these verses of Khushhal Khan:

The flowers of the parterre hang down their heads, and they say:
 The heart-ravisher hath appropriated to herself all admiration.

Solomon compares the beloved to a palm-tree; and Theocritus likens Helen to the cypress in the garden: this last is a favourite similitude in Eastern poetry. Thus Firdausi:

Tall as the graceful cypress, and as bright
 As ever struck a ravished lover's sight;

and Hafiz:

Abashed by thy majestic mien,
 The cypress casts a gloomy shade;

and the Turkish poet 'Arif:

Though I'm far now from the shadow of thy love, O cypress straight!

In the "Popular Poetry of Persia," translated by Dr. Alex. Chodzko, are these lines, said to be borrowed from Sa'di:

Who is walking there--thou, or a tall cypress?
 Or is it an angel in human shape?

[312]

This last line recalls a similar thought, but far more beautifully expressed, which occurs in The King's Quair (or Book), by James I., of Scotland: the spelling is modernised:

Ah, sweet! are you a worldly creature,
 Or heavenly thing in likeness of nature?
 Or are you god Cupid his own princess,
 And coming are to loose me out of band?
 Or are you very Nature the goddess,
 That have depainted with your heavenly hand
 This garden full of flowers as they stand?

The following description of a female divinity, from the Megha Duta, contains some of the similitudes above noticed:

Goddess beloved! how vainly I explore
 The world to trace the semblance I adore:
 Thy graceful form the flexile tendril shows,
 And like thy locks the peacock's plumage glows;
 Mild as thy cheeks, the moon's new beams appear,
 And those soft eyes adorn the timid deer;
 In rippling brooks thy curling brows I see,
 But only view combined these charms in thee.

When Abla smiles, "between her teeth is a mixture of wine and honey": "she passes the night with musk under her veil, and its fragrance is increased by the still fresher essence of her breath." Solomon says that the lips of the beloved "drop as the honey-comb;" her mouth is "like wine that goeth down sweetly;" her garments have the fragrance of Lebanon. And the Ottoman Fazil Beg, in a fine poem on the Circassian Women, says: "Their lips and cheeks are taverns of wine."

An abject slave is the lover: "I will kiss the earth where thou art!" exclaims our poet. And Hafiz, in the same spirit (according to Richardson's paraphrase):

O for one heavenly glance of that dear maid!
  How would my raptured heart with joy rebound!
 Down to her feet I'd lowly bend my head,
  And with my eyebrows sweep the hallowed ground.

The phantom of his beloved appearing to Antara during the watches of the night is a source of great consolation to him. "O Abla!" he exclaims, "let thy visionary form appear to me, and spread soft slumber over my distracted heart!" This phantom-visitation is frequently alluded to in the mystical poetry of the East, which is externally erotic-- bacchanalian and anacreontic--but possessed of a deep, recondite, spiritual signification, like the Song of Solomon. In every line of the Persian poet Hafiz, for instance, and in the Afghan poetry from which citations have been made, the natural parallels are maintained

[313]

between the details of the inward and spiritual and those of the outward and sensual. The whole system of Persian Mystic Theology--Sufiism, or dervish-doctrine--is set forth in the Mesnevi, a grand poem in six long books; full of noble poetry, varied as that of our own Shakspeare; composed by the celebrated Jelalu-'d-Din, the founder of the sect known in Europe as the "Dancing Dervishes," from their gyrations in performing their acts of public worship. Professor E. H. Palmer has published a few selections from this great work ("Song of the Reed," &c. London: N. Trubner & Co.), rendered into graceful English verse, that "dwells, like bells, upon the ear." And Messrs. Trubner & Co. have recently issued proposals for the publication, by subscription, of a complete translation in English verse, by Mr. J. W. Redhouse, of the First Book of the Mesnevi, together with some two hundred anecdotes of the author from El-Eflaki, a contemporary of Jelalu-'d-Din. This important project has already met with sufficient encouragement to ensure the issue of the work.

In Oriental poetry the zephyr is often the messenger of love. "O western breeze!" exclaims Abla, "blow to my country and give tidings of me to the hero of Abs!"--"O may the western breeze tell thee of my ardent wish to return home!" says Antara. Thus, too, in the old Scottish ballad, entitled, "Willie's drowned in Yarrow":

O gentle wind, that bloweth south,
  From where my love repaireth,
Convey a kiss from his clear mouth,
  And tell me how he fareth!

The ancients, it is well known, placed the seat of Love in the liver; and so Antara says: "Ask my burning sighs that mount on high; they will tell thee of the flaming passion in my liver." An epigram in the seventh book of the Anthologia is to the same purpose:

Cease, Love, to wound my liver and my heart;
  If I must suffer, choose some other part.

Theocritus, in his 13th Idyll, speaking of Hercules, says: "In his liver Love had fixed a wound;" Anacreon tells how the god of Love drew his bow, and "the dart pierced through my liver and my heart;" and Horace (B. 1, Ode 2) says: "Burning Love . . cloth in thy cankered liver rage." But this notion was not confined to the ancients. Shakspeare says:

Alas! then Love may be called appetite,
  No motion of the liver, but the palate.

The "bird of the tamarisk"--the turtle-dove--is frequently invoked by Antara, to bear witness to his passion, to sympathize with his griefs: this bird is considered in the East as the pattern of conjugal affection. Thus, in the Megha Duta:

On some cool terrace, where the turtle-dove
  In gentle accents breathes connubial love.

[314]

The hero's passion for Abla is often described as a consuming flame: "Quit me not," he conjures the turtle-dove--"quit me not till I die of love, the victim of passion, of absence and separation." Our great dramatist affirms that "men have died, and worms have eaten them, but not for love." Had Shakspeare never heard of the gallant Troubadour Geoffrey Rudel, who died for love--and love, too, from hearsay description of the beauty of the Countess of Tripoli? Barton, in his History of English Poetry, tells the sad story: how the poet sailed for Tripoli; fell sick on the voyage from the fever of expectation; was taken ashore at Tripoli, dying; how the Countess, hearing of his arrival, hastened to the shore and took him by the hand, but the poet could only murmur his satisfaction at having seen her, and expired. The Countess very properly made him a handsome funeral, and erected a tomb of porphyry over his remains, inscribed with an epitaph in Arabic verse.--"Dying for love," says Richardson, "is considered amongst us as a mere poetic figure; and we certainly can support the reality by few examples; but in Eastern countries it seems to be something more: many words in the Arabic and Persian languages which express Love implying also Melancholy, Madness, and Death."

Another story of dying for love--or from grief at the loss of a beloved one--is furnished by Oriental writers in their accounts of the reign of Yezid II., the ninth Khalif of the house of 'Umayya. This monarch was passionately fond of a beautiful and amiable singing-girl named Hababa; and one day, while they were at dinner together, Yezid playfully threw a grape at her, which she took up and put in her mouth, to eat it; but the grape, slipping down her throat, stuck across the passage and choked her, almost instantly. The melancholy accident so affected Yezid that he fell into an excess of grief, and was inconsolable for the loss of so amiable a creature. He would not suffer her body to be buried for several days, and even the tomb could not cure his frenzy. He ordered her grave to be opened, and the body of the girl to be once more exposed to his view. In short, being incapable of moderating his grief, he survived her only fifteen days, and before he expired he ordered his remains to be deposited in a grave near that of his darling. This happened in the year of the Hijra 105 (A.D. 723).

Mr. Payne's translation of the pathetic verses on Aziza's Tomb, which occur in the "Thousand and One Nights," maybe appropriately cited in this connection:

I PASSED by a ruined tomb in the midst of a garden way,
  Upon whose letterless stone seven blood-red anemones lay.
"Who sleeps in this unmarked grave?" I said; and the earth: "Bend low;
  For a lover lies here and waits for the Resurrection Day."
"God keep thee, O victim of love!" I said, "and bring thee to dwell
  In the highest of all the heavens of Paradise, I pray!
How wretched are lovers all, even in the sepulchre,
  For their very tombs are covered with ruin and decay!
Lo! if I might, I would plant thee a garden round about,
  And with my streaming tears the thirst of its flowers allay!

[315]

The loves of Layla and Majnun, by the celebrated Persian poet Nizami, are to Orientals what the story of Romeo and Juliet is to us. Majnun signifies, frantic, mad, from love. The poetry of Nizami, like the best Oriental poetry of the present day, is mystical; but the common people chant the Sufi songs as if there was in them no more than meets the ear.

It is instructive as well as interesting to observe resemblances of thought and expression in the poetry of different nations and ages wide apart. No doubt, modern Oriental poets have adopted many of their similitudes from earlier poetry. But the discovery of such similitudes in the works of great poets of different countries and times tends to show us that there are certain subjects on which minds cast in a large and comprehensive mould always think nearly alike; that human thought moves, so to say, in certain grooves; and that the same objects suggest similar ideas to different minds, which find expression in language almost identical, whether the poet be a rude Arab or a cultured European.

NOTES ON KA'B'S MANTLE POEM.
BY THE TRANSLATOR.

PREFACE, p. 307, l. 1-10.--KA'B, the Poet, and MUHAMMAD, the Lawgiver, were descended, by sixteen and seventeen degrees respectively (not seventeen and fifteen, as stated in the Preface), from Ilyas, the son of Mudhar, the son of Nizar, the son of 'Adnan; as is shown in the subjoined genealogies, both from An-Nawawi's "Biographical Dictionary," edited by Wustenfeld: Gottingen, 1842-47. That of Muhammad is identical with what is found in p. 1, text, of "The Life of Muhammed" of Ibn Hisham, by the same editor; London, 1867. The transliterations are by the translator. Sir W. Jones, in his "Genealogy of the Seven Arabian Poets," puts "Mozeinah" (read, Muzayna) in the place of 'Amr, as No. 3, in the descent of Zuhayr, the father of Ka'b. Muzayna may have been a surname of 'Amr, as Abu Sulma was that of Rabi'a.

Sir W. Jones adds a name, "'Awamer," between Qaratz and Riyah--by him written "Kerth" and "Reiahh"--but Nawawi has it not.

    ILYaS.

1.
MUDRIKA.
1.
TaBIKHA.
2.
Khuzayma.
2.
'Udd.
3.
Kinana.

[316]

3.
'Amr.
4.
an-Nadzr.
4.
'Uthman.
5.
Malik.
5.
Latim.
6.
Fihr-Quraysh.
6.
Hudhma.
7.
Galib.
7.
Thawr.
8.
Lu'ayy.
8.
Tha'laba.
9.
Ka'b.
9.
Khalawa.
10.
Murra.
10.
Mazin.
11.
Kilab
11.
al-Harith.
12.
Qusayy.
12.
Qaratz.
13.
'Abdu-Manaf.
13.
Riyah.
14.
Hashim.

[317]

14.
Abu Sulma, Rabi'a.
15.
'Abdu-'l Muttalib.
15.
Zuhayr.
16.
'Abdu-'llah.
16.
KA'B.
17.
MUHAMMAD.

l. 11. The orthography "Abu-Solma" is erroneous--a result of the Hebraizing proclivities of early European Arabists.

v. 1. The name Beatrice is a fair equivalent to the Arabian original Su'ad (i.e. happy), and conveys a more definite impression to the English reader.

v. 10. "Promises of 'Urqub" is an Arabian proverb, about equivalent to our "Fudge."

v. 20. From the genealogy of the Poet's camel we are to understand that there were two brothers and a sister: one of the brothers, himself got out of the sister, gets the filly out of her also;--he is thus father and brother; the other brother is paternal and maternal uncle.

v. 25. This verse is very obscure in the original, and has many variants. It seems to intimate that the Poet's imaginary camel had never foaled, had never had a full udder, had never been sucked or milked. The best commentary consulted explains that the "whisking" is to drive away flies.

v. 29. The rocks are supposed to be so hot that a "piebald locust" cannot bear them: he touches them with his feet, and withdraws; but he is tired also; so he again tries to alight, and is again and again repelled by the hot rock.

v. 31. The Poet's mother is pictured as beating her breast with her two hands alternately, tearing her flesh and her clothes, on hearing that the Prophet had doomed her elder son, whose enemies derived pleasure in tormenting her with assurances that he is already as good as dead. The other "bereaved ones" are probably mothers of warriors killed in the recent wars against Muhammad.

v. 34. The Poet here, by a poetical amplification, calls himself the son of his grandfather, or, by a contraction, omits his father's name. All Israelites are "Sons of Abraham."

v. 35. Here he recounts how he was refused protection by an old friend; and how (v. 36) he resolved to appeal to the Prophet himself, saying (v. 37) that, "after all, a man can die but once."

v. 38. This verse is held to be "the verse of the Poem"--that is, it recites the pith of the reason why the Poem was composed: "pardon is hoped for from the Apostle of God." Twice does the Poet, in this verse, skilfully use the expression, "Apostle of God," thereby reminding the Prophet of his conversion to Islam.

v. 41. Muhammad was born in the year when Abraha, viceroy of Arabia Felix for the King of Ethiopia, advanced against Makka with an elephant in his train, to destroy the sacred temple of the pagan city, he and his sovereign being Christians. Arrived in front of the city, the elephant refused to obey his leader and advance to the attack. Abraha was obliged to withdraw, and his army perished in a way very variously explained. The elephant of Abraha is said to have seen and heard an angel threatening him, should he advance; but Ka'b was deterred by no dissuasions, for who was more terrible than the incensed Apostle, whose pardon was hoped for?

v. 51. The Qur'an styles Muhammad "a Light from God."

v. 52. The "small band of Quraysh" were those who had abandoned Makka and migrated to Madina for the faith. Their "spokesman," who commanded them to depart, was Muhammad himself.

v. 55. By "shirts of the tissue of David" is meant coats of mail; for tradition asserts that David was divinely taught, and was very skilful in the manufacture of link armour.

Muhammad subsequently objected to Ka'b that his Poem had in it not one word of praise for the "auxiliaries" of Madina, whereas they were in every way worthy of eulogy, and had felt hurt by being excluded from his panegyric of the "emigrants." Thereupon the Poet indited in their special honour a series of verses, and praised them for the fidelity with which they had carried out their promise to assist the Prophet to the death, and the steadfastness they had shown on many a trying occasion on his behalf.

NOTES ON EL-BUSIRI'S MANTLE POEM.
BY THE TRANSLATOR.

vv. 1-7. The old Arabian poets of pagan times usually began their eclogues with some kind of amatory address to a real or imaginary mistress. This was discountenanced by Islam, and El-Busiri, in his first seven couplets, introduces a friend who chides him for being in love, and for attempting to conceal the fact.

vv. 8-11. In the four following verses the poet acknowledges his secret passion, and the uselessness of his attempts to suppress its manifestation.

[319]

vv. 12-28. In these verses the poet laments the shortcomings of his life. The "dominating spirit" (v. 13) of the ethics of Islam is what in Christian phraseology is termed "the flesh," and "the lusts of the flesh"; and what is commonly spoken of as "the passions." Muslim moralists teach that, in the course of a penitent's life, his spirit (nefs), or "flesh," goes through three stages. At first it is the "spirit dominant" (en-nefsu 'l-emmara). It then commands despotically, and its behests are implicitly obeyed by the subject will. Presently, by the exercise of self-control, and by the divine aid, the spirit is deprived of its despotic power, and it subsides into the condition of a grumbler, an upbraider (en-nefsu 'l-levvama), that submits to the strengthening resolve of the reforming man--though not without bitter complainings of the inutility of self-restraint--of the cruelty inflicted on the sufferer by the mortifications of self-denial. Lastly, however, when the virtuous man reaches the saintly goal of perfected righteousness, he has in his turn become the sovereign commander over his lusts and passions; his spirit has become submissive (en-nefsu'l-mutma'inna) to his pious will: he has but to resolve, with GOD'S aid, on good thoughts, good words, good deeds, and his now submissive spirit at once leaps with humble joy and alacrity to put in docile practice what the divine ordinances require.--The remaining verses in this section of the Poem portray the struggle with that "dominant spirit," the poet's regret that he has not laid up a treasure of good works, and an exhortation to others to resist the flesh and its inordinate desires. Verse 18 is worthy of careful remark.

v. 29. With this verse the poet begins his enumeration of the virtues of Muhammad, which he ought to have sought to imitate in his nightly devotions and (v. 30) his long fastings. It is a practice with those who fast long in the East to bind large round stones between their girdles and the pits of their stomachs and flanks, so as to quiet the gnawings of hunger.

v. 31-58. With v. 31 the poet begins to recite the traditionary miracles of the Prophet: how, when he, before his mission, used to retire to the mountains around Makka for meditation and prayer, those mountains found voices, and used to entice him to forego his holy purpose, by revealing to him where gold was to be found within their recesses, that would exalt him above all his fellow-townsmen in wealth and influence: v. 33 recites the pregnant idea, not found in the Qur'an, that the whole material creation was drawn forth out of nothing by GOD, merely to manifest the divine love towards the first of created things, the light of the spirit of Muhammad. Verse 35 begins the list of the Prophet's titles, as celebrated throughout the Muslim world. "GOD'S Beloved One" (habibu 'llah) is his highest, most sacred, and most special style; as Adam is called "the Elect of GOD"; Noah, "the Saved of GOD"; Abraham, "the Friend of GOD" Moses, "the Interlocutor of GOD"; and Jesus, "the Spirit of GOD," as also "the Word of GOD." Muhammad is held to have been a prophet to demons as well as to all mankind. In v. 39 is intimated the boundless science said to have been communicated to him direct from God when he was admitted to the divine presence, sole of all created beings, on the occasion of his celebrated "Night Journey." These laudations continue in special items down to v. 58,

[320]

which mentions the sanctity of the Prophet's tomb at Madina (not at Makka, as is generally supposed), and the blessedness of the pilgrim who reverently visits it.

vv. 59-71. With verse 59 commences a recitation of the prodigies told in traditions to have taken place when Muhammad was born, "in the year of the Elephant," when Abraha advanced against Makka with his elephant, threatening to destroy the "Cubical House" (as the Temple there is designated), said to have been built by Adam and rebuilt by Abraham. The palace of Chosroes at Ctesiphon split, and many of its pinnacles fell; the Fire of the Magi went out, the Tigris receded, and the Lake of Sawa went dry; (v. 65) the genii moaned aloud, and meteors gleamed in the sky. If calculated back, it would perhaps be found that our August or November meteors were in profusion at that time; but Islam has invested them with a poetical significance. They are flaming bolts, hurled by the angels that watch the approaches to heaven, who with these missiles drive back the demons that lurk about to overhear the secrets of Paradise and the divine counsels, as talked over by the watchers. By means of the information thus surreptitiously gained, those demons were, until then, wont to beguile mankind through oracles and soothsayers; but thenceforward such eavesdropping was to be prevented; and the genii in flight are likened to the above mentioned discomfited array of Abraha, and also to the defeated Makka forces of Badr, who turned their backs when Muhammad cast handfuls of pebbles towards them in the fight. The pebbles in his hands proclaimed audibly the unity of GOD, as though each had been a Jonah cast forth from the whale's belly.

vv. 72-75. Other miracles of Muhammad previous to his mission.

vv. 76-79. The "Cave" was that in which Muhammad and his firmest friend Abu Bakr, the father of his only virgin wife 'A'isha, and the first of his successors as Caliph, were concealed for a time on the occasion of their "Flight," or emigration, from Makka to Madina, when his townsmen had determined to rid themselves of his preaching by the shedding of his blood. A spider covered the cave entrance with a dense web, and a dove built its nest and laid eggs in front of the cavern; so that the pursuers judged it useless to search a place so evidently untenanted. Abu Bakr, hearing their horses' footsteps approach, whispered: "What shall we do--two against many?" Muhammad replied: "Nay, we are three: GOD is with us." Abu Bakr's chief title through all future time is that of "the Companion in the Cave."

vv. 80, 81. In the East it is customary to kiss the hand that bestows a gift or favour; and the Poet, in imagination, kisses the hand of the Prophet, from whom he has received much and hopes more.

vv. 82-90. More of the miracles attributed to the Prophet.

vv. 91-104. "Miracles of the Truth" are the verses of the Qur'an. Each verse--nay, each word that has an attributive sense--is held to be, and is commonly termed, "a miracle," "a sign," "a wonder" (ayet). The idea of "a verse" is never held of them by Muslims. The Qur'an is believed to be eternal in its signification, inherent in GOD'S essence, though its visible and audible words were "brought into new existence" when revealed or promulgated. Each of these distichs of the Poem has a definite allusion.--'Ad is the name of a pre-Semitic nation of Arabia Felix, whose cyclopean constructions remain to this day the wonder of the simple Arab, and of the rare European traveller. That nation is said to have been destroyed by a hot blast.--"Iram" is the mysterious earthly paradise, usually invisible to mortal eyes, but reported to have been occasionally seen in the sandy desert, at no very great distance from the present British stronghold, Aden (which word is the very name of "Eden")The Qur'an and Islam are each styled "the Cable of GOD."--The "Tank" is a traditional reservoir in Paradise, where the traces of worldly sin will be washed from the faces of those justified.--The "Straight Path" is, of course, Righteousness; but common ignorance describes it as a bridge spanning the gulf between this world and heaven.--The "Balance" is one of the names of the Qur'an, but commonly supposed to be the weighing-machine in which men's good and bad actions will be set against each other in the last Judgment.

vv. 105-115. A description of the "Night Journey" of Muhammad, in the spirit, from Makka to Jerusalem, and thence, through all the heavens, to GOD'S own sacred presence, from which even Gabriel has to keep at a distance lest he be consumed.

vv. 116-134. The feats of Muhammad after that event: his battles and his victories. The Poet tells his hearers to ask for details of those who were vanquished: of Hunayn, the great battle after Makka had submitted; of Badr and Uhud (Ohod), his two first fights.--v. 130. The "lances of Khatt" are bamboo spears imported from India at Khatt, an ancient Arabian port on the Persian Gulf, whence their name.--v. 131. "Who have a mark that distinguishes them"--in the scars on their foreheads, produced by frequent prostration in worship (not prayer).--v. 132. The odour of warriors in buff and armour is, doubtless, "as a nosegay" to their valiant leader, and to their companions-in-arms on the battle-field.

vv. 135-139. Other glories of Muhammad. The "words of GOD" are the words of the Qur'an, and the "Demonstration" is one of its names.--v. 139. The "Illiterate One" is the title of which Muhammad is usually said to have been most proud; for, by reason of his lack of worldly scholarship, the wondrous rhetorical elegancies and deep significancies of the Qur'anic passages amount to the greatest of miracles. He was himself an "orphan"-- fatherless ere he was born, or soon after, and motherless when only six years of age; being cared for, at first, by his grandfather, 'Abdu-'l-Muttalib, and after him by one of his paternal uncles, Abu-Talib.

vv. 140-161. The Poet's account of the reason why he composed the Poem, and invocation of the Prophet's intercession for him. The mention, in v. 151, of Zuhayr the poet (father of Ka'b, the author of the first and only real "Mantle Poem") and his eulogy of Harim, by whom he was richly rewarded, is as much as to say that he himself hopes to be spiritually rewarded for the present panegyric. (Zuhayr sings the praises of Harim, son of Salma, in the 18th eclogue, p. 99 of Ahlwardt's Divans, published by Messrs. Trubner & Co., of London.)--The concluding two verses of the section are an expression of confiding reliance.--vv. 157-161. The usual concluding prayer for GOD'S grace upon the Prophet, his family, companions, and all succeeding Muslims.

THE L POEM OF THE FOREIGNER.
(LAMIYYATU-'L-'AJAM, BY ET-TUGRA'I)
TRANSLATED BY J. W. REDHOUSE, ESQ.

[On comparing the following translation of the famous poem of Et-Tugra'i, which Mr. Redhouse has obligingly made for this volume, with Dr. Carlyle's rendering (pp. <page 153>-<page 161>), it will be observed that, in a few instances, the true meaning of the original is lost in the metrical version. Some particulars regarding the author, &c., are given in pp. <page 433>-<page 435>.]

FIRM-ROOTEDNESS of view has protected me from precipitancy; and the ornament of excellence has embellished me when void of trinkets.

2. My honour at the last, and my honour at the first, are equal; for the sun that inclines towards a fair altitude in the morning resembles the sun in its decline.

3. In what might consist a residence in Bagdad?--I have no home therein; I have neither she nor he-camel there.

4. Distant from my friends; empty-handed; isolated: I still am as a sword-blade, the two flat sides of which are bare of sheath-coverings.

5. There is no sincere friend unto whom to make plaint of my sorrow; nor a companion unto whom my joy may be communicated.

6. My absence from home has grown long; so that my saddle-camel has moaned, and her saddle, and the heel of my limber spear.

7. My famished beast has shrieked from fatigue, and has groaned for what my saddle-beasts have thrown off; and the riders have been contentious in blame of me.

8. I wish for the open hand of wealth, that I may have its help to pay off debts that I owe, as a point of exalted feeling.

9. But Fortune inverts my wishes, and makes me contented with a return home, instead of riches following on earnest endeavour.

10. And then, that well-proportioned man, like the upper part of a spear, holding his like between his leg and his saddle: not pusillanimous, and not depending on another;

11. Pleasant in his jesting; bitter in his earnest; in the firmness of whose valour there is mixed the tenderness of amatory converse;

12. From the watering-places of whose eyeballs I had driven away the flocks of drowsiness, though the night incited the herds of sleep to men's eyeballs;

13. The riders being inclined over their saddles, through heaviness, [some] coming to themselves, and others fuddled with the wine of drowsiness.

14. Then I said: "Shall I call thee to a momentous event, that thou mayest succour me, and wilt thou refuse me in the great misfortune?

15. "Dost thou sleep, leaving me, while the eye of the Pleiades is sleepless? And dost thou turn away from me, when the dye of night turns not?

16. "Then wilt thou help me in a folly I have taken into my head? (for at times folly scares away from cowardice).

17. "Verily I wish to visit the tribe by night at Idzam; whereas the archers of the tribe from Thu'al have already shielded it:

18. "They shield therein, with bright swords and brown pliant lances, [maidens] with black tresses, yellow trinkets [of gold], and crimson vestments [of silk].

19. "Then march with us under the safeguard of the night, at random; for a fragrant puff shall guide us to their dwelling-places.

20. "For the beloved one is where the enemies and the lions are crouched down around the lairs of the antelopes, the thickets of which are shafts of spears.

21. "We are bound towards a growing damsel in the bend of the valley, the spear-heads of whose eyelashes have been tempered with the waters of coquetry and of the darkness of her eyelid borders.

22. "The commendatory conversations of generous men have already multiplied concerning her, as to the noble qualities [in a woman] of cowardice and avarice.

23. "The fire of love rises by night in feverish hearts [livers], through their women; and that of hospitality, on the hill-tops, through their men.

24. "Their women slay the emaciated of their lovers, who struggle not; the men slaughter noble steeds and camels [as food for guests].

25. "Those stung with their spears are cured in their tents with a draught of the pond of wine and of honey [of the lips of their maidens].

[324]

26. "Perhaps a second visit to that bend of the valley [see v. 21] will cause to creep along a breath of cure for my ills.

27. "I do not dislike the gaping spear-thrust, when paired with a shot from the arrows of wide eyes.

28. "Neither do I fear the glancing blades [eyes] that help me to flashes from the interstices of blinds and curtains;

29. "Neither do I part with does [women] with whom I hold tender converse, even though lions of the thickets menace me with evil.

30. "The love of safety turns the effort of its possessor from high objects, and incites man to sloth.

31. "Therefore, if thou incline to it, then take thou to thyself a burrow in the earth, or a ladder to the atmosphere, and isolate thyself;

32. "And leave the broad ocean of ambition to those who dare ride thereon; contenting thee with some slight moisture.

33. "The contentment of the lowly, with a sorry livelihood, is abjectness; the glory of docile she-camels is in their most accelerated pace.

34. "Drive thou them, then, at a swift pace, into the very throats of the deserts; they emulating with their nose-bands the doubled bits [of horses]."

35. Verily, all grave matters have given me to understand that glory resides in migrations [and they speak truly in that respect].

36. If in the glory of a repair there were an attainment of desire, the sun would never move from the sign of Aries [his house of exaltation].

37. I would cry out to Fortune, were I in company of a listener; but Fortune is occupied in [other] matters, and ignores me.

38. It may be that, if my superiority and the defectuosity of those [others] should appear to its eye, it would sleep in respect of them, or would awake in respect of me.

39. I amuse my soul with desires which I entertain. How narrow is life, were it not for the expansion of desire!

40. I was not pleased with my livelihood when the days were fortunate. How, then, can I be satisfied, when they are retrograding in haste?

[325]

41. My knowledge has risen in my own estimation to a degree of preciousness in value; therefore have I protected it from the cheap rate of an every-day commodity.

42. It is a customary thing in a sword to be [esteemed] beautiful through its damaskeening; but it will not act, save in the hands of a hero. [I am such a sword-blade, with my knowledge; but, to show this, I must be used.]

43. I should not have chosen that my time should be lengthened unto me, until I should see the prosperity of ragamuffins and the vile.

44. People have, however, got before me whose run was behind my paces when I walked with leisure.

45. This is the reward of the man whose fellows have passed away before him, and who still has craved a long respite of his doom.

46. And if they who are inferior to me have risen above me, no wonder!--I have a precedent in the lower position of the sun than that of Saturn [in the Ptolemaic system of the spheres].

47. Then be patient therewith, without hatching stratagems or feeling vexed. In the forthcoming event of time there is that which will make thee independent of stratagems.

48. Thy most virulent enemy is the nearest of those to whom thou hast trusted. Then beware of men, and associate with them upon [terms of] distrust.

49. For verily the lord of the world, and the unique one thereof, is he who leans not for support upon any man in the world.

50. And thy good opinion of the days is a weakness; then, hold a bad opinion, and be in fear of them.

51. Honesty has sunk into the earth, and dishonesty has spread abroad; while between word and action an interval as wide as perjury has opened out.

52. Thy truthfulness hath the falsehood of mankind shamed with men; for can the crooked be fitted to the straight?

53. If there were anything useful in their firm adherence to their promises, the sword would outrun the chider.

54. O thou, who comest to drink of the remnant of a life, the whole of which is turbid!-- thou hast expended thy clear and pure water in thy pristine days.

55. Wherefore inconsiderately rushest thou into the depth of the sea on which thou ridest, whereas one sip of a trickling spring would suffice thee?

56. The possession of contentment is not feared for; neither therein is want felt for auxiliaries or for attendants.

57. Dost thou seek for permanency in an abode that has no durability? Hast thou ever heard of a shadow that did not pass away?

58. And, O thou who art aware of the secrets informed thereof! be silent!--for in silence is there an escape from mistakes.

59. They have fostered thee for a matter which, if thou hast comprehended it, should make thee beware of pasturing among the loose cattle.

The End.

Printed in Great Britain
by Amazon.co.uk, Ltd.,
Marston Gate.